Azores

the Bradt Travel Guide

David Sayers

With a foreword by Ben Fogle

edition
5

www.bradtguides.com

Bradt Travel Guides Ltd, UK
The Globe Pequot Press Inc, USA

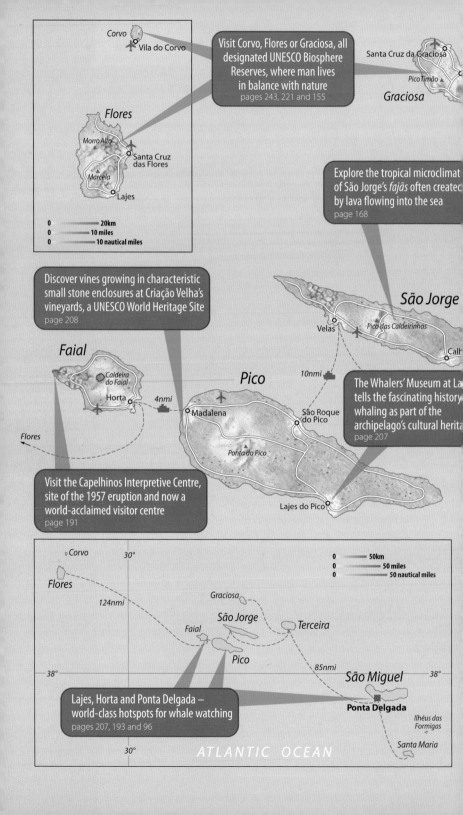

Corvo

Vila do Corvo

Visit Corvo, Flores or Graciosa, all
designated UNESCO Biosphere
Reserves, where man lives
in balance with nature
pages 243, 221 and 155

Santa Cruz da Graciosa

Pico Timão ▲

Graciosa

Flores

Morro Alto

Santa Cruz
das Flores

Marcela

Lajes

0	20km
0	10 miles
0	10 nautical miles

Explore the tropical microclimat
of São Jorge's *fajãs* often createc
by lava flowing into the sea
page 168

Discover vines growing in characteristic
small stone enclosures at Criação Velha's
vineyards, a UNESCO World Heritage Site
page 208

São Jorge

Velas

Pico das Caldeirinhas

Calh

Faial

Caldeira
do Faial

Horta

Pico

4nmi

Madalena

São Roque
do Pico

10nmi

The Whalers' Museum at La
tells the fascinating history
whaling as part of the
archipelago's cultural herita
page 207

Flores

Ponta do Pico

Lajes do Pico

Visit the Capelhinos Interpretive Centre,
site of the 1957 eruption and now a
world-acclaimed visitor centre
page 191

Corvo

30°

Flores

124nmi

Graciosa

São Jorge

Terceira

Faial

Pico

85nmi

São Miguel

38°   38°

Ponta Delgada

Ilhéus das
Formigas

0	50km
0	50 miles
0	50 nautical miles

Lajes, Horta and Ponta Delgada –
world-class hotspots for whale watching
pages 207, 193 and 96

Santa Maria

30°

ATLANTIC OCEAN

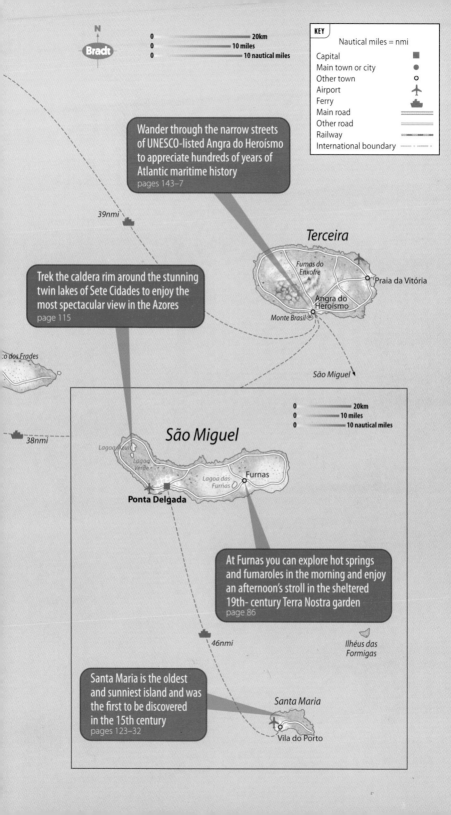

Wander through the narrow streets of UNESCO-listed Angra do Heroísmo to appreciate hundreds of years of Atlantic maritime history
pages 143–7

Trek the caldera rim around the stunning twin lakes of Sete Cidades to enjoy the most spectacular view in the Azores
page 115

At Furnas you can explore hot springs and fumaroles in the morning and enjoy an afternoon's stroll in the sheltered 19th-century Terra Nostra garden
page 86

Santa Maria is the oldest and sunniest island and was the first to be discovered in the 15th century
pages 123–32

KEY

Nautical miles = nmi

Capital	■
Main town or city	●
Other town	○
Airport	✈
Ferry	⛴
Main road	──
Other road	──
Railway	──
International boundary	─·─·─

N

Bradt

0 ──────── 20km
0 ──────── 10 miles
0 ──────── 10 nautical miles

0 ──────── 20km
0 ──────── 10 miles
0 ──────── 10 nautical miles

Terceira

Fumas do Enxofre

Praia da Vitória

Angra do Heroísmo

Monte Brasil

39nmi

...o dos Frades

São Miguel

38nmi

São Miguel

Lagoa Azul

Lagoa Verde

Lagoa das Furnas

Furnas

Ponta Delgada

46nmi

Ilhéus das Formigas

Santa Maria

Vila do Porto

Azores
Don't miss...

Small-scale charm
Little chapels or *impérios* like this one on Terceira act as the hub of the island's exuberant religious festivals
(AT/S) pages 27 and 29

Climbing Pico
On top of the world on the summit of Pico Mountain
(JD/D) page 202

Awe-inspiring views
Lake Fogo, or Fire Lake, ascending from the south coast is one of the most popular walks on São Miguel
(A/S) page 109

tranquillity and timelessness
Farmers still use ponies to bring the milk churns down from the higher fields
(SS)

Whale and dolphin watching
Some 25 species of cetaceans have been sighted off the Azores, making the archipelago one of the world's viewing hotspots
(PJ/S) page 11

Azores in colour

above   Pico's wines were once sent to the Russian Tsar; now the vineyards are a **UNESCO** World Heritage Site and are still producing good wines (RG/S) page 210

left   This short trail on São Miguel leads from Lagoa do Canário to the most breathtaking viewpoint in all the islands: a bird's-eye view of Sete Cidades (SS) page 107

below   Motoring is always a pleasure as the scenery is ever-changing and roads almost empty (TZ/S)

above On São Miguel, many roads laid down in the early last century were landscaped with plane trees, hydrangeas, azaleas and roses (HD/S)

right The distinct low, stone base and squat, conical tower immediately identifies this windmill as belonging to Corvo (SS) page 28

below A Faial-type windmill on Pico (RD/FLPA) page 28

find the real Azores

AUTHOR

David Sayers is a horticulturist who studied at Kew and overseas, and has spent a lifetime exploring the world for plants. Abandoning gardening after 20 years and graduating in social sciences, he worked in social policy and corporate planning, at the same time using annual leave to lead adventure/botanical holidays to the Himalayas for Thomas Cook and others. In 1982 he formed a company specialising in botanical and garden travel and for 26 years arranged and led tours worldwide. In 1984, he offered the Azores for the first time and led the first ever tour group to climb Pico and to visit São Jorge, Flores and Corvo. He now writes on botanical travel.

ILLUSTRATOR

Hedvika Fraser comes from Prague and has lived in Britain for the past 40 years. Formerly a science editor and translator, a childhood fascination with orchids led to painting them in watercolour, and the charm of the Azores led her to the line drawings illustrating this guide.

AUTHOR'S STORY

For me the Azores were an immediate *coup de foudre*. The scenery is very beautiful, I could never tire of walking the hills, there is an interesting flora, the geology is fascinating, the natives are extra friendly, and there is blissful peace. I was spending months each year in distant countries where travel is hard work, and to suddenly find all the natural attractions with the wonderful bonus of good coffee, excellent wines, a comfortable bed and easy flight seemed a paradise. It still does, even after 30 years. The long-established Azorean travel agent Albano Cymbron and I pioneered a series of walks (and even marked the routes with blobs of red paint), and in 1991, wrote and jointly published a modest guide to six of the islands. We sold 2,000 copies. A year later I was invited to advise on the restoration of the Terra Nostra garden in Furnas, one of the great gems of Azorean heritage. This developed into a major project, and from there came two more garden restorations, this time for the Ponta Delgada Municipality. Friendships have matured over the years, and the islands remain as lovely as ever – what more could one wish for. Now three entire islands have been recognised by UNESCO as Biosphere Reserves for their balance between man, nature and sustainable development. Someone else must have fallen in love with the Azores!

I hope this guide will help you discover some of the hidden delights of this little-known cluster of islands, and that you will have a memorable holiday. And maybe go back again!

PUBLISHER'S FOREWORD   *Hilary Bradt*

Many years ago I used to visit bookshops in Europe to sell the early Bradt guides. There was (and still is) one in Brussels with the mysterious name L'Anticyclone des Azores. That was the first time I'd heard of the Azores and its climate-influencing weather patterns. Now this archipelago is known and loved by the many visitors who come for the whale watching or to walk in the green, flower-covered mountains. I've known David Sayers for almost as long as I've known that Brussels bookshop and he has had a distinctly bright and sunny influence on our island coverage! I'm proud to be publishing this fifth edition of his successful book.

Fifth edition published November 2013. First published 2001.

Bradt Travel Guides Ltd
IDC House, The Vale, Chalfont St Peter, Bucks SL9 9RZ, England.
www.bradtguides.com
Published in the USA by The Globe Pequot Press Inc, PO Box 480, Guilford, Connecticut 06437-0480

Text copyright © 2013 David Sayers
Maps copyright © 2013 Bradt Travel Guides Ltd
Illustrations copyright © 2013 Individual photographers and artists
Project managers: Greg Dickinson and Claire Strange
Cover image research: Pepi Bluck

British Library Cataloguing in Publication Data
A catalogue record for this book is available from the British Library

ISBN: 978 1 84162 468 6 (print)
e-ISBN: 978 1 84162 776 2 (e-pub)
e-ISBN: 978 1 84162 678 9 (mobi)

Photographs AWL Images: Mauricio Abreu (MA/AWL); Carina Costa (CC); Dreamstime: Gunold Brunbauer (GB/D), Jaime Debrum (JD/D); FLPA: Reinhard Dirscher (RD/FLPA); Shutterstock: AMA (AMA/S), ArjaKo's (A/S), Yulia B (YB/S), Hemmer Danke (HD/S), Mikael Damkier (MD/S), Rafal Gadomski (RG/S), Miroslav Hladik (MH/S), Pierre J (PJ/S), Rui Vale Sousa (RVS/S), Anibal Trajo (AT/S), Lois Viegas (LV/S), Tony Zelenoff (TZ/S); SuperStock (SS)
Front cover Pasture fields on Terceira (MA/AWL)
Back cover A view towards Sete Cidades (SS)
Title page Windmill on São Miguel (RVS/S); preparing a flower carpet at Vila Franca do Campo (SS); a sperm whale swims past Pico Mountain (HD/S)

Illustrations Hedvika Fraser   **Maps** David McCutcheon FBCart.S

Typeset from the author's disc by Wakewing, High Wycombe
Production managed by Jellyfish Print Solutions and manufactured in India

Acknowledgements

As with the earlier editions, I am much indebted to Albano Cymbron and increasingly to his daughter Catarina, of the Melo Agency in Ponta Delgada, for facts, insights and contributions about Azorean life and history and for their unstinted time and practical support. Also to them go my thanks for invaluable introductions to kind and generous people throughout the islands who have helped me in so many different ways. To Helena Carvalho and Cristina Valcorba in the Melo office for their continuing help. Finally to this stalwart team, my thanks for making all my travel arrangements.

For invaluable textual contributions to this guide and for their time and interest I am most grateful to Dr Isabel Soares de Albergaria from São Miguel who contributed the pages on art and architecture and thus revealed some of the treasures that might otherwise have remained hidden; to António Pedroso from São Jorge for providing many cultural anecdotes; to Monique Cymbron from São Miguel for her Azorean kitchen; to Luis Silva for delving into the history of the Azorean cow; and to geologist Pedro Freire of Geo-fun in Ponta Delgada who generously gave his knowledge and time to steer me through the lava flows of volcanic history.

Vital practical support was given by the Azores Regional Directorate of Tourism in Horta, whose continuing interest in this guide I gratefully acknowledge. I am indebted to Sunvil for international flights, to SATA for domestic flights, and to hoteliers for their generous hospitality throughout the islands and especially Hotel Talisman in Ponta Delgada and Casa do António in Velas. Following earlier editions I remain amazed and thankful at the patience of Sandra Dart of the Azores Regional Tourism Office for her continuing prompt replies to my many emails. My thanks also go to the local tourism officers on Pico, Santa Maria, Flores and Graciosa, and especially to Rui Costa on Terceira for unfailing help and long friendship. Also to Katt Rita on Corvo.

For all the illustrations and for her indulgent support at home during my many and often extended visits to the islands, I express heartfelt thanks to my partner Hedvika Fraser.

Lastly, and central to the whole project, the ebullient team at Bradt Travel Guides.

Contents

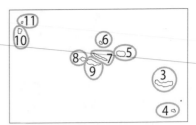

FOLLOW BRADT

Follow Bradt on Facebook and Twitter for the latest news, special offers and competitions.

 www.facebook.com/BradtTravelGuides
 @BradtGuides

LIST OF MAPS

THE NEXT EDITION

At Bradt Travel Guides we're aware that guidebooks start to go out of date on the day they're published – and that you, our readers, are out there in the field doing research of your own. You'll find out before us when a fine new family-run hotel opens or a favourite restaurant changes hands and goes downhill. So why not write and tell us about your experiences? Contact us on 📞 01753 893444 or e info@bradtguides.com. We will forward emails to the author who may post 'one-off updates' on the Bradt website at www.bradtguides.com/guidebook-updates. Alternatively you can add a review of the book to www.bradtguides.com or Amazon.

Foreword

By Ben Fogle

For me the Azores represents a bite-sized piece of a national identity. The islands offer a taste of Portugal wrapped up in their own unique Atlantic geography and geology. The island archipelago has been described as like heaven and hell: defined both by a lush green environment and by the fiery belly of the earth.

It's a heady mix that can overwhelm the senses. Birds, plants, whales and dolphins, combined with Portuguese architecture, are akin to heaven; sulphurous water bubbling up from deep underground, thick volcanic ash and pumice that blanket vast swathes of land, and black lava flows, frozen like fossils that dip into the turgid Atlantic Ocean, are all reminiscent of hell.

It is truly astonishing to think that these islands emerged from the ocean relatively recently in geological terms and that all the flora and fauna are immigrants, migrating half way across the Atlantic, borne on the ocean current or in the wind.

The Azores is a hauntingly beautiful chain of nine islands spread over more than 600km of ocean, half way between Lisbon and New York. In some ways the Azores is to Portugal what the Outer Hebrides is to Scotland – a remote archipelago many miles offshore – but there the similarities end. Where the Hebrides are flat, sandy isles, the Azores islands are rugged and volcanic, dominated by their geology and influenced by the warm Gulf Stream that has created an ecosystem unlike anywhere else.

The Azores High is responsible for the unique ecology of this archipelago. This area of high pressure is semi permanent and ensures the islands are more tropical than you might expect. It combines with the warm ocean currents of the Gulf Stream, creating a subtropical climate.

Ponta da Ferraria must rate as one of the greatest places in the world for a saltwater swim. A natural swimming pool formed by lava lies next to the ocean but is heated by a bubbling spring that pumps water into the pool at 61°C. Indeed, the water in the pool is too hot to swim in at low tide and is only cool enough when it mixes with crashing Atlantic waves that tumble in at high tide, bringing the temperature down to a comfortable 28°C. It is the perfect combination of exhilaration and relaxation.

One of the most memorable experiences for me was my first visit to Terra Nostra Garden on São Miguel, the main island. In 1770, Thomas Hickling built a summer house on a small hill overlooking a thermal-spring swimming pool. Thirty acres of rich gardens were planted in the ensuing years, and now there are more than 2,500 trees, abundant ferns, a formal flower garden, a garden devoted to cycads and another to camellias. The garden thrives in the subtropical climate and it is now simply breathtaking.

Not far away is Furnas where boiling pools and steaming vents offer a portal to Middle Earth. For decades, if not centuries, families have come here to cook the famous *cozido nas caldeiras* in huge pots buried in the volcanic sand; prized cooking spots are passed down from generation to generation. Holes about a metre deep have been dug into the hot earth into which a container is lowered. Filled with different meats, sausage, vegetables, kale, potato and cabbage, the pot is left to cook gently for seven hours. The long, slow simmer ensures that meat becomes tender and flavours meld. This simple form of cooking, in my eyes, is symbolic of how the land and the geology have shaped the unique culture and heritage of these islands.

Volcanic activity has, of course, cast, moulded and created these unique islands, and Faial is an example of how the Azores has been changed by the power of the earth. The western tip of the island exemplifies this, its entire landscape formed by the great eruption in 1957–58. Walking on this moon-like terrain is like stepping onto another planet. On the face of it, it is a bleak, soulless place, but it takes on a gritty beauty that overcomes most visitors.

Perhaps one of the most iconic activities in the Azores is to climb the summit of the tallest peak, Pico Mountain, at 2,351m. The 5km journey begins at Cabeço das Cabras at 1,231m. The difficulty of the ascent varies according to the weather, but the views from the summit are well worth the six-hour round trip. No matter how many mountains you have climbed there is something utterly mesmerising about looking out over thousands of miles of ocean and cloud below.

Most people associate the Azores with whales. Indeed, the ocean around the islands offers one of the best habitats in the world for marine mammals and more than 24 species have been identified off the coast. For many years, until the 1980s, sperm whales were hunted commercially in the Azores from small boats with hand-held harpoons. Fortunately, today whale hunting has been replaced by whale watching. Short-finned pilot whales and sperm whales are the most common in the Azores and can be seen all year round.

Early one morning on my last trip I headed out to sea in a fast rigid inflatable boat. Dressed in wet-weather gear to protect me from the ocean spray, I travelled out deep into the Atlantic Ocean. The boat leapt from wave to wave, directed from the same observation huts used by the hunters of previous decades. The difference was that I was armed with a camera rather than a harpoon gun.

There can be few sights as moving as that of a breaching sperm whale. These marine mammals can measure up to 20m and are surprisingly elusive considering their size. Persevere, however, and you will be rewarded with an experience that will, quite literally, take your breath away.

Whale watching, swimming, bathing in hot springs, eating volcano-cooked food, mountain biking, kayaking, walking, bird watching, visiting tea plantations, island hopping … the list of eco-friendly activities available on the Azores is endless. In an era when more and more people are looking for something different from their holiday, the islands of the Azores really are at the forefront of the 'natural' travel movement.

Ben Fogle

Introduction

It is perhaps strange to think there is a cluster of nine small islands, isolated but thriving, lying between Lisbon and New York and surrounded by the great Atlantic Ocean.

Very much part of Europe and members of the European Union, they have many of the accoutrements of modern life: the latest fashion trainers, cars, second homes, and the very latest communications technology connecting home computers with the internet.

Yet few people are aware of the Azores's existence and many of those who are hold an image of dry, sun-baked volcanic islands like Lanzarote in the Canaries. And they almost always assume they belong to Spain.

The Azores are Europe's best-kept secret: verdant, tranquil, diverse, exquisitely beautiful, always welcoming. Further south and close to the African coast lies Madeira, Portugal's more familiar Atlantic island; sunnier and with less rain and cloud but considerably more developed for tourism, and famous for its well-promoted flowers and gardens. It was going to Madeira that aroused my curiosity about those other far-off islands; a flight from Funchal took me to Ponta Delgada, and back to an ambience that possibly could have been found in Madeira half a century ago. One needs to take the Azores at their own speed. Fight it, and you will be frustrated; relax along with it and you will return a different person. Old-World courtesy prevails, a reminder of the many tiny niceties of life that have been sacrificed to the exigencies of faster lifestyles.

Since they were first settled in the 15th century, each island has developed at a different speed, depending upon the quality of its harbour, terrain, crops, and its distance from the others. Today this is reflected in their diversity, each island offering the visitor its own individual character that makes the Azores such a varied entity.

All the islands are green, the flowers are mostly sophisticated and subtle, the gardens are steeped in history and, like the flowers, are more cerebral than flamboyant. While some main towns have their roads and traffic, just a short distance away men ride horses to their pastures and pony carts filled with milk churns clatter over cobbles. Flashing neon lights are rare, streets are narrow, shops modest and in keeping with the streetscape, coffee bars are numerous while nightclubs are few. The islands reflect their turbulent geological past and offer rural landscapes enhanced by rocky or precipitous coasts surrounded by an often travel-brochure-blue sea. Religious and secular festivals riot through the calendar and touch the lives of every island and islander. There are sailing regattas, golf tournaments, big-game fishing tournaments, cycle races, car rallies and other events that come as rather a surprise and largely leave the non-enthusiasts in happy oblivion. There is so much to explore, so much to experience; these islands should be savoured like a rare wine.

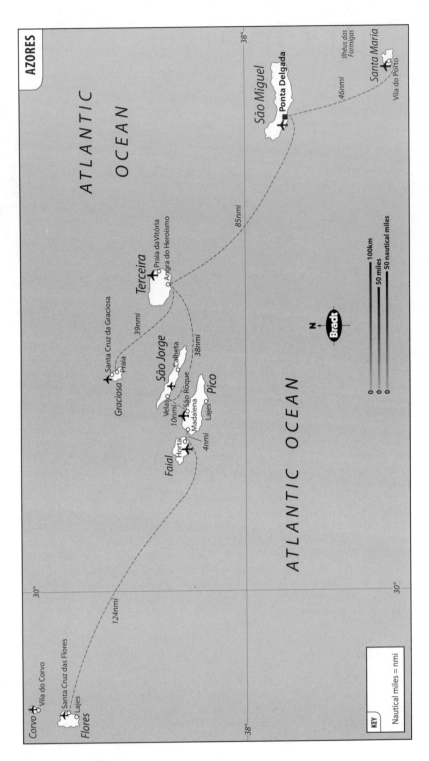

AZORES

ATLANTIC OCEAN

ATLANTIC OCEAN

Corvo
Vila do Corvo

Flores
Santa Cruz das Flores
Lajes

124nmi

Graciosa
Santa Cruz da Graciosa
Praia

39nmi

São Jorge
Velas
Calheta
10nmi

Faial
Horta
4nmi

Pico
São Roque
Madalena
Lajes
38nmi

Terceira
Praia da Vitória
Angra do Heroísmo

85nmi

São Miguel
Ponta Delgada

46nmi

Santa Maria
Ilhéus das Formigas
Vila do Porto

N
Bradt

0 100km
0 50 miles
0 50 nautical miles

KEY
Nautical miles = nmi

x

Part One

GENERAL INFORMATION

AZORES ARCHIPELAGO AT A GLANCE

Islands São Miguel, Santa Maria, Terceira, Graciosa, São Jorge, Faial, Pico, Flores, Corvo

Location In the Atlantic Ocean, approximately 1,500km from Lisbon and 3,900km from the east coast of North America

Size Nine islands varying from 17km^2 (Corvo) to 746km^2 (São Miguel), spread across some 600km of ocean

Climate Temperate, maritime climate with agreeable temperatures ranging from 13–14°C in Jan/Feb to 22–23°C in Jul/Aug. Rain throughout the year; light cloud common.

Status Autonomous region of Portugal

Population 247,000

Economy Major earners are beef, dairy products, fishing and tourism

Language Portuguese

Religion Roman Catholic

Currency Euro

Rate of exchange £1 = €1.15, US$1 = €0.75 (July 2013)

Time GMT –1; 4 hours later than US Eastern Standard Time

Electricity 220 volts

International telephone code +351

Flag Blue and white block colour. At the centre is a goshawk, with nine golden stars. In the left corner is the national coat of arms.

Coat of arms The shield is silver with a red border, and includes a goshawk and nine golden stars.

National anthem *Hino da Região Autónoma dos Açores* (Anthem to Autonomy)

Motto *Antes morrer livres que em paz sujeitos* ('Better to die free than live enslaved')

Public holidays See page 61

1

Background Information

GEOGRAPHY AND CLIMATE

LOCATION The nine islands of the Azores – regarded as the westernmost point of Europe – are spread over some 600km of ocean (the Economic Free Zone is about 940km²) and are located roughly 1,500km or two hours' flying time from Lisbon and about 3,900km or five hours from the east coast of North America. Running along a southeast to northwest axis they lie on either side of the line of latitude that links Lisbon with New York, and are between latitudes 36–39°N and longitudes 25–31°W. The total population is approximately 247,000. The islands separate conveniently into three groups: the Eastern Group of São Miguel and Santa Maria; the Central Group of Terceira, Graciosa, São Jorge, Pico and Faial; and the Western Group of Flores and Corvo. The islands closest to each other are Pico and Faial at just 6km apart. In area, they range from Corvo at 17km² to São Miguel at 746km². Highest altitudes vary from 412m on Graciosa to 2,351m on Pico.

CLIMATE For small islands the weather, especially when in the middle of a large ocean, is all-important. For the busy city worker, as everywhere, the weather impacts little on a daily basis, and for the visitor rain is but a passing nuisance. However, for farmers even a relatively short dry period causes problems because the volcanic soils are very quick-draining, while a rough sea means the coastal fishermen cannot go out, there is no income for them, and no fresh fish for the villages.

The Azores have a mild and equable climate, surrounded as they are by a huge expanse of sea and influenced by the warm Gulf Stream. This means that the temperature is pleasant at any time of year. The average winter temperature is 13°C, only sometimes dropping to around 4°C at night; frosts occur only above 1,000m. In summer, the average temperature is 23°C, with a maximum of 27°C.

Rain can and does fall in every month, but it is seldom persistent; and one can drive from rain through a world of rainbows into sunshine. There is a saying in the islands that you can have all four seasons in one day and this is amazingly true. If it is raining in the morning, do not despair – there could be clear skies and sunshine by lunchtime. Of course, the reverse is often true! The annual rainfall increases westwards and ranges from 700mm in Ponta Delgada on São Miguel to 1,600mm in Santa Cruz on Flores. Average humidity is around 80–85%, but can go up to 100%. Flowers love it! Many days are still or with a gentle breeze. However, winds can occasionally be strong and this is especially noticeable on exposed mountains. A winter gale can also bring an invigorating chill, but the scudding clouds and turbulent seas can be inspiring for the visitor.

For swimmers, the sea temperatures also vary relatively little and you will often see people bathing off the beaches throughout the winter, when the lowest sea temperatures are 15–16°C in February and March. The highest are in August and September, with an average of around 22–24°C.

NATURAL HISTORY AND CONSERVATION

It was not until the middle of the 19th century that the first studies of the flora, fauna and oceanographics took place, when the Azores were frequently visited by scientists. In 1841 and 1845, the British war vessel HMS *Styx*, led by Captain Vidal, undertook hydrographic studies of the Azores, drawing up the first map where the islands appear correctly surveyed and with their positions correctly given. HMS *Beagle* stopped in Terceira and São Miguel on its return from voyaging round the world, enabling Charles Darwin to make shore excursions. In 1850, HMS *Rattlesnake*, on the way home from a four-year voyage surveying the Coral Sea and the New Guinea coast, sailed into Horta for six days' recuperation. It had taken almost nine weeks to travel from the Falkland Islands, their last landfall, and the islands' plentiful supplies were much needed for the health of the crew and passengers. The ship's assistant surgeon and naturalist was Thomas Huxley, who later famously defended Darwin and his theory of evolution; during their week in port, he made the ascent of Pico. Prince Albert I of Monaco (1848–1922) stayed several times on the islands making oceanographic studies, then a new scientific discipline, and exploring the caldera on Graciosa. There are references to these studies in the Oceanographic Museum in Monaco.

Many of the remaining patches of native vegetation are now in protected zones and you might see notices to this effect. The vegetation of the islands, particularly

HOW THE WEATHER WORKS

Of the few things generally known about the Azores, the 'Azores High' probably tops the list. This is an area of high pressure or anticyclone that is semi-permanent.

Very simply, warm moist air rises over the tropics leading to low pressure there; this warm moist air then moves north towards the sub-tropical latitudes and cools. It then descends, increasing the pressure over the sub-tropical latitudes, at the same time becoming drier and resulting in largely clear skies. This tropical/sub-tropical circulation varies little in position; in summer it is more northerly, in winter and spring more southerly, usually lying to the south or southwest of the archipelago. This high-pressure belt is part of the global circulatory system and is called the Hadley cell. In the north Atlantic it is centred close to the Azores for most of the time, hence the 'Azores High'. The reason it is centred there is because the Azores lie roughly midway between the influence of the African and American continents. Landmasses distort the process and strong summer heating at these latitudes can cause, for example, low pressure in the northern summer over southeast Asia and India and bring monsoon rains. Surface layers of the ocean do not heat up in the same way as the land does, and therefore allow the high-pressure belt to persist.

Sometimes the 'Azores High' extends northeast towards the British Isles, especially when they have a good summer. In winter it can sometimes recede southwards, if the jet stream is also further south. Occasionally it disappears altogether to be replaced by low pressure, while often, at the same time, high pressure dominates northern Europe, giving cold weather in winter and hot, often eventually thundery weather in summer.

In the Azores the weather is influenced by the strength and location of this high, particularly in summer. A strong high gives pleasant, warm weather with on Pico, Terceira and São Miguel, is interesting not only because it represents communities that were once widespread in parts of Europe millions of years ago, but also because very few aspects of its ecology and biology have been studied and the opportunities for simple observation and research are considerable. There is a desire to know what is happening in amongst the evergreens. Many stretches of coastal cliff are protected zones, mostly for seabirds; again you might see the signs. The marine environment is similarly protected.

You may be curious to know what the yellow plastic traps are for that you may see around the islands. These are pheromone traps for the rather colourful iridescent copper and green Japanese beetle, a very serious pest about 15mm long and 10mm wide. Not a problem in its native Japan, where there are natural predators, it was accidentally introduced into the USA in the early 1900s and in the 1970s arrived in the Azores, thought to be from a military aircraft landing at Lajes on Terceira. The larval stage is mostly spent in lawns and pastureland feeding on roots, and the adult eats the foliage of many plants including vines, roses, oak and fruit trees.

GEOLOGY The archipelago is formed from the upper sections of volcanoes. In the mid-Atlantic, tectonic plates are pulling apart on the ocean bed. The gap between them is filled by molten volcanic material that rises from the Earth's mantle and continuously forms new oceanic crust. This extrusion wells up and forms an enormous underwater mountain chain or mid-ocean ridge, and the sea floor spreads. The **Mid-Atlantic Ridge** runs from the Arctic to the Antarctic, meeting on its way the Indian Ocean Ridge off the southern tip of Africa. Along its length

little wind. A weak high gives weather that is changeable and wet, and you can tell when a depression is coming by a sudden drop in the barometer and a southerly wind, veering from southwest to northwest. A low approaches with steadily lowering and thickening cloud. The wind increases, bringing heavier cloud and rain showers, and then often torrential rain, by which time all sight of any nearby island has vanished. Then comes a break, the wind changes direction, and blue skies return. Finally, it all calms down, and the high reasserts itself. This drama might sometimes be over within a few hours and, if you are on land with a good vantage point, it can be fun to watch the rain squalls skating across the ocean. Winds come from the west, travelling eastwards, and this is reflected in the higher rainfall of the Western Group. In early summer, winds are mainly from the southwest and by July and August are predominantly northeasterly, gentle and with frequent calms. By September they return to the southwest and become gradually stronger. Occasionally bad storms hit the islands, but mostly they follow a narrow path. As you drive round the islands from time to time you will see cryptomeria trees snapped off like broken toothpicks.

Another major climatic influence on the Azores is the ocean currents, especially those originating from the Gulf Stream. This is a movement of warm water of equatorial and tropical origin into the colder northern waters of the Atlantic. West of the Azores, the Gulf Stream splits into two main branches: the North Atlantic Current that passes north of the islands, and the Azores Current passing to the south. This Gulf Stream gives the Azores their warm temperate climate. A further complication is the North Atlantic Oscillation (NAO), a northern equivalent of El Niño, which concerns atmospheric circulation.

lie Iceland, the largest landmass created from oceanic crust, the Azores, Ascension, Saint Helena and Tristan da Cunha islands. Mid-ocean ridges occur beneath all our major oceans, and only in exceptional cases are there so many eruptions that they build up to appear above sea level and form islands. Much more frequent activity occurs under the ocean's surface on the seabed than is seen on the surface of the islands. Seamounts constantly rise and fall, and new lava pressure ridges are formed.

In the Azores, giant linear ridges have been created, conspicuously Pico and São Jorge, and these are among the largest such volcanic ridges actively forming anywhere on our planet. With the ocean floor roughly between 1,000m and 3,000m below sea level, it is fun to try to imagine the landscape that would confront the traveller if the Atlantic Ocean could be emptied.

The situation is more complicated because, near the Azores, three plates meet in a T-shaped triple junction. The North American, African and Eurasian plates meet at a point between the Western and Central groups of islands, between Flores and Faial. Flores and Corvo are on the North American Plate. The Mid-Atlantic Ridge forms two legs of the 'T' and the other islands are alongside a spreading centre called the **Terceira Rift**, formed about 36 million years ago. It is not certain on which plates, African or Eurasian, the remaining islands belong or whether some might be on an Azorean microplate.

The seismic tremors felt in the islands are mostly caused by magma flowing up through the cracks left in the Earth's crust as the plates separate. At times these tremors, measuring less than 5.0 on the Richter scale, will occur with surprising frequency. Six of the islands have all been subject to **eruptions and earthquakes** within recent history, but the remaining three, Santa Maria, Flores and Corvo, are now considered inactive.

Of the central and eastern islands, Santa Maria was the first to rise above the sea some five million years ago but changes in sea level and tectonic activity caused it to submerge. A million years later, the Formigas islets and what is now the eastern end of São Miguel rose above the sea and Santa Maria reappeared. It was during this period of submergence that the island acquired its marine fossils, the only island to have them. The oldest part of São Miguel is around Pico da Vara in the east; at the far western end, Sete Cidades began around 290,000 years ago, at the same time as Água de Pau started out from the ocean bed. Thus São Miguel was once two islands, only becoming united when the Picos region north of what is now Ponta Delgada began a long series of eruptions starting 50,000 years ago. Terceira, Graciosa, São Jorge and Faial are all younger than a million years, Pico being the youngest at a mere 300,000 years or less. The two western isles, Flores and Corvo, lie on the western flanks of the Mid-Atlantic Ridge; the oldest rocks on Flores date to around 2.5 million years and are below sea level; the youngest are about 3,000 years old.

In 1811, about a mile off the coast of São Miguel opposite Ferraria, a new island appeared. One hundred metres tall and about 1.5km long, it took about a month to create. The British frigate *Sabrina* was in the area and her commanding officer, Captain Tillard, landed on the still-steaming island, planted a Union Jack, named the island '**Sabrina**' and claimed it as British territory! Unfortunately for his credibility, when the next surveyors arrived, there was no trace of the island; in just four months the sea had washed it away and all that remains now is a bank 40m below sea level. Most recently, in 1957, an eruption began just off the west coast of Faial that added a further 2km² of land to that island.

More information about the volcanoes and how the islands were formed is given in the chapters on the individual islands. See also www.azoresgeopark.com, the website of the Azores Geopark Association, a non-profit association established in

2010 and based in Horta with wide objectives concerning the environment, socio-economic, cultural and sustainable balanced development of the Azores. A geopark is a defined area with an exceptional geological heritage that is a base promoting the population's wellbeing at the same time as respecting the environment. There is a network of Geosites on the nine islands and surrounding sea floor representing the geodiversity of the archipelago, and the website lists the principal sites together with various tourist routes (these yet to be developed).

COLONISATION Oceanic islands such as the Azores differ from continental islands in that they are usually basaltic volcanoes, distant from the mainland and surrounded by vast oceans. They have to gain their flora and fauna by invasion, unlike continental islands that are close to geologically diverse landmasses to which they were once attached. The flora and fauna of an oceanic island is therefore distinct because it is made up of those organisms that can cross oceans. This barrier filters out many potential colonists so that the Azores lack certain groups, such as mammals (excluding bats), that are important on the mainland.

Not only has half the Atlantic Ocean to be crossed to reach the Azores from the nearest land, but on arrival landfall is extremely tough, on a new, raw, volcanic island presenting hardened flows of lava or desert-like ash. How tough a challenge it is to colonise new ash deposits can be seen at Capelinhos on Faial. This area was engulfed and enlarged by an eruption in 1957. When you stand by the remains of the old lighthouse and the wind drives sharp volcanic sand into your face with stinging force, look at the few plants that are establishing. There is *Arundo donax*, planted and artificially aided by humans, and the human-sponsored evening primrose. Left entirely to nature, colonisation takes a long time.

Winds and sea brought life to the Azores. Ocean currents transported marine organisms and shoreline animals to scavenge and survive upon what the sea washed ashore, along with others such as land crabs that have a marine larval stage. Travelling on prevailing winds and also the jet stream came spores of ferns, algae, fungi, lichens and mosses, seeds and microscopic animals, even spiders and other insects. All lightweight and adapted to wind dispersal, they landed in the Azores, even falling to earth in raindrops. Ground-nesting seabirds deposited their guano, providing further food for scavenging invertebrates and micro-organisms while rain slowly washed out minerals from the lava, all helping to create a very fertile soil. Currents, prevailing winds and distance from landmasses all influence which organisms will become established on an island, and where they, or their ancestors, came from. Land birds that have wandered or been blown off course by storms will bring seeds, either in their stomachs or attached to their bodies. For the early colonists, survival would have been a harsh process, but it needed only some to succeed.

Slowly these first organisms changed the bare habitat by contributing organic matter to form soil. By retaining moisture, and modifying light, temperature and exposure, they enabled later arrivals to establish, thus slowly creating a more hospitable environment which in turn would allow further colonists to establish. They had to be adaptable, able to adjust to climatic variations and different food sources, and to survive both competition from other species and many other challenges in a new habitat. Variation in some species may have allowed them to adapt better to the conditions, thus leading over time to new species and subspecies. Today, there are 60 endemic plant species in the Azores, unique to the islands and found nowhere else in the world.

The Azores, along with the other archipelagos of Madeira, the Savage Islands, the Canaries and the Cape Verdes, comprise the region known as Macaronesia.

The most characteristic vegetation is the dense evergreen forest, or laurisilva. It is a representative relic of the evergreen forests that grew in late Tertiary times (around 2.75 million years ago) in what is now southern Europe and northwest Africa. Possibly because of the Azores' oceanic climate, these forests escaped the extremes of climatic changes and thus survived while elsewhere they became extinct.

Colonisation and evolution never cease. New plants will arrive – see *Two Bullies*, opposite – and others will be eliminated by changing circumstances. Islands are living laboratories where the processes of dispersal, immigration, establishment, adaptation and extinction can all be studied. These are just some of the reasons why areas need to be protected from human depredation so that they may be there for future generations of students and provide an account of the changes going on around us.

THE VEGETATION The dense evergreen forest that once covered much of the islands has long been cleared for agriculture and settlement. Visually the quite extensive plantations of the exotic conifer *Cryptomeria japonica* now add considerably to the aesthetics of the Azorean landscape since tree cover within the lifetime of elderly islanders has been very considerably less than it is today. Planted to reduce erosion, lessen water loss, provide shelter for cattle and produce timber, these plantations are a substantial if sometimes controversial plus. Emigration has left many previously cultivated areas abandoned, to be invaded by a mix of native *Myrica faya*, *Erica azorica* and introduced and subsequently naturalised *Pittosporum undulatum* and, encouragingly, some other **native species** such as the endemic *Picconia azorica*. There is a tremendous battle raging, because *Myrica faya* is light-demanding, and must fight with the pittosporum for survival.

The native vegetation remains in a number of isolated areas. Evergreen forest is found as remnant forest or as individual species surviving in hedgerows above the 500m contour. The quite different coastal region of steep cliffs, of lava flows, agricultural land and seashore have their own mix of native, endemic and introduced exotic species.

The Azores archipelago has a total of 850 or more **plant species**, most of which have been introduced by humans. Of the total, some 300 are native, and of these possibly 60 species are endemic, found nowhere else in the world. Of the 11 species of native trees, eight are endemic to the Azores, and two others are found elsewhere only in Madeira. Dominant species of the forest include holly (*Ilex perado* ssp. *azorica*), juniper (*Juniperus brevifolia*), tree heather (*Erica azorica*) and laurel (*Laurus azorica*). Growing in the mountains at altitudes where the hillsides are often embraced by cloud, such vegetation is called **cloudforest**; often the trunks and branches are adorned with epiphytic ferns, while bryophytes (mosses and liverworts) can be exuberant, sometimes even thriving on the leaves as epiphylls.

The largest area remaining of undisturbed forest is on Terceira, on the Caldeira de Santa Bárbara and a small area between Juncal, Pico Alto and Serra do Labaçal, not the easiest to access for the relaxed naturalist on holiday. The forests of the Caldeira de Santa Bárbara, at over 800m, are often cloud-covered and are largely dominated by juniper (*Juniperus brevifolia*), although all of the Azorean tree species can be found in gullies and other places. Areas of natural grassland are to be seen inside the caldera and endemic grasses such as fescue (*Festuca jubata*) and soft-grass *Holcus rigidus* are to be found growing with endemic herbaceous species such as *Tolpis azorica*. However, the caldeira is a reserved area and to visit one should contact the Mountaineering Society in Angra do Heroísma (see page 141) and book a local guide as there are no trails and the weather can suddenly close in within 20 minutes.

São Miguel's only remaining area of natural forest can at least be easily seen! It is to be found at the eastern end of the island, and covers about 600ha on Pico da Vara.

Pico has the most accessible of all native forest, although little remains and that in small patches, often where the ground is badly tumbled with small boulder-sized lava and has therefore escaped the predations of farmer and cattle. There are patches of *Viburnum tinus* ssp. *subcordatum*, *Euphorbia stygiana*, *Ilex perado*, *Vaccinium cylindraceum*, *Frangula azorica*, *Hedera helix* ssp. *canariensis*, *Juniperus brevifolia* and its green-branched parasite *Arceuthobium azoricum* and occasionally, in the loose gravel at the edge of the asphalt road, *Thymus caespititius*.

The coastal flora has been badly disturbed by numerous developments and in places by the escape and spread of garden ornamentals such as the several members of the succulent Aizoaceae. However, while some of the species are endangered, none is on the verge of extinction and all are to be found, often in places where one least expects them, and in the most inhospitable sites. All the islands have suitable habitats. Characteristic species include the endemic grass *Festuca petraea* and the rush *Juncus acutus*. Widely located but found in small concentrations by the coast is one of the most handsome of all Azorean endemics, the perennial, slightly shrubby *Azorina vidalii*.

(See also *Appendix 2*, *Flora*, for an aid to identifying plants you are likely to see, and the website www.horta.uac.pt/species/plantae.)

Two bullies Amid all the excitement of introducing new plants into the show gardens of São Miguel came two very gardenworthy species which have more than outlived their mid 19th-century patrons. From the middle altitudes of the Himalaya came the **Kahili ginger**, *Hedychium gardnerianum*, a handsome plant about 1.5m tall with beautiful, sweetly scented, terminal spikes of orange-yellow spidery flowers. Away from its native habitat it found itself in the Azores in a permanently moist climate, with nothing to limit its growth. It has become a superbly aggressive invader: it can adapt to various Azorean habitats; it is a strongly competitive plant; cut it down and it can quickly recover; it produces abundant efficiently dispersed seeds; can easily reproduce vegetatively; and once established it dominates the site for many years. As a consequence it has smothered areas of native vegetation, prevents the re-establishment of desirable species and has invaded large areas of cryptomeria forest – a real pest, and very difficult to eradicate. The second garden delight is **Gunnera tinctoria**, one of the 'giant rhubarbs' from South America. You will see this invading parts of the Furnas Valley and especially the pastures high above; also Lake Fogo, a protected area for flora, and Sete Cidades. Deeply rooted and with a strong constitution, it covers hectares of pastures; the occasional container-load taken to Holland for sale to garden centres makes little impact.

THE BIRDS Studies have shown that the Azores are one of the least attractive birdwatching destinations in terms of numbers of birds that might be seen and the cost per bird seen! Almost without exception there are no full species in the Azores that cannot be seen closer to, or on, continental Europe. However, for the independent birdwatching traveller, there are some 150 species recorded for the islands plus 35 breeding species; of these breeding species, ten are endemic subspecies and one is an endemic species. Of the total number of species, 45 have a regular presence in the archipelago, and seven have been introduced. The subspecies present a substantial challenge, even to the experts. In addition, birds which are blown off course when migrating between North and Central America occasionally add exotic interest. Such incidences can be expected to increase as the weather becomes more turbulent with climate change and September to November 2005 proved an especially suitable time following the several hurricanes to hit North America, particularly hurricane Rita. American waders and waterfowl were known but now land birds like wood warblers are being recorded for the first time.

Two regular migrants are the common tern and the black-headed gull. The first arrives in April and stays until October, when the black-headed gull arrives, remaining until spring. The beautiful glaucous gull (*Larus hyperboreus*) can also be seen in winter where it stays in Madalena harbour on Pico. Along the coast where lava has flowed into the sea and shallow pools form, wagtails, rock doves, turnstones, dunlins, little egrets, whimbrels and other waders come to feed. On stacks and, importantly for breeding, small offshore islets where nests are protected from predators, gulls and terns crowd together. There are few sandy beaches in the Azores, but here may be seen Kentish plovers (*Charadius alexandrinus*), although one of the best places to see them is at Santa Maria airport! Steep sea cliffs are important nesting sites for shearwaters; in some places the rocky faces are over 300m high and are made up of layers of lava, scoriae and cinders. It is in the cinder layer where the circular nesting holes may be seen. Cory's shearwater (*Calonectris diomedea*) is quite common on all the islands and during the daytime it is possible to see them at sea interacting with dolphins and big fish such as tuna; it is usually absent from mid-November to February. Like the shearwater, terns are also regular breeders and the endangered roseate tern (*Sterna dougalii*) mixes in breeding colonies with the common tern (*Sterna hirundo*); the latter can often be seen catching and feeding on small fish in the harbours.

Inland there are habitats of fields surrounded by hedges or stone walls, extensive areas of lava where vines are often planted, areas where native erica or myrica predominate or where introduced pittosporum or eucalyptus have invaded, and many areas of planted conifer forest. Above 600m conditions generally are very wet and humid; pockets of native evergreen forest remain, surrounded by cattle pastures. Birds are everywhere, including chaffinches, blackbirds, blackcaps, grey wagtails and canaries.

If you walk quietly through wooded areas you may chance upon the shy and diminutive goldcrest (*Regulus regulus*); there are three subspecies on different islands, distinguished by the colour of their plumage. One of the prettiest birds is the Azores grey wagtail (*Motacilla cinerea particiae*). Often running about on quiet roads or near a water fountain, the wagging tail and bright yellow underparts are unmistakable. It is a paler yellow and has a slightly longer bill than its Madeiran counterpart. The blackbird (*Turdus merula azorensis*) is darker and glossier than the European bird while the female has feathers of a deeper brown, and the chaffinch (*Fringilla coelebs moreleti*) has a different colour and song from that found on the mainland. The sparrow (*Passer domesticus*) is most frequently seen and was introduced in the 1940s – on one island even the name of the Italian ship that brought the stowaways is known. The starling (*Sternus vulgaris granti*) is the next bird most often seen, particularly at dusk when great flocks of them soar around large Canary Island palms prior to roosting. Incidentally, these palms are sometimes favoured homes for bats. Memorable is the song of the canary, especially in concert with the sound of cowbells. These pleasurable brown-and-yellow birds (*Serinus canaria*), endemic to Macaronesia, take exception to common sparrows and, since their immigration, have largely moved away from urban areas to the fields and higher places where they flock and serenade the walker.

The Azorean bullfinch (*Pyrrhula murina*) (*priolo* in Portuguese) is the bird that receives all the promotional publicity, and it is rare. Once common, it was shot almost to extinction long ago, mainly by the fruit farmers who also killed chaffinch, canary, blackbird and blackcap because they viewed them as agricultural pests and the government paid compensation on the number of beaks presented. The *priolo* can now be seen with much patience in the reserve of Pico da Vara on São Miguel amid the dense evergreen forest. (See also page 74, the Priolo Environmental Centre.) With a considerably higher profile is the endemic Azorean buzzard that, when misidentified by the early settlers, gave its false name to the islands; *açor* in Portuguese means 'goshawk'. Another explanation suggests that when the first settlers arrived they found the birds so tame they came to hand like goshawks. Anyway, *Buteo buteo rothschildi* has been in the islands for a very considerable time and subjective observation suggests their number has increased over the past few years. They are frequently seen soaring over the countryside, and it is possible to get quite close to them when they perch on telegraph poles or buildings.

Seabirds, especially the rarer species, may often best be seen from the inter-island ferries. For other birdwatching areas please see under the individual islands. There is an excellent website (*www.birdingazores.com*) – see page 269 for details.

WHALES AND OTHER CETACEANS Cetaceans, from the Greek meaning 'sea monster', are members of the order Cetaceae, commonly known as whales and dolphins. Altogether there are a little over 80 species worldwide, and some 25 species have been sighted off the Azores. They are mammals, have lungs and nostrils (blowholes), suckle their young and have front flippers evolved from forelegs. Within the Cetaceae are two subgroups: the toothed whales and the baleen whales. The former have teeth and a single blowhole while the latter have, instead of teeth, a horny baleen or plate descending from the upper jaw and paired blowholes. This difference is important when feeding; the toothed whales eat larger prey such as cephalopods and fish and the baleen whales use their comb-like plates to filter very small fish and the shrimp-like krill. Many of these filter-feeding whales often undertake long migrations because they need warm waters for the growth and development of their young, but they also need the food resources that concentrate in colder waters.

The mid-Atlantic location of the steep-sided volcanic islands of the Azores causes great upswellings of coldwater currents from the ocean depths which meet the warm waters of the Gulf Stream, producing nutrient-rich waters. The species most readily identified with the Azores is the sperm whale or cachalote (*Physeter macrocephalus*), the largest of all toothed whales. Other toothed whales frequently seen during the main season are Cuvier's beaked whale (*Ziphius caviostris*), northern bottlenose whale (*Hyperodon ampullatus*), short-finned pilot whale (*Globicephala macrorhynchus*) and Sowerby's beaked whale (*Mesoplodon bidens*).

Dolphins seen regularly are common Atlantic (*Delphinus delphis*), bottlenose (*Tursiops truncates*), Risso's (*Grampus griseus*), Atlantic spotted (*Stenella frontalis*) and striped (*Stenella coeruleoalba*). Since 2001 observations of baleen or great whales have increased, during early April to late June. Species include fin (*Balaenoptera musculus*), sei (*Balaenoptera borealis*), humpback (*Megeptera novaeangliae*) and the blue whale (*Balaenoptera musculus*), thought to be the largest animal ever to have lived on Earth. The Azores are claimed to be the European hotspot for the number of cetacean species seen.

CONSERVATION The Azores Regional Government has committed to a policy focused on the environment and national heritage – sites of high botanical, fauna, ecological, landscape and geological interest – and the surrounding marine

In the Azores only sperm whales were hunted, the largest of the toothed whales, with males growing to 20m. First used for lamps and candle wax, sperm whale oil gave the brightest glow free of any disagreeable odour. Other uses over time included watch oil, and lubricants for delicate instruments, cosmetics, textiles (preventing fibres from unravelling when twisted into threads), an early equivalent of WD40, soap, jute, varnish, explosives and paint, and for margarine until the 1960s, when it was replaced with vegetable oils.

The first known organised commercial whaling was done in the Bay of Biscay by the Basques, who, from the 10th century, hunted migrating right whales (*Eubaleana glacialis*) that passed inshore. The whales were spied by lookouts onshore, and they were hunted from land-based small boats. Six hundred years later the right whales had declined in number and the catches were small, so the Basques went cod fishing instead, in the Grand Bank area of Westfoundland, where they discovered large numbers of whales. These they hunted, as did the Dutch, British and Germans. From a larger ship small boats were used to approach the whales and harpoon them. The carcasses were then towed ashore, where the blubber was processed for eventual use as lighting oil, lubrication, soap and paint. Within a century the whale numbers declined here as well so that the ships had to search further afield, and the blubber was processed on board. In the early 18th century, the American colonists began hunting whales, especially the sperm whale, near their shores. Soon they began to explore and profitably exploit more distant Atlantic waters and by 1765 reached the Azores, then known as the Western Islands Ground. The whaling here was so good they continued to visit in spite of the Spanish and French privateers and numerous pirates who infested the Azorean waters, and even when they were having to make three- or four-year-long voyages to the Indian and Pacific oceans and beyond to make the search profitable. It soon became the practice for the American ships to recruit from the islands, where the local fishermen made outstanding boatmen. The British whalers out of Dundee and other towns on their way to the Greenland fisheries likewise called in at Orkney or Shetland to make up their crews. By the 1800s, American whalers were regularly calling at Horta for victuals and water, and also to tranship barrels of oil. This golden age of American whaling, when New Bedford was known as 'the city that lit the world', continued until the 1850s; whale oil was becoming unaffordable and the start of the American petroleum industry in 1859 producing kerosene for lighting soon began to replace it. At the same time, the American Civil War, beginning in 1861, played havoc with the whaling fleet, Confederacy ships capturing or destroying many of the vessels, frequently off the Azores. The year 1927 saw the last of the American whalers out of New Bedford.

The Azoreans, so long accustomed to small boats from childhood, excelled in the jobs of lookouts, boatmen and harpooners in the small boats lowered to hunt and kill the whales, and in time could be found as a majority of the crew; some became officers and captains. Yet it was a desperately arduous life with often poor food and conditions, low pay, and increasingly long voyages. It was, however, an escape from compulsory military service, and between voyages they could settle in New England and send money home to dependants in the islands.

Sperm whaling far off the Brazil coast began in the late 1700s, funded from mainland Portugal, and there were other schemes tried off the coast of Mozambique and the Cape Verdes. In 1840, subsidised voyages went as far as

New Zealand, but Portugal never established a deep-sea industry. There were attempts to fit out whale ships in the Azores, but there was never much capital available in the islands and the maintenance costs made little economic sense against the by now increasing and successful shore whaling.

It is not certain when shore whaling began in the Azores. Previously, an occasional whale had been taken, but it was not soundly established until the 1850s, in Faial, coinciding with the demise of the American fleets. It soon spread to Pico and by the end of the 19th century this island was catching the most whales, and did so until the end of the practice. The advent of shore whaling also coincided with the failure of the wine industry which so badly affected Pico, and this was the probable stimulus. Pico established several whaling companies, all competing with each other, and obtained concessions from other islands to whale so that, by 1908, there were whale boats in Terceira, Graciosa and Faial. Flores and São Miguel began whaling a couple of decades after Pico, the latter with its whale station and try-works at Capelas, which benefited from the greater number of whales that passed its shores than those of the Central and Western groups. Corvo, with its dangerous coastline a major disadvantage for whaling, caught few whales and these were mostly taken to Flores for processing (working-up). Santa Maria was also whaling, but it lapsed in the 20th century, only to be revived just before World War II, with the highest catch per boat of all the islands, while São Jorge became as active as Faial during the first 40 years of the 20th century.

The crew had a captain, the *mestre*, who was helmsman, and a *trancado* or harpooner, who was also the first oarsman and occupied the bow of the boat. The five oarsmen completing the crew sat between the captain and the harpooner. It was an exceedingly dangerous occupation, going far out to sea in a small open boat and then closing to kill the huge animal, first with the harpoon and then with lances. This meant risking disaster from the great flukes or, less likely but very possible, to be upturned by an unexpected rising of the whale below the keel or for an angry animal to try to bite the boat. Between as many as ten and 30 smashed boats each year have been reported from one whaling station alone. Lookouts or *vigias* were positioned on vantage points around the coast and each arc of search overlapped to thoroughly watch the sea to a distance of 30 or 35 miles, from dawn to late afternoon throughout the year. Records indicate the best time was around 06.00. On sighting a blow a rocket was fired from the *vigia* to let the whalemen know to launch their boats, and also a white flag. If a kill was made, the flag was flown at half-mast to warn the try-works to get ready for processing. The boats would sail or row out, in later years to be towed out by motor launch, guided by large sheets laid out on the cliffs or by radio telephone. Once the whale felt the harpoon it went away very fast or dived, taking out line at a rapid rate; friction could set it on fire, so water was poured over it. Sails and mast had to be rapidly lowered while taking care to stay clear of the running line down the middle of the boat between each man's rowing position; not to do so could result in the loss of a leg or worse. Once several hundred feet of line had been taken out and the pace began to slacken, the line would be fixed to the loggerhead, a post at the back of the boat. With the line fixed, the whale would feel the drag and take off again to tow the whalers at around 25–30km/h, often called the 'Nantucket sleigh ride', which was another dangerous period because the whale could veer or

continued overleaf

1

double back and capsize the boat. When the whale tired, rope was taken in, but let out if the whale surged again. Since a whale in one breath can exchange 85–90% of air, an objective was to break the animal's breathing pattern to prevent it from diving deeply. Eventually the whale tired sufficiently for the boat to close, when lances were used for the kill.

The most important modern innovation was the gradual introduction from 1909 of motorised tow-boats, enabling several boats to be rapidly towed to the whale regardless of unfavourable winds once it was sighted by the lookouts; this greatly extended their range. The engine noise would have scared off the whales, so the last mile was covered by sail, oars and finally by paddle to within harpooning range. Among other advantages, it enabled longer chases without becoming benighted at sea and in possibly deteriorating weather; it also offered support in case of an emergency such as if a whale boat was smashed by the whale. Finally, it towed the dead whales back to shore, a backbreaking task formerly done by the whaling boat under oars. Although harpoon guns and exploding lances were used to hunt whales, the Azorean whalemen stayed with the hand harpoon and lance. Similarly, processing or *saving* of the dead whale changed little; first the whale was *cut in*, meaning the blubber was cut up or *flensed* with the animal either beached, or tied alongside a jetty using cutting-spades, ropes and at most a hand capstan. With the blubber and spermaceti removed, these were then *tried out*, by being placed into try-pots or iron cauldrons to melt and reduce over a basalt oven to make sperm oil and 'head oil'. The carcass, with its meat and bone, was simply towed back out to sea and abandoned. It was not until 1934 that sufficient capital became available to invest in modern processing equipment using powered winches and pressure cookers when the whole animal was utilised. Just after World War II radio-telephones were first used for communication between the lookouts and the motor tow-boats, purchased from the US military, who sold off the stock very cheaply.

In the Azores the owners of a whalery might take half the profits, with the balance shared between the whalemen. Importantly, income was supplemented

environment. The Azores have one of the richest marine ecosystems in the world, including some eight hydrothermal vents of the Mid-Atlantic Ridge.

Designating areas to be protected began in 1972 with the Faial caldera and two years later Lagoa do Fogo on São Miguel. In the next decades there followed forest nature reserves with a wider remit, and the first marine reserves. Today, visitors see onsite noticeboards declaring protected areas, often followed by a run of acronyms.

The European Union's Natura 2000 (*http://ec.europa.eu/environment/nature/natura2000/index_en.htm*) is a network of sites in a European-wide partnership at the heart of which are two Directives. The 1979 Birds Directive seeks the establishment of Special Protection Areas (SPAs) for birds, aiming to protect and manage areas important for rare and vulnerable species because they use them for breeding, feeding, wintering or migration; the 1992 Habitats Directive requires Special Areas of Conservation (SACs) to be designated to provide increased protection and management for rare and vulnerable animals, plants and habitats. These Natura 2000 sites now cover about 20% of the European territory and, as their website says, most European citizens will not live far from a Natura 2000 site. There are further acronyms, including Site of Community Importance (SCI), which contributes to the from small-scale farming, ie: some crops, one or two animals, some fishing. The whale boats or *canoas* were American to begin with, and 1894 saw the first one built in the Azores, on Pico. The Azores design evolved to be longer, accommodating a seventh, extra crew, to have larger sails and other technical differences.

As with so many island enterprises, the commercial success of whaling suffered market vicissitudes beyond the control of the islanders. New substitute products, prices, and in the late 1940s the big Antarctic sperm whale catches, impacted upon Azorean sales, but markets during the two world wars and the Korean War saw high demand. In 1935, 99 sperm whales were taken, and in 1969, 263 was the last of the peak catches. In terms of world totals, the Azorean catches made little impact, but depleted stocks are part of the history of whaling and some species were driven almost to extinction – annual catches in the 1930s were over 40,000 whales – and the Washington Convention of 1946 was an attempt to regulate whaling. As the century continued the numbers allowed to be caught were reduced substantially, but economics, declining stocks, falling prices and the ready availability of substitutes caused nations to abandon whaling. By 1954, Azorean whaling was seen as a relic industry. The factory on São Miguel closed in 1972, and whaling ceased in the Eastern Group of islands. The International Whaling Commission in 1982 agreed zero commercial quotas, but Norway and Japan, and now Iceland, continue. Whale hunting in the Azores became a very minor affair, and had ceased altogether by the mid 1980s. I remember standing on the quay at Lajes on Pico watching in the shallows a huge jawbone slowly being grazed by sea creatures; it must have belonged to one of the very last whales to be caught.

Today, the annual whaleman's festival, *Festa dos baleeiros*, continues to be held on the first Sunday in August in the tiny church on Monte da Guia, above Porto Pim in Horta. In Lajes do Pico there is also a whaler's festival, and still some of the old whaling villages beautifully maintain old *canoas* and sometimes even commission new ones, especially for sailing races. There is an annual regatta, when opportunities are given for people to sail in a whale boat.

maintenance or restoration of a natural habitat or species or biological diversity, and also contributes significantly to Natura 2000. The rich geological and volcanic heritage is recognised by selected locations under Regional Natural Monuments (RNMs). Most recently, to better administer and manage the protected areas the regional government established three management units: Island Nature Parks – on all nine islands; Marine Parks; and Local Protected Areas, created by local municipalities to safeguard local parks, gardens, lookouts and the Recreational Forest Reserves.

At the same time the OSPAR Convention for the Protection of the Marine Environment of the northeast Atlantic (*www.ospar.org*) is creating in conjunction with Natura 2000 a network of Marine Protected Areas (MPAs) that are both ecologically coherent and well managed. The northeast Atlantic has been divided into five regions. In the wider Atlantic region six MPAs have been established, four in collaboration with Portugal, covering a total area of 285,000km², protecting a series of seamounts and sections of the Mid-Atlantic Ridge and hosting a range of vulnerable deep-sea habitats and species. This is of special significance for the Azores since their maritime area is greater than their terrestrial. Member states are expected to pay for the management of their sites, but there are various community funds that can assist.

The presence of onsite wardens, rangers, professional naturalists and voluntary workers is still in its infancy throughout the Azores. Exceptions are the Capelinhos eruption site of 1958, the base supervising access to Pico Mountain, lava caves on Terceira, Pico and Graciosa, the whaling centres of Lajes on Pico and Horta on Faial, and the Priolo Environmental Centre on São Miguel.

Most recently, the islands of Corvo, Flores and Graciosa have been recognised by UNESCO as Biosphere Reserves; these are protected areas intended to demonstrate an equilibrium between man and nature, conservation and sustainable development. Finally, there are proposals afoot to have sites along the Mid-Atlantic Ridge declared World Heritage Sites. With the islands' increasing emphasis on renewable sources of energy, conservation strategies and environmental management, it is hoped the Azores could in time become a model for future sustainability.

HISTORY

DISCOVERY The islands were pristine until the 15th century; there were no indigenous peoples, and no-one had ever settled there. They were known to

THE STRATEGIC IMPORTANCE OF THE AZORES

From their initial settlement in the 15th century, the Azores have played a pivotal role in the history of the Atlantic. On Terceira, the Bay of Angra (Angra meaning 'Anchorage') provided protection and was soon defended, later by the great fortress of São Filipe and smaller São Sebastião. By the early 1500s, it was an obligatory port of call for the fleets serving Africa and the East and West Indies and for 300 years was a link between Europe and the New World.

When Spain overran Portugal, the 'Reprisal Pirates' of England sought to capture their treasure ships, and to protect them the Spanish in 1555 formed the first convoy system, with merchant ships defended by armed escorts.

Powerful nations must have long coveted the Azores for their strategic location. However, one enthusiast in the early 1800s proposed that Britain should acquire the archipelago, not only for use as a base between Africa and America and as a staging post in the transportation of troops to the Cape of Good Hope and the East Indies, but also because at the time the British Empire had no colony that produced wine(!), and that São Miguel and Terceira would make excellent penal colonies with transportation costs much less than the long voyage to Australia.

In November 1914, Portugal declared war on Germany, co-operating closely with the Allies, thus giving them access to the ports in Horta and Ponta Delgada for anti-submarine warfare and a safe harbour for repairs and refuelling convoys – convoys being a repeat of the Spanish strategy centuries earlier. In World War II, agreement to the use of the facilities in the Azores came much later as President Salazar was very reluctant to give Nazi Germany cause to invade mainland Portugal. Churchill famously called upon the Treaty of Eternal Friendship of 1373, or Treaty of Windsor; this was between England's King Edward III and King D João I of Portugal and was further sealed a year later when King João married Philippa of Lancaster, daughter of John of Gaunt. Reinforced from time to time through the following centuries, the treaty is still in force today after more than 600 years, and is the oldest alliance between any two countries. Negotiations were time-consuming, but eventually Britain was allowed by August 1943 to develop the exist, for in the *Medici Atlas* of 1351 the seven islands of the Central and Eastern groups are shown. Less than a century later the **Portuguese 'Age of Discoveries'** began and Portuguese explorers made the first recorded landfalls on Madeira (c1419), the Azores (c1427), Cape Verde (1456–60), Saint Helena and Ascension (1501–02) and Tristan da Cunha (c1506). Bartolomeu Dias rounded the Cape of Good Hope in 1488 and thus opened access to the Indian Ocean, and Pedro Álvares Cabral landed in Brazil in 1500, to say nothing of the numerous inland expeditions in Africa and elsewhere. It is not known for certain who discovered the islands for the Portuguese, nor the exact dates; numerous stories abound from which to take your choice. One I rather like which caps the debate is that a caravel came upon them by chance when sailing homewards from the west coast of Africa using the trade winds. Another is that the Infante Dom Henrique (Prince Henry 'the Navigator') ordered one Gonçalo Velho Cabral to sail westwards to find the islands he thought must exist. Cabral found only the Formigas rocks ('The Ants'), and went back home, getting a low mark from the Sagres Management School. Sent out again the following year, and sailing 15 miles distant from the Formigas, a much better prospect came into view. Since it was 15 August, the Feast of the Assumption, he called the island he reached first Santa Maria and was later

earth strip at Lajes on Terceira. Known as *aerovaca*, these simple airstrips were on several of the islands and regularly grazed by cattle. This time the farmers on Terceira were not only losing pasture, but to greater consternation there was also an *aguardente* (firewater) factory in the middle of the site. Marsden matting, an interlocking perforated metal sheet, was used initially to make a 6,000ft runway. Soon afterwards, the United States military were also allowed to use Lajes and they later made it a permanent airfield for heavy transports as the eventual liberation of Europe drew closer. A second airbase was needed and the US was given permission under cover of Pan American Airways so that it would seem Portugal was building it for post-war communications. Work began towards the end of 1944 and three A-shaped runways were built. Access to the Azores proved vital to the Allies in protecting the Atlantic convoys from German U-boats. There was a north Atlantic route which had protection from bases in Newfoundland and Iceland, and a southern route, but these left the mid-Atlantic as an undefended black hole; significantly, it was also the shortest crossing, saving time and vital fuel. Enemy U-boats prowled the seas around the Azores and Allied shipping losses were appalling. With the Lajes base the odds were turned, U-boats were sunk and shipping losses dramatically dropped and eventually the wolf packs were called off. Had Hitler built more U-boats as his admirals wanted, and implemented the Nazi plan to invade the Azores, how different might the outcome have been.

By 1947, all military operations had been transferred to Lajes, leaving Santa Maria an important stop for commercial transatlantic flights until the 1970s, when newer aircraft could cross non-stop. The only airstrip in the Azores long enough, it even hosted an occasional visit from Concorde. In 1948/49, Lajes was used in the Berlin airlift to counter the Soviet blockade, and this experience influenced the decision to negotiate long-term use by the American military for a base. It also continues as a Portuguese airbase. Portugal was one of the founding members of NATO, and in Ponta Delgada there is a NATO naval fuel depot and terminal.

appointed governor. São Miguel was supposedly discovered when an escaped slave clambered up a hill and saw a much larger island in the distance; this was settled around 1444. By chance some unknown mariners spotted a third island, and with a stroke of originality called it Terceira, 'Third Island'. Another version is that Prince Henry sent out caravels, date unknown, to find the islands and they discovered five, later named Santa Maria, São Miguel, Terceira, Faial and Pico. Most popular accounts give the Portuguese explorer Diogo de Silves the credit for finding the first island, Santa Maria, in 1427. In 1439, Alfonso V sanctioned Henry to settle seven islands, so they must have been discovered before that year. Flores and Corvo were certainly added last.

SETTLEMENT Colonisation of the islands was undertaken in a typically medieval way. King Alfonso V granted them to his nephew, the Infante Dom Henrique (Henry the Navigator) as Master of the Military Order of Avis, of Crusades origin. It was this Order of Avis that financially supported the discoveries of the 15th century and for reward was given the new lands to explore and populate. The Infante in

THE AZOREAN COW   *Luis Silva*

In the 15th century, when the islands were first settled, one of the first things that was done was to introduce many Portuguese domestic animals. Of these the cow was extremely important because she not only provided milk and meat but was also a hardworking animal around the farm, for ploughing, carting, etc. Some of the distinct cattle breeds that were imported from Portugal include Alentejana, Mirandesa, Minhota and Algarvia. There is also historical suggestion that some cows were imported from Flanders but there is no information on specific breeds. Importation would have continued until the numbers reached a reproductive level that was self-sustaining, and then probably stopped. The following five centuries of cross-breeding between the original breeds imported from Portugal and Flanders evolved into a distinct breed known today as Ramo Grande. This Ramo Grande breed dominated on most of the islands. Then, in the 1950s, Friesians were imported from England and later on from the USA and soon after that an artificial insemination programme was set up on Terceira and São Miguel. By the 1980s, there were quite a few importations of dairy heifers (Holsteins) and beef breeds (Limousin, Charolais and Fleckview) from Germany, England, Holland, France and Canada. A small number of Jersey heifers have since been added, plus Jersey embryo transfers. Consequently, and in a very short time, the Azorean breed became almost extinct.

Fortunately, in the area of Ramo Grande on Terceira, a group of farmers continued to maintain small herds of these animals. Today there is increasing interest in the conservation of this Azorean genetic heritage, and in its potential for producing beef; its specific characteristics have been defined and all individuals are now registered. At present, the genetic line in the Azores is mostly Holsteins for dairy and Limousin and Charolais for beef. Just recently, the Azores University, through its Agricultural Sciences Department, has concluded from a study of various dairy breeds that Jerseys would be the most suitable for the region. Hopefully, the Azorean Ramo Grande will survive the effects of globalisation and someday might even contribute its distinctive characters to future breeding.

turn delegated control over administration, defence, justice and land grants to the Captain Donatário (donatory or lord proprietor, the Portuguese equivalent of a colonial governor), together with the revenue from certain taxes, and the monopoly control over mills, salt and the ovens for baking bread. The king retained oversight of customs, control of selected taxes and of the death penalty.

The usual practice was followed when discovering islands; cattle, goats and pigs were landed to provide future food, and also very likely to begin the tremendous task of penetrating the dense vegetation. The first islands to be populated were Santa Maria and São Miguel, followed by Terceira in about 1450. Settlers came from mainland Portugal, particularly the Algarve and Alentejo, and from Madeira. Portugal's population was only 1.5 million, so Henry encouraged **immigration from Flanders**, and in 1466 Faial and Pico were settled by Flemings, under the Captain Donatário Josse Van der Huertere, and a few years later Flores by Willem Van der Hagen; for a time, these islands became known in northern Europe as the Flemish Islands because so many settled there, refugees from the scourges of the Hundred Years' War.

The first settlers faced an enormous task and probably used fire to begin to clear the vegetation. On some of the islands this would have revealed a very stony soil, and especially on Pico it must have been heartbreaking. Huge neatly piled stacks of stones metres square and 2m tall remain testimony to this tenacity and determination, as do the numerous stone walls. With such an inhospitable coastline, wherever it was possible to land must have dictated the location of those first settlements. Looking at them today, some still appear daunting, often at the foot of steep cliffs or ravines. Farming slowly spread across the islands as the vegetation was cleared and by the next century there was a surplus of production for export: wheat for the Portuguese garrison in north Africa, sugar and woad for dyeing to Flanders. Each island grew more of the crops that best suited its climate and terrain. However, by the end of the 17th century, the peasants were eating the introduced American corn (maize) and yams, so freeing the wheat crop for export for townspeople and cash export.

During the middle of the 16th century, vessels returning from India using the westerly trade winds passed through the Azores, but it was at the beginning of the Portuguese colonisation of Brazil and the discovery of America when the islands began their great development, mainly in the coastal village of Angra on Terceira because it offered sheltered anchorage. It became a principal port for exporting Azorean produce, and significantly an assembly port for ships returning from Brazil laden with valuable cargoes. Here they would form convoys for the journey to Lisbon, protected by warships against the marauding pirates.

In 1580, Spanish Castile annexed Portugal and the Azores supported Dom António, the next in line to the throne, who, with French help, held out on Terceira, becoming the last Portuguese resistance to Castilian power. The Spaniards defeated the French fleet off Terceira in July 1582 and the following year overran the islands. In 1591, the Spanish were attacked by the English, giving rise to the famous Tennyson poem *The Revenge* (see page 223). Liberated in 1640, the islands became an important staging post for British trade and for British naval strategy, until the opening of the Suez Canal over 200 years later.

Although so distant from the Portuguese mainland, the Azores nevertheless have often played an important part in Portuguese history. They contributed to the conquest, defence and supply of the Portuguese strongholds on the north African coast, caravels stopped in the Azores on their return from India, they supported the ships sailing to the Americas, and they strongly resisted Spanish domination between 1580 and 1640. Two centuries later the islands featured in the Liberals' struggle with the Absolutists; two presidents in the First Republic came from the Azores and, most recently, the islands provided important bases for the Allies in the two world wars, and in the Gulf War.

WOAD, PASTEL AND ORCHIL

For me, and I suspect for many, the name woad brings to mind school lessons telling of Boadicea and her warriors painted blue doing battle with the Roman invaders. Knowledge of the dye goes back to the Ancients, and the Greeks and Romans used it medicinally – it is a good astringent. In the cabbage family, *Isatis tinctoria* is a greyish, medium-tall biennial herb native to eastern Europe and western Asia; cultivated in Europe since the 10th century, it may now be found naturalised as a relict of former cultivation. First the leaves and stems were washed and dried, then ground in a mill; the powder thus obtained was again wetted and again sun-dried. The resultant concentrated black and granular extract was then formed into cakes and large balls called pastel. By the 13th century, French Languedoc became a main area of woad cultivation, centred on Toulouse, making the city very wealthy. It was from here the plant was introduced into the Azores at the end of the 15th century, where it was grown for almost 200 years, but only 100 of these were economically important. Woad's success was linked to the fortunes of the European textile industry, and the Azores and the English textile towns, especially Exeter, enjoyed a mutually profitable trade and more than a dozen English merchants lived in Ponta Delgada. At its peak, it is thought that woad was grown on more than 30% of São Miguel's arable land. Unfortunately, the dye constituent indigotin in woad is the same as in a dye plant in the pea family, *Indigofera*, or indigo, and being chemically inert they can both dye the same textiles; indigo also is much less vulnerable to fading, and was thus ideal for military uniforms. Limited supplies had come from India, but when the Portuguese discovered the sea route to India, imports rose. The woad lobby was considerable, imports were banned and in England indigo dye was prohibited for over 100 years, until 1685. Because it was so valuable, the French began its cultivation on their Caribbean islands; the climate was ideal, and the crop demanded slaves. Britain followed in Jamaica and South Carolina, and by the middle of the 17th century, cheap imports and heavy taxes imposed by Lisbon had killed the Azorean pastel trade, and the resident English merchants slowly dwindled.

Orchil or archil, *urzela* in Portuguese, is the source of a dye prepared from certain lichens of several genera. The Cape Verde Islands were a major producer, using it to dye their cotton trade cloth, but the discovery of abundant supplies in the early 19th century in Angola and Mozambique killed their market. In the Azores the lichen *Roccella tinctoria* is found on maritime rocks and when processed with stale urine (or ammonia) and dried it was sold in powder form, later known as cudbear, or as a paste, which gives a purple-red colour. Lichen dyes change colour in reaction to acids or bases – red to acid and blue to alkaline – and are used in litmus paper, while Orcein from *Roccella tinctoria* is used to make a purple stain for studying chromosomes. Never as significant in the Azores as pastel, its export was short-lived; indeed, one commentator claimed the revenue went as pin money to the queen!

GOVERNMENT AND POLITICS with Albano Cymbron

Initially, except for a period during the Spanish occupation, the Azores had no central government, and it was not until 1766 that a governor and captain-general for the whole group were appointed by the **Marquis of Pombal**. He was very much a man of the 18th-century Enlightenment, and had lived for several years in the main capitals of Europe, so was well aware how backward Portugal had become. He became Prime Minister of Portugal in 1750 and implemented economic and educational reforms, abolished slavery, revised the tax system and introduced commercial regulation. He implemented a new administrative system throughout the kingdom, creating districts or provinces. The Azores became a single province, governed by the captain-general (*capitão-general*), with Angra on Terceira – the archipelago's capital – doing away with the semi-feudal privileges of the various donatories and the islands losing their autonomous captaincies. While this may have been logical in Lisbon, it went against the vigorous individualism of the islands and greatly displeased the people of São Miguel, for theirs was the largest and richest island and they were accustomed to resolving their problems directly with the central government. Under the new arrangement, each island was totally independent of the others, and for approximately 60 years this regime prevailed; it was a time of struggle and indiscipline between the governor in Terceira and the other islands, mainly São Miguel.

In 1807, Napoleon's forces invaded Portugal; Napoleon wanted to stop **Anglo-Portuguese trade** and demanded Portugal blockade the ports, but the Portuguese refused to comply, so beginning the **Peninsular War**. The Portuguese royal family, their court and important citizens fled to Brazil and made Rio de Janeiro the capital of Portugal, leaving Portugal to a military junta with orders not to resist. In 1808, British and Portuguese troops under Sir Arthur Wellesley (the later Duke of Wellington) gained control over Lisbon and a treaty allowed the French to withdraw. In the meantime Napoleon forced the Spanish King Charles IV to abdicate and replaced him with his brother, Joseph Bonaparte. Also in 1808, the French invaded a second time, and again Wellesley repelled them, forcing them to retreat to Galicia. Their third and last invasion in 1810 ended with their defeat at the Battle of Busacco, near Coimbra and they were eventually forced to retreat to Spain, from where they were finally evicted in 1814. The consequences were considerable, with the Azores playing a valiant part, but it would take many long years for Portugal to recover from the ravages of the war.

Liberal ideas resulting from the French Revolution spread to Portugal with the French invasion and found fertile ground in a country that was in a deplorable state, its king and government in Brazil, and in their absence Lisbon ruled by the English Marshal Beresford and British commercial interests. The economy was in crisis, previously being dependent on a trade monopoly with Brazil and now, with the king residing there, this commerce had been opened to all friendly countries with the English benefiting most. Lisbon felt it was a colony of Brazil.

A **Liberal revolution** quickly spread from its beginnings in Oporto, demanding the return of the royal court, a constitutional monarchy and that Brazil revert to its old status of colony trading exclusively with Portugal. Beresford was replaced by a junta and in 1821, a Constituent Assembly was elected in Lisbon, the same year as the publication of the first Liberal constitution. A few months later the king, João VI, returned to Lisbon leaving his son, Dom Pedro, Regent of Brazil. In September, the assembly voted to abolish the Kingdom of Brazil and so bring it under direct control of Lisbon; the following year Brazil declared its independence, and Dom Pedro its first emperor.

Under the new constitution, adopted in 1822, deputies were elected by the people (landowners and merchants) and the king had no powers, not even to dissolve parliament. This was strongly opposed by João VI's queen, Carlota-Joaquina, who, together with her son Dom Miguel, prompted a countrywide insurgency against it in the name of Absolutism and a call for the king to abdicate. It was a very troubled time, as is common with any change of regime, with revolts against revolts with either the Traditionalists (Absolutists) or the Liberals in power. João VI died in 1826 and eventually in 1828, the youngest brother of Dom Miguel was declared king absolute, totally against the constitution only recently accepted by the crown. Liberals dissatisfied with or persecuted by the absolutist regime withdrew to Terceira, which remained loyal to the Liberal cause against the central government.

Meanwhile, in Brazil, following a political crisis King Pedro abdicated in favour of his son, Pedro II in 1831, and crossed to Europe to oppose his brother Dom Miguel. Going first to England where there were many exiled Portuguese Liberals, he moved in 1832 to Terceira, which he used as his base for the coming invasion of Portugal, and formed an interim **government-in-exile**. In July, he led a military force including the French and English, and took Oporto in the north, with the Duke of Terceira capturing Lisbon. Final victory came in 1834.

Reforms followed, and a new administration for the Azores was created by making the islands a province of Portugal, with Angra the capital. São Miguel strongly opposed the consequent dominance of Terceira and this was eventually resolved by first creating two districts, and then three. São Miguel and Santa Maria came under Ponta Delgada District, while Angra administered the islands of Terceira, Graciosa and São Jorge. Horta District presided over Faial, Pico, Flores and Corvo. Each district was independent of the others and managed its affairs directly with the central government in Lisbon. The provincial governor was appointed by Lisbon. So began the process of territorial division which later led to the creation of further autonomous districts that lasted until 1974. Interestingly, it was resentment over taxes that prompted the first ideas that the islands should have autonomy. This first occurred in 1869 with the **'Dízimo' tax** that obliged people to pay 10% of their earnings to the Church. Later came a tax on the alcohol produced in the Azores, introduced to protect the same industry on the mainland.

Prime Minister, and later President, Salazar led the authoritarian right-wing government which controlled Portugal from 1932 to 1974. He established public order which was previously lacking, and the political and financial stability for economic growth. A basic education was provided for everyone, and a substantial investment made in infrastructure. Many of the often very attractive schools in the Azores owe their origins to this period. His dictatorship followed a strict Catholic social doctrine opposed to class struggle and economic dominance, with a secret police to counter opposition. On his death a leftish military coup slowly changed the regime to a democracy leading to free elections and in 1976, the first constitutional government.

In 1976, the Azores became an autonomous region with its own government of Regional Assembly and Executive. The Executive or Regional Government is responsible politically to the Regional Legislative Assembly. The region elects five deputies to the national parliament in Lisbon. The Regional Government has 51 deputies elected every four years and meets in Horta. The President of the Azores, whose official residence is in Ponta Delgada, is the leader of the party with the greatest number of elected deputies. There are nine regional secretaries, each in charge of a department, eg: Finance and Planning, Tourism and Environment. The secretariats, or ministries, are based in Ponta Delgada, Angra do Heroísmo and Horta. Each island is divided into district councils, from six on São Miguel to just one on each of the smallest islands, which are in turn divided into parishes. The islands' autonomy includes responsibility for their economy. Education, health, the army, police and judiciary are controlled directly by the national government in Lisbon. The Portuguese government is represented by the Minister of the Republic who maintains residency in Angra do Heroísmo, Terceira. The Azores have one MEP.

ECONOMY

During the 30 years before the 2008 economic crisis in Europe, island infrastructure was given priority, and new airports, harbours and telecommunication systems were completed. The Azores, or at least Ponta Delgada, has changed hugely in the past few years with new industrial/commercial estates on the outskirts and many new shops in the town. Everywhere in the islands one frequently saw the European Union flag on a hoarding announcing funds for some new development, from further new port facilities to a tiny family enterprise for rural tourism. While some of the road building may be questioned, such as the recently finished highway to Nordeste on São Miguel and the asphalt surfacing of many of the minor farm tracks throughout the islands that once were easy and enjoyable walking trails, the airfields, new port facilities for cruise liners and tourism will pay dividends. But with the economic crisis have come austerity measures, with substantial increases in personal and corporate taxation, VAT rises and cuts in government budgets. Portugal was quick to try to reduce its budget deficit, and to meet the conditions of its EU bail out, but with forecasts of continuing reduced growth times are lean. However, the Azores, while affected, are faring better than the mainland and Maderia due to lower debts, although there have been many job losses in the construction industry. Apart from the public sector, the greatest contribution to GDP has been and remains the export of cattle and dairy products. Then there are minor crops of pineapples, potatoes, wine, tobacco and tea; all labour intensive. Tourism has long been gaining in importance, and while 2013 is likely to see a continuing downturn in the number of visitors, new markets to target have been identified. Although proportionately small, Azorean fishing is also artisanal, providing a relatively large number of jobs per tonne of fish landed. Given their different characters, it is not surprising economic activities have different relevance for individual islands. Dairy and beef are more relevant for Graciosa and São Jorge, fishing is more important to Faial and Pico, tourism for São Miguel, Pico, Faial and Flores, and other exports on the more diversified São Miguel. Transfer payments are important to Corvo because of its small size, to Terceira for its military airbase (although this will change if the USA implements its proposed reduction to 10% of its present strength), and to Santa Maria, which hosts the air control of the north Atlantic.

ENERGY The Azores have been dependent upon imported oil to generate electricity but are now increasingly seeking and exploiting energy from geothermal, wind and solar sources. The first hydro-electric plant was built on São Miguel in 1899 and ran until 1950.

In 1975 the Institute of Geosciences of the Azores was founded and in the following year began drilling wells down to 1,500m on São Miguel. The first pilot geothermal plant generating 3MW opened in 1980 and this success led to the exploration of the Ribeira Grande field. Now some 40% of São Miguel's electricity is from geothermal sources, development of a new geostation has commenced on Terceira, and exploration is planned for six of the other islands.

ISLAND SIZE AND APPROXIMATE POPULATION (CENSUS 2011)				
	Length (km)	Breadth (km)	Surface Area (km²)	Population
São Miguel	65	14	746	137,800
Pico	42	15	447	14,100
Terceira	29	17.5	382	56,400
São Jorge	56	8	246	9,100
Faial	21	14	173	15,000
Flores	17	12.5	143	3,800
Santa Maria	17	9.5	97	5,500
Graciosa	12.5	8.5	61	4,400
Corvo	6.5	4	17	430

Nine separate islands in the archipelago means nine isolated energy grids, each with specific characteristics and possible solutions for renewable energy. Flores generates almost 50% from renewables (33% hydro), São Miguel 44% (mostly geothermal), and Terceira 8.5% from wind, the island's Serra do Cume wind farm setting a world record for generation in 2010. On Graciosa the German company Younicos has a project using a combination of wind and solar power supplemented with energy storage systems which by 2014 will supply the island with its own totally carbon-free electricity. It will have a back-up system operating on vegetable oil, produced locally. Tiny Corvo is pressing ahead with solar panels and heat pumps to replace imports of liquefied petroleum gas; 150 homes will be fitted by mid 2013. By 2018 the Azores aims to generate 75% of its electricity from renewables.

POPULATION

The total population of the Azores is just over 246,000 (2011 census), an increase of 1.79% over the past decade. Movement within the islands varies, with some islands or towns losing populations while others increased.

For centuries emigration has played a major part in the life of the islands. Overpopulation and economic hardship have been the underlying cause. Since the early days numerous initiatives were tried to find crops that could be exported to give a cash income to the islands. Many succeeded, only to be dashed by changing world markets, war in Europe or America, or pest and disease, leaving thriving communities destitute. Other natural disasters like earthquakes and eruptions drove islanders away after their homes and fields had been destroyed, even up until the 1980s. As a result there are large populations of Azoreans in Canada, the US, Brazil and many elsewhere. Emigration ceased with the entry of Portugal to the EEC.

EMIGRATION Emigration deeply impacted upon the psychology and economics of the Azores over the centuries and is integral to the culture of the islands.

Following the decline in commerce with India, exploration of Brazil was encouraged, and sugar plantations were established in the northeast. In 1746, King João V announced a package of incentives to promote settlement in the south: land, tools, seeds, two cows and a mare. As a result some 6,000 Azorean peasant farmers and fishermen settled in a period of six years, mainly in the state of Santa Catarina.

Throughout Azorean history poverty and lack of opportunity have been the main driving forces underlying the need to emigrate. Fundamental to this was overpopulation, eased by a wave of emigration, the population then only to increase again. By the 19th century, the land was the only source of income for the islanders, but land tenure did not offer opportunities for individuals to better themselves, and landowners were conservative and not open to innovation, so crop yields were low.

For a young man living in a close-knit community on a small island in a vast sea, with no big city experience or that of a faster way of life, and speaking only Portuguese, emigration must have been a daunting prospect.

Around 1800, the Portuguese government introduced compulsory military conscription for 14 year olds. Pay was poor, advantages few, and this, coupled with the trap of peasant land tenure, spurred many to emigrate. At the same time American ships increasingly visited the Azores, including whalers, and very many young males escaped by joining the crew and eventually landing often years later in America via the east-coast whaling ports. Then disease and pests struck the grape vines, and later came the collapse of the orange crop, disasters that led to huge migrations.

With Brazil less inviting after gaining its independence, America offered better jobs and opportunities, and many Azoreans had already settled there from the whaling ships. By 1920, there were over 100,000 Azoreans in the United States, those from São Miguel having settled mostly on the east coast and Rhode Island, while people from the Central Group of islands made for California.

Immigration then virtually ceased due to new US immigration laws. In 1957, Capelinhos Volcano erupted on Faial, destroying villages and farmland. The US, under President Kennedy, passed refugee laws for Azoreans, and Canada also opened its doors. The emigrants were not only refugees from the volcano, but many were also economic migrants since the Azorean population was at its highest ever, at around 350,000 and nearly 100,000 more than it is today. At the same time many middle-class people emigrated to join their families, because whole family groups had gone, leaving many individuals alone.

Between 1878 and 1888, 17 ships carried 11,057 immigrants from the Azores and Madeira halfway round the world, including rounding Cape Horn, to Hawaii for work in the cane fields. Unlike to other destinations, this was the only mass immigration and contact was lost with the Azores. Only in the 1980s was contact resumed by the Azorean regional authorities, although the community had kept alive their Portuguese names and traditions such as the Holy Ghost celebrations.

Bermuda, another warm-temperate archipelago with geological origins linked to the Mid-Atlantic Ridge, was from the second half of the 19th century a popular destination of choice for Azoreans, especially from São Miguel, peaking in the 1960s and 1970s. Permanent residence was never permitted, and a contract of employment was essential to obtaining a visa. Most worked in Hamilton, either in tourism or gardening.

Repeatedly through history, some Azorean migrants have returned to their home island, with material goods and money to build a new house or maybe refurbish an old family holding. Both hardy and hardworking, the Azoreans' work reputation has a long pedigree and their labour has always been welcomed. But the generations that have been born abroad, while recognising their ancestral links with the islands, often visit now as American tourists along with their American culture, sadly a price that perhaps has to be paid. On the other hand, some are returning permanently, preferring to raise their young children in the Azores. This quality of life in the islands, where few are wealthy, but rich in a traditional way, where there is little crime and the landscape beautiful, is ironically now attracting foreign nationals seeking tranquil retirement.

LANGUAGE

Portuguese is both the national and native language, but there are strong regional dialects and vocabulary that often mother-tongue Portuguese-speakers from the mainland find difficult to understand. Natives of each island can be quickly recognised by fellow Azoreans, and even from which part of an island they come. Try learning Portuguese before you travel; you may get by with just English in Lisbon, but stay in Furnas on São Miguel and you will be in difficulty. While in Furnas learn some new vocabulary and then try the words out in Ponta Delgada. Pronounce them in every different way you can imagine, and finally you are taught another new word for the same thing. Generally, of course, you can manage with just English, but it is mostly in smaller cafés that it is useful to speak Portuguese, and in villages to ask the way. Some taxi drivers are fluent in English; many know enough to get by, but many speak only Portuguese. In the towns very many people speak English, it is a standard subject in school, and there are numerous Azoreans who have worked abroad. There are English-language television channels as well, CNN, BBC World, and films. Some French is spoken in Faial and Flores. Worldwide, Portuguese is the third-most widely spoken European language. (See *Appendix 1*, page 249, for a list of useful phrases.)

RELIGION

The Azores have been Catholic from their first settlement. The rare Protestant churches were built much later, for example in Ponta Delgada on São Miguel in the 19th century, primarily in response to the mainly English merchants who came to live on the islands to manage the orange trade. Although very much a minority, there was also a strong Jewish presence from the early days, with some Jews originating from north Africa. The Catholic parish priests were very influential, and the religious orders, especially the Franciscans, built many convents and churches and organised the first schools. In modern times it is the older parishioners who mostly make up church congregations, although young people still make up the numbers on festival days.

CULTURE

ARCHITECTURE AND ART *With thanks to Dr Isabel Soares de Albergaria*

Secular architecture Architecture in the Azores is an offshoot of the designs known in continental Portugal, sharing the simplicity of form common to the Mediterranean. It does, however, have its own characteristics. The most obvious are the easy integration of the buildings in the landscape and the structure of the settlements, in which streets tend to converge in small irregular squares where stand the most imposing buildings, the church and town hall. Until very recently most houses were modest in size and appearance and had distinctive features: they were built of stone, with a characteristic contrast between whitewash and black basalt.

Vernacular architecture, less affected by variations in style and the dictates of fashion, perhaps best reflects the Azoreans' relationship with their island environment. Their isolation, the simple agrarian way of life and the use of naturally available materials have led to very simple, almost rudimentary, designs for both houses and utilitarian buildings such as barns, cowsheds and mills. These, together with the small shrines and chapels have, through the centuries, gradually developed their own style and form, leading to regional styles.

As you go around the different islands variations emerge: Santa Maria has white houses with coloured bars marking the shapes and windows and Algarve-style prismatic chimneys, while on Pico, houses are black with no plaster on the walls and balconies running along the upper floors are accessed via outside staircases. On Terceira a long house is common, with its row of windows and doors with the kitchen at one end indicated by the presence of the broad chimneys called *de mãos postas* ('with joined hands'). On São Miguel low window–door–window-style houses are more frequent, similar to those in the Alentejo or, in some areas, houses with their gable end directly on the street. Variations can also be seen in the generally very simple decorative elements, focused around the windows and doors: mouldings of curved lines; the *aventais* (aprons) of the windows outlined in black; the characteristic staircase eye-windows decorated with geometric motifs, possibly Arabic in influence; or the windows with wrought-iron balconies, with a more cultivated influence. Another very common element, especially in the islands of the Central Group, is the bands of basalt that cut vertically and horizontally across the façades, as a form of proof against earthquakes.

It is not possible to talk about popular Azorean architecture without mentioning one of the most peculiar and unique aspects of its heritage: the *impérios* (small chapels) of the Holy Spirit. Linked to an age-old religion, which existed in the Azores from the times of their earliest settlement, the impérios are fundamental to the ritual practices of this extraordinary cult that on the mainland disappeared long ago. Here again variations can be seen between the various islands, but the most famous are the impérios on Terceira, immediately recognisable for their festive appearance, bright colours and designs, and triangular pediment.

Religious architecture On approaching any Azorean village from the sea, the most prominent feature is always the more or less imposing façade of a church. The most notable in this respect is the view of Horta on Faial, with the façades of the parish church, the Convent of São Francisco and the beautiful façade of the Carmelite monastery dominating the group of houses and 'gazing out to sea'. Hills near the villages are often topped by little pilgrimage chapels; of the many that are to be found scattered through the islands is the group of chapels and pilgrimage houses of Nossa Senhora da Ajuda above the small town of Santa Cruz da Graciosa, among which is also what is perhaps the best example of a fortified church with huge buttresses, decorative battlements and ribbed vaults inside.

In spite of limited resources, religious art in the Azores always had the benefit of fine talents and this enabled the islands to keep up with the artistic developments of mainland Portugal. The initial period, characterised by Gothic-Manueline architecture which lasted until the mid 16th century, is represented by almost all the surviving early parish churches of the main towns; for example the parish churches of São Sebastião in Ponta Delgada and of São Sebastião on Terceira. Then followed a long period of Portuguese classicism, known as *estilo chão* (plain architecture) because of its bare, austere and purely functional style exemplified by the Cathedral of Angra, and the Parish Church of Santa Cruz on Graciosa. The majority of monastic buildings in the Azores belong to this group, in spite of the decorative alterations many of them underwent during the Baroque period, of which examples include Nossa Senhora da Graça in Ponta Delgada and São Boaventura in Santa Cruz on Flores.

The religious way of life, with its ritual of offerings, processions and pilgrimages, had its origins in the mendicant orders established in the early Middle Ages in continental Europe. Monks came to the Azores during the early phase of settlement

From the writings of early travellers to the Azores it appears that at least until the end of the 16th century only watermills, *moinhos de água*, were present in the islands, and that the windmills were a later innovation. Old long-disused watermills are still abundant and often now hidden beneath the vigorous growth of ginger lilies that also like the humid stream beds. The mills were built either over streams or below specially constructed dams, or were even seasonal, relying upon the heavier winter rains to drive them.

Like so many aspects of the archipelago, individual islands developed their own style of windmills, and there were at least eight different versions, of which four are still extant.

SÃO MIGUEL TYPE These are similar to the so-called 'Dutch' type and are found mainly on São Miguel, Santa Maria and Graciosa, with small differences between those on each island. They have a conical stone-built base with a wooden semi-ovoid rotating roof, and have four cloth-covered sails.

FAIAL TYPE This has a truncated cone-shaped stone base with a substantial timber upper structure called a *casota*, or 'little house'. Access is by a staircase which also acts as a central tail to the *casota*. Originally it should have had a long mast with a pointed tip and eight crossed poles tied by guides and wire fasteners for triangular cloth sails, without bars. Today it is almost always of the square type, or is even replaced by rotors of two or four vanes. This type is to be seen on Faial and Pico.

SÃO JORGE TYPE São Jorge has two types of windmill: the mechanical mill now most commonly seen is a modified form of an earlier mill. This earlier version had four triangular sails made of cloth without lattice work. The later, adapted version has a stone-built conical base upon which is a narrow vertical mill providing an elevated support for the rotor of either two or four blades. This small mill can either rotate or be fixed, in which case only the dome rotates. The narrow tail leads either from the body of the mill or its dome, reaching to the ground.

CORVO TYPE Corvo's distinctive type has a low stone base and a squat conical tower, almost always rendered and whitewashed. The tower is built well inside the edges of the base so there is a wide ledge all round. The mast is long and pointed, leans upwards at a low angle and has eight sail poles with guides and fasteners for triangular cloth sails. Internal access is through a door in the tower reached by an external stone stairway rising from the ledge.

(15th century), the Franciscans being the most prominent; their monasteries soon sprang up in every town and city. Later on the Jesuits joined them. Soon after receiving papal approval, in 1540, the Company of Jesus promoted the building of great and elaborate colleges for the whole Portuguese Empire, including the islands. By royal initiative, the Colégio da Ascenção in Angra (the present Palácio dos Capitães-Generais) was founded in 1570, then the Colégio de Ponta Delgada, dedicated to All Saints (1591) and only much later, in 1680, the Colégio de São Francisco Xavier in Horta (today the seat of the parish church, municipal hall, treasury and museum). The present churches of Angra and Ponta Delgada are not, however, the original ones, there being various reconstructions and additions in later years.

Baroque architecture is well represented in the islands, particularly on São Miguel. It was dominant throughout the 18th and early 19th centuries, and is characterised by exuberant sculptural and decorative forms. Monastery churches entirely rebuilt or substantially altered (for example the Monastery dos Frades in Lagoa, São Miguel; Santo André, c1744; Esperança, 1740–86 and Conceição (Carmo), c1754, Ponta Delgada; São Gonçalo, Angra, 1730–50) use black basalt in capricious curves, highly indented mouldings, twisted columns, garlands and medallions, which form the new decorative language. The reconstruction of the Parish Church of São Pedro de Ponta Delgada (1737–42) was developed on an octagonal plan, original for the period, and the idea was repeated in the Parish Church of Fajã de Baixo. The Church of Santo Espírito, on the island of Santa Maria (18th century), is another example of originality, this time with the application of a dense and compact decoration, which is reminiscent of South American Baroque. Private chapels were often associated with the construction of Baroque manor houses such as Santa Catarina in Ponta Delgada; also of the 18th century were extravagant Baroque *misericórdias*, institutions for the poor offering medical care, food and other charitable benefits.

Military architecture Because of their strategic location between Europe and the New World the Azores were important for shipping, especially the returning treasure ships, but the islands were constantly threatened by corsairs. During the reigns of Dom João III and Dom Sebastião in the mid 16th century, a series of fortifications were begun 3km apart around the coast, with São Miguel, Terceira and Flores the most fortified. Construction was inspired by Renaissance technology and supervised by Italian military engineers and examples are São Brás in Ponta Delgada and Santa Cruz in Horta. In Angra on Terceira the castle of São Filipe, later renamed São João Baptista, was built during Philippine sovereignty (1580–1640), again as part of a general defence plan; construction was supervised by the Portuguese military engineer João de Vilhena and the Italian fortification specialist Tiburzio Spanochi, and was only completed after the Restoration. Practically impregnable, the castle benefited from the natural situation of Monte Brasil and included, on the landward side of the isthmus, a defensive platform with bulwarks and powerful curtain walls with deep moats. By this device the forces loyal to the Spanish crown were able to resist for long months after the King of Portugal took power.

Surprisingly few vestiges of this vast military effort are left to us. This is probably due to two factors. First, the quality of the constructions varied since often, with an attack imminent, the work was organised by the town hall and executed by the population using the materials and technology immediately to hand. Second, advances in warfare made many buildings obsolete, so that they were abandoned and left to the mercy of the elements and vandalism. Only more recently has the historical and architectural value of this heritage been recognised and efforts are slowly being made to save it from total ruin.

PAINTING AND DECORATIVE ARTS Most paintings, carvings, glazed tiles, furniture and gold artefacts in the Azores come from studios abroad following commissions made in a religious context. Only in a few cases is the artist or school, those who commissioned the item and the iconographic association known to us. On the whole, however, the quality of the work is comparable to the rest of Portugal, with the obvious exception of the royal court.

As with the architecture, genuinely Gothic artefacts are extremely rare. One of them is the triptych of the Virgin Mary in the Church of Dos Anjos (on Santa Maria), a portable altarpiece that according to tradition belonged to Christopher Columbus, on which Gothic designs can be distinguished. Another example is the murals of the Church of São Sebastião on Terceira.

Later 16th-century **Flemish art** is much more visible in the archipelago, both in works imported from the workshops of Antwerp, Brussels and Mechelen, and in works of local artists who succumbed to a veritable passion for the Flemish style. This fashion spread throughout the Portuguese territory, largely because of the privileged relationship Iberia had with this northern European region in the 15th and 16th centuries. In the Azores the Flemish influence was exercised directly by Flemish settlers and through a significant trade in woad and urzela, two dye plants used in the textile industry.

Imported Flemish art includes numerous small sculptures such as the *Virgin and Child* (Horta Museum), *St Sebastian tied to a dry tree trunk* (Ponta Delgada Museum), or the larger sculpture *Our Lady of the Miracles* in the Church of Vila do Corvo, all from Mechelen. More elaborate and emotionally charged is the *Crucifixion and Saint Mary Magdalen* (Horta Museum), a delicate work that must have come from the hands of a Brussels artist around 1520. Another theatrical composition is the *Christ being taken down from the Cross*, probably also from the 15th century, now exhibited in the Church of the Altares on Terceira. A moving group presents the scene of *Our Lady, St John and the Holy Women*, with Roman soldiers and citizens; at the bottom you can see skulls, the bones of Adam and some souls from purgatory. Probably also of Flemish influence, but from the first half of the 17th century, is the magnificent sculpture of *Our Lady of the Tears* (Church of São Pedro, Ponta Delgada), a powerfully modelled work of great expressiveness.

Among paintings, the triptych of *Saint Andrew* (Church of Nossa Senhora da Estrela, Ribeira Grande), which came from the chapel of the same name, is a 16th-century work whose Flemish affiliation is obvious in the drawing and sculptural appearance of the figures, the warm colours and delicate play of light on the background landscape, made in perspective. Although more archaic, the Flemish influence is visible also in the magnificent triptych of the *Adoration of the Magi* (Angra Museum) and in the painting of *Saint Ursula and the Eleven Thousand Virgins*, commissioned by the Jesuits of Angra perhaps in the late 16th century, in which a mannerist style is already evident.

The 16th-century purely Portuguese painting also achieved very high standards. Some exceptionally good works of this period can be seen in the Azores, including the polyptych in the Church of Santa Cruz da Graciosa depicting scenes from the Passion of Christ and the *Legend of Vera Cruz*, and showing all the signs of the late-Renaissance pathos that characterises this work. In the Carlos Machado Museum in Ponta Delgada there are two paintings from the Coimbra studio of Manuel Vicente and Vicente Gil, with Gothic-style features, as well as the polyptych of the

Holy Martyrs of Lisbon, by an anonymous artist but from a major Lisbon studio, closer to the Italian Renaissance style.

The **Counter-Reformation** movement, the setting up of the Inquisition in Portugal (1547) and Catholic orthodoxy dictated by the Council of Trent (1545–63) dealt a serious blow to artistic expression; painting became increasingly conventional. Altarpieces developed a tendency for compositional repetition and the command of anatomical detail became somewhat precarious. In spite of that there were still some worthwhile works of art, linked to the Italian or Spanish school. These include *Our Lady with Angel Musicians*, commissioned by Ponta Delgada Jesuits from Vasco Pereira for the Church of Ponta Delgada (now in the Carlos Machado Museum) and produced in Seville in 1604, and a set of Mannerist paintings by Francisco Álvares in the sacristy of the Church of São Pedro (Ponta Delgada). Outstanding is the group of eight paintings representing the infancy of Christ, painted by an anonymous artist for the Church of São Gonçalo in Angra; it is already linked to the early Baroque and shows a clear Italian influence. Simultaneously with the imposition of artistic conventionality ran the taste for luxury and ostentation in religious rituals; this led to churches being covered in gilded carvings, panels of glazed tiles and altars adorned with gold, silver and marble.

Sailing ships arriving from the **Orient** brought into the Azores new riches; marble figurines of the Good Shepherd in the meditative pose of the Buddha or Virgins in Glory with oriental features and a hieratic pose of which a collection can be seen in the Carlos Machado Museum. Others include Indo-Portuguese counters with inlays of marble and mother-of-pearl (examples in Angra Museum and the Palácio de Sant'Ana in Ponta Delgada) and bookcases designed to hold the plainsong books (Ponta Delgada parish church, Angra Cathedral). In the same way Chinese porcelain – pots, vases, plates and platters – sent by the Companhia das Índias from the 17th to the 19th centuries was also imported, as were Hindu tapestries which greatly influenced the designs of glazed tiles. Worthy of special mention in the context of Hindu–Portuguese art originating from the Malabar coast (Goa) and Sri Lanka are the two paintings in the Church of Santa Cruz da Graciosa, depicting St Francisco Xavier and Saint Inácio de Loyola dressed in long robes with golden adornments, brought in during the 17th century.

Portuguese art makes great use of the **glazed tiles** that bring colour and brightness to architectural space and can be used to depict natural scenes, tell stories in narrative sequences or extend architectural patterns by illusion. There was no local production in the Azores, so the existing tiles are the product of commissions from the mainland where they have been made for centuries. After the phase of Hispano-Arabic glazed tiles, some 16th-century examples of which are in various Azorean chapels (the most complete comes from Seville and is now in the Casa da Cultura at Ribeira Grande), Portuguese glazed tile-making expanded, patterns diversified and new techniques developed. There are polychrome altar fronts with a symmetrical composition and plant motifs, directly inspired by oriental textiles, which were in former Azorean shrines and chapels. Good examples are in the Carlos Machado Museum; the sets are full of peacocks, vases of flowers and friezes of exotic animals. There is also the pediment of the private chapel of the Chaves, now in the Palácio de Sant'Ana in Ponta Delgada; another is from the chapel of Anjos, on the island of Santa Maria, dating from 1679. Equally abundant are the wall coverings with blue, white and yellow glazed tiles, called *padronagem de tapete*; they repeat stylised plant motifs, applied inside decorative borders. A fine example of these is the 17th- and 18th-century glazed tiles that completely line the beautiful chapel of the Monastery of Caloura (São Miguel). Entirely Mannerist are the tiles from the sacristy of the

One day on São Jorge I was sitting over a coffee with António Pedroso, an old friend who lives in a beautifully restored town house in Velas. António is an artist, a collector and restorer of antiques, a church organist and much else. He told me that rural children were given responsibility at an early age. A farmer, for example, would give his young son a small calf to look after and when it was ready for market the boy was allowed to keep the money and reinvest it in more calves, thus gaining in his early years a good introduction to the economic world. He continued, reminiscing about the time of his own childhood not so many years ago, and I asked him to write it down. Here is what he sent me:

Life on São Jorge island has changed out of all recognition in the last two or three decades. Before the 1970s, there was no mains electricity and no mod-cons. Life was simple and harsh and people had to create their own amusements. Two major events, one many miles away, the other local, changed all that.

First, there was a revolution in Portugal in 1975 and the liberation of Angola from Portuguese rule, when hundreds of ex-patriots returned from Angola. Although some spent only a few years there, most did quite well and a handful became quite rich, but in the upheaval all lost everything; on returning home to the Azores via mainland Portugal financial support was granted to them to begin a new life. Many of them re-emigrated to the United States or Canada, but some remained on São Jorge. Abroad they were used to big country ways and big cities like Luanda with busy, aggressive markets, so when they started new businesses in the Azores, they had a considerable effect on the traditionally run local economy. The second event literally shook the island to its roots. A big earthquake in 1980 destroyed a large area of São Jorge and financial aid again came to the island to help with reconstruction. The two events had a profound effect on the life of the locals. And as always, some changes were good and others bad.

All water had to be brought in from outside water pumps; women had to ensure the supply, sometimes helped in the heavy task by the children. Water was transported in pottery jars which the women carried on their heads. In most developed countries, life without electricity is something to be experienced for fun during holidays or something to be read about; only the oldest people remember it as an everyday fact. Those born in the countryside of São Jorge, however, had the luxury of mains electricity as late as 30 years ago. Before then, there were no refrigerators and no television, and people had much more time for each other. There was enough time for everything.

January, with its relatively cold weather, was the pig-killing season and as such, a time for friends and families to join together. Whole communities participated in the organisation. Preparations started well ahead with cleaning all the required tools and utensils for carving, salting and boiling, including pottery jars in which the meat would be stored, to be used in the coming months. Next, women would concentrate on peeling and chopping a mountain of onions and parsley for various sausages. The men would meanwhile go in search of armfuls of wild heath (*Erica azorica*), needed to burn off pig bristles. On the chosen day, the men would arrive very early, while it was still dark, to be received by the owners of the house, and the pig, and offered a little warming refreshment – usually *aguardente* and *biscoito* (sweet bread).

The pig, quite oblivious to its fate, would be released from its pen and charge, squealing happily with the unexpected freedom, up the village street, pursued by equally merrily squealing men. The fatal blow would come suddenly and then all would turn into purposeful activity. All blood would be caught in a pan, to be mixed with green onions and rice for black sausage, *morcelas*. Skin bristles would be burnt off with heath twigs; alternatively, the carcass would be scalded with boiling water and bristles rubbed off with pieces of basalt. The beast would then be opened, the heart and liver taken out to be cooked immediately for communal lunch, and the intestines would be cleaned with copious quantities of lemons and oranges, and used later as tender sausage casings. After thorough cleaning, the pig would be hung from sturdy hooks in a cellar or another cool part of the house, the empty belly secured open with bamboo canes to air, to rest until the following day when it would be cut up for further processing.

After this exhausting effort, a big meal would be served in the evening to the family and friends, and half the village would join later in a masquerade, accompanied by Portuguese guitar playing, singing and dancing. Next day the carcass would be cut up, large portions salted and stored or cooked and stored, small bits of meat and pork fat would be made into another type of sausage, *linguiça*, that would be hung on hooks in a huge chimney and smoked with bacon joints. All traditional Azorean houses had chimneys built for this purpose. Nowadays a pig of a required size can be dispatched by an efficient butcher at any time, fresh cuts simply stored in a refrigerator or freezer and natural (or artificial) casings, all nicely prepared, bought in a slaughterhouse. Much cleaner, much quicker and much less fun.

São Jorge is relatively mountainous and most villages nestle among pastures at the altitude of 400–500m. Low down near the sea are the *fajãs*, flat areas at the foot of the cliffs. Shelter here results in a microclimate favourable to plants; coffee, tropical fruit, figs and grapes can be grown and most local farmers produce their own wine. During February and March, families traditionally used to move to the *fajãs* for a time to take care of the vines, dig the land and plant potatoes. For this purpose there was often a simple second house built in the vicinity, frequently with a small barn attached, just good enough to provide accommodation for the farmer and one or two milking cows. Between the fields in the *fajã* or higher up on the cliffs, quantities of *Pittosporum undulatum* and other evergreens provided a plentiful supply of green leaves that the cows consumed with relish. This also being the carnival season, children had school holidays and could help their parents in the fields. Not everything was work, of course; the usual way of enjoying the *Carnaval* day was to play with water, of which there is no shortage in the *fajãs*, and if you got soaked, no matter, the weather was much warmer here than higher up in the villages.

September was the time to make wine and to pick up figs and loquats for *aguardente*, and time for moving down again. The families would move with oxcarts heaped with mattresses (usually made of strong linen stuffed with corn leaves), blankets, pottery and all the other paraphernalia, women and children sitting on top of all that. Every *fajã* had a small chapel and various patron days meant a big festivity with a mass and a procession; on the Saturday before there would be a bullfight in the street. In the evening there would be theatre and folk

continued overleaf

1

music. A bullfight in a *fajã* was always a very colourful affair: the highest walls around the street would become crowded with viewers, especially women carrying coloured umbrellas to protect them from the sun, with green vineyards, black basalt stone walls and the blue sea providing an impressionistic backdrop. The bull was the star of the festival, and was never hurt. The same could not always be said about the people; if the bull jumped into someone's garden, a hilarious scene ensued with umbrellas flying, people running or climbing fig trees.

The only industry on the island was and is cheese production; however, since all cattle including milking cows are kept on pastures all the year round, milk production drops off in winter and there is enough for cheese only between March and October. In the past when milk was not pasteurised, all farmers kept one or two cows in the barn to ensure a supply of fresh milk for the family in winter. Modern islanders simply buy their pasteurised milk at the supermarket and farmers drive to the *fajãs* whenever work needs to be done; only a few old ones still keep the tradition of twice-yearly migration.

October was a traditional cereal harvest season, neighbours helping neighbours and whole families engaged. Ripe corn would be cut in the field, loaded on to oxcarts and brought to barns (*palheiros*) built on each farm usually from basalt blocks; most barns had a ground floor where the wheat or maize was milled, and a first floor where straw and maize ears were stored. In the evening young people would sit together and clean the husk from the cobs, with much singing and teasing of each other, or dreaming of the future, while the village elders would sit, doze, or tell stories from the past. Suddenly a girl cries 'A red one!' – she has just found a red grain that entitles her to a kiss from everyone, but with the strict chaperoning of unmarried girls, it is a wonderful opportunity to receive a kiss from the one dear to her heart. No-one can object.

Theatres, folk dances and philharmonic orchestras have always been much enjoyed on the island during the long winter nights in spite of – or perhaps because of – an otherwise hard life. The traditional theatre had no place for women, men usually performing all the roles and, similarly, participation in some folk dances was the preserve of the men. Even now, with the pervasive influence of television, São Jorge maintains 15 orchestras, each with 40 to 60 musicians. Although nobody wants to miss an opportunity to participate in cultural events, it is becoming increasingly difficult to find dedicated players; practice must now be organised so that it does not interfere with television broadcasts of football matches and soap operas.

Church of São José de Ponta Delgada, Church of São Roque (São Miguel), chapel of the Almas of the Church of São Francisco de Vila do Porto (Santa Maria) and Church of Conceição de Angra (Terceira).

In the **Baroque** period glazed tiles reached their zenith in terms of figurative, narrative compositions in blue and white. There are many examples. Among the finest are the panels in the lower choir of the Church of Esperança (Ponta Delgada) by António de Oliveira Bernardes, dated 1712 and relating scenes from the Passion of Christ; and the tiling of the main chapel in the Church of São José (Ponta Delgada) and in the Church of São Francisco in Horta: both illustrate the life of St Francis of Assisi and date from the same period. Also in Horta and worthy of special mention is the set from the parish church (former church of the Jesuit monastery) with scenes relating the life of Saint Inácio de Loyola. In Angra the glazed tiles which

People on São Jorge worked very hard; men outside, tending the cows in the pastures and working in the fields, while women stayed mainly in the house; one exception was the village of Toledo, where men preferred a good sleep and sent their womenfolk to tend the cows! Generally, however, women were busy at home, taking care of the children, looking after the house and processing wool and flax and weaving. Most houses had a loom on which women would make bedcovers and material for clothes, or they would knit socks and pullovers. Dyes for the wool were made from plants; wool would be boiled with the appropriate plant material and sometimes salt for colour fixing. The following were commonly used: *Erica azorica*, green; *Juniperus brevifolia*, reddish-grey; *Rocella tinctoria* (urzela, a lichen), wine red; and onion skins, light-brown. Men in turn would gather suitable cedarwood for homemade galoshes for which women would make the uppers. Straw was used to make hats; this was done especially on Pico, and at the beginning of summer many women from Pico would come selling hats.

On this island of black lava rocks, many women were always seen in black. Religious custom demanded that any widow had to dress in black for the rest of her life. Apart from black clothes, a widow had to wear a black-fringed square shawl and have her head covered by a triangular woollen scarf. After a loss of a parent, black was obligatory for two or three years; the loss of a brother meant black clothes for a year.

Many women therefore spent most of their life in black. The rule was less strict for the men: mourning was expressed by a simple black band on the upper arm, except for Sundays when they all took out their black suits; this was usually the suit made for the wedding and used until the last journey to the cemetery. In the last 20 years young people have adopted the colour black as a fashion statement, and under the American influence, the widows are changing slowly to wearing grey and even some colours, but in the countryside the traditional black persists.

All expenses associated with a wedding and the related festivities were borne by the bride's parents, who provided the dowry including all linen for the new house. The groom's duty was to pay for the house and the rings. Business was a male activity but women held the purse strings, particularly in the countryside. This was not just because the women were house managers but also because they could often read better than men, who were sometimes illiterate. Thus women exercised a big influence on the organisation of rural life.

line the Church of São Roque (c1725) are worth seeing; in Livramento there is a fine picture depicting the Sermon of St Anthony to the Fishes; and the chapel of the Santíssimo Sacramento in the Church of Nossa Senhora do Monte do Carmo, with an excellent allegorical composition on the Eucharist, is one of the finest works in the archipelago, made in Lisbon around 1740.

The **Rococo** period is represented in the Azores by some top-quality pieces. The return of polychromy, the spread of borders, bands, garlands, shells and other forms of decorative framing of great linear elegance, make the aesthetics of this Baroque period easily identifiable. The little Church of Santa Bárbara das Manadas on the island of São Jorge has one of the finest sets of polychrome glazed tiles with *rocaille* (shell) motifs, as well as a set of locally made carvings and paintings, which make this church a precious example of the alliance between cultivated and naïve art. Other examples of Rococo glazed tiles are in São Pedro de Alcântara at Lajes do Pico and in the Church of Santa Cruz da Graciosa. In the Piedade chapel in the Church of São José (Ponta Delgada) the Rococo glazed tiles are combined with mouldings consisting of gilded carvings on white backgrounds.

Azorean Baroque is not expressed just in richly decorated glazed tiles; the entire church interior is usually full of gilded carvings, paintings and painted wood. The history of carving also goes back a long way but again it peaked in the Baroque period, especially during the reign of King John (Dom João V), when many shipments of gold came from Brazil, enabling the carvings to be gilded. The Renaissance retables (carved and sometimes painted panels behind the altar) are replaced by the Baroque-style ornamentation with twisted columns, fluttering angels, birds pecking at grapes and drawn-back curtains. Examples can be found in almost every church; particularly rich are the carvings in the Church of São Gonçalo, Angra; in the main chapel of the Church of Esperança, Ponta Delgada, which covers the whole vault; in the Parish Church of Horta; and the most imposing of all the Azorean retables, the one in the main chapel of the Church of the Jesuits in Ponta Delgada, already in transition to Rococo style.

The range of **devotional sculptures** is impressive, if not always of great quality. In addition to the gallery of Catholic saints and tutelary figures, the Virgins in Glory are a favourite theme; Horta parish church contains one of the most spectacular examples. Other subjects include the Holy Family, scenes dedicated to the cycle of Christ's Passion, including *pietàs*, and nativities such as in the churches of São Miguel in Vila Franca do Campo and Angústias in Horta.

Throughout this period in which religious art dominated, gold work was associated with liturgical ritual. A vast range of ornaments and precious objects including chalices, salvers, monstrances, incense boats, censers, chandeliers, candlesticks, crucifixes, processional crosses, etc, today fill the church treasuries and are still used in worship. Only a few genuinely old pieces have survived the centuries of constant plundering by pirates, for whom churches and monasteries were a particularly rewarding target. The processional cross of the Church das Altares on Terceira is a late Gothic rarity, Flemish-made; also unique is the altar front in wrought silver in the chapel of the Sacramento in Angra Cathedral (17th century), probably Spanish in origin. Much more common, yet having enormous symbolic significance for the Azoreans, are the Crowns of the Holy Spirit in wrought silver, some dating back to the 17th century. In material riches and artistic value, however, nothing surpasses the treasury of Senhor Santo Cristo (Santuário da Esperança, Ponta Delgada). Consisting essentially of five pieces (*Glory, Crown, Sceptre, Cords* and *Reliquary*) that accompany the figure of Ecce Homo, originally designed and made in the 18th century during the reign of João V, it was later enriched with new gifts from the faithful. The *Glory* stands out, a fabulous piece weighing 4.85kg; it is made of gold-plated platinum and contains 6,842 precious stones, among them four extremely rare topazes from Brazil. Made in Lisbon by the finest goldsmiths of João V, the *Glory* presents a complete lesson in theology, containing the symbols of the Trinity, Redemption and the Passion of Christ, all executed with wonderful precision and detail.

Progressively moving away from the religious context, the 19th and 20th centuries finally began to place art in the service of a bourgeois public with secular ideas. The initially timid decorative schemes that the Azorean nobility used in their manor houses and town houses (an unusual example dating from the 1940s is the glazed tile panels alluding to the loss of independence and restoration of Portugal, in the Palácio Bettencourt in Angra) gradually expanded and diversified. The new urban and Liberal bourgeoisie, grown rich on the orange trade, contracted artists to paint their portraits and indulged in luxurious furniture, porcelain and textiles bought in England or France. Ambitious artists went to Paris to receive a proper academic training; such was the case with Marciano Henriques da Silva (1831–73) and Duarte Maia (1867–1922), the first a romantic, the second a naturalist, with work in the Carlos Machado Museum, Ponta Delgada.

The **20th century** began with a new generation of artists who gathered in Paris, the city of light, along with many others seeking inspiration from the artistic avant-garde. Two Azoreans stand out: **Domingos Rebelo** (1891–1975) and **Ernesto Canto da Maia** (1890–1981). Rebelo, a painter, caricaturist and ceramicist, followed a path that diverged from the vanguard, focusing all his attention on local reality, on the landscapes, appearances and attitudes of the simple and common people that he perceived as the most authentic aspect of this landscape, and capturing them with the detail of an ethnographer. His most famous work, *Os Emigrantes* (*The Emigrants*), portrays with contained feeling the drama experienced by thousands of Azoreans obliged to leave the islands in search of a better future (his paintings may be seen in the Palácio da Conceição, Museu Carlos Machado, Arte Contemporânea in Lisbon, Viseu, Caldas da Rainha, The Gulbenkian Foundation for Modern Art and in countless private collections).

Sculptor Canto da Maia embraced Parisian life with enthusiasm, showing in his synthetic and graphic style traces of the symbolism and stylised decorativeness of the 1920s and 1930s. Even so, his work reflects the deeper quest of a probing mind, meditating upon the themes of life, death and love. (Examples of his works are to be found in the Museu Carlos Machado, The Gulbenkian Foundation, Musée des Années 30, Boulogne, and the Musée Jeu de Paume, Paris, as well as in various public spaces.)

In 1901, Carlos and Amélia, the Portuguese royal couple, officially visited the Azores. Their temporary residence was to be the Palácio de Sant'Ana in Ponta Delgada, and the occasion was a perfect excuse for the most complete decorative renovation that had ever been carried out in a non-religious context. From 1915 to the late 1930s, painters, sculptors, decorators and carvers, both Azorean and from the continent, worked at Sant'Ana. Worth examining are the enormous paintings in the vestibule by Ernesto Condeixa, referring to the royal visit; the frieze in the former armoury; a bas-relief in gilded plaster of Paris by Canto da Maia; and the dining room lined with magnificent carved panelling and furniture entirely made by local artists. There are also extensive glazed-tile pictures made by the painter Jorge Colaço.

In the second half of the 20th century, particularly in the last two decades, Azorean arts blossomed. Art exhibitions and galleries of fine arts were supported and new art programmes initiated. Throughout its history, Azorean art has mirrored movements in Europe, and developed its own style affected by local conditions and materials. In the 21st century, the internet adds to the external influences, while artists and photographers pursue contemporary Azorean themes and concerns.

FESTIVALS These are many, both religious and secular, and take place on all the islands, mostly during the summer months. They are listed in each island's chapter; some festivals are common to all the islands, while others are island-specific. Some dates are fixed, others change each year, and you should check with the tourist information office. Visitors during the summer months will be very unlucky not to chance upon one during their stay; they are often joyful occasions and the kindness and generosity given to strangers make for happy memories.

The most important festival that is celebrated throughout the archipelago is that of the Holy Ghost (Espírito Santo), held six weeks after Easter on the seventh Sunday. It can also be repeated on the following Sunday if enough people have made promises to make the festival, and if emigrants come back to visit in the summer it can again be celebrated. Of 13th-century medieval origin imported from the mainland, it is one of the most traditional, although each island and each village has its own variation. On the chosen day, offerings of bread, meat and wine are distributed among the needy, followed by a procession through the town or village. You may notice small chapels called *impérios* in most of the villages at road junctions or on prominent corners. These are a source of great pride and they form the centrepoint of the **Espírito Santo Festival**. This festival is under the direction of a local group of men, a brotherhood, who undertake the care of the impérios and the giving of food to the poor, an important feature of Espírito Santo. Above the doors of most impérios you will find symbols: the crown, the sceptre, the dove and a red banner. The symbols are also to be found on the silver crowns which are worn by the *imperador*, the member of the brotherhood in charge of that day's festivities. Several *imperadores* may be crowned in each village during the festival season and each has the honour of guarding the crown and sceptre on a throne in his home until the next procession. Some of these precious village crowns and sceptres are many hundreds of years old. Fireworks signal the end of the opening church service

FESTIVAL OF THE HOLY GHOST AS CELEBRATED ON SÃO JORGE

The Festival of the Holy Ghost differs a little from island to island and from village to village and São Jorge celebrates the festival in its own way. Every village that has a church also has a small chapel called an *império*. The festival extends beyond its religious role; it is also a good excuse to have a great time.

The old traditions can still be enjoyed in the village of Rosais; they are centred on the *Carro das bandeiras* – an oxcart carrying a boat constructed from bamboo canes and green leaves and decorated on all sides with paper flowers, with colourful flags waving from long canes on the top. The carts are not just decorative, they have an important role: to bring to the império wine, sweet bread, cheese and lupin seeds. The lupin seeds have to be soaked in seawater for three tides, after which they are boiled. The festive food is then served free to all visitors during Saturday. Usually there are two carts and much rivalry exists between the two competing teams of villagers. The ornaments with which the horns of the oxen are decorated are kept strictly secret until the festive day and can never be repeated.

Independent of the religious festival is Mordomia, in which anyone in the village can participate, after joining one of many local groups. Donations of corn and other products are made, usually the previous year, and sold, and the proceeds are used to help with the preparation of the festival. The remaining expenses are divided between the members of individual organising groups. Mordomias are organised by most villages on São Jorge, so don't be surprised if you see cars stopped in the middle of the street to be offered some wine and sweet bread. These celebrations take place on the Saturday before the Festival of the Holy Ghost.

The organiser of the religious festival is called the *imperador* and is usually someone who has undertaken the work voluntarily. These types of festivals are increasingly expensive to organise because in some villages, like Beira and Topo, there is a tradition to invite anyone who passes through to eat for free. In the and the start of a procession from the church to the império led by the crowned imperador. Music is provided by the local brass marching band, or *filarmonica*. These bands are a major part of village life in the Azores, where there are more such groups than in all of Portugal. After the procession a beef-based broth, called *sopas do Espírito Santo*, is served along with another Azorean food with a strong tradition: *massa sovada*, a slightly sweet bread made in homes by groups of women taking turns during hours of hand-kneading. This festival, brought by the first settlers to the islands in the early 1400s, is seldom seen in Europe today, but is celebrated by communities of Azorean ancestry around the world, especially in the US, including Hawaii, and in Canada.

Other festivals are for saints' days or for vows made long ago to God. The most colourful is the Festival of Corpus Christi, and the preparation is as interesting as the procession. This takes place in June. Early in the morning many baskets of various small colourful flowers and finely chopped soft branch tips of the conifer *Cryptomeria japonica* are brought in and laid out in geometrical patterns upon the roadway using wooden templates, the colours all kept in separate shapes. The flowers and petals are frequently sprayed with water to keep them fresh and to stop the wind from disturbing the patterns or blowing them away. Sometimes dyed woodshavings are also used. Summer flowers in baskets and pots adorn balconies, and bright bedcovers hanging from windows add further colour. The procession is

past people did not have cars to get about and only local people came for the meal. Now the feast can attract many people from the entire island and it can be crowded. The village of Manadas has its festivities at lunchtime on the Thursday before the Holy Ghost day. Food is served on long tables, sometimes outside in the street. There is a special Holy Spirit soup, wine, *alcatra* sweet bread and sweet rice for dessert.

In Rosais you can also see the *foliões*: two or three men, one or two playing the drums and the other one singing in front of the império and walking up and down the square. The singing is improvised, sometimes repeated; it can be about God and the kindness of the Holy Ghost, or it can praise the organisation. The musicians are accompanied by the *cavaleiro*, a young man with two helpers. The cavaleiro carries a flag and the helpers bring two huge loaves of bread, called the castles, usually quite hard because they are so big (100cm x 50cm). On Sunday afternoon after the mass and the procession, the foliões and the cavaleiro perform a traditional dance with the bread, to the accompaniment of the drums and the singing. After that there is a merry game for all. The cavaleiro comes out of the império with a cake or dolls made of sweet bread in his hands, and attempts a dance, to be accosted suddenly by someone trying to steal the cake and run away with it. The helpers must then run behind and try to touch the thief with a rod. If they succeed, the thief has to return the cake; if he escapes, the cake is his. The more people take part, the more fun there is to be had.

In Norte Grande, each evening of that week a big dog-whelk shell is used to call everyone to the imperador's house. The sound carries round the entire village. The imperador then invites the guests to sing the rosary at his house, where he keeps an altar made especially for this event. It is decorated with candles and flowers and at the top is the crown of the Holy Ghost. The rosary is sung in a way unique to this event. After the rosary, the imperador offers sweets and drinks to all comers.

led by the priest under a pallium escorted by his followers and many small children dressed as angels. Much less formal is the June Festival of São João, marked with picnics at the many barbecue sites throughout the islands. The secular festivals get bigger every year and are celebrated by music, dance, arts, local culture, food stalls and sporting events. Music includes not only folk, but also pop groups from the mainland and Brazil, something not always viewed with enthusiasm by everyone.

Tourada à corda – **bullfights on a rope** In the Portuguese version of bullfighting, the bulls are not killed and the only blood spilt is that of overconfident humans! Terceira is especially noted for its *tourada à corda*, but other islands also participate.

The organisers have introduced regulations and planned a classification system for the bulls. No more than four bulls are allowed at any one event. Each must be at least three years old, and can appear only once for no more than 30 minutes. Cloaks and similar items are allowed, but anything that could cause injury to the bulls is banned. Action can only take place during daylight, and in the late afternoon/early evening. In practice, they mostly start around 18.00, beginning on 1 May until 15 October, almost daily during July and August, with some 50 runs in the latter month.

The bull is at the end of a long rope that is held by several men to try to keep him under some control. The fun comes in approaching the bull as close as one dares and then outmanoeuvring him while keeping clear of his horns. I vividly recall one year watching on a quayside when the bull really got up speed and chased five boys the length of the quay. Having nowhere else to go, they leapt off the end into the harbour and the bull had so much momentum he could not stop and went in on top of them to a tremendous cheer from the crowd and creating a huge tidal wave. The bull appeared to rather enjoy it, a nice cooling swim to the slipway at the end of a warm afternoon! Terceira and Graciosa both have bullrings, but here the bull is let loose without a rope.

These events have become very popular, with over 200 meetings each year. Dating back to the 16th century, in the past it was not only an entertainment but also an excuse for people from different villages to meet, both socially and for business. Animals could be bought and sold, goods traded or exchanged, youths could demonstrate to the girls their dash and courage with the bulls, there would be refreshment stalls and it was all huge fun. It still is.

2

Practical Information

The islands are very green and in the middle of the Atlantic. This means the weather is variable, and while at any time there can be a week or more of continuous glorious sunshine and blue skies, it can also be fickle.

You will be welcomed everywhere and find that English is widely spoken in the main towns, but when you enter a café away from the main centres or seek directions out in the country you might have fun trying to communicate. You should also be very safe, for there is little crime or street violence, although drugs and alcohol are problems locally.

Ferry services and domestic flights keep reasonably well to the timetables except for understandable delays through bad weather – in the case of aircraft this can just be wind affecting certain of the airports. Communications are excellent, the islands and their public facilities are very clean, and standards are high.

The cost of many items is greater than in mainland Portugal but compared with northern Europe prices for the visitor are reasonable, and the budget traveller can, with care, get by. In winter it gets dark about 18.30, in summer about 21.00, and time is Greenwich Mean Time –1.

WHEN TO VISIT

There are small variations between the individual islands, with Santa Maria seen as the sunniest, while the western islands are the wettest. June and July are the warmest months and should have the most stable weather. April and September normally tend to be the most changeable, but all the old patterns are changing, like everywhere else in the world. Every month is a delight in the Azores and even in January we have enjoyed our ritual walker's lunch of local cheese, fresh bread and a bottle of wine, sitting in a field in bright sunshine without jackets or jerseys.

The time to go depends upon what you want to do. If it is to do with the sea – inter-island ferry travel, whale watching, sailing or fishing – then you need to go in the summer months between mid-April and early October. People swim throughout the year, but the popular times for the beaches are again the summer months and into October, but remember the Azores are not beach destinations. Regarding flowers, there will always be something of interest but for the beautiful and spectacular hedgerows you should consider June and July to see them at their best, and for native species May to September is the best time. For walking, the whole year is good, but the rain in winter is usually colder than in summer! In winter you will also have to take extra care in the mountains. In summer there are more eating places open and they keep longer daytime opening hours. During the high season of July and August hotels throughout the islands are usually fully booked and the casual traveller may have difficulty in getting accommodation. The same goes for car rental. In summer it is impossible to rent a car on arrival and advance reservation is essential; similarly for bicycles. Increasingly this is becoming the situation for June and September. In addition to inbound tourists, many Azoreans who emigrated to North America come back to see relatives, while second and third generations return to discover their roots. March and April, still low season, are beautiful months because spring is early in the Azores and by now nature is wide awake; autumn is a much longer season than in northern Europe and October and November have lovely warm days while the golden hues of falling leaves prevail into December. And December is the Christmas festival season, when every town is festooned with lights and decorations in a very Azorean way that is so charming and does not hint of commercialism.

HIGHLIGHTS

The greatest attraction for many is the tranquillity and the lack of pollution: the quiet rural scenes of small houses, the pastures, the grazing cows on a stage of lush green grass and the backdrop of a deep blue sea, farmers on horseback with milk churns hanging from their saddles, the little pony cart clattering along the cobbles with more milk churns, the cattle dogs perched on top. Then the scenery is so lovely and ever-changing, from sea to coast and often spectacular cliffs, to pastures or stony vineyards, up into forest and hills of often conical shape until culminating in a volcano's caldera and other heights lost in cloud. Blue hydrangeas and the Azores may have become a cliché but to see an island seeming as if a fisherman's net with extra-large holes had been thrown over it creating a pattern of blue lines and enclosures remains, all the same, a remarkable sight.

Even the largest towns, including busy Ponta Delgada, have an irresistible allure that urges the visitor to explore them. Many ordinary street buildings have an elegant simplicity with lovely adornments of wrought-iron balconies or perhaps some ornamented basalt carving while grander places may show a more ornate Manueline influence. Small retailers are modest and sometimes do not advertise their presence while often the stock is held in the shop's dark recess so that it is difficult to decide what it is they are selling. The narrow cobbled backstreets have constricted pavements while bigger thoroughfares have grander ones; whatever their size they are made of small squares of black basalt and imported white granite that is used to make designs appropriate to the place: caravels, whaling boats, whales, fish, figures dressed in the no-longer-worn *capote* or cloak, windmills, sheaves of corn – there is no end to the *pavior's* enterprise. For the foot-weary there are street cafés and good ice creams to enjoy while seated watching island life pass by, or many a quiet church for contemplation.

Certain islands are perfect for exploring by car, and endless hours can be spent discovering rural roads or following up those that do not appear on maps. There are so many tempting places to park the car and just lean on a fence post and enjoy a view or listen to the birds. Should you tire of rural scenery, then comes the satisfying contrast of dropping down to the coast and into a little village; maybe at its centre is the main church, a tiny public garden with its bandstand, and a café, or perhaps you have chanced upon a fishing village with a harbour and nearby natural swimming pools for an ocean swim and a fish restaurant to follow.

Whale watching has become tremendously popular since it first began on Pico years ago and uses the old expertise of the lookouts to spy the cetaceans. It is a truly world-class cetacean hotspot and between 6% and 10% of all known cetacean species can sometimes be seen in a single three-hour trip. Numerous enterprises now offer the experience. Diving offers a range of opportunities, from wrecks to sea cliffs and extraordinary underwater lava formations, and several companies offer their services. Many small fishing boats can be seen, either drawn up on the harbour quays or gently bobbing a short distance offshore, and if you feel tempted there are fishermen registered to take you out to fish for your supper. At the other end of the spectrum, the Azores are renowned internationally for sport- or big-game fishing, especially for blue marlin, and many world-record catches have been made, although of course these are for putting back and not for eating.

Going hand in hand with the tranquillity and clean environment is walking or cycling, the finest way to acquire a real feel for the islands. Several companies offer

A MESSAGE FROM MELO, AN AZOREAN TRAVEL AGENT

Slow down, relax and enjoy yourself.

As the Azores are so little known beyond Portugal and so many visitors arrive at this archipelago with mixed ideas of what to expect, most are surprised to discover how green the islands are. At the same time we are not a place for sun-drenched holidays, entertainment or busy nightlife. Please accept the Azores, their landscape and many interests for what they are and not what you might have expected them to be. If this is your approach right from the start, we are sure the islands will give you a lifetime of happy memories of your visit.

Slow down and adapt to our way of doing things. We do not have the bustling pressures found in other places of Europe; we have our own scale, and things still get done, although they may take a little longer. It is time for you to relax and enjoy yourself.

HOLIDAY ITINERARY Sometimes arrangements are affected by events beyond our control, and planes and ferries are rescheduled or cancelled. Please be flexible about your itinerary, because everything will be solved and we are here to look after you. Do contact your travel agent in the Azores if you have any questions; please don't feel you are left on your own.

MEETING THE AZOREAN PEOPLE Travel slowly and enjoy our ways of living should our paths cross when out in the countryside or in a café. Even if the Azoreans do not speak your language, they always try to communicate.

SAFETY Everywhere in the Azores you still feel safe from crime. However, like anywhere else, it is wise to always lock your car and take normal care of your valuables. When out walking in the hills, do be careful of the weather; if thick mist suddenly appears it is easy to lose your way, and make sure you have warm clothing.

COMPLAINTS/PROBLEMS If you have any complaints during your stay, please let your tour operator's representative in the Azores or your Azores travel agent know about it immediately, not at the end of your holiday when it may be too late to improve things.

FINALLY Please think of us as your friends, not guides or travel agents, and of yourselves as our guests, not tourists. We shall enjoy having you as much as we hope you will enjoy being with us.

organised cycling tours, and it is often possible to hire bicycles. There are short walks and long walks, in the mountains, along the coast, sometimes on narrow trails, at other times on seldom-used farm roads. The views are always changing, and relics of the past are everywhere, from wheel-worn donkey paths hidden beneath the summer's flush of vegetation to abandoned farmhouses and crumbling watermills. Hiking routes are slowly being signposted, but there is still a long way to go before access and waymarking is reliable on all islands. Some published walks are short and not linked to transport, and the descriptions can be vague, but the whole trails programme is under review. Winter storms cause landslides, and vegetation is so lush that in a very few weeks paths are concealed. For all walks it is best to check with the local tourist information office or your Azorean travel agent that the walk is clear before setting out; also the official trails website (*www.trails-azores.com*). One gets the impression some routes are devised by office-based bureaucrats, and not by a practical ranger or forester on the ground. However, if you are prepared to risk some possible frustration and the need to fall back upon your own sense of direction, you will enjoy many a memorable walk. For those who prefer, guides are available through the local travel agencies (see page 46).

The golf course at Furnas (see page 98) on São Miguel must be one of the world's most intimate and exquisitely beautiful courses, given its mountain setting with sheltering forests and numerous elegant tree ferns. It is little known, but for any golfer who values the environment and surroundings in which he or she plays, this course cannot fail to impress. However, it is not without hidden challenges, for its luxuriant vegetation reflects its relationship with the clouds, and it can be quite entertaining to drive off into a white mist that has suddenly descended and might well instantly clear to give advantage to your opponent. There are two other equally green courses to play, both at much lower altitudes, on São Miguel and Terceira; see pages 98 and 143.

PLANNING AN ITINERARY: WHICH ISLANDS?

The pace of the Azores is slow, and slowly is how one should discover them. There are nine islands and if you were to attempt to see them all in one visit to the archipelago you would need several weeks to do them justice. Should you try to visit too many islands in a short period you will end up spending a disproportionate amount of time waiting in airports. If you have just a week, then you might be well advised to concentrate on the largest and most diverse island, São Miguel. If you have more time, maybe combine São Miguel with Faial, and Pico with perhaps Terceira as well for your first visit (these islands will easily take up two weeks) and then see other islands on return visits! Various islands suit different means of touring.

If you like to hire a car and take your time exploring then São Miguel, Santa Maria, Terceira, Pico, São Jorge and Flores would make the best choices.

If you prefer to tour by taxi and public bus then much of São Miguel can be accessed by bus. Graciosa is small, there are buses, but distances are so short taxi fares are reasonable. Terceira means the city of Angra, for which you do not need a car, and adjacent Monte Brasil can also be explored on foot. A half-day taxi tour would provide a glimpse of many of the other highlights. Faial offers Horta and nearby attractions, and a half-day taxi tour will take in the island's main features. Pico can be visited in a day from Horta, with a half-day tour seeing the western sector.

For walking, São Jorge has long been supreme, but São Miguel and Faial are fast catching up. Then comes Flores, followed by Pico if you want to climb the mountain. For cycling, São Miguel is the most developed. São Miguel is best for gardens and

Pico has the most accessible native flora. Birdwatchers should give priority to São Miguel, São Jorge, Pico and especially Flores and Corvo in the autumn, although the old quarry at Praia on Terceira is also excellent for rare waders at this time.

TOUR OPERATORS

The Azores are very popular with the Scandinavians and Germans, after which come the Spanish and Dutch, then the Americans, British (with 10,158 visitors in 2011) and French, and of course there is a very heavy Portuguese tourist traffic from the mainland, which makes up the vast majority of visitors. For years it has been mostly small companies that have offered this destination, but now big tour operators are also doing so. Tour operators in their brochures sell the Azores for their tranquillity, landscapes and the islands' way of life, and their retailers should know these qualities. Earlier, the average high-street travel agent knew little about the Azores, and the poor inbound agents in the islands found themselves at the receiving end of irate complaints from clients who had just arrived to realise that there was no constantly blazing sun and endless sandy beaches; this is changing, but still some visitors arrive ill-informed. For those who wish to travel out of the main season or go to different islands from those offered in the standard package, some of the operators will be able to make a bespoke tour programme for you. There are over 20 UK tour operators offering the Azores, including the following:

UK
Archipelago Choice 1b Museum Sq, Keswick, Cumbria CA12 5DZ; ☎01768 775672; e info@ azoreschoice.com; www.azoreschoice.com

Biosphere Expeditions Sprat's Water, near Carlton Colville, Broads National Park, Norfolk NR33 8BP; ☎0870 446 080; e uk@biosphere-expeditions.org; www.biosphere-expeditions. org. Arranges hands-on conservation projects collecting data on whales, dolphins & turtles.

Explore Worldwide Nelson Hse, 55 Victoria Rd, Farnborough, Hants GU14 7PA; ☎0845 013 1539; e res@explore.com; www.explore.co.uk

Naturetrek Cheriton Mill, Hants SO24 ONG; ☎01962 733051; e info@naturetrek.co.uk; www. naturetrek.co.uk

Saga Holidays Ltd The Saga Bldg, Enbrook Park, Folkstone, Kent CT20 3SE; ☎0800 096 0074; www.saga.co.uk

Sunvil Sunvil Hse, Upper Sq, Old Isleworth, Middx TW7 7BJ; ☎020 8758 4722; e discovery@ sunvil.co.uk; www.sunvil.co.uk/azores. One of the leading promoters of responsible tourism, offering the Azores since 1990.

Wexas Travel 45–49 Brompton Rd, London SW3 1DE; ☎020 7590 0610; e travel@wexas.com; www.wexas.com

Whale Watch Azores 5 Old Parr Cl, Banbury, Oxon OX16 5HY; ☎0208 144 2560; e info@ whalewatchazores.com; www. whalewatchazores.com

CANADA
Karavaniers Monde 108 rue du Square Gallery, Bureau 104, Montreal, Québec H3C 3R3; ☎+1 514 281 0799/877 477 0799; e expeditions@ karavaniers.com; www.karavaniers.com

Sunmed Holidays Inc 5245 Dundas St W, Toronto, Ontario M9B 1A5; ☎+1 416 234 0774; e info@sunmedholidays.com; www.sunmedholidays.com

DENMARK
Svante Rejser Tvendersgade 6, DK-1363 Copenhagen; ☎+45 3315 2525; e info@svante.dk; www.svante.dk

FRANCE
Arts et Vie 251 rue de Vaugirard, 75015 Paris; ☎+33 1 40 43 20 21; e info@artsetvie.com; www.artsetvie.com

Atalante 5 rue du Sommerard, 75005 Paris; ☎+33 1 55 42 81 00; e paris@atalante.fr; www.atalante.fr

Donatello 10 rue Daunou, 75002 Paris; ☎+33 (0) 826 10 2005; e serviceclient@donatello-to. com; www.donatello.fr

2

GERMANY

Bayerisches Pilgerbüro GmbH Dachauer Str 9, 80335 Munich; ☎ +49 89 545 8110; e bp@ pilgerreisen.de; www.pilgerreisen.de

Berge & Meer Touristik GmbH Andréestraße 27, 56578 Rengsdorf; ☎ +49 60 316 2062; e online@berge-meer.de; www.berge-meer.de

Olimar Reisen Vertriebs GmbH Glockengasse 2, 50667 Cologne; ☎ +49 22 120 5900; e info@ olimar.com; www.olimar.com

Reisen mit Sinnen Roseggerstrasse 59, 44137 Dortmund; ☎ +49 23 158 97920; e oneworld@ reisenmitsinnen.de; www.reisenmitsinnen.de

TUI Otto-Lilienthal-Strasse 17, D-28199 Bremen; ☎ +49 18 05 884 266; e internet.service@ tui.com; www.tui.com

Wikinger Reisen Kölner Str 20, 58135 Hagen; ☎ +49 23 31/90 47 42; e mail@wikinger.de; www. wikinger-reisen.de

NETHERLANDS

Girassol Vakanties Prinsengracht 783–785, 1017 JZ Amsterdam; ☎ +31 20 42 80 555; e info@ girassolvakanties.nl; www.girassolvakanties.nl

SNP Bijleveldsingel 26, Nijmegen; ☎ +31 24 32 77 000; e sales@snp.nl; www.snp.nl

US

Abreu Tours 875 Av of the Americas, Suite 206 New York, NY 10001; ☎ +1 800 223 1580/212 760 3301; e info@abreu-tours.com; www.abreu-tours. com

Azores Express PO Box 2819, South Main St, Fall River, MA 02721; ☎ +1 800 762 9995; e res.info@ azores-express.com; www.azores-express.com

Easy Rider Tours PO Box 228, Newburyport, MA 01950; ☎ +1 800 488 8332; e info@ easyridertours.com; www.easyridertours.com

LOCAL TRAVEL AGENTS There are several travel agents in the Azores, offering the usual services of car hire, hotel reservations, airport transfers, etc; these offer certain other activities.

Geo-fun Av Infante D Henrique (by S Brás Fort) Ponta Delgada, m 919 931 562/919 000 056; e info@geo-fun.com; www.geo-fun.com. A small company focused on active tourism with a special interest in geology, birds & flowers, offering day excursions with a naturalist leader.

Melo Agência de Viagens Rua de Sta Luzia 7–11, 9500-114 Ponta Delgada, São Miguel; ☎ 296 205 385; e geral@melo-lda.pt; www.melotravel. com. Established in 1971 & the first company to offer walking holidays in the Azores. They have self-guided programmes for nature lovers. They also pioneered cycling holidays & offer an 8-day package. For whale watching, daily departures in

season are offered from São Miguel, Faial & Pico, & a 7-night package on Pico. Again for individual travellers, 3-, 4- & 5-island tours are available, together with a tailor-made service.

Teles Agência de Viagens Rua da Sé 138, 9700-191 Angra do Heroísmo, Terceira; ☎ 295 213 236; e angra@telestravel.com; www.telestravel.com. Offers a variety of packages from 2 to 10 nights to various islands, an 8-night golf package to Terceira & São Miguel, a week whale watching on Pico, & various anti-stress, recuperation & revitalisation health programmes at the Hotel do Caracol on Terceira.

TOURIST INFORMATION

AZORES TOURISM AUTHORITY The Regional Directorate of Tourism for the Azores headquarters is in Horta, on Faial (*Direcção Regional de Turismo, Rua Ernesto Rebelo 14, 9900-112 Horta*). It has branch information offices on all the islands, and publishes informative brochures on each island illustrated with excellent photographs, together with various other publications. Compiled each year are lists of approved hotels, *residenciais* and rural accommodation, available upon request by letter or by email (e *acoresturismo@mail.telepac.pt*; *www. visitazores.com*).

A tourist helpline is available on ☎ 808 781 212; it is a general number for the whole region.

⛵ São Miguel [102 D4] Av Infante D Henrique, Ponta Delgada; 📞 296 308 625/26/27, plus an airport branch office; 📞 296 284 569, plus a small seasonal office by the hot springs in Furnas; 📞 296 584 525

⛵ Santa Maria Airport; 📞 296 886 355, plus a seasonal office at the ferry quay

⛵ Terceira [145 D3] Rua Direita 70–74, Angra do Heroísmo; 📞 295 213 393, plus a branch office at Lajes airport; 📞 295 513 140

⛵ Graciosa Rua Caastilho 7, Santa Cruz da Graciosa; 📞 295 712 509

⛵ São Jorge [174 F2] Rua Conselheiro Dr José Pereira, Velas; 📞 295 412 440

⛵ Faial [194 C3] Rua Vasco da Gama, Horta; 📞 292 292 237, and at the new ferry terminal; 📞 292 293 097, plus a seasonal office at the airport

⛵ Pico [map page 212] Ferry quay, Madalena; 📞 292 623 524, plus a temporary summer cabin by the church

⛵ Flores [map page 229] Santa Cruz das Flores; 📞 292 592 369

⛵ Corvo At the interpretation centre; 📞 292 596 051

RED TAPE

Portugal with the Azores are full members of the European Union, and nationals of other EU countries do not require a visa.

Should you need consular assistance during your stay, these are the contact numbers of those consulates represented in the Azores. Largely these responsibilities are undertaken by private individuals in an honorary capacity without official premises. They can issue emergency passports and contact relatives.

🏛 UK 13 Largo Vasco Bensaúde, Ponta Delgada; 📞 296 283 192; e Antonio.CastroFreire-honcon@ fconet.fco.gov.uk; www.ukinportugal.fco.gov.uk

🏛 USA Av Príncipe do Mónaco, Ponta Delgada; 📞 296 282 216; e CabralAI@state.gov

🏛 Brazil Casa da Eira, Estrada Velha da Ribeira Grande, São Roque, Ponta Delgada; 📞 296 381 425

🏛 Canada 27 Rua António José de Almeida, Ponta Delgada; 📞 296 281 488; e canadapdl@ mail.telepac.pt

🏛 Denmark Praceta Gonçalo Velho Cabral, 8 - 1° Ponta Delgada; 📞 296 284 291; e willem.rieff@ cmjrieff.pt

🏛 Finland 63 Rua Machado dos Santos, Ponta Delgada; 📞 296 628 736; e fredericopascoa-77a@ adv.oa.pt

🏛 France 73 Rua Manuel Inácio Correia, 2° Esq°, Ponta Delgada; 📞 296 629 511; e migueldaguiar@ gmail.com

6 Rua Walter Bensaúde, Horta, Faial; 📞 292 392 780; e rbraz@financor.pt

🏛 Germany 5 Rua da Lombinha, 9555-100 Ginetes, São Miguel; 📞 296 295 426

🏛 Italy 35 Rua Luís Soares de Sousa, Ponta Delgada; 📞 296 284 558

🏛 Netherlands 92 Rua da Pranchincha, Ponta Delgada; 📞 296 201 580; e rbraz@financor.pt

🏛 Norway 61 Largo da Matriz, Ponta Delgada; 📞 296 205 030; e jloazevedo@mail.elepac.pt

🏛 Sweden 47 Av Infante D Henrique, 1° Esq°, Ponta Delgada; m 915 600 985; e colegio27@ gmail.com

GETTING THERE AND AWAY

BY AIR From the UK there are direct flights with SATA Internacional (*www.sata. pt*) from Gatwick every Saturday between April and October, with a flying time of three hours 45 minutes. TAP Air Portugal (*www.flytap.com*) has departures throughout the year from Heathrow or Gatwick changing in Lisbon to Ponta Delgada, and with less frequency from Lisbon to Horta (on Faial), Lajes (Terceira), Santa Maria and Pico. Flying via Lisbon has the advantage that you can fly to one island and return from certain others, thus saving you an inter-island flight or two and maybe some hours out of your holiday waiting at airports; you can also break your return journey and spend some nights in Lisbon. Flights take approximately two hours to Lisbon and another two hours from Lisbon to the Azores.

From the rest of Europe there are direct flights from Frankfurt, Munich, Gran Canaria, Amsterdam, Copenhagen, Paris and from Portugal Faro, Lisbon, Porto and Funchal (Madeira).

From the US and Canada there are direct SATA flights throughout the year from Boston and Toronto to Ponta Delgada and more in summer, and codeshare flights via various cities to/from other US and Canadian cities.

BY SEA

By cruise ship About 100 cruise ships are currently calling in at the Azores, and this number is expected to increase with expanding facilities. Three ports now take large cruise ships, with Ponta Delgada receiving the most cruise visitors. Small-ship cruises also operate, visiting all nine islands using onboard Zodiac craft for some excursions. It was in 1867 that the first scheduled cruise ship put in at Horta, steaming from New York on a five-month cruise to the Mediterranean.

Ponta Delgada (São Miguel) The largest town in the Azores now has a new terminal complex – Portas do Mar or Gateways of the Sea, opened in 2008. From the pier into town is just a 200m walk. The tourist information office is on the pier, and around the promenade are shops, a bank and pharmacy, bars and restaurants. Various onshore tours are available, going to some of the places described in the respective chapters of this guide.

Horta (Faial) The cruise ship quay is located about a 1km walk along the harbourfront. Tourist information is available on the quayside. Bus excursions take in Capelinhos, site of the last volcano eruption and the excellent new visitor centre.

Praia da Vitória (Terceira) Cruise ships dock 4km from the town (usually covered by bus excursions!). Tourist information is available in town, and excursions to Angra do Heroísmo and other highlights start from the quay.

By yacht Facilities are concentrated in the four principal ports, the most popular of which for transatlantic yachts is Horta on Faial. Opened in 1986, and having held the European Blue Flag since 1987, it can take 300 vessels and claims to be the fourth-most-visited ocean marina. Second-most popular is Ponta Delgada on São Miguel, with a new marina taking 470 yachts, followed by Praia da Vitória on Terceira. All three provide fuel, water, waste handling and repair services. There are also small marinas opened in recent years at Velas on São Jorge, Madalena on Pico, Lajes on Flores and Vila do Porto on Santa Maria. The website www.noonsite. com/Countries/Azores gives latest information on facilities, immigration, etc, and anchorages on the other islands.

HEALTH *with Dr Felicity Nicholson*

All EU nationals visiting the Azores are entitled to the reciprocal arrangements covering medical care and expenses but will need the appropriate documentation. Dental treatment will mostly have to be paid for. British nationals should have their European Health Insurance Card (EHIC), obtainable by phone (ℕ *0845 606 2030*), online (*www.dh.gov.uk/travellers*), or from the post office and some travel clinics. You should in any case have additional private travel insurance. Pregnant women, travellers with pre-existing illnesses and those travelling with children or going to remote areas should identify healthcare facilities prior to departure. However, larger hotels and tour company representatives are usually able to provide addresses for local services. The Foreign and Commonwealth Office (*www.fco.gov.uk*) can provide details of the nearest relevant embassy or consulate for emergencies.

Hospitals in the Azores are modern and equivalent to normal European standards. They are located on São Miguel, Terceira and Faial. On certain islands where there are limited services emergency medical cases have to be flown either to Faial or Terceira. Health centres (*centros médicos*) provide non-hospital treatment.

Pharmacies are widespread, but you should always take a sufficient supply of prescription drugs to more than last the length of your holiday. When travelling, do not pack them all in your suitcase; always make sure you have enough tablets and any medical equipment you use regularly in your hand luggage. The pharmacies in larger towns will have a rota for out-of-business-hours opening; if you need anything, ask at your hotel or a police station to see which one is open.

LONG-HAUL FLIGHTS, CLOTS AND DVT

Any prolonged immobility, including travel by land or air, can result in deep-vein thrombosis (DVT) with the risk of embolus to the lungs. Certain factors can increase the risk and these include:

- Having a previous clot or a close relative with a history
- People over 40, with increased risk in over 80s
- Recent major operation or varicose-veins surgery
- Cancer
- Stroke
- Heart disease
- Obesity
- Pregnancy
- Hormone therapy
- Heavy smokers
- Severe varicose veins
- People who are tall (over 6ft/1.8m) or short (under 5ft/1.5m)

A deep-vein thrombosis causes painful swelling and redness of the calf or sometimes the thigh. It is only dangerous if a clot travels to the lungs (pulmonary embolus). Symptoms of a pulmonary embolus (PE) – which commonly start three to ten days after a long flight – include chest pain, shortness of breath, and sometimes coughing up small amounts of blood. Anyone who thinks that they might have a DVT needs to see a doctor immediately.

PREVENTION OF DVT
- Keep mobile before and during the flight; move around every couple of hours
- Drink plenty of fluids during the flight
- Avoid taking sleeping pills and excessive tea, coffee and alcohol
- Consider wearing flight socks or support stockings (see *www.legshealth.com*)

If you think you are at increased risk of a clot, ask your doctor if it is safe to travel.

Tap water in the hotels is generally safe to drink; on some islands it tastes better than some bottled waters I can think of. However, if you are in any doubt then drink bottled or treated water (boiled or with chlorine drops/tablets). Mineral water is widely sold by the bottle, imported mostly from the mainland, but also sourced locally.

It is wise to be up to date with routine vaccinations. Occasionally hepatitis A may also be recommended, which will depend more on lifestyle and/or occupation.

A few cases of leishmaniasis from sand flies and west Nile fever from mosquitoes have been reported from the Azores. The only way these diseases can be avoided is by using a good DEET-based insect repellent – ideally containing 50–55% DEET (eg: the Repel range).

Rabies is not considered a risk in the Azores in terrestrial animals, but all bites from animals should be assessed carefully. Rabies vaccine is only recommended for travellers involved in activities that could bring them into direct contact with bats. These travellers include wildlife professionals, researchers, veterinarians, or adventure travellers visiting areas where bats are commonly found.

TRAVEL CLINICS AND HEALTH INFORMATION A full list of current travel clinic websites worldwide is available on www.istm.org. For other journey preparation information, consult www.nathnac.org/ds/map_world.aspx or http://wwwnc.cdc. gov/travel/(US). Information about various medications may be found on www. netdoctor.co.uk/travel. All advice found online should be used in conjunction with expert advice received prior to or during travel.

DISABLED TRAVELLERS

The Azores are not geared towards travellers with mobility problems, since narrow cobbled streets and a lack of ramped kerbs don't create a wheelchair-friendly environment. However, latest developments do recognise the difficulties, and some hotels have facilities. Airports have wheelchairs for use on site. New museums are adapted, with some offering information in Braille.

SAFETY

The Azores are considered to be one of the safest places in the world and crime is, on the whole, limited to minor thievery in Ponta Delgada. However, you should sensibly take the same precautions as you would at home.

WHAT TO TAKE

The clothes you take need to correspond with the quickly changing weather so always remember you are in the mid-Atlantic! In summer generally the temperatures are very comfortable and at sea level it is doubtful if you will need a jersey. In winter, there will be days when you also do not need a jersey, but then for many days at sea level there will be times when you are very pleased to have one, as well as a windproof jacket. At all times you will need to be prepared for weather changes, so a raincoat is recommended, although in summer you may find it too warm and prefer to have an umbrella. It can also be very humid. Many of the streets are cobbled, so wear sensible shoes; you will be handicapped in high heels or fashion shoes. Generally, townspeople dress smartly casual, and cotton items are popular. In the evening, men will wear ties and jackets in the more expensive hotels and restaurants.

Away from the coast you should always take a windproof and waterproof jacket for the mountains, warmer ones in winter. The same applies if you are making any ferry journeys and like to stay on deck. Walkers will need their favoured walking shoes or boots. Waterproofs in the mountains are fine, but at low altitudes many find them too warm and a poncho style may be more comfortable. Always ensure you have sufficient warm clothing if you are going into the mountains. Always take water with you. You might find a whistle useful to keep in touch with straying companions should the clouds descend and kill visibility. A mobile phone can be an asset.

Hotel laundry services are very good, but for same-day service a 50% surcharge is usually levied, and beware of weekends and public holidays. Increasingly, hairdryers are provided in hotel bedrooms, but this should certainly not be relied upon, and in the cheaper hotels there is not always a shaver socket. The electricity supply is 220V, the standard in western Europe, and the plugs are the usual continental European two-pin.

Budget travellers should take a towel as those provided are often thin and very small, and a universal basin plug.

Photographers using a digital SLR camera could usefully take a standard UV filter to minimise glare off the sea – and protect the lens at the same time. In winter the light is wonderfully clear and sharp and there are some dramatic results to be had.

MONEY

Portugal is a member of the European Monetary Union and the currency is the euro. Travellers' cheques are accepted by most banks in the major currencies. Most banks in the main centres have ATMs and this is certainly the fastest way to obtain cash. *Levantamentos* (withdrawals) is the word you need! Some machines now automatically recognise UK cards. Credit cards, especially Visa, are accepted in hotels and some shops but not in all restaurants or the smaller cafés/bars.

Banks are generally open between 08.30 and 14.30 Monday to Friday, but are closed on Saturday and Sunday and public holidays.

TIPPING In the Azores it is not normal to leave a 10% tip, as only the newer and more expensive restaurants might include such a service charge. A small tip can be left on the table, one or two euros, but it does depend on the category of the restaurant. If you do wish to give a tip, consider a euro to hotel porters, but tipping taxi drivers or guides is not a common or 'must-do' thing.

BUDGETING

At present most overseas visitors come to the Azores on a pre-purchased package bought from their travel agent so they know roughly what their costs are going to be. UK prices start at around £600 for a seven-night stay on a bed-and-breakfast basis including transfers, and £790 for 14 nights on São Miguel. Cycling, walking,

2

ADMISSION CHARGES

Admission to museums throughout the Azores is often free or very modest; occasionally it is €5 or so and any admission charge over this amount is shown in the text.

whale and dolphin watching, and fly-drive tours are available. Given the present economic downturn, special offers can also be found out of the peak season.

The Azores are not a cheap-flight destination. Having arrived, you will find a wide range of accommodation, from one- to five-star hotels and apartment hotels, to small *residencias* and camping sites. Five islands have youth hostels. The most visited islands, São Miguel, Terceira, Faial and Pico, are more expensive than the others. Using ferries to travel between the islands is cheaper and more fun than flying, but you do need to be prepared for changes in the timetables and these can be complicated. Using buses will be considerably cheaper than taxis, but they can be neither very convenient nor always available, as they cater mainly to local people going to and from work.

Hiring general guides is expensive and in the busy summer months they are usually already occupied with pre-booked clients and tour groups. If you need a guide, then the cheapest way is often to contact the local travel agencies, who may be able to assemble individual clients to make a small tour group – for example, a full-day tour by minibus from Ponta Delgada to Furnas including a hot-springs lunch costs around €65 per person (see page 46 for local travel agencies).

Often there is not a huge difference between the prices various restaurants charge, and those that are more expensive are indicated in this book. Eating in smaller bars/cafés will be cheaper than the tourist restaurants and hotels and lunches can be delicious picnics with island products from the local supermarket or market. In fact, restaurant portions are so generous that a light picnic for one meal is often preferable.

Two budget travellers can expect to spend around €100 each per day in the high season. This roughly breaks down into: accommodation (shared room, usually includes breakfast) €70; supermarket lunch €12 per person; dinner including wine €38 per person; bus fares, occasional taxi, say a daily average of €15 per person, excluding inter-island travel.

For two travellers who like reasonable comfort and enjoy spending time over dinner, then allow: €130 for accommodation; a light lunch with wine €17 per person; dinner €30 per person – which adds up to a daily budget of around €112 per person plus excursions/taxis.

GETTING AROUND

INTER-ISLAND TRAVEL Most visitors coming by air from Europe or North America arrive in Ponta Delgada on São Miguel or Lajes on Terceira, much less often Horta on Faial.

By air Flights are inevitably subject to the weather, and can be delayed or cancelled. When it happens, it is bad luck and you simply have to be philosophical about it and make sure there is a good book to hand. Getting between the islands is not always straightforward, especially in winter, but more flights are being introduced every year, and independent travellers should spend time studying the SATA website (*www.sata.pt*). Most flights between each island take about 30 minutes, except São Miguel to Flores, which takes 80 minutes. For travellers with an international SATA air ticket, the airline offers some advanced purchase reductions; again see their website.

Eastern Group There are direct flights between Santa Maria and São Miguel and São Miguel to Terceira, and from São Miguel to Faial, Pico, São Jorge and Flores, direct on certain days, otherwise via Terceira.

Western Group Flores has direct flights with Faial, Terceira and São Miguel and Corvo. You must allow spare days around these flights in case of cancellation through bad weather, especially if your visit there is towards the end of your holiday and you have a fixed international flight to catch. Visits to the Western Group are best seen as the main objective of a two-week holiday and can be combined easily with Faial and Pico.

Central Group There are direct flights from Terceira to São Miguel, Santa Maria, Faial, Pico, São Jorge, Graciosa and Flores.

The structure of the air fares favours linking São Miguel, Terceira, Faial and Pico; flights to the other islands will be more expensive. SATA Air Açores offers tourists with an already purchased international air ticket a discount on inter-island fares, but the flights cannot be changed once booked. Staying over ten days triggers a discount of 10%. Single flights between islands start from around €87.

By ferry Taking a boat is great fun if you have the time; there are always seabirds to look out for, and if you are lucky there is a chance of seeing dolphins or maybe even a whale. Tickets can be purchased at the quayside office 30 minutes before departure, or for longer journeys from travel agents in advance.

Throughout the year there are several sailings daily between Horta (Faial) and Madalena (Pico), a 30-minute crossing, costing around €4.

In summer, there is a daily Horta–Velas (São Jorge) service via Pico (Madalena and some sailings also via São Roque), less often in winter. The single fare is around €16, and the journey time is 105 minutes. This means that, in summer at least, it is quite possible to make day excursions to São Jorge from Faial or Pico, and vice versa.

On certain days expect services between Terceira and Velas, taking 4.5 hours. In summer there has been a ferry service between the Eastern and Central island groups, even very infrequently to Flores. Distances did not allow regular sailings on set days and, of course, all is subject to the weather so flexibility is needed if planning a holiday using ferries. Unfortunately the Azores do not have a ship of their own and therefore rely on chartering a vessel: in 2009, it was several weeks late arriving from the UK. It is frustratingly difficult to organise journeys in advance and local travel agents are understandably very reluctant to commit themselves. In 30 years of visiting, I have never managed more than Santa Maria to São Miguel, made possible because there are sometimes summer weekend excursions between the islands.

For details of the current ferry services, check the websites (*www.atlanticoline.pt* and *www.transmacor.pt*).

By car As in Portugal, driving is on the right. At crossroads vehicles approaching from the right have priority. There is a maximum speed limit of 80km/h, 50km/h in built-up areas. Seat belts have to be worn at all times, including the rear passengers.

The new main roads are good but the small country roads can be pot-holed and narrow. One thing to be very careful about when driving in fog or low cloud and poor visibility is the Azorean black-and-white cow wandering on the road, either singly or in a scattered herd; in such conditions they are superbly camouflaged! Many of the minor roads are not signposted. Diversions for roadworks are signposted, but if the sign disappears after a few days it is seldom replaced because by then it is assumed everyone knows the way!

For UK drivers, a full driving licence is required and those aged under 25 years should check minimum requirements for hiring a car at the time of making a booking. Citizens from non-European countries similarly require a driving licence, along with a passport or other form of official identification. Normally there is no upper age limit but again this should be checked at the time of booking. In peak summer season there is a shortage of hire cars, and reservations should be made well in advance.

There are many car-hire companies in the Azores, and some are very small. Three well-established firms with their main offices in Ponta Delgada are:

Autatlantis ✆296 205 340 (reservations);
e info@autatlantis.com; www.autatlantis.com
Hertz Airport, Ponta Delgada;✆296 205 435;
e reservas@hertz.pt; www.hertz.pt

Ilha Verde ✆296 304 891 (reservations);
e reserve@ilhaverde.com; www.ilhaverde.com

Alternatively, your travel agent can of course make arrangements for you on all the islands.

Prices for car hire range per day for three to seven days according to season from around €38 per day for the cheapest group A, up to about €67 for group D, and may be paid for in advance. Prices can differ between islands. Rates do not include insurance, CDW, TP, PAI and Super CDW. It should be noted that car-hire companies do not allow their vehicles to be taken on board the ferries.

Several islands have scooter hire, but this is not for the faint-hearted or inexperienced. However, it is a cheap way to get around and rental starts from around €20 per day. A driving licence is again required and helmets are supplied and must be worn. Bicycles are also available, but for these and motor scooters check with the tourist office for latest rental companies.

By bus Some islands are better served than others. On São Miguel you can see a lot of the island by public bus. You can make a circuit on the islands of Faial and Pico, and some trips by bus on Terceira and São Jorge. For details see the *Getting around* section for the individual island. For the other four islands, bus services are not very convenient.

ACCOMMODATION

This varies hugely, from standard comfort in conventional hotels, apartment hotels, resort hotels and interesting hotels, to the simple family hotel, and finally delightful old manor houses with character. Until recently there were no five-star hotels, the islands' hoteliers always preferring to provide a higher standard than conventional classification leads guests to expect. There is now a five-star hotel on Terceira. In addition to hotels, there are also self-catering apartments and cottages, small guesthouses and bed-and-breakfast establishments.

Accommodation has hugely improved and expanded over the past few years; São Miguel has seen the biggest increase in new hotels, mostly around Ponta Delgada, with some in other parts of the island. Angra on Terceira and Horta on Faial have also seen a substantial increase in the number of new places to stay.

There is also new accommodation on all the other islands. Many hotels now have suites, with quite a number offering special rates for children, or for an extra bed in a room. All this building has greatly eased the acute shortage of beds in the peak season, but of course it creates a surplus in the winter months – another reason to come off-season!

Finally, a *pensão* or *residencial* can be a relatively old and small town hotel, and furnishings may be a little spartan and gloomy. However, in the last few years many have been refurbished to a high standard and offer good value for money.

I have graded the hotels according to the price of a double room in high season. Low-season rates can fall between €25 and €50 a night. The high season is generally from 1 June to 30 September, with more specific details covered in each island chapter. The majority of rooms are priced between €100 and €170. Single-room rates are generally only a little below the double-room rate. Many hotels offer special deals; check their websites for the latest offers.

There are now too many small guesthouses to list, but I have mentioned the occasional one that has come to my attention; they can be in the centre of a village, surrounded by pastures, or by the sea. The owners have formed an association and have an excellent website (*www.casasacorianas.com*), with photographs and details of all the houses with online reservation available.

All islands have official campsites, most with amenities and nominal charges, and some are very attractive. Details are given under the respective islands. The sites are very popular with the local people – it's just nice to get away from home for a couple of days or so, read a book, go fishing, find a good restaurant or eat outside at the barbecues provided. They are also very popular with teenagers in the school holidays.

Five islands (São Miguel, Santa Maria, Terceira, Pico and São Jorge) have youth hostels; see the website www.pousadasjuvacores.com.

EATING AND DRINKING

EATING Eating out in the Azores is a very variable experience and is often surprising. Sometimes you can strike it lucky in the more expensive eateries and be given a sophisticated and well-presented dish, depending on who is cooking that night; you will soon conclude it is rather a lottery. In the medium-priced restaurants there can again be surprises. Some islands are definitely better than others for eateries, and often a single establishment can shine like a beacon.

Sadly it cannot be claimed that the islands are a gastronomic delight, but this is changing. The lower and mid-priced restaurants all seem to share the same menu so that after a week you are beginning to look for novelties. To do so, instead of simply looking down one menu, menus of all the restaurants have to be examined – at least in Angra, Ponta Delgada and Horta where there are many restaurants to

THE AZOREAN KITCHEN   *Monique Cymbron, São Miguel*

The Azorean kitchen has more or less maintained the flavours of the Portuguese kitchen from the time of the Discoveries. There does not seem to be any influence from the early Breton or Flemish population. History tells us that they kept their language only for a generation and the same seems to be true about their food. One of the reasons may be that the Portuguese have always kept in touch with their continental homeland while other settlers perhaps did not.

The Azorean staple is soup. In the old times the main meal of poor rural inhabitants was often simply a thick vegetable soup with *chouriço* and bread. People are now better off but soup is still served as a starter twice a day, the thicker the better. There is a variety of vegetable soups, one of the most famous being *caldo verde*, a potato soup with finely shredded cabbage leaves cooked in it. Chicken broth is also popular and sometimes fish soup. Until the 1950s, the rural social structure was very archaic and the limited economic possibilities of the population meant that fish was the basic component of daily meals, meat being a luxury served only on festive days, where tradition decreed three dishes of chicken, pork and beef, some boiled, others roasted, should be served.

Interestingly, on the island of São Miguel all dishes are flavoured with hot pepper (*pimenta*) in different forms: powdered, salted or as a paste.

Cod is one of the main raw materials in the islands. According to Portuguese tradition, there are 365 different recipes for cod, one for each day of the year. Even at formal dinners, it is usual to prepare a codfish dish. There is *bacalhau à Brás* (fried potatoes, small pieces of boiled cod mixed with scrambled eggs), *bacalhau com natas* (fried potatoes, small pieces of codfish, olive oil-based béchamel sauce and cream on top), or *bacalhau na chapa* (a thick piece of codfish baked in the oven with olive oil, onion, garlic and red pepper).

There is a large variety of local fish. Small fish, *chicharros*, was regarded in former times as food of the poor since it was very cheap and eaten fried almost daily for lunch, on its own or with a garlic and lemon sauce or a hot pepper sauce, or parsley, olive oil and onions (green sauce). Recently its price rose astronomically – no-one could explain why the fish almost completely disappeared, only to return. Many medium-sized fish appear on restaurant menus, fried, grilled, steamed, sometimes filleted. They include *abrotea*, white hake, and *cherne*, 'wreck fish'. These are considered the best of the white fish. They are huge, so they appear mostly filleted. In summer one can find fresh tuna which is sliced as steaks and served fried. Swordfish (*espadarte*) is also a dark-flesh fish that is usually served fried.

As for seafood (*marisqueira*), octopus cooked in the regional wine, *vinho de cheiro*, is very popular, as is barbecued European squid. There are *cracas* (a type of barnacle), a seafood typical of the Azores but increasingly rare, now found only in restaurants specialising in seafood. They are eaten as an appetiser, the tiny morsels retrieved with a special hooked tool from the shell that clings to a piece of rock. *Lapas* (limpets) are another shellfish eaten in various ways, most commonly baked with garlic and lemon juice. Rice with *lapas* is also popular, or *lapas de molho Afonso* spicy sauce. There is *cavaco*, an endemic kind of crab, and *lagosta* (spiny lobster), and shrimps that are mostly imported.

choose from. With such a good growing climate there should be a wonderful range of vegetables on offer but it seems most townspeople prefer simply to buy from the supermarket rather than grow much for themselves, and the supermarkets are

For meat, pork, beef and chicken are all on the menu. Typical dishes here are *cozido à portuguesa* – pork, beef and chicken mixed mostly with cabbage, root vegetables and potatoes, all cooked together. Many restaurants serve this dish once a week as the dish of the day. In Furnas, *cozido* is a speciality but here it is cooked slowly in volcanic heat in the ground and called *cozido nas caldeiras*. Terceira has *alcatra*, a special meat dish cooked in wine and spices.

A meal in an Azorean restaurant is often preceded with cheese, bread and pepper sauce offered while waiting for the meal. A local cheese is usually given: on Faial and Pico the cheese will be *São João do Pico*; on São Jorge it is *São Jorge*, a strong sharp-flavoured cheese, considered to be the best in the Azores. On Terceira the *Castelinhos* cheese and on São Miguel the *Agua Retorta* cheese or a fresh white cheese with the ever-present *massa de pimenta* are served.

The most typical appetiser on Faial, Pico and São Jorge is blood sausage with yams, a tropical vegetable cultivated on all the islands, while on São Miguel blood sausage comes with fresh pineapple.

Religious festivals have their own special dishes. During the Holy Spirit Festival, a meat broth with bread is cooked in the islands of the Central Group. During the carnival, *malassados*, a rich dough, like that for doughnuts, is deep-fried and sugared. *Massa sovado*, sweet bread somewhere between bread and cake, is baked year-round.

Formerly, village people ate only home-baked bread, because corn was widely cultivated to feed both humans and animals. Corn bread is a greyish, moist kind of bread that tends to mould rather quickly. Typical local restaurants often serve both corn and wheat bread. White Azorean bread tends to be too dry; the so-called home-baked bread, a big round loaf, is better.

There is a great variety of locally grown fruit in the Azores and many fruits were introduced following the disease that attacked orange trees in the last century. Pineapples were cultivated but it was soon found that the climate was not warm enough for outdoor growing, so greenhouses were built to obtain a reasonable crop. The Azores are now the only place in the world where pineapples are grown commercially in greenhouses. Economically they cannot compete with pineapples imported from Africa and South America and are heavily subsidised. They are generally sweet and juicy but can be acidic in winter. Again, the Azorean climate is a little too cool for bananas, which are generally smaller and sometimes brownish, but compensate by being sweet.

Other tropical fruits such as avocado, guava, mango, papaya, annona, maracujá (passion fruit) and diospyros (persimmon) are also grown. Citrus fruits including oranges, mandarins, clementines and lemons are still grown in quantity. While bananas and pineapples are ripening all the year round, the others are mostly winter fruit starting in October and available until May or June. Typical summer fruits such as apples, pears, plums and peaches do not grow too well in the islands. A lack of a definite cold period means poor flowering; thus cherries do not crop at all, although insects are abundant in summer, since insecticides are not generally used. Only in the higher altitudes such as the Furnas Valley can one get a reasonable crop.

Generally, most restaurants open for both lunch and dinner and the usual hours are 12.00–15.00 and 18.30–23.00. Depending on which town or island, they are closed all day either Sunday (especially Ponta Delgada) or Monday, but there is always somewhere open.

Prices range from €8.00 to €12.00 per plate for lunch and €12.00 to €17.00 for dinner while desserts are around €2–3. Some places have special lunchtime offers for around €7.00, including coffee. There are some restaurants that offer buffet meals only which often include a selection of regional dishes for €7.00 to €12.00 per person, excluding dessert and drinks.

Most hotels offer a buffet meal from around €18.00 per person, excluding drinks, plus an a-la-carte menu.

not very adventurous. This is then reflected in the restaurants, which is no excuse, however, for serving rice and chips in combination, together with tinned diced mixed vegetables. Salads are mostly lettuce, some tomato, sliced onion, maybe grated carrot and if you are lucky some cucumber, rarely all together; dressing is usually left to you, from a bottle of olive oil and vinegar. Hotels often offer more variety, and can be very good, but even the best can include some of the routine ingredients cooked unimaginatively. Hopefully the new catering school by the cruise terminal in Ponta Delgada (see page 89) will bring change.

Portions are generally huge, sometimes overpoweringly so, especially meat. Fish including seafood is usually excellent, but there is a danger of fish being smothered in sauces or garlic so killing natural flavours. If you cannot find it plain grilled, often the most reliable ploy is to find it done as a local version of *bouillabaisse*; the *alcatra* on Terceira is an excellent example, and they make it with meat as well. *Bacalhau* (dried cod), the traditional village dishes and Azorean sausages can be very good indeed, as can the spicy *chouriço* (smoked sausage) and the black blood sausage, *morcelas*, with pineapple, but not too often in the same week!

Mercifully Azorean cheeses are excellent and quality mainland Portuguese wines have been unsung for far too long, leaving the diner feeling very content with the world. Some chocolate desserts can be gorgeous. Whenever I am able I tend to seek the least pretentious, smallest, tucked-away place I can find and there often discover superb Azorean fish cooked faultlessly to reveal the flavours only really fresh fish can give. Often, too, such places give amazingly good value for money although, like the fish, they are disappearing.

Restaurants are often tucked away down narrow alleyways and labelling them on maps is liable to confuse, rather than aid, a hungry traveller, but locals are friendly – don't hesitate to ask for directions.

DRINKING The settlers in the Azores had their priorities well ordered because wine has been produced since the very early days. On Pico grape varieties brought by the first settlers from mainland Portugal failed to acclimatise. The Verdelho grape was imported around 1500, possibly from Sicily, or maybe from Madeira, or perhaps by a Jesuit from Italy.

Vines were first planted on a large scale in the 16th century by the Catholic orders of Franciscans and Carmelites and by Jesuits in the following century. On Pico the vines were brought to Silveira, but here the surrounding land was too good for grapes and needed for essential foods such as wheat. Instead they went to the geologically youngest area of the island where the ground was very poor and stony, around the west coast. It is so heavily lava-strewn that it was only with great labour and difficulty sufficient stones were cleared, using them to make what became the characteristic walls, or *currais*, of small enclosures that provide such wonderful shelter from salty winds and at the same time extra heat. Surplus stone was neatly stacked into rectangular piles called *richeiros*. This was done mainly along the western edge of the island and now, almost half a millennium later, it is a protected zone because of its history. Other interesting features of this extraordinary memorial to the energy and persistence of the islanders include the *decansadouros*, the resting places for those carrying full baskets of grapes; made of stone, they are in two levels, one for those carrying on their heads and those carrying baskets on their shoulders. At the height of production some 30,000 barrels or 15 million litres were produced annually. Among the countries it was exported to were Britain and famously to the Russian tsars, apparently by a German trading family. Quite what this wine was is not known as there were very few written records kept about how it was produced. However, Edward Boid, visiting in 1832, wrote that the merchants in Horta took the Pico wine and mixed it with wine from São Jorge and added brandy. It was then heated to between 110°F and 130°F for four to six months, during which time any evaporation from the casks was topped up with more wine and brandy. It seems that different blends were produced for different markets.

Because of the rocky terrain, transport of the barrels was difficult, and to get them onto the waiting ships, wooden boards were laid over rocks that had previously been cut and roughly levelled. You might see old stone slipways or *rola-pipas* used to get the barrels into the sea, where they were then towed out to the waiting ship. The best Pico wine was said to be 'so good it should be drunk in the middle of a prayer'.

When disease struck in the mid 1800s the first vines were replaced with the hardy Isabella grape whose strong aroma gave rise to the *vinho de cheiro* – fragrant wine. This is widely made throughout the islands for village consumption, and many a walker has staggered onward under the influence of spontaneous hospitality.

Twenty years or so ago small-scale experiments were conducted with new continental varieties, and some old stone enclosures replaced by long, straight rows supported by wires that always looked impressively immaculate in their level

ORDERING COFFEE

In the Azores coffee comes in different strengths and sizes, but all bar one are made from the same amount of coffee, just different dilution rates.

Café normal A strong, small cup
Café duplo Two strong small cups in one small cup
Café curto Strong coffee with a little water in a small cup
Café carioca A larger but weaker coffee, again served in a small cup
Café chávena cheia Strong coffee with plenty of water served in a small cup
Café chávena grande Strong coffee with more water served in a larger cup
Café chávena grande com leite Strong coffee with milk served in a larger cup
Café garoto Strong coffee with milk served in a small cup
Café galão The nearest to caffé latte and served in a tall glass
Café galão escuro A stronger version (*escuro* meaning 'dark')
Café galão claro A weaker version (*claro* meaning 'light')

fields of cinders. However, it is the traditional method with its long history that is the remarkable showpiece and has most recently been rejuvenated in a number of ways, firstly by recognising various areas of vine growing and production – the Zonas Vitivinícolas – and secondly by the establishment of a Regional Commission based in Madalena to guarantee quality and production methods, and certification. Named quality wines produced in a demarcated area are designated VLQPRD (*vinhos licorosos de qualidade produzidos em região determinada*), which covers *vinhos licorosos* or fortified sweetened wines recommended as an *aperitivo*, and includes the white table wine Pedras Brancas from Graciosa, now happily much reduced in price from a few years ago. The VLQPRD include the Brum wine from Biscoitos on Terceira and Pico's Lajido. Also from Pico is a more versatile red wine from Verdelho and Arinto grapes called Czar. Finally there are the certified Azores Regional Wines (Vinho Regional Açores): the whites Viosinho and Gouveio, Frei Gigante, Terras de Lava and Maresia from Pico, Moledo from Terceira and the red from Pico, simply labelled Cabernet Sauvignon and Merlot.

On Pico the Cooperativa Vitivinicola da Ilha do Pico now has some 250 small growers. Their winery can be visited. Wine production is far from conventional, not just because of the lava habitat but also because complications affecting acidity, sugar content, maturation and other aspects are created by the extremes of cold air falling from Pico Mountain and the sun on the rocks and the salt in the air.

Terceira's first true vineyard was planted more than 400 years ago. A certain Pero Anes do Canto was in charge of the Portuguese navy and owned land at Biscoitos and it was he who introduced a Verdelho grape from Sicily. Production took off and records for 1693 show that taverns in Angra sold over 1,000 barrels of 500 litres each of Verdelho wine. It seems the same quantity was also sold to the island's eight convents! This may have been a translation error, but wine was certainly exported to the Portuguese colonies. Subsequent introduction of the Baco variety helped make the vineyards more resistant to disease.

Legislation ensures urban development is limited in the Biscoitos region to protect the vine-growing area. In 1993, the Biscoitos Society of Verdelho Wines was founded with the objective of promoting the Verdelho wines of Biscoitos as well as all of the quality wines of the Azores. Members are founders, honorary members, brothers and novices and wear a blue cape with a gold trim, blue representing the colour of the Azorean flag and gold the colour of the Verdelho. The society's coat of arms in addition to the Azores arms includes a *tambolhadeira*, a drinking cup resembling the traditional clay *taladeira* used in Terceira to taste the new wine, a ritual that takes place on St Martin's Day. The Brum family wine museum at Biscoitos is open to visitors (see page 141).

Graciosa quietly produces wine from two wineries. Under the Terras da Conde name with its distinctive label showing a windmill comes a red and a white table wine, a welcome *aperitivo* and an excellent *aguardente*. The company was founded over 70 years ago and has its own vineyards, growing mainly Arinto on *vinho brava* stock. The winery welcomes visitors. The second producer is the Adega Cooperativa da Ilha Graciosa, begun in 1960 with an initial production of 200,000 litres of dry white wine. By the 1980s, this had languished and production ceased for a time but now with government support the situation is reversed, and its white table wine Pedras Brancas has certified status.

Several liqueur wines are also made, especially São Miguel's well-known *Maracujá* liqueur (passion fruit). This, mixed half and half with *aguardente* – fire and passion – is a great ending to a typical feast of traditional Azorean dishes! Others are made from local fruit such as Japanese plum (*Eriobotrya japonica*, the loquat), figs and blackberries. This last, called *Amora*, is less sweet than the others, and imbibed not in moderation has the kick of an island donkey.

PUBLIC HOLIDAYS AND FESTIVALS

The main public holidays are 1 January; 25 April (marking the Revolution of 1974); Good Friday and Easter Sunday; 1 May (Labour Day); 24 May (Autonomy Day); 3 June (Corpus Christi); 10 June (National Day of Portugal); 15 August (Feast of the Assumption); 5 October (Proclamation of the Republic); 1 November (All Saints' Day); 1 December (Restoration of Independence); 8 December (Feast of the Immaculate Conception); and 25 December (Christmas Day). There are also municipal holidays, each municipality taking them on different dates so that there are some 18 of these during the summer, but they should not significantly affect the visitor.

New Year's Eve is celebrated throughout the islands and in Ponta Delgada there are fireworks and brass bands, and sometimes a rock band. More modest celebrations are also held in Angra do Heroísmo and Horta and smaller towns.

Carnival is another islands-wide celebration, in Ponta Delgada marked by grand balls on 20 February and 23 February and a matinée masquerade ball on 21 February. Visitors are welcome, but tickets need to be pre-booked. On 24 February, the last day of this five-day festival ends with a water battle at the marina.

Portugal's second-largest religious festival takes place in Ponta Delgada on the fifth Sunday after Easter, the **Festas de Santo Cristo dos Milagres** (Christ of the Miracles). There are many festivals in August throughout the islands and two of the most important are the **Sea Week** with music and sailing regattas based on Horta between 5 August and 12 August, and **Whaler's Week** on Pico during the last week of that month. The **Angra Jazz Festival** (*www.angrajazz.com*) is held every year in early October when performers come from both Europe and America to play for several days.

There are festivals throughout the year, and the principal ones are detailed in the following chapters for the individual islands.

SHOPPING

In addition to the handicrafts (see below), cheeses from the islands are always a popular purchase. Homemade jams are as good as or better than grandmother's, while tea from the two tea estates on São Miguel is a very original gift and easiest of all to carry home. Somewhat heavier are one or two fresh pineapples in a presentation box, and island wine, *aperitivos*, liqueurs and *aguardentes*. For food gifts try the supermarkets, and at the airports on São Miguel and Faial there is at least one shop selling Azorean products, and new outlets are appearing all the time. Also, check out the main markets in Ponta Delgada and Horta. Azorean tea can also be purchased direct from the estates (see page 110). Please note that many shops close from 13.00 on Saturday until Monday morning.

HANDICRAFTS – *ARTESANATO* There are many items common to all or most of the islands, with their own variations, while some handicrafts are specific to one island or village. All use natural raw materials; you cannot fail to see charming corn dollies or *escravela japonesa*, folk figures made from maize husks, wickerwork baskets, ceramics, various items from cut basalt, embroidery, delicate flowers made from fish scales or fig pith, simple rugs made from maize or rags, and superb woven bedspreads made on São Jorge. There are also models of whales and items to do

Scrimshaw is an art born of boredom and loneliness on the whaling ships of the 19th century and links the Azores to many countries. Ships' crews would while away their time engraving on whales' teeth, and then rubbing lamp black into the lines to bring up the design. In the Azores this tradition continued, using the teeth taken from whales killed off the islands and brought ashore for processing. It has all but disappeared because time passes and also the supply of teeth is diminishing. Fifteen years ago divers could still find them on the seabed near old whaling stations on Pico and on Madeira, but now such finds are rare.

Modern artists sand down the tooth ridges, then use car polish to coat the tooth. A layer of Indian ink is applied to blacken the surface to be engraved. Machine-powered needles are used to engrave through the ink, the polish, and into the tooth. The engraved lines appear white and Indian ink is then applied a second time and this time it enters the unwaxed lines that form the design. The first coat of black is then removed.

with whaling, and some scrimshaw (products made from whale teeth; see box above). Shops do offer whalebone items, but please be aware it is illegal to take these products out of Portugal and their purchase encourages this trade. Several shops now sell items made from environmentally friendly alternative materials. Something new is very attractive local jewellery made from basalt, ladies' earrings, brooches and necklaces, but only a few jewellers stock them.

ARTS AND ENTERTAINMENT

Entertainment is very modest, but the number of places to go out in the evening is increasing, although their names are not emblazoned across the night sky and they are still relatively few in number. In larger towns on summer evenings there will often be rock, jazz and folk bands playing in the public squares or by the harbour. There are a handful of pubs, again scattered widely. A lively nightlife thrives, but is much more private than commercial and has a quite different meaning from that in the big city. There can be evening dress balls and other social events associated with the many organisations that thrive in the islands, of which the casual visitor remains unaware. As you travel around the islands you will see many barbecue sites at *miradouros* and in sylvan roadside glades. In summer these are busy after office hours when family and friends meet for an alfresco supper and evening together. At weekends and holidays they will again all be occupied, as will the woodland picnic sites laid out in so many lovely places by the forestry services. Summer is for outdoor living, which is also when the festivals and folklore gatherings mostly take place. Very noticeably over the past few years cafés and bars have put out tables and chairs on the pavement, especially around the new marinas and quaysides and pedestrianised squares, so that now friends and families stay out late quietly enjoying a beer, bottle of wine or coffee. On a balmy summer evening the visitor can enjoy a promenade around the main harbours with their pretty lights reflecting on the water, or sit in a garden square and nibble a snack from a street stall or watch the world go by from a pavement café. During your stay in Ponta Delgada check whether there is anything on at the recently restored **Teatro Micaelense** (*www. teatromicaelense.pt*); this offers a wide range of cultural events throughout the year, from ballet, musicals, *fado*, jazz and chamber recitals to fully staged operas, the programmes often linked with the Coliseums in Lisbon and Oporto. In Horta, on Faial, the *teatro* near the main square has also been recently restored and offers a mix of Hollywood and art cinema together with occasional orchestral and jazz music.

ACTIVITIES

WALKING Walking in the mid-Atlantic is a most wonderful experience. Whether you are high in the mountains, following a coastal walk, or merely strolling along a country lane, there is a purity in the air, an exhilaration in the light, and ever-changing cloud patterns. In places trails lie dark and dank between 2m-tall embankments, with hedges of cryptomeria, pittosporum and endemic shrubs, while the banks themselves are moss-covered or draped with soft green curtains of selaginella, a primitive fern ally. At other times when high up in the mountains the scene is more akin to moorland, with low-growing grasses, rushes and mossy flushes in the wetter areas, and elsewhere a knee-high scrub of heather, and often a view of the distant sea. Perhaps best of all is to file along a narrow path contouring a steep sea cliff, when the views are spectacular, very special and pure Azores. However, gentler walks along farm roads through patchworks of pastures with the sight of healthy, contented cows out to grass all year, and past farm buildings with ever-changing rural scenes, are equally as satisfying in their different way. A recent survey of visitors from the UK showed that 80% came principally for walking.

Buried beneath the vigorous alien vegetation of the islands lie many old cobbled trails, used long ago by the islanders to travel between the villages by donkey, oxcart and horse. Before the advent of roads these trails were the economic and social lifelines for the villages, for the fishermen carrying basketloads of fish to inland villages, for the workers walking to their fields, to the vineyards, their fruit and orange orchards, and for religious pilgrimages. The history and stories they could tell are as lost to the visitor as is the dustiest archive in the deepest cellar. Maybe one day local historians will make all this tangible and readily accessible, but meanwhile all we have are brief glimpses of this earlier age. If old trails happen to lead to pastures or to vineyards then their weathered surfaces can still be seen, perhaps for just a few metres, maybe for 100m or more. They are there for the observant traveller to find, and then to let the imagination fill in the stories. Certainly if these hidden paths could be rediscovered they would make wonderful walks and stories for our time and century. And if time and tide have in part destroyed them, then maybe new routes could be found to link them.

At present we are still losing walks, but gaining new ones. For years unsurfaced farm tracks were given asphalt surfaces with the help of EU funding; great for the farmer, but bad news for the walking tourist. Seismic tremors and flash floods cause human tragedies, and also send favourite walks permanently into memory, their imprint on the landscape forever destroyed by nature. Whether our pioneering efforts and appeals over the years have influenced the authorities one does not know, but recently waymarking and maintenance of walking routes has at last been taken seriously and there are now some 60 official walks covering all the islands; 28 on São Miguel, and between two and six on each of the others. This is tremendous news, and hopefully they will now go from strength to strength. These trails vary in length from 2km to 17km. Some are circular; others follow some of the old inter-village paths. Unfortunately cows like to use the marker poles as scratching posts and pushed sideways they do not always point in the right direction, while walls with paint marks get knocked down, so one still needs to keep a good sense of direction! There are descriptive brochures for each trail available from the local tourist offices, and all can be downloaded from the website www.trails-azores.com which is an excellent service, because should any walks be made impassable by storms, etc, then updates are regularly posted. At present the texts are not as detailed as they should be, and how one accesses the walks or gets home afterwards is often frustratingly vague, but again one should be able to work it out without too much difficulty. All the trails are at the time of writing under review, and in the future one hopes the best will be fully maintained and waymarked.

While all the islands now have attractive walks, the best are on São Jorge, São Miguel and Flores, and new trails on Pico and Faial are rightly proving very popular. Pico also offers the ascent of Pico Mountain, the highest in Portugal. In the relevant island chapters, I have described my own favourite walks.

Remember always to take with you sensible kit – layers for warmth, a waterproof/windproof outer jacket, and sun protection. Always take water, and for some of the walks where the route takes you across lava or the few arid areas, take double the normal quantity. A most useful item to have with you in the Azores is a mobile phone to call a taxi at the end of a walk.

CYCLING Next to walking, this is the finest way to get to know the islands, following quiet rural lanes and passing through pretty villages for frequent pit-stops. Autatlantis (*www.autatlantis.com*) offers cycle hire at €12 per day or €6 per day in conjunction with its car hire, and €10 or €6 respectively per day for three to eight days' hire from their outlet in Vila Franco do Campo on São Miguel. Some travel agencies in the Azores offer fully supported eight-day packages with two-centred accommodation and daily transfers for around £800 excluding flights, while UK and other tour operators offer all-inclusive cycling holidays.

WHALE AND DOLPHIN WATCHING Whale and dolphin watching has become a major focus of ecotourism and the increase in its popularity is phenomenal; it's the fastest-growing tourist activity worldwide. Beginning as a commercial enterprise in 1955 on the southern California coast, it is claimed whale watching is now organised in about 120 countries with 13 million participants – 2008 figures; its popularity continues. For some economies, it has become an industry in its own right; divide the number of whales viewed into the cash generated, and each whale must be worth a small fortune. Good news in support of the conservation argument for, in this role, whales are more valuable than if they were hunted and killed. Another important plus is that in many places commercial whale watching has become a recognised tool for education, and is supporting research by the observations and recordings made during whale-watching trips and other inputs. All the more extraordinary that, with government subsidy, Norway, Iceland and Japan continue to hunt and kill them commercially and at the same time offer whale-watching trips! How I should like to translate the calls of the whales and know the word they have for us.

It is essential that these 'subjects' of our recreational curiosity are viewed with the respect they deserve. In the Azores, whale and dolphin watching has become a much-advertised and popular activity and there are now many operators offering whale-watching trips; some have more than one boat. This brings into question what effect this has on the cetaceans; they are sensitive animals surviving in a very tough environment doing the things we do, finding food, rearing young and socialising. They have highly sensitive hearing and are distressed when their communication is interfered with, when speedboats tear around them, gunning their engines. Bothering them by too close a contact and in other ways can alter their migration patterns, separate groups and interfere with their reproduction. What the stress thresholds are is not known and more research is needed, so given our ignorance the best policy is: don't do it unless you know it is harmless. Swimming with cetaceans is controversial and is banned in several countries.

A 2011 estimate revealed that some 48,000 people went whale watching in the

WHALE- AND DOLPHIN-WATCHING ETIQUETTE

Legislation has been passed in the Azores to regulate the increasing demand for whale and dolphin watching but supervising behaviour out at sea and out of sight is not easy. You, the client whale watcher, can do this by reporting back any malpractice you encounter. The new economic significance of whale watching and the widening concern and support from those who participate is likely to do more than anything else to help protect these animals on the world stage and change political opinions.

- Cetaceans should not be chased.
- Boats should approach by maintaining direction parallel and slightly to the rear of the cetaceans, keeping an open field of 180° to the front of them.
- When approaching, boats should avoid changes in direction, keep to slow speeds of under 10 knots and when 400m from the area reduce to 4 knots.
- A maximum of only two boats are permitted inside a radius of 400m around an individual whale or group of whales.
- It is prohibited to approach cetaceans closer than 50m; when they are resting they may not be approached at all.
- Only one boat at a time is permitted to approach to the minimum distance of 50m from the whales, and the engine should be kept on low revs.
- Boats should not come between animals in groups thereby separating them, especially the young.
- Whales with small calves should not be approached closer than 100m.
- Movements of all boats must always be on the same side, parallel to and a little to the rear of the animals.
- The maximum time to be spent in the area observing is 30 minutes near the animal.
- After observation, boats must depart from the area to the rear of the animals, and maintain a slow speed within 400m of them.
- No swimming is allowed with cetaceans.
- Skippers must explain to clients the dangers of swimming with dolphins and that they do this at their own risk (there is no insurance available).
- When swimming with dolphins, one extra crew member, apart from the skipper, must be allocated for surveillance of swimmers at all times and be equipped for swimming.
- Only two swimmers with dolphins should be allowed in the water at the same time and they should be equipped with snorkels; they must remain quietly on the surface and not touch the dolphins.
- Swimming time with dolphins is limited to 15 minutes maximum.
- The boat's motor must be in neutral at all times when swimmers are in the water.

Azores that year, supporting 53 boats and 195 jobs. This is but a small window into the situation worldwide, and it is pleasing to note that the Azorean government has passed regulations controlling the number of boats allowed, passenger safety, and visitor behaviour when near the animals. The regulations also aim to encourage the companies involved to work more closely together, reduce competition and limit the number of boats around any one pod.

If you are going to visit them, there is an accepted etiquette to follow (see box, page 65). Rather than book a trip at random, study the notes about what you should know before you go out to sea, and how your boat crew should handle the situation. When you have absorbed these, check out the operators, ask the right questions, and when you find one that suits you, go ahead. Check whether they have an experienced biologist on board at all times; ask how many people they take as a maximum, if there is shade from the sun, a lavatory, and if drinking water is supplied. You can also ask if you are contributing to scientific research by choosing their boat.

For those who do not like the idea of venturing into the mid-Atlantic in a small rigid inflatable boat and enduring three hours banging into the waves as you speed along, there are now larger, more comfortable vessels that have cabins and decks where you can move around. You are no less likely to see whales and dolphins this way and your view from the raised decks of these vessels is much better. Seeing whales and dolphins out at sea is a memorable and special experience; to really get the most out of your boat trip, do your homework first, read up about the creatures, be informed; only then should you intrude upon them and with a clearer conscience.

Because of the weather, the main season is from April to October, although cetaceans may be seen throughout the year and you may find there are opportunities in winter. With over 27 species now recorded in Azorean waters out of a total of some 83 species of whales, dolphins and porpoises, this makes the Azores one of the world's top places to observe them. In January 2009, the first northern right whale for 110 years was recorded in the Azores, five miles south of Faial. The islands best placed and with organised excursions are Pico, Faial and São Miguel.

Typically there are two departures each day, around 09.00 and 15.00, each lasting about three hours. Thirty minutes before departure there is usually a pre-trip briefing. The cost varies, but is generally around €40–50 per person. A seven-night whale-watching programme staying on Pico costs from around £580 excluding flights. Typically this would be: arrive and briefing on day 1; further briefing and talks on history of whaling, etc, and afternoon whale-watching boat trip on day 2; then days 3–6 morning boat trip with afternoons free for optional land-based activities or at leisure; and final day flexible, allowing for any replacement boat trips if earlier bad weather caused cancellations. Several tour operators offer whale-watching packages including international flights and various extras on São Miguel, Faial and Pico from around £880.

Should you like more information, then the Whale and Dolphin Conservation Society, the world's most active charity dedicated to the conservation and welfare of all whales, dolphins and porpoises, has an excellent website (*www.wdcs.org*).

SWIMMING The steep rocky sea coasts mean that swimming opportunities are mostly focused on small beaches, little bays and a combination of natural and manmade rock pools. The more popular locations often have changing facilities and sometimes lifeguards, while amenities are improving rapidly all the time. The coveted European Blue Flags signifying the beaches or swimming areas that meet stringent standards have been awarded to many sites in the Azores. Few of the natural swimming places are really suitable for non-swimmers, and nowhere have

I become more aware of so many very young children participating in swimming lessons in municipal pools. There are various adverse conditions and dangerous currents unknown to the visitor and swimming should be enjoyed only in clearly designated areas. Please be very aware of the coded flags flying according to prevailing conditions on designated swimming beaches:

Green	Safe to swim
Yellow	Be careful, no swimming
Red	Danger, keep out of the water
Chequered	Beach temporarily without a lifeguard

Many hotels have conventional swimming pools and recent investment has created attractive public pools near some of the main population centres, while local municipalities have created simpler facilities, often modifying rocky sea-washed locations – many with natural built-in wave machines! Seldom, however, around any of the sites is shade provided from the sun. But the sheer diversity of opportunities to swim is remarkable, from the sea and rock pools, formal and indoor pools, volcanic lakes, to a naturally warm geothermal pool.

DIVING For a long time few people thought of the Azores as a diving destination, and I wrote in the last edition of this guide that it is still in its infancy and really virgin territory. Now it is recognised, and being rated as among the best in the world! The seabed, being of volcanic origin, offers large areas of lava and various volcanic debris, tunnels, arches, vertical cliffs, small caves and rock needles while the Gulf Stream brings together both Atlantic and tropical fish. Large schools of fish may often be seen – barracuda, mackerel, trigger fish – and very large sting rays as well as occasional giant mantas, together with a diversity of other marine organisms. With a visibility range of up to 20m, the great joy of diving off the Azores is that you never know what you are going to see.

Because the weather is unpredictable dives usually take place in the mornings when the sea is most likely to be at its calmest. June to November are the best months, but diving can be enjoyed in any month.

There are now specialist companies listed on all the islands except Corvo, offering shore dives with easy access to the water, and boat dives. Experienced divers are catered for as well as those less experienced, and instruction is available for beginners and refreshers. Night diving is also offered. Single dives start from around €40 and ten dives €330 plus hire of dive gear, and tour operators offer a week's diving with accommodation and international flights from £940. For Seamounts, 45nmi (nautical miles) offshore, two dives cost around €220. For those who prefer to snorkel, both instruction and tours are available. Up-to-date details of diving companies can be found at www.azoresweb.com/diving_azores.html.

COASTAL FISHING Open-boat fishing with a guide is available out of Faial, São Miguel, and from other islands offering bottom-fishing, jigging, trawling live bait and sea fly fishing. Species include mackerel, barracuda, bonito, scabbard fish, sea bream and more, depending on the depth. The cost is around €200 for a maximum of three persons for a half day's (four–five hours) boat hire.

SPORT OR GAME FISHING The Azores marine environment attracts large fish including 'granders', a fishing term for blue marlin weighing 1,000lb or more, and many world records have been caught in these waters. The season usually runs from early July to mid-October when the water temperature is above 20°C and the weather is generally warm and calm. Apart from the Atlantic blue marlin, various tuna species, several different sharks and numerous white marlin, there are also small game fish. With an instructor and skipper prices are around €980 per day for a group of up to four. (See pages 45–6 for details of operators.)

CAR RALLIES Several rallies are held annually in the islands and those wishing to attend should make sure they have their hotel accommodation booked well in advance. Anyone coming to the Azores for a quiet holiday should plan their itinerary accordingly! Dates vary each year and should be checked with your tour operator or the Azores Directorate of Tourism. Normally, they are:

São Miguel	Late February: Sata Rali Açores
Santa Maria	First or second weekend of August, usually one week before the big religious festivities of 15 August: Rali de Santa Maria
Terceira	Around 20–21 April: Rally Sical
	Around 14–15 September: Rally Ilha Lilás
Graciosa	Mid-July: car rally
Faial	End of May or early June: Rali Ilha Azul
	Mid-November: Rali do Faial Além Mar
Pico	Towards end of October: Rali Ilha do Pico Além Mar

SAILING Skippered boat charter is available on São Miguel. With a minimum of four people, maximum six, prices are around €85 per person with a minimum charge of €425 for a full day sailing along the south coast of São Miguel; to the Formigas islets €150 or €750; to Santa Maria for the weekend €200 or €1,000. For further information, see the website www.azoressailing.com.

Inclusive sailing holidays from the UK, including international flights, sailing between and around São Miguel and Terceira with an option to extend to Santa Maria, start from around £1,200; around the three central islands of Faial, Pico and São Jorge from around £1,000.

These notes are made for the land visitor: sailors have their own cruising guides! Apparently the first American pleasure yacht to cross the Atlantic called in at Horta on its way to the Mediterranean in 1867, and in 1895 Joshua Slocum put into Horta while making the first single-handed circumnavigation of the world. Since then small boat arrivals have increased and with the construction of marinas and onshore facilities the number of yachts now visiting Horta is around 1,400 annually. Many are doing the milk-run, bringing boats over from Bermuda or the West Indies to the Mediterranean or similar for the summer, allowing their owners who do not like real sailing to fly across later. The Azores are also a major focus for several famous international races, and there are also local yachting events. The calendar is something like this:

Last Saturday in April	Competitors windsurf from Velas to Cais do Pico and then cycle via the coast road to Madalena and then kayak to Horta.
First week in July	Faial yacht club organises a race for cruising yachts from Horta to Velas on São Jorge and back, including an overnight party in Velas!
End of July	Atlantis Cup: São Miguel to Terceira.
Beginning first	Semana do Mar or Sea Week, with events connected with

Sunday in August	the sea as well as other cultural events.
Every four years	The famous Azores and Back race organised by the Royal Cornwall Yacht Club every four years since 1975, binding Falmouth with Ponta Delgada. For further details, see www.azab.co.uk.
Every two years	Race from Brittany to Horta and back is organised by Société Nautique.
Further events	Include the Yachting World ARC Europe rally from the Canaries to the West Indies; Canaries–Bermuda–Horta–Ponta Delgada to either Plymouth or the Algarve; Rotterdam–Horta and back by Dutch Sports Planning International; rally by Ocean Cruising Club of England.

GARDENS Portuguese gardeners took their inspiration from the Romans and Moors, as well as the Italians and French, and later the romantic English style of the 19th century, and made their own landscape style. Combined with the unchanging skills and methods of Azorean gardeners, the historic gardens in the Azores offer a special charm. Around the mid 1850s there was a veritable outbreak of garden development and of these one garden on Terceira and five gardens on São Miguel are open to visitors. The owners of three gardens in Ponta Delgada vied with each other to have the latest introductions and the rarest plants, importing plants from famous nurseries in Belgium, France and England, and from mainland Portugal and Brazil. Architects and gardeners were invited from overseas to superintend the landscaping, including from Britain David Mocatta, who studied under Sir John Soane and designed several of the stations for the London to Brighton railway; Peter Wallace, a gardener to the Duke of Devonshire at Chatsworth and who later died in Ceylon; Jean-Pierre Barillet-Deschamps, a leading French horticulturist who worked with Haussmann and transformed Paris, creating the Jardin du Luxembourg and Parc Monceau among many others; Georges Aumont, designer of the Barbieux Park in Lille; and Francisco Gabriel, who came from the famous Makoy nursery in Liege and introduced to the Terceira garden (see page 146) many plants from Parisian and Belgian nurseries.

RECREATIONAL FOREST RESERVES These areas have been designated for public recreation and are found on all islands except Corvo. Dominated by *Cryptomeria japonica* forest often along with oaks, chestnut and other deciduous species, often there are camellias or azaleas too and more recently native species have been introduced as part of a broader educational and conservation programme. These mature habitats offer peaceful places for a relaxed and tranquil walk or a picnic, and often a loo. I have listed in this guide those I think have special merit for the overseas visitor. They are generally open 08.00–19.00 Monday–Friday and 10.00–20.00 Saturday and Sunday in summer, 08.00–16.00 Monday–Friday in winter.

OTHER ACTIVITIES These include kayaking, canyoning, horseriding and other physical pursuits. Tour operators offer specific packages including international flights, some local travel agencies offer some of the activities, and at least one company specialises in these services, working with small groups since 2003: **Picos de Adventura** (*Av João B Mota Amaral, Ponta Delgada;* \ *296 283 288;* e *geral@picosdeaventura.com; www.picosdeaventura.com*), near the Hotel Marina Atlântico. Prices start from around €70 a day.

Canyoning This is walking in streams, rappelling down waterfalls and generally getting wet in a diversity of geological settings. Because this is usually the only way to experience some of these places, there is often undisturbed native vegetation and rare plants plus birds as a bonus. Barely heard of just a few years ago, this activity has now burgeoned and has an enthusiastic local following as well as organised expeditions for visitors. There are at least 53 bolted routes of various difficulty levels and three islands are especially good; on São Miguel the challenges are less steep, Flores has the greatest diversity, and São Jorge offers the hardest routes as most are accessible only by boat.

Kayaking and canoeing This is largely done on the caldera lakes of Sete Cidades and Furnas on São Miguel, and on the open sea exploring small islets, visiting caves and watching seabirds off the islands of Terceira and Flores. On Flores there is a spectacular coastline and waterfalls to enjoy and, by contrast, Terceira offers the bay of Praia and along the southeast coast with its many sandy shallow bays and is emerging as one of the best locations. Organised trips are either half-day or full-day, with experienced guides.

Horseriding There are programmes available throughout the year for both beginners and experienced riders. You can take a one-hour gentle walk across farmland, half- and full-day rides or a whole week programme on São Miguel, and there are opportunities on some of the other islands.

Family holidays With so many different things to see and do, the Azores are a perfect family destination, particularly as children generally receive an especially warm welcome from the islanders. The sheer variety of swimming opportunities must be a highlight, from the sandy beaches on São Miguel, Santa Maria and Faial, the artificial rock pools on all the islands, swimming pools both public and in hotels, to the warm thermal pool of Terra Nostra in Furnas. Whale-watching trips will be another highlight. Then there is cycling and other sporting activities, lovely walks with birds, flowers, geology and dramatic landscapes to study, many and varied museums to visit, and so on. Browse this guide, and perhaps do some additional online research, and you will find several holidays' worth of things to do!

MEDIA AND COMMUNICATIONS

POST Postal services are efficient and reliable. A postcard sent by ordinary mail on a Monday at the airport in Ponta Delgada was delivered two days later in rural England, but realistically expect cards and letters to take around three to five days from Ponta Delgada or Lajes on Terceira, possibly longer from the other islands. You can recognise a post office by the sign *Correio*, or *CTT*. Opening hours are 08.30–12.30 and 14.00–18.30 Monday–Friday. There are post office counters at these airports: Terceira, São Miguel and Faial. There are two levels of service, and outside post offices you will see two post boxes, one for ordinary mail and one for blue mail.

The rates are:

Ordinary domestic   Up to 20g, €0.36; 20–50g, €0.57
Ordinary mail abroad Up to 20g, Europe €0.70; rest of the world €0.80
Blue mail priority   Up to 20g, €0.50; Europe and the rest of the world up to 20g, €1.90;

TELEPHONE The telephone service is excellent. The international code for the Azores (Portugal) is 351. The islands also have codes: 296 for São Miguel and Santa Maria; 295 for Terceira, São Jorge and Graciosa; 292 for Faial, Pico, Flores and Corvo. You need to dial the whole nine-figure number no matter where you are.

Off-peak (economic) time is from 21.00 to 09.00. The cheapest way to make a call is to buy a telephone chargecard and use a public callbox. Many public phone boxes also accept debit or credit cards and, once inserted, there is a button with a flag to press until your chosen instruction language appears.

Mobile reception is generally very good, though the mountains do create blank spots.

A **tourist helpline** is available on ☎ 808 781 212.

NEWSPAPERS AND BROADCASTING The main daily newspapers are *Açoreano Oriental* and *Diário Insular*, in Portuguese, both of which can be seen online at www.allyoucanread.com/azores-newspaper-portugal/. *Azores News* is an English-language free newspaper published occasionally in Horta offering always interesting snippets of news about the islands and which can usually be found in hotel lobbies.

Portuguese state-owned RTP (Rádio e Televisão de Portugal) provides local radio and television in the Azores. Most hotels have at least one English-speaking television news service, usually CNN, but the BBC World Service is also available, depending on the hotel.

INTERNET Interest in IT is considerable and there are clubs on all the islands offering internet access and various courses; not so helpful for the visitor. The larger hotels offer internet services, either via sockets in the rooms or in their business centre, or in the lobby. Wi-Fi systems are common in airports and main towns. Many require payment (such as the 'PT' network run by the Post Office) but some are free and often very fast. Many areas of the Azores now have ADSL broadband.

Internet cafés can be found at the following locations:

Ponta Delgada (São Miguel)	First-floor bookshop in the Solomar Shopping Centre, Infante D Henriques
Angra (Terceira)	Centro Cultural de Congressos de Angra, Canada Novo; ⊕ 10.00–22.00; no charge
Vila do Porto (Santa Maria)	Main St, No 88, next to the SATA office; ⊕ 10.00–21.00; no charge
Horta (Faial)	Hotel do Canal; ⊕ access 24/7, open to non-residents
Lajes (Flores)	Public library; ⊕ 09.00–17.00; no charge

BUYING A PROPERTY

Just a few nationals from northern Europe have bought houses and are living permanently in the Azores. Some have holiday homes and there appear not to be any eccentric barriers to ownership. Until recently there was little evidence of estate agents, but they are now appearing, along with rental and property management services. Just put 'Azores property' into your search engine. The best way is: first, decide which island, and then get to know it and ask around.

CULTURAL ETIQUETTE

Through the ages the Azoreans have had plenty of contact with the outside world, from pirates to tourists, and from their own travels for work abroad, family members in mainland Portugal, business, higher education and so on. For all this, the communities remain tight-knit, especially in rural areas. It is also a country with strong Catholic traditions. Simple courtesy and respect remain refreshingly important and the visitor will find these greatly contribute to first impressions. Boorish behaviour is not appreciated and will not go unremarked. Neither will topless sunbathing, or changing on the beach – use the cabins provided.

PHOTOGRAPHY If you are taking photographs of people, then do ask first; your smile will in most cases be returned and permission granted (see box below).

TRAVELLING POSITIVELY

If you have enjoyed your visit and the islands' hospitality, you may have the feeling you would like to say thank you, and give something back.

The **Portuguese Society for the Study of Birds (Sociedade Portuguesa para o Estudo das Aves) (SPEA)** (*SPEA – Açores, Apartado 14, 9630 Nordeste, São Miguel;* \ *296 488 455;* m *915 836 123;* e *acores@spea.pt; www.spea.pt*) is a not-for-profit organisation promoting the study and conservation of birds in Portugal. They are

EQUIPMENT Although with some thought and an eye for composition you can take reasonable photos with a 'point-and-shoot' camera, you need an SLR camera if you are at all serious about photography. Modern SLRs tend to be very clever, with automatic programmes for almost every possible situation, but remember that these programmes are limited in the sense that the camera cannot think, but only makes calculations. Every starting amateur photographer should read a photographic manual for beginners and get to grips with such basics as the relationship between aperture and shutter speed.

Digital SLRs come in different formats, which refer to the size of the sensor. The format of the future is the full-size sensor, but at present all full-size sensor cameras are in the higher price bracket. Different lenses are designed to accommodate the camera sensor sizes.

Always buy the best lens you can afford. The lens determines the quality of your photo more than the camera body. Fixed fast lenses are ideal, but very costly. A zoom lens makes it easier to change composition without changing lenses the whole time. If you carry only one lens with a full-size sensor camera, a 28–70mm or similar zoom should be ideal. This corresponds to a 17–55mm or similar for a camera with a smaller sensor. For a second lens, a lightweight telephoto zoom will be excellent for candid shots and varying your composition. Wildlife photography will be very frustrating if you don't have at least a 300mm lens. For a small loss of quality, tele-converters are a cheap and compact way to increase your focal length: a 300mm lens with a 1.4x converter becomes 420mm, and with a 2x it becomes 600mm. Note, however, that 1.4x and 2x tele-converters reduce the speed of your lens.

For wildlife photography from a safari vehicle, a solid beanbag, which you can make yourself very cheaply, will be necessary to avoid blurred images, and is more useful than a tripod. A clamp with a tripod head screwed onto it can be attached to the vehicle as well. Modern dedicated flash units are easy to use; aside from the obvious need to flash when you photograph at night, you can improve a lot of photos in difficult 'high contrast' or very dull light with some fill-in flash. It pays to have a proper flash unit as opposed to a built-in camera flash.

very active in the Azores and need all the support and help they can get since there is much to do to protect and regenerate wildlife habitats in the islands.

Early farmers killed the once locally abundant endemic Azorean bullfinch or *priolo*, *Pyrrhula murina*, to save their crops, especially oranges, from its attacks. However, from the 1920s, forest clearance and general habitat destruction, together with the invasion of alien plant species destroying its food plants plus probable predation by rats and feral cats, made this small bird increasingly rare. It is now confined to about 6km² of native forest on Pico da Vara and Serra da Tronqueira in the east of São Miguel. Long thought to be down to between only 200 and 300 individuals, in 2008 the first full census was made and the estimate revised to 775 individuals. Under the 2009 IUCN Red List, the *priolo* was officially categorised as 'Critically Endangered', because of its small population and limited distribution.

The area where it survives is designated a Special Protection Area under the EU Wild Birds Directive and is included in the São Miguel Natural Island Park. Since 2003, SPEA, along with governmental agencies and municipalities, have undertaken conservation work in the *priolo*'s main distribution area; they have recovered its habitat, the Azores laurel forest or laurisilva, by controlling invasive plant species

The resolution of digital cameras is improving the whole time and even the most basic digital SLRs are more than adequate for ordinary prints and enlargements. For professional reproduction, cameras with a resolution up to 24 megapixels are available.

Memory space is important. The number of pictures you can fit on a memory card depends on the quality you choose. Calculate in advance how many pictures you can fit on a card and either take enough cards to last for your trip, or take a storage drive onto which you can download the content. A laptop gives the advantage that you can see your pictures properly at the end of each day and edit and delete rejects, but a storage device is lighter and less bulky.

Bear in mind that digital camera batteries, computers and other storage devices need charging, so make sure you have all the chargers, cables and converters with you. Most hotels have charging points, but do enquire about this in advance.

LIGHT The most striking outdoor photographs are often taken during the hour or two of 'golden light', after dawn and before sunset. Shooting in low light may enforce the use of very low shutter speeds, in which case a tripod might be required to avoid camera shake. Some top digital SLR's now give good results with minimal grain when shooting at very high ISO settings which makes low light photography a lot easier and reduces the need of a tripod in many situations.

With careful handling, side lighting and back lighting can produce stunning effects, especially in soft light and at sunrise or sunset. Generally, however, it is best to shoot with the sun behind you. When photographing animals or people in the harsh midday sun, images taken in light but even shade are likely to be more effective than those taken in direct sunlight or patchy shade, since the latter conditions create too much contrast.

Ariadne Van Zandbergen is a professional travel and wildlife photographer specialising in Africa. She runs The Africa Image Library. For photo requests, visit www. africaimagelibrary.com or contact her by email at ℮ info@africaimagelibrary.com.

Father Américo, the founder of the charity 'Os Meninos de Rua' (Street Boys), dedicated his life to the service of the poor and needy. For some time, he was in charge of the 'Soup for the Poor' in Coimbra (Portugal), where he established the first 'Casa do Gaiato' (House for Boys – *gaiato* is a common word for a boy) in Miranda do Corvo in 1940.

Currently, the eight existing Casas do Gaiato (five in Portugal, two in Angola and one in Mozambique) take in youngsters deprived of a normal family life. In the Azores, Casa do Gaiato is a sheltered home for boys and girls, dependent mainly on government funding but supplemented by charitable donations. The institution currently cares for 31 boys and girls, living in three houses: the Capelas House, the Transition House and the Monte Alegre House. The Capelas is the main building which houses administrative services as well as 15 boys between the ages of seven and 16. Its activities are focused on agriculture and husbandry, providing practical training for the boys and supplying the centre with fresh produce. A further seven boys between the ages of 18 and 21 live in the Transition House. All these youngsters attend a government school, while those not academically gifted also undergo a home-schooling programme.

The Casas do Gaiato have resident staff on 24-hour shifts including housekeepers/cooks, and a specialised team manages educational matters and organises volunteers, visits, children's events, etc. This work is supplemented by a farmer, a teacher and a psychologist who offers group or individual counselling and psychotherapy. The youngsters are provided with the basic necessities and offered finance for tuition, school fees, transport, medical expenses, sports activities, etc.

You can help the Casas do Gaiato in their quest to help children from deprived backgrounds either by contacting them in Capelas, São Miguel (*House Gaiato of São Miguel, Rua Monte Alegre, 9545-148 Capelas, São Miguel, Azores;* ☏ *296 298 326*), or by sending a donation to: IBAN PT50 0038 0000 0598 9823 3010 8.

and planting native species to increase its desperately needed food supplies. This is a long-term commitment. This work allowed the *priolo*'s population to increase up to 1,000 individuals in 2013, allowing it to be downgraded to only 'Endangered' by the IUCN. SPEA's work has also contributed to sustainable development of the territory by restoring peatland areas in the Planalto dos Graminhais and promoting sustainable tourism in the territory. In 2012, the 'Lands of Priolo' (Nordeste and Povoação municipalities) were awarded the European Charter of Sustainable Tourism.

The society's first ever visitor/interpretative centre is located within the protected area, in the Cancela do Cinzeiro Forest Recreational Reserve. The **Priolo Environmental Centre** (m *918 536 123;* e *centropriolo@spea.pt;* ⊕ *May–Sep 10.00–18.00 Tue–Sun; Feb–Apr & Oct–Nov 12.00–17.00 Sat & Sun; other times available by appointment*) offers information about the flora and fauna of the Serra da Tronqueira and Pico da Vara and especially about the *priolo*, with temporary exhibitions, a nearby small garden of native plant species, and facilities for its education programme for schools and the local population. In addition, there is a shop with merchandising.

Visitors are made very welcome, and the centre may be reached via the unsurfaced road off the main Povoação to Nordeste road, either just beyond Povoação, or from above the village of Lomba da Pedreira, or from Nordeste (ten minutes). You can find more information about the centre and its activities at the website http://centropriolo. spea.pt. Membership is available to families or individuals. Members receive the society's magazine three times a year and news of regular field trips (free to members).

Your financial donation and/or your participation in voluntary work (educational activities, fieldwork activities, professional or academic visits) are fundamental for the success of the project and for the conservation of the *priolo* and its habitat.

Bradt Travel Guides

Claim 20% discount on your next Bradt book when you order from www.bradtguides.com quoting the code BRADT20

Africa

Africa Overland	£16.99
Algeria	£15.99
Angola	£18.99
Botswana	£16.99
Burkina Faso	£17.99
Cameroon	£15.99
Cape Verde	£15.99
Congo	£16.99
Eritrea	£15.99
Ethiopia	£17.99
Ethiopia Highlights	£15.99
Ghana	£15.99
Kenya Highlights	£15.99
Madagascar	£16.99
Madagascar Highlights	£15.99
Malawi	£15.99
Mali	£14.99
Mauritius, Rodrigues & Réunion	£16.99
Mozambique	£15.99
Namibia	£15.99
Nigeria	£17.99
North Africa: Roman Coast	£15.99
Rwanda	£16.99
São Tomé & Príncipe	£14.99
Seychelles	£16.99
Sierra Leone	£16.99
Somaliland	£15.99
South Africa Highlights	£15.99
Sudan	£16.99
Swaziland	£15.99
Tanzania Safari Guide	£17.99
Tanzania, Northern	£14.99
Uganda	£16.99
Zambia	£18.99
Zanzibar	£15.99
Zimbabwe	£15.99

The Americas and the Caribbean

Alaska	£15.99
Amazon Highlights	£15.99
Argentina	£16.99
Bahia	£14.99
Cayman Islands	£14.99
Chile Highlights	£15.99
Colombia	£17.99
Dominica	£15.99
Grenada, Carriacou & Petite Martinique	£15.99
Guyana	£15.99
Haiti	£16.99
Nova Scotia	£15.99
Panama	£14.99
Paraguay	£15.99
Peru Highlights	£15.99
Turks & Caicos Islands	£14.99
Uruguay	£15.99
USA by Rail	£15.99
Venezuela	£16.99
Yukon	£14.99

British Isles

Britain from the Rails	£14.99
Bus-Pass Britain	£15.99
Eccentric Britain	£16.99
Eccentric Cambridge	£9.99
Eccentric London	£14.99
Eccentric Oxford	£9.99
Sacred Britain	£16.99
Slow: Cornwall	£14.99
Slow: Cotswolds	£14.99
Slow: Devon & Exmoor	£14.99
Slow: Dorset	£14.99
Slow: New Forest	£9.99
Slow: Norfolk & Suffolk	£14.99
Slow: North Yorkshire	£14.99
Slow: Northumberland	£14.99
Slow: Sussex & South Downs National Park	£14.99

Europe

Abruzzo	£16.99
Albania	£16.99
Armenia	£15.99
Azores	£14.99
Belarus	£15.99
Bosnia & Herzegovina	£15.99
Bratislava	£9.99
Budapest	£9.99
Croatia	£15.99
Cross-Channel France: Nord-Pas de Calais	£13.99
Cyprus see North Cyprus	
Estonia	£14.99
Faroe Islands	£16.99
Flanders	£15.99
Georgia	£15.99
Greece: The Peloponnese	£14.99
Hungary	£15.99
Iceland	£15.99
Istria	£13.99
Kosovo	£15.99
Lapland	£15.99
Liguria	£15.99
Lille	£9.99
Lithuania	£14.99
Luxembourg	£14.99
Macedonia	£16.99
Malta & Gozo	£14.99
Montenegro	£14.99
North Cyprus	£13.99
Serbia	£15.99
Slovakia	£14.99
Slovenia	£13.99
Svalbard: Spitsbergen, Jan Mayen, Franz Jozef Land	£17.99
Switzerland Without a Car	£15.99
Transylvania	£15.99
Ukraine	£16.99

Middle East, Asia and Australasia

Bangladesh	£17.99
Borneo	£17.99
Eastern Turkey	£16.99
Iran	£15.99
Israel	£15.99
Jordan	£16.99
Kazakhstan	£16.99
Kyrgyzstan	£16.99
Lake Baikal	£15.99
Lebanon	£15.99
Maldives	£15.99
Mongolia	£16.99
North Korea	£14.99
Oman	£15.99
Palestine	£15.99
Shangri-La: A Travel Guide to the Himalayan Dream	£14.99
Sri Lanka	£15.99
Syria	£15.99
Taiwan	£16.99
Tajikistan	£15.99
Tibet	£17.99
Yemen	£14.99

Wildlife

Antarctica: A Guide to the Wildlife	£15.99
Arctic: A Guide to Coastal Wildlife	£16.99
Australian Wildlife	£14.99
East African Wildlife	£19.99
Galápagos Wildlife	£16.99
Madagascar Wildlife	£16.99
Pantanal Wildlife	£16.99
Southern African Wildlife	£19.99
Sri Lankan Wildlife	£15.99

Pictorials and other guides

100 Alien Invaders	£16.99
100 Animals to See Before They Die	£16.99
100 Bizarre Animals	£16.99
Eccentric Australia	£12.99
Northern Lights	£6.99
Swimming with Dolphins, Tracking Gorillas	£15.99
The Northwest Passage	£14.99
Tips on Tipping	£6.99
Total Solar Eclipse 2012 & 2013	£6.99
Wildlife & Conservation Volunteering: The Complete Guide	£13.99

Travel literature

A Glimpse of Eternal Snows	£11.99
A Tourist in the Arab Spring	£9.99
Connemara Mollie	£9.99
Fakirs, Feluccas and Femmes Fatales	£9.99
Madagascar: The Eighth Continent	£11.99
The Marsh Lions	£9.99
The Two-Year Mountain	£9.99
The Urban Circus	£9.99
Up the Creek	£9.99

Part Two

EASTERN GROUP

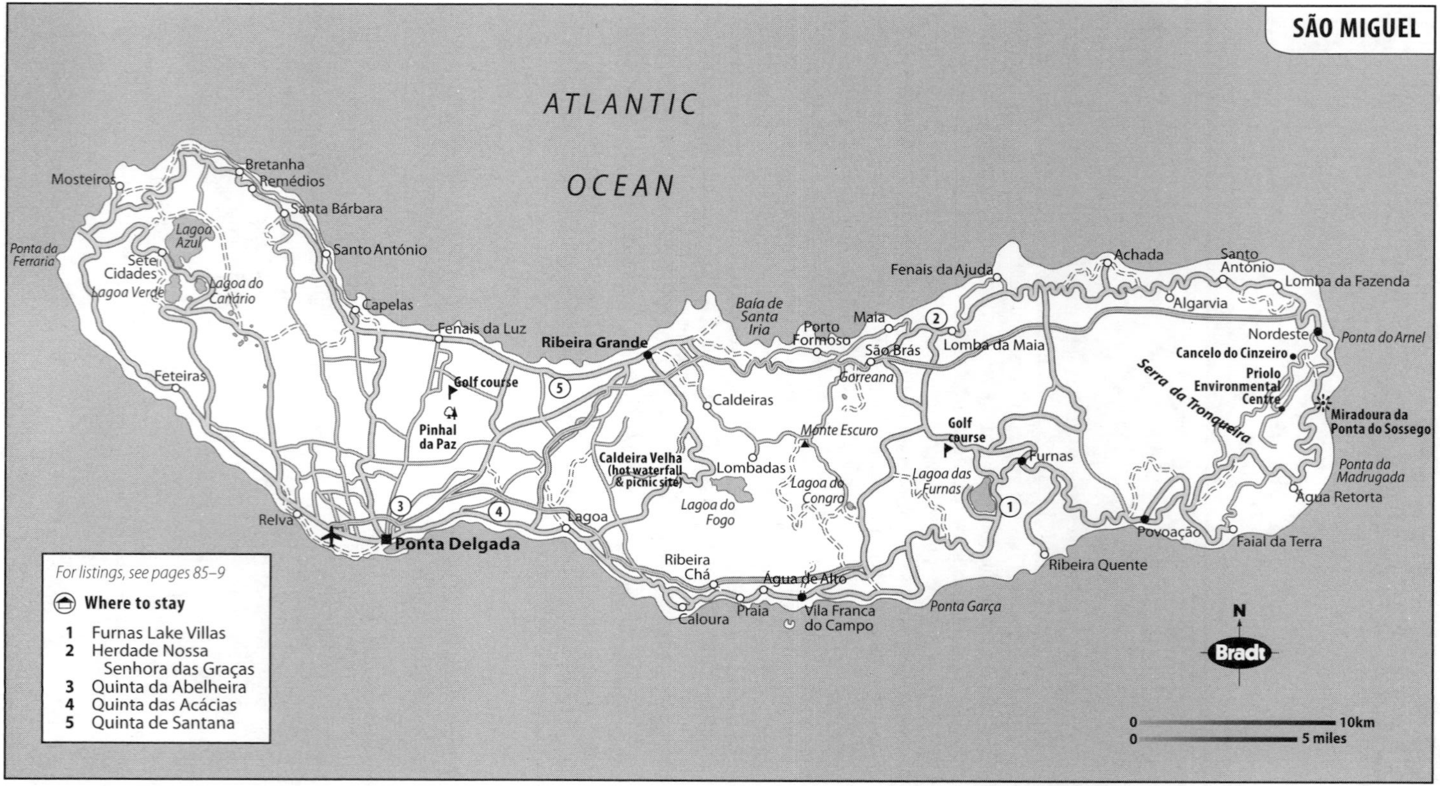

SÃO MIGUEL

ATLANTIC
OCEAN

Ponta do Ferraria
Mosteiros
Bretanha
Remédios
Santa Bárbara
Sete Cidades
Lagoa Azul
Lagoa do Canário
Lagoa Verde
Feteiras
Santo António
Capelas
Fenais da Luz
Relva
Ponta Delgada
Golf course
Pinhal da Paz
Santo António
Ribeira Grande
Caldeira Velha (hot waterfall & picnic site)
Lagoa
Lagoa do Fogo
Caldeiras
Baía de Santa Iria
Porto Formoso
Fenais da Ajuda
São Brás
Mata
Botrenha
Lombadas
Monte Escuro
Lagoa do Congro
Lagoa das Furnas
Golf course
Furnas
Lomba da Maia
Achada
Santo António
Algarvia
Nordeste
Lomba da Fazenda
Ponta do Arnel
Cancelo do Cinzeiro
Priolo Environmental Centre
Serra da Tronqueira
Miradoura da Ponta do Sossego
Ponta da Madrugada
Água Retorta
Faial da Terra
Povoação
Ribeira Quente
Ponta Garça
Vila Franca do Campo
Água de Alto
Praia
Ribeira Chã
Caloura

N

Bradt

0   5 miles
0   10km

For listings, see pages 85–9

🏠 **Where to stay**
1 Furnas Lake Villas
2 Herdade Nossa
   Senhora das Graças
3 Quinta da Abelheira
4 Quinta das Acácias
5 Quinta de Santana

78

3

São Miguel

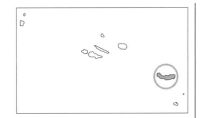

With photographs of the lakes of Sete Cidades appearing in so many travel brochures and promotions, São Miguel has become the best-known island of the archipelago; it is also the largest, and has the greatest diversity of interests. It also has the largest town in the Azores, Ponta Delgada, and the busiest harbour. Although all the islands are green, São Miguel is known as the *Ilha Verde*, the 'Green Island', after the central area that has very good soil and is highly productive. There is a varied coastline, from small bays with black sand to precipitous sea cliffs and a mountain wilderness area of endemic plants on Pico da Vara, the highest point at 1,103m. Ponta Delgada, the principal town, is very charming and the pedestrianised streets, cafés, shops and long esplanade around the harbour all go to make it an enjoyable place to explore.

More cosmopolitan than the other islands, São Miguel has in recent years become increasingly sophisticated and is now the focus for the archipelago. Ponta Delgada's airport, towards the island's southwest, receives most of the international air traffic. Yet, in spite of new marinas, new hotels, a second golf course, numerous restaurants, out-of-town supermarkets and so on, considerable rural charm is still to be found.

Most famous are the two lakes of Sete Cidades, one blue, the other green, in the caldera that dominates the western topography, which have mythological origins. Ribeira Grande has a charming town centre that you pass through to reach the only tea estates in Europe, Gorreana and Chã Porto Formoso, midway along the north coast. In the southeast the small spa of Furnas, which has changed little physically over the years, is a must. Here, bubbling hot springs and fumaroles together with the smell of sulphur remind you that you are on a volcano in spite of the verdant surroundings; in fact you are in the centre of another large crater. Twenty-two mineral waters, all with different tastes, spout out of the ground; some have elaborate manmade ornamental surrounds, while others just flow from between the native heather bushes. The 30-acre garden of the Terra Nostra Garden Hotel, mostly dating from 150 years ago but with beginnings in the late 18th century, with its naturally warm thermal swimming pool and meandering walks beneath some 2,000 trees, is contact with the genteel life of earlier centuries. In the far northeast is Nordeste, a region not often visited by tourists, which has a spectacularly beautiful coast when viewed from the several splendid viewpoints and picnic sites. Vila Franca do Campo in the middle of the south coast was São Miguel's first capital, and is still a thriving and pretty town; the town square and the nearby harbour should be seen before taking a coffee and trying the local *queijadas* or Vila Franca cake. Pineapples are still grown under glass, and a nursery can be visited near Ponta Delgada.

If you have a full week to spend exploring São Miguel, you will depart still leaving unseen places for your next visit. If you have the time and are entering and leaving the Azores through Ponta Delgada, it is a good idea to spend the first two or three nights of your holiday in Furnas, and then the last two or maybe three nights in Ponta Delgada. This way you can get a real feel for the island and its diversity, and Furnas is an ideal place to begin to relax, unwind and get into a holiday mood.

BACKGROUND

GEOLOGY Now the largest island of the archipelago, São Miguel was once two islands as evidenced by the two large volcanic massifs, one at each end, and the low central area that emerged later from the sea following further eruptions. About four million years ago, the first island appeared, from an eruption on the seabed 2,000m below sea level. Erosion has given us today a broad upland of thick basaltic flows, probably originating as a shield volcano (one gently sloping and built of lava from many closely spaced vents and fissures) with frequent eruptions, with Pico da Vara the highest point. Towards the edge of this upland the stratovolcano (a steep-sided cone of layered lava flows and other volcanic products) of Povoação developed about three million years ago, and the caldera is thought to have occurred in two stages about 820,000 and 700,000 years ago, but the southern wall is lost.

Approximately one million years ago, a stratovolcano from the sea added more land. About 18,000 years ago its caldera collapsed, and later – some 13,500 years ago – further collapsed to form an inner caldera; it may be that there was a third, even later,

THE ORANGE TRADE

Even today there is evidence of the great orange-growing industry that dominated several of the islands in the 19th century; look in the numerous small gardens with their tall enclosing hedges of banksias and pittosporum. Grand town houses also reflect the wealth this crop generated, and the development of the countryside by land purchase for rural estates is significant history.

Far less known are the implications all these oranges had for transportation between the Azores and England, the major export customer. Citrus was a luxury fruit, available in season from November to May only, and its peak of desirability for the Victorians was Christmas, when oranges and lemons were the fruit to have displayed on the table. And most of these came from the Azores.

'Buy my fresh St Michael's' was a common streetseller's cry, although it is doubtful that, like today, many customers would have known where 'St Michael's' was. Oranges were grown in the Azores already by the 16th century, brought in from Lisbon, in turn introduced by Portugal's Indian viceroys. From 1600 to 1800, the citrus trade steadily increased, with most oranges coming from Valencia and lemons from Sicily, but it was the ending of the Napoleonic Wars that accelerated exports from the Azores so that by the mid 1800s, several hundred ships and several thousand seamen were employed in the trade. The topsail schooner was the favoured ship, one that could travel fast, for oranges are a quickly perishable cargo. The ships were of small tonnage since a larger vessel would have been no advantage; the boxes of oranges could not be stacked high otherwise those at the bottom would have spoilt, and the boats were loaded in the open roadsteads, so speed was essential. Also, should a large consignment have arrived in one ship, the quantity would have swamped the market and reduced the price. In 1854, 60 million oranges and 15 million lemons were exported to London alone, using at least 70 vessels.

collapse. There were three lakes. A series of explosive eruptions followed, with the largest throwing out a huge volume of pumice from a vent in a flat area which today gives us one of the most loved places of the entire archipelago – Furnas. In 1630, a violent eruption lasting just a few days sent a pyroclastic flow, a fiery avalanche of hot gases, rocks, pumice and ash down the gorge to Ribeira Quente into the sea to form a small delta, and distributed pumice and ash over a wide area. Two of the lakes disappeared and the surviving lake was probably dammed, resulting in Lake Furnas now being almost 100m above Furnas village. It is thought the average interval between eruptions over the past almost 3,000 years is just 362 years.

Around 290,000 years ago, two stratovolcanoes began to form on the ocean floor, one to form the separate Sete Cidades Volcano to the west and Água de Pau Volcano to add to the already extant island to the east. Água de Pau, more or less in the middle of São Miguel, is known for its much-visited lake of fire, the Lagoa do Fogo, 250m below the caldera rim. With more than 200,000 years of eruptive history, its most vigorous period of growth was between 100,000 and 40,000 years ago, with the caldera enclosing a lake formed some 15,000 years ago. It has a history of violent eruptions followed by long periods of dormancy. Plinian eruptions, explosions of gas, steam and ash followed by pyroclastic flows, occurred over the following millennia. The most recent happened in 1563, over a period of six days, burying crops and houses in ash and lapilli, small volcanic stones, together with further destruction from the associated earthquakes. Four days after this eruption

At first English merchants came out to the Azores at the start of the season to supervise purchase and loading, but by the mid 19th century many, along with their families, lived permanently on São Miguel in their large houses. Each fruit was picked as it turned from green to yellow and was wrapped in a dry sheathing leaf of the Indian corn cob. Loading was done with small boats from the shore taking the boxes out to the waiting ships. Speed in loading was vital, for should bad weather suddenly blow in, the vessel would have to stand out to sea only part-loaded, and several days might pass before loading could be completed. Typically a crew of not more than six under a master ran the ship, and it was tough sailing during winter in the north Atlantic. The average sailing time was 10–14 days, but it could sometimes be done in seven days. An added anxiety for the voyage home was to inspect the boxes daily for rotten fruit, since a clean cargo meant a bonus for the master. Today such an event would have been spun to equal the fame of the tea clippers, but there was a race each year to deliver the first oranges of the season. It is recorded that the first ship home sold all its cargo within six hours at three guineas a box (£3.15). When others arrived, 47 ships within 40 hours, the price fell to 4/6d (22½p).

These schooners flourished until about 1860; steam was already transporting lemons from Sicily by the early 1850s, but there was no harbour suitable in Ponta Delgada for steam ships, a real problem in bad weather if they had to stand off burning coal, with no bunkering facilities onshore. About ten years later, harbour construction began and the schooners' days were numbered, with an ever-decreasing number being chartered up until about 1870. Then, in the 1880s, disease struck the orange trees and harvests plummeted, by which time supplies from other countries, including California and Florida, became available, from orchards established with parent trees taken from the Azores.

began, another started to the northwest in Pico Queimado, of Hawaiian type, with lava fountains and scorieae or cinders, which flowed down to engulf the village of Ribeira Seca, just west of Ribeira Grande. There you can see the fountain and the surrounding lava.

Sete Cidades Volcano is now 14km across at sea level. The early eruptions of dark basalt were slowly followed by pale-grey trachyte, only later to be succeeded by violent explosions that can be seen in the abundant layers of pumice. The caldera collapsed about 22,000 years ago, and remained quiet for 17,000 years although there was activity around its flanks. Some 5,000 years ago, eruptions again began in the caldera, creating a number of broad cones including those containing the crater lakes of Lagoa Rasa and Lagoa de Santiago; these craters together with other sites within Sete Cidades erupted again at later periods, as did numerous satellite vents on the outer lower slopes. The last eruption on Sete Cidades was around the middle of the 15th century, with more recent 19th-century eruptions out to sea northwest from the Ponta da Ferraria. At Ferraria you can see an example of a littoral cone, a secondary cone caused by steam trapped under lava which has flowed into the sea.

The middle region, the Região dos Picos or Complexo dos Picos, which unites the two islands by joining Sete Cidades to Água de Pau, began to form about 50,000 years ago. In contrast with the stratovolcano and their collapsed calderas of São Miguel's two extremities, volcanism here is fissural, and produced about 250 cinder cones and domes, and ash-covered lava flows that are now cultivated. These fissures, or cracks so deep they allow magma to reach the surface, are in places close enough that some of the cinder cones are joined together while smaller, separate cones are as high as 200m. These cones lie in a broad band parallel with the south coast and some 5km inland, and are a most conspicuous landscape feature when seen from an aeroplane coming in to land at Ponta Delgada airport, or from the ferry arriving from Santa Maria. The dominant cone, distinguished by its double hump, erupted about 4,400 years ago. During the past 3,000 years, more than 18 eruptions have occurred. This bridging fissure zone, together with the volcanoes of Sete Cidades, Fogo and Furnas, are all potentially active zones, and only the very far eastern end of the island is considered inactive.

HISTORY São Miguel's first settlers came from the Estremadura, Alentejo and Algarve provinces of Portugal, and there were also Madeirans, Jews, Moors and French. The first capital was Vila Franca do Campo, but in 1522 a severe earthquake and mudslide that killed most of the 5,000 inhabitants was so destructive that the island's principal port, Ponta Delgada, which was also sited on the more geologically stable area of the island, took precedence and became the capital in 1546. Already there were some wealthy merchants, trading with mainland Portugal, Madeira, the Canaries, Flanders and elsewhere; some 25 English merchant ships are recorded as having visited in one year. Early crops included wheat, woad and sugarcane, and there were also dairy products. The port area was fortified during the 16th and 17th centuries against the frequent attacks by pirates and corsairs. Terceira was the key island in maritime trade and journeys, but with the restoration of Portuguese independence in 1640, São Miguel became the commercial centre although there were many economic difficulties. During the 18th and early 19th centuries, the island prospered, much of the time through the development of the new export crop, oranges, and many substantial homes and churches were built. In 1831–32, resistance to the Absolutist regime was organised from the island and it was from Ponta Delgada that the Liberal expedition with some 3,500 Azoreans sailed to northern Portugal.

Around 1860, oranges began to lose their share of the British market, partly to cheaper sources of supply from mainland Portugal and Spain, and partly because the orange trees succumbed to disease. This eventually caused an economic crisis and resulted in emigration to the Americas. New crops such as tea, pineapples, chicory, sugarbeet and tobacco then began to be introduced, together with livestock and, later, the development of fishing. Work began in 1861 to improve the port in Ponta Delgada which later stimulated industrial development, but it was after World War II in 1947 that it was greatly expanded. The basalt city gateway was removed to its present position in the nearby square (see pages 101–2), and the new Avenida do Infante D Henrique and the colonnaded buildings along the seafront transformed the town's appearance: truly a piece of excellent town planning much enjoyed today by townspeople and visitors alike.

GETTING AROUND

For travel to São Miguel, see pages 47 and 52–3.

BY CAR/TAXI Island tours by taxi generally fall into two separate programmes. One covers Sete Cidades in the west, often a half-day tour, while the second is a full day going to Ribeira Grande and the tea estates on the north coast, followed by Furnas and Vila Franca on the south coast, combined with some viewpoints in the mountains on the way, depending upon the route taken. Visitors with a rented car can also advantageously divide their touring of São Miguel into three sectors: the western part including Sete Cidades and the northern coast to Capelas; the central area of Ribeira Grande, Lagoa do Fogo and Vila Franca; and the eastern part embracing Nordeste, Povoação and Furnas.

BY BUS São Miguel has a good bus service, with services running along both the north and south coasts. With an early start it is possible to enjoy a full day in Nordeste, Furnas, Povoação, Ribeira Grande, Sete Cidades and Capelas. The timetable changes little from year to year, but to be safe and to use the buses most effectively, get a current timetable from the tourist office (www.smigueltransportes.com). The schedules may not always be very convenient for tourists, but they work well in combination with taxis, perhaps taking a bus for the outward journey and a taxi for the return. They are rewarding because you see details of everyday life, and they slowly meander through villages that perhaps you would not otherwise see. The following times from Ponta Delgada are for the buses most useful to visitors. There are three private bus companies.

CRP – Caetano Raposa and Pereira

🚌 **To Ribeira Grande** (45 mins): 07.35, 08.15, 08.25, 09.15, 11.30, then hourly to 16.30, 17.15, 17.45, 18.10, 18.40, 19.15, 21.15, 23.15 Mon–Fri; 08.15, 10.00, 11.30, 13.30, 15.30, 17.30, 19.00, 21.15, 23.15 Sat; 08.30, 10.00, 12.30, 14.30, 16.30, 18.30, 21.15, 23.15 Sun

🚌 **From Ribeira Grande:** 07.15, 07.45, 08.15, 10.00, 12.15, 12.45, 13.45, 15.45, 16.45, 17.45, 22.00 Mon–Fri; 07.00, 07.45, 12.30, 15.30, 17.30, 22.00 Sat; 07.00, 08.45, 10.15, 11.30, 12.30, 14.45, 16.45, 18.00, 18.30, 22.00 Sun

🚌 **To Furnas via Ribeira Grande & the north coast** (about 85 mins): 07.15, 15.15 daily

🚌 **From Furnas:** 09.10, 17.10 daily

🚌 **To Nordeste** (105 mins): 06.45, 11.00, 16.15 (mid-Jun–mid-Sep 18.30) Mon–Fri; 06.45, 16.15 Sat & Sun

🚌 **From Nordeste:** 06.45, 11.30, 16.00 Mon–Fri; 06.45, 14.30 Sat; 06.45, 16.00 Sun

Varela and Companhia

🚌 **To Vila Franca** (35 mins): 07.00, 07.25, 11.00, 12.35, 15.00, 17.40, 19.00 Mon–Fri; 08.00, 11.00, 12.40, 17.30 Sat; 10.00, 12.30, 17.30 Sun

From Vila Franca: 06.30, 07.20, 08.00, 09.00, 09.50, 13.00, 14.45, 16.25, 17.40 Mon–Fri; 07.10, 08.10, 10.00, 12.00, 15.00 Sat; 08.10, 15.00, 16.30 Sun

To Povoação (via Furnas along the south coast) (2 hours): 09.00, 13.45, 16.00 Mon–Fri; 09.00, 15.00 Sat & Sun

From Povoação (via Furnas): 06.40, 08.30, 10.15, 16.00 Mon–Fri; 11.00, 17.00 Sat & Sun

To Fajã de Baixo (20 mins): 07.15, 07.45, 08.15, 10.00, 12.15, 12.45, 13.45, 15.45, 16.45, 17.45, 22.00 Mon–Fri; 07.00, 07.45, 12.30, 15.30, 17.30, 22.00 Sat; 07.00, 08.45, 10.15, 11.30, 12.30, 14.45, 16.45, 18.00, 18.30, 22.00 Sun

From Fajã de Baixo: 07.55, 08.25, 09.10, 10.35, 12.35, 13.05, 13.30, 14.25, 16.35, 17.30, 18.40, 20.30 Mon–Fri; 08.00, 10.35, 12.35, 13.30, 17.50 Sat; 11.15, 13.30, 14.35, 17.05 Sun

Auto Viaçao Micaelense

To Sete Cidades (75 mins): 08.25, 18.50 Mon–Fri; 07.15, 14.35 Sat; 08.30, 16.15 Sun

From Sete Cidades (transfer in Varzea): 07.00, 09.30, 16.25 Mon–Fri; 08.55, 16.25 Sat; 10.45, 18.05 Sun

To Capelas (30 mins): 07.45, 10.15, 15.30, 18.00, 19.05, 21.30 Mon–Fri; 07.15, 09.30, 12.00, 14.00, 17.30 Sat; 08.30, 13.10, 16.15, 20.10 Sun

From Capelas: 07.00, 08.55, 12.30, 18.00, 22.30 Mon–Fri; 07.00, 08.55, 13.02, 15.06, 22.30 Sat; 07.25, 10.06, 11.50, 15.20, 19.07 Sun

All buses from Ponta Delgada leave from the esplanade – Avenida Infante Dom Henrique – near the post office. Bus stops for Capelas and Sete Cidades are on the north side; the others are on the south harbourside nearer the fort.

By bus to Furnas Depart Ponta Delgada 07.15, arrive Furnas 09.00 via the north coast. The journey ends at the big school; walk to the end of this road and turn left to the Terra Nostra garden. This allows plenty of time to enjoy the famous garden, walk through the village to see the spa and on to the fumaroles, and time for lunch

BUS EXCURSION TO NORDESTE

Departing Ponta Delgada at 06.45 in November; the streets are empty and there is only one other passenger and me waiting. After the strong and often howling winds of the previous two days, the pre-dawn gentle warm breeze softly caresses the face and is quite welcome. Travelling through town we soon pick up more passengers and, with the streets empty of traffic, and to a glorious fiery sunrise, we hurtle along and are passing the Gorreana tea estate after 40 minutes. Then come the many charming villages along the coast. We are now into rugged country, formed by volcanoes and subsequent erosion that has created a series of deep valleys and ravines. On the land between these ravines many of the villages have been established, but sadly we do not turn off and descend to their centres. It would just take too much time, and the bus is too long to wind easily through the narrow roads, although we do go down to Achada and have great problems negotiating a parked tractor. Circling the connecting loops to the new highway can be quite confusing, but one feels sorry for the many tour buses that stick to the highway and miss the fun. The bus becomes quite full as we get nearer to Nordeste, where it terminates. Arriving at 09.00, it gives a comfortable seven hours for exploration before catching the 16.00 return bus. This is time enough to visit the two museums, walk along to the *miradouro* overlooking the Ponta do Arnel with its handsome lighthouse, and wander up to the forest park, perhaps with a picnic lunch. Should you miss the last bus back, it is €50 by taxi to Ponta Delgada!

– maybe try the *cozido*, the Furnas speciality (see page 113 for details). Return 16.30 on the bus coming from Povoação (bus stop by the café before the entrance to the garden), via the south coast, arriving 18.00. Alternatively, get the bus starting from Furnas by the school at 17.10.

By bus to Nordeste This makes for a very happy full-day excursion, with the opportunity to see the north coast and a little of its villages, and explore the small town of Nordeste; all for a very modest fare. (See box opposite for an account of this trip.)

⌂ WHERE TO STAY

The principal hotels in Ponta Delgada I have grouped into: those in the west, in the centre and the east of the town. All are within 10–15 minutes' walk of the town centre, but those in the west are convenient for the public buses and those in the east for the marina and swimming pools. For price code details, see page 55. For location of listings see map, pages 78 and 102–3.

PONTA DELGADA See *Ponta Delgada* map, pages 102–3.

In the west

⌂ **Royal Garden** (193 rooms) Rua de Lisboa; ☎296 307 300; e royalgardenhotel@investacor. com. An extra couple of minutes' walk to town over the following 2 establishments, but a well-designed building with lots of light & feeling of space, built round an attractive inner enclosed garden planted with bamboos & cloud trees. Indoor & outdoor pools, tennis court, sauna, Turkish bath & gymnasium, off-street parking. €€€€€

⌂ **Hotel Vila Nova** (102 rooms) Rua João Francisco Cabral; ☎296 301 600; e vilanova@ hotelcanadiano.com; www.hoteisplatano.com. Family owned & run, a nicely fitted, comfortable, modern hotel suited for both holiday & business use. Buffet restaurant, gymnasium, outdoor heated pool, parking. €€€€

⌂ **Hotel Ponta Delgada** (50 rooms) Rua João Francisco Cabral; ☎296 209 480; e hotelpdl@hotelpdl.com; www.hotelpdl.com. Some rooms with disabled facilities. Swimming pool, bar, restaurant next door, hairdresser, parking. €€€

In the centre

⌂ **São Miguel Park Hotel** (163 rooms) Rua Manuel Augusto Amaral; ☎296 306 000; e smgparkhotel.reservas@bensaude.pt; www.bensaude.pt. Situated towards the rear of the town with a good view over Ponta Delgada.

Rooms all have balconies. Pool, fitness room, restaurant, bar. €€€€€

⌂ **Hotel Camões** (36 rooms) Largo de Camões; ☎296 209 580; www.hotelcamoes.com. A very solid old manor house inventively converted to a high standard modern hotel in a traditional Portuguese style. Although right in town, just below the market, & very convenient, it is quiet. Restaurant serves light lunches & evening meals; open to non-residents. Very popular – you need to book well in advance. €€€€

⌂ **Hotel do Colégio** (55 rooms) Rua Carvalho Araújo 39; ☎296 306 600; e hoteldocolegio@mail. telepac.pt; www.hoteldocolegio.com. Converted from a former convent, this is conveniently located in a quiet & narrow street. Good bar, restaurant, courtyard pool, Turkish bath, gymnasium, parking. €€€€

⌂ **Hotel Talisman** (53 rooms) Rua Marquês da Praia e Monforte; ☎296 308 500; www. hoteltalisman.com. The hotel is charming, stylishly converted in Art Deco style from an 18th-century town house by a French architect in 1992, & later enlarged & refurbished with roof-top pool & lift. It is right in town on a pedestrianised street, a quite different place to stay. €€€€

⌂ **Hotel Canadiano** (50 rooms) Rua do Contador; ☎296 287 421; e canadiano@ hoteisplatano.com; www.hoteisplatano.com. Rooms are all very spacious, most facing an inner open courtyard. Very friendly, bar, breakfast room, room service menu, buffet bistro, coffee shop, lounge, parking. Near the museum, but foot

In 1770 the noted orange farmer Thomas Hickling built a simple summer house on the high mound overlooking what is now the thermal swimming pool at Furnas. It was surrounded by trees which would have sheltered fashionable summer parties and music; of those trees, I believe the old pollarded English oak in the corner by the pool is the only one that remains, and is therefore probably the oldest tree in the garden. Hickling died in 1834, and it was not until 1848 that the Visconde da Praia purchased the property and on the mound built the present house. The Viscondessa was a keen gardener, and over the years they enlarged the estate and laid out the garden in a grand style with water, dark groves of trees and parterres of flowers. After the Visconde's death in 1872, his son enhanced the house and laid out the garden more or less as it is today with its serpentine canal and grottoes, and walks. New tree species were introduced from around the world so many of these now-mature trees are at most 140 years old.

The newly built Terra Nostra Hotel (see opposite) opened in 1935, and soon after, Vasco Bensaúde, who was a very keen gardener, purchased the now-neglected garden; the family's company still owns it today. With a head gardener from Scotland and a veritable army of workmen, he totally refurbished the house and restored the garden within two years. World War II came and ended the fashionable life of Furnas based on the hotel, casino, spa and gardens, and the place continued to slumber for years afterwards until tourism once more asserted itself.

In 1990, restoration began once again, this time with English gardeners, and a team of tree surgeons climbed vertically the equivalent of Mount Everest from sea level working on the 2,500 trees while local engineers refurbished the canals. Many new trees were planted, a garden of Azorean native species begun and, significantly, a collection of Malesian rhododendrons was planted. This is the only garden in Europe that can grow, out of doors without protection, these tender rhododendrons native to tropical mountains; they flower intermittently all year and come in spectacular colours and some are perfumed. The head gardener, Fernando Costa, continues with new developments: a fern garden, a formal flower garden, a garden devoted to cycads and most recently an ever-expanding collection of camellias.

access for a short stretch is along a busy narrow road. €€€

⌂ **Hotel Comfort Inn** (46 rooms) Rua Dr Bruno Tavares; e hotelhelp@choicehotels.com; www.comfortinn.com. Close to the university, with business centre & associated services, & very convenient for town. High season May–Oct. €€€

In the east

⌂ **Hotel Marina Atlântico** (184 rooms) Av Infante D Henrique; ☎296 307 900; www. hotelmarinaatlantico.com. Next to the Hotel Açores Atlântico, this is a smart hotel with external detailing influenced by the adjacent marina with,

dare I say it, decking. A pedestrian bridge crosses the main road to give easy access to the marina & public swimming pools, & a 10-min harbour promenade walk into the centre of town. Indoor & outdoor pools, health club, sauna, jacuzzi, Turkish bath, reading room, parking. €€€€€€

⌂ **The Lince Azores Great Hotel** (154 rooms) Av D João III 29; ☎296 630 000; e info@thelince-azores.com; www.thelince-azores.com/en/. On the edge of the main part of town, & a few minutes' walk down to the harbour promenade & marina. Rooms are designated smoking & non-smoking. Restaurant, sauna, jacuzzi, gym, swimming pool. €€€€€€

🏠 **Hotel Açores Atlântico** (130 rooms & suites) Av Infante D Henrique; ☏ 296 302 200; e reservas@bensaude.pt; www.bensaude.pt; closed Nov–end Mar. Almost all rooms have balconies, some sea-facing. Restaurant, bar, piano bar, indoor swimming pool, fitness room, sauna, hairdresser, conference & banqueting rooms, computer centre, free parking. On the main seafront road at the eastern end of town but still just a short walk from the centre. €€€€€

🏠 **Hotel Azores VIP Executive** (229 rooms) Rotunda de São Gonçalo Papa Terra; ☏ 296 000 100; e res.azores@viphotels.com; www.viphotels.com. Offers a great range of services, but unless you have a car it is a tedious walk into town. €€€€

Residenciais Several residenciais, some very small, are scattered throughout Ponta Delgada. This one is long established and very central:

🏠 **Residencial Sete Cidades** (34 rooms) Rua do Contador 20; ☏ 296 287 344; e residencial_sete_cidades@hotmail.com; www.residencialsetecidades.com. Centrally located. €

Youth hostel
🏠 Rua São Francisco Xavier; ☏ 296 629 431; e pja.acores@sapo.pt. In town, with easy access to shops & transport. The hostel has 90 beds in shared rooms & 2 family rooms with bathroom. Twin room with private bath €.

CAPELAS
🏠 **Solar do Conde** (27 3- & 4-bed cottages & 4 suites in main building) Rua do Rosário 36, 9545-142 Capelas; ☏ 296 298 887; e reservas@solardocondehotel.com; www.solardocondehotel.com. On the north coast, about 20 mins' drive from Ponta Delgada & 6km from the golf course. 4 suites in the main building, 27 cottages, some with open fires, all with kitchens & in a garden setting. Excellent restaurant. Small pool. €€€€

ÁGUA DE PAU
🏠 **Hotel Caloura** (80 rooms & suites) Rua do Jubileu, 9560-206 Água de Pau; ☏ 296 960 900; e info@calourahotel.com; www.calourahotel.com. An oceanfront resort 17km from Ponta Delgada offering double rooms including junior suites for

4 people, most with private terrace; panoramic restaurant, bar, swimming pool, fitness room, sauna, scuba-diving base, boating & tennis. The location is stunning, & you can walk the narrow roads round to the pretty unspoiled harbour with its fishing boats & simple swimming facilities. Formerly an area of tiny vineyards, these have largely been removed in favour of pasture & very expensive housing. Sheltered & a sun trap, it is ideal for a winter holiday, but you will need a car if you want to explore the island. €€€€

ÁGUA DE ALTO
🏠 **Hotel Bahia Palace** (102 rooms) Água de Alto, 9680 Vila Franca do Campo; ☏ 296 539 130; e bahiapalace@azoresnet.com; www.hotelbahiapalace.com. On a little flat promontory by the sea 4km from the nearest town. Spacious common rooms & large suites & junior suites with sun terraces & sea-facing, cocktail lounge, restaurant & grill, pool & good black-sand beach for sea swimming. €€€€

VILA FRANCO DO CAMPO
🏠 **Hotel Marina** (46 rooms, 3 suites) Rua Eng Manuel António Martins Mota, Vinha d'Areia, 9680-029 Vila Franca do Campo; ☏ 296 539 200; e hotelmarina@mail.telepac.pt; www.maisturismo.pt. Right beside the seaside, with an extra view of the Aquapark next door with water slides & pools. Rooms all have balconies, panoramic restaurant, bar & pool. €€€

FURNAS
🏠 **Terra Nostra Garden Hotel** (79 rooms) Rua Padre José Jacinto Botelho 5, 9675-061 Furnas; ☏ 296 549 090; e recepcao.htnl@bensaude.pt; www.bensaude.pt. The hotel dates back to the 1930s & has a very strong period atmosphere. There is a new wing with large balconied rooms looking into the garden. Rooms in the original part of the hotel either overlook the garden or the front road with a view to the old casino & its little formal garden. The hotel was completely refurbished winter 2012/13. There is a restaurant, bar, comfortable residents' lounge, indoor heated pool & outdoor thermally heated pool. Residents have free access to the famous garden at all times. €€€€€

🏠 **Residencial Vista do Vale** (24 rooms) Rua da Palha 56, 9675-042 Furnas; ☏ 296 549 030;

⏱ 1 Apr–30 Sep. In a quiet location tucked away on the edge of Furnas near the forest department's nursery, with views over the village rooftops & the valley, giving the visitor a real feeling of living in the village. Only breakfast served, but restaurants are a short walk away. €

POVOAÇÃO
🏠 **Hotel do Mar** (36 rooms) Rua Gonçalo Velho, 9650-411 Povoação; ✆ 296 550 010; e hoteldomar@ hoteldomar.com; www.hoteldomar.com. Located close to the sea near the harbour. Rooms have balcony & sea view, bar, outdoor pool. €€€

MANOR HOUSES
In recent years, large country houses have begun to take in paying guests. There are now too many to detail here, but the Azores Tourism Authority (see page 46) provides lists. The following are three establishments that I know or that have been recommended.

🏠 **Herdade Nossa Senhora das Graças** (4 rooms & 2 apts) Estaleiro, 9625-000 Lomba da Maia; m 961 127350; e reservas@nsgracas.com; www.virtualacores.com/nsgracas. 47km from the airport, garden, rustic golf. Feedback from Nico Olofsen in Amsterdam says it all: 'The 1920s' house is situated in farmland far off the beaten track & Lomba da Maia, the nearest village, can be reached by a farm road in about 30 mins' walk. Visitors are given a warm welcome & hospitality standards are high, with splendid evening meals with authentic Azorean flavours. The surroundings & peace are overwhelming, but a car would be useful as there is only 1 bus a day to Furnas & 1 to Lomba da Maia. English & German spoken.' €€
🏠 **Quinta da Abelheira** (8 rooms, family room, 1 apt) Pico da Abelheira 17, Fajã de Baixo, 9500-701 Ponta Delgada; ✆ 296 630 180/1; e info@

quintadaabelheira.com; www.quintadaabelheira. com. On the eastern side of Ponta Delgada & just a 10-min drive to the centre, yet very quiet. A lovely old house, traditionally furnished, some rooms within the house, others purpose built in an adjacent annexe. Games room & pool. Relaxing garden, decorated with tiled panels from 1932 & illustrated quotes from the Azorean poets. Dinner provided with 24hrs' notice. No facilities for children. €€
🏠 **Quinta de Santana** (21 apts) Canada da Meca, 9600 Rabo de Peixe; ✆ 296 491 241; e bookings@qsantana.com; www.virtualazores. com/quinta-santana. On the north coast west of Ribeira Grande, a large property with purpose-built units nicely laid out & ideal for family use. Equipped children's play area, swimming pool, & garden estate with enticing paths & lots of hidden areas to explore. €€

SELF-CATERING
🏠 **Quinta da mó** (3 separate 1-bed houses & restored watermill with 3 bedrooms) 66 Ruas das Águas Quentes, Furnas; ✆ 296 912 295; e reservas@quintadamo.com. Secluded accommodation with full facilities & bicycles within a luxuriant & very different garden crossed by a briskly flowing stream in Furnas village. €€€€€ (2 persons), €€€€€€ (6 persons)
🏠 **Furnas Lake Villas** (10 timber chalets sleeping 2+2 or 4+2) Estrada Regional do Sul, Lagoa das Furnas; ✆ 292 584 107; e reservas@ furnaslakevillas.pt; www.furnaslakevillas.pt. Comfortable, well fitted, TV, internet & a wood-burning stove, on a spacious site near Furnas Lake with a pool surrounded by mountains. Canoe & cycle rental. Special packages offered. €€€€ (2 persons)
🏠 **Quinta dos Curubas** Estrada Regional, Ribeira Seca, Vila Franco do Campo; m 961

739880; e geral@quintadoscurubas.com; www.quintadoscurubas.com. Self-catering 5 1-bedroomed timber chalets that can sleep 2+2 children, or 2 chalets attached, set in a large garden property on a hillside overlooking Vila Franca & its bay. Very comfortable with all mod-cons. Free use of 3 bicycles, free access to the produce from the owner's vegetable garden, welcome pack of basic foodstuffs included, special deals for 7-night stay. See also ad on page 122. €€€
🏠 **Casas do Frade** (9 cottages) Rua do Traitro 11, 13, 15, Lombas da Fazenda, near Nordeste; ✆ 296 487 001; e info@casasdofrade.com; www. casasdofrade.com. This is a small & very pretty complex of old cottages simply furnished & made comfortable; each has a double bedroom, living room, kitchen & bathroom. On the edge of the village & just 3km from Nordeste, it is a quite

lovely rural scene. In March, sitting on the little stone terrace in brilliant sun looking over meadows as lush & green as they can possibly be, bordered by trees, a few tiny houses & a blue sea beyond, the only sound that of cow bells & wild canaries, it would be hard to find a simpler place for a hideaway. €€ (per night each cottage)

🏠 **Quinta das Acácias** (1x2-bed, 5x1-bed cottages) 74 Rua da Lapinha, Livramento, 9500-605 Ponta Delgada; 📞296 642 166; e contact@

quintadasacacias.net; www.quintadasacacias. net. Fully equipped cottages set in a beautifully maintained garden that was once a quarry. Terraces create gardens on different levels, thus providing privacy. Carefully sited seating makes this remarkable garden of trees, flowers & sculptures a place to slowly enjoy, a great place to chill out yet just 8km from Ponta Delgada town centre. Long-term stays available 1 Oct–31 May. €€ (per cottage)

CAMPING

⛺ **Campsite Furnas** 📞296 549 010. In a lovely position overlooking the fumaroles, but a rather confused site with hideously built facilities, tennis court, children's play area, small snack bar & large surfaced car park that mercifully weeds are already beginning to green over.

⛺ **Nordeste, Ribeira do Guilherme** [map page 78] 📞296 480 060. Just before you reach Nordeste coming from the north road & tucked away at the bottom of a river valley, this pretty campsite is beneath trees by a stream with many watermills. Showers & WCs. Semi-natural swimming pool near the sea.

WHERE TO EAT

São Miguel has many restaurants, and several of the hotels also have restaurants open to non-residents. There are also good places to be found tucked away in several of the villages around the island; for details see under the respective village. Now very popular are the new eateries along the promenade next to Ponta Delgada's marina near the ferry terminal. In Ponta Delgada there are far too many to list, or even for your author to assess on your behalf, but here are some first thoughts. For location of listings see map, pages 102–3.

In approximate order of increasing cost:

✘ **Snack Bar Água** Na Boca Rua Aljube; 📞296 282 334; ⏰ 08.00–20.00. A small place near the main church, off the Rua da Misericórdia. Excellent lunchtime sandwiches & good-value *prato do dia*.

✘ **Bom Apetite** 48 Tavares Resendes St, just up from the Hotel Talisman; 📞296 285 508; ⏰ Tue–Sun. Modestly priced, nothing fancy, & shark is a speciality.

✘ **Restaurante Rotas Ilha Verde** Rua Pedro Homem; 📞296 628 560; www.rotasilha.blogspot. com ⏰ 12.00–15.00 & 19.00–midnight Mon–Fri, 19.00–02.00 Sat, closed Sun. Vegetarian, especially salads.

✘ **Casa de Pasto Avião** Rua Comandante Jaime de Sousa; 📞296 285 740; ⏰ Mon–Sat. 'The place looks very simple but the food is really great & not expensive at all', according to feedback from a reader in Rome.

✘ **Restaurante Nacional** Rua Açoreana Oriental; 📞296 629 949; ⏰ Mon–Sat. Long established.

✘ **Alcides** Rua Hintze Ribeiro; 📞296 282 677. Has a reputation for its beef, & a reader recommends the steak & blue mackerel.

✘ **Hotel Talisman** Rua Marquês da Praia e Monforte; 📞296 629 502; ⏰ Mon–Sat. In summer you should reserve a table. Ever popular, one of Ponta Delgada's better restaurants.

✘ **London Restaurante** 21 Rua Ernesto Canto, 📞296 282 500. Another long-established & very civilised eatery. Offers free transport from & to your hotel.

✘ **Anfiteatro Restaurant & Lounge** Pavilao do Mar; 📞296 206 150; ⏰ 12.00–22.00 daily. This is a Restaurant School & a chance for fine dining in the Azores, contemporary cuisine & fusion. A bit difficult to find, it is hidden beneath the amphitheatre used for summer outdoor concerts; walk round the new ferry access road. There is a lounge/café/bar on the ground floor, & the dining room is on the first floor overlooking the harbour

& waterfront. The students are getting very good reviews & fine dining for 2 costs around €60 (but can go up to €40 pp) for 3 courses, a bottle of wine & coffee.

NIGHTLIFE

Although Ponta Delgada is by far the most important and busiest town in the Azores, nightlife mercifully remains mostly quiet and traditional so you can fully appreciate how civilised everything is and enjoy an evening promenade by the harbour after a good dinner. In summer things can get quite lively, however, with popular music events in the city's squares and by the marina. One evening I chanced across a formally seated audience in front of the town hall listening to a Brazilian choir giving a lovely concert beneath the stars, and afterwards discovered colourful folk music and dancing in the nearby Campo S Francisco.

The **Teatro Micaelense** [103 E3] (*www.teatromicaelense.pt*) offers a wide range of cultural events throughout the year, from ballet, musicals, *fado*, jazz and chamber recitals to fully staged operas, the programmes often linked with the Coliseums in Lisbon and Porto.

FESTIVALS ON SÃO MIGUEL

One of the most important festivals is that of **Senhor Santo Cristo dos Milagres** (literally Lord Holy Christ of Miracles) to whom intense devotion was given during the 17th century when the island was racked by frequent earthquakes and tremors, and whose celebration has strengthened through the centuries. The monastery and nearby 'Square of 5th of October' are illuminated and the street decorated with flowers and at the end of the week, on the fifth Sunday after Easter, a large procession passes round the town with the crown of golden thorns at the front. Behind come men in religious clothes, some barefoot, some carrying large, very heavy candles to declare their thanks for a blessing received during a period of affliction. These are followed by youth organisations with their brightly coloured banners, children, some dressed as angels, priests, then the figure of Senhor Santo Cristo dos Milagres carried under a dossel of velvet and gold decorated with 18th-century woven flowers.

A much less conspicuous celebration, but one that perhaps makes a greater impression upon the visitor by its gravity and simplicity, is that of the **Lenten pilgrims**. During the seven weeks of Lent, groups of men led by a 'master' walk right round the island and pray at the churches and chapels dedicated to Our Lady. As they walk they say the Ave Maria; you can ask them to say one for you, but in return you must say as many yourself as there are men walking in the group.

Of great significance in the religious calendar is the **Holy Ghost Festival** that climaxes on the seventh Sunday after Easter. It is a festival with German origins when an Imperial Brotherhood was set up to help people in times of calamity; it spread widely in Christian Europe including Portugal. On São Miguel its importance grew after the tragic consequences of the earthquake that virtually destroyed Vila Franca do Campo in 1522. The **Procession of Bom Jesus da Pedra** is one of the oldest religious festivals and attracts many emigrants from around the world.

Cantar às Estrelas, Our Lady of the Stars, is celebrated by singing at night in the streets in thanks for the star that guided the Three Kings to Bethlehem.

In May is the festival of **São Miguel Arcanjo** which has been celebrated for more than 400 years. Its secular content involves a procession of different professional groups – fishermen, potters, shoemakers, barbers and farmers, etc. The **Festival of**

OTHER PRACTICALITIES

Emergency ☎112
Police [103 E4] Ponta Delgada; ☎296 282 022
Hospital [102 C5] ☎296 203 000
Tourist information office [102 D4]
Av Infante D Henrique, Ponta Delgada; ☎296 285 743
Post office [102 D4] Praça Vasco da Gama; ☎296 201 050

Private tour guide Rui Medieros m 962 275 8186; e rm@vivazores.com; www. azoresprivatetours. com
SATA Air Açores [103 E4] Av Infante D Henrique, Ponta Delgada; ☎296 209 720
TAP Air Portugal [103 E4] Av Infante D Henrique, Ponta Delgada; ☎296 205 233
Airport information ☎296 205 414; lost and found, ☎296 205 413

WHAT TO SEE AND DO

MUSEUMS

Ponta Delgada Museums seem to be opening all the time and they are all most charmingly staged, often in picturesque settings. The majority cover social history,

São João on 24 June is also Vila Franca's municipal holiday; celebrations continue for a week with marching bands, dances, bonfires and barbecues.

Cantar às Estrelas Ribeira Grande; beginning of Feb
Festa de São José Ponta Delgada; procession 3rd week of Mar
Easter Mar/Apr
Festa Sr dos Enfermos Furnas; end of Apr. *The streets are covered with azaleas & other flowers for the procession.*
Festa de São Pedro Gonçalves – Festa do Irró Vila Franca; end of Apr. *The fishermen process down to the harbour.*
Festa do Sr Santo Cristo dos Milagres Ponta Delgada; 5th Sunday after Easter
Festa da Flor Ribeira Grande; May. *Flower festival.*
Festas do Espírito Santo May to Sep; intermittent
Festas de São João da Vila Vila Franca; middle of June. *With popular singing groups & food stalls, dancing, bonfires & barbecues.*
Império da Trindade Ponta Delgada; 3rd week of Jun. *Ending of the Holy Ghost Festival.*
Festa do Corpo de Deus Povoação; last week of Jun
Cavalhadas de São Pedro Ribeira Grande; last week of Jun. *Horsemen pay tribute to St Peter in traditional song asking protection for the island's governor.*
Semana do Chicharro Ribeira Quente; middle of Jul. *Fishing festival.*
Festa de N Sra de Lurdes Capelas; end of Jul
Festa de Santana Furnas; end of Jul
Festa de São Nicolau Sete Cidades; middle of Aug
Festa de N Sra dos Anjos Água de Pau/Fajã de Baixo; middle of Aug
Festa de N Sra da Conceição Mosteiros; 3rd week of Aug
Semana da Cultura Povoação; last week of Aug. *Handicrafts & other activities.*
Festa de Bom Jesus da Pedra Vila Franca; last week of Aug. *One of the oldest religious festivals, attracting many emigrants from around the world.*
Festival de Bandas Povoação; 1st week of Oct. *Road show.*
Dia das Montras Ponta Delgada; 2nd week of Dec. *Shop windows are dressed for Christmas and prizes awarded for the best.*

3

but there is also the excellent Wheat Museum, Tobacco Museum and the innovative Microbial Museum.

Museu Carlos Machado [103 E3] (*Rua João Moreira, Ponta Delgada*) Founded in 1876, this important museum is in the former convent of Santo André, named after the first patron saint of Ponta Delgada. Intended to house Clarissa nuns in the late 16th century, it has undergone several structural changes and its present appearance dates from the first half of the 19th century. The museum is named after its founder, Carlos Machado. Sadly it has been closed for several years and reopening is uncertain; check for developments. Meanwhile there are two associated museums which house some of the collection, the Santa Barbara Centre and the Igreja do Colégio (see below for further details).

Núcleo de Santa Bárbara or Santa Barbara Centre [103 E3] (*Rua Dr Carlos Machado, Ponta Delgada, adjacent to the Carlos Machado Museum;* \ *296 202 930;* ⊕ *10.00–12.30 & 14.00–17.30 Tue–Fri, 14.00–17.30 Sat & Sun*) Permanent and temporary exhibitions, guided tour available by appointment.

Igreja do Colégio (Museum of Sacred Art) [102 D3] (*By the Antero de Quental memorial garden, Ponta Delgada;* ⊕ *10.00–12.30 & 14.00–17.30 Tue–Fri, 14.00–17.30 Sat & Sun*) The church has the two most important examples of 18th-century Portuguese art: the magnificent carved altarpiece is the greatest wooden monument in Portugal, begun after 1737 and left partially gilded in 1760 when the Jesuits were banished; the tiled panels are 5m high and depict Eucharistic allegories framed by Baroque ornamentation. For these two works alone it is well worth visiting.

Museu Militar dos Açores [102 C5] (*Forte de São Brás, at the western end of the harbour in Ponta Delgada);* \ *296 304 920;* ⊕ *10.00–15.00 Tue–Fri, 13.00–17.30 Sat; admission price nominal)* The Military Museum of the Azores has displays of uniforms, World War II guns used to defend the harbour, various historical armaments going back 200 years, military communications, field equipment and medical services. Opened to the public only in 2006, the museum, while modest, affords fascinating access to the fort itself which is alone well worth the visit.

Around the island

Oficina-Museu M J Melo (*Rua do Loural 56, 9545-137 Capelas;* \ *296 298 202;* ⊕ *09.00–12.00 & 13.00–18.00 Mon–Sat)* This is a most remarkable and extensive display of recreated bygone retail and artisan shops in the style of a street, all done by a retired schoolteacher of Capelas. Not only has Senhor Melo made the museum, he has also financed it, without any grant-aid. It is in part of his house, and from the outside does not look at all like a museum. You will find Rua do Loural up from the main square of Rossio, in Capelas village. Well worth visiting.

Museu de Emigração (*On the right-hand side of the main road into Ribeira Grande from Ponta Delgada, next to the market, in a large building with museum flags flying;* \ *296 470 770; www.mea.cm-ribeiragrande.pt;* ⊕ *09.30–12.30 & 13.30–17.00 Mon–Fri)* This museum stages permanent and changing exhibitions concerning different topics to do with the emigrants. The show I saw displayed the tools and domestic items of the Azores at the end of the 18th and early 19th centuries contrasted with the items introduced by the returning emigrants, mainly tableware and glassware, and linen made in New Bedford but with typical

Azorean crochet designs. The large car park opposite, behind the wall, used to be the cattle market.

Casa de Cultura da Ribeira Grande (*Rua São Vicente, Ribeira Grande;* \ *296 470 730;* ⊕ *08.30–17.30 Mon–Fri*) Recommended, providing a good insight into life as it was in the past.

Casa da Arcano (*Rua João d'Horta, Matriz, Ribeira Grande;* \ *296 473 339;* ⊕ *09.00–17.00 Mon–Fri*) On the road off to the left of the large Chapel of Santa Luzia, the focus of this new museum is an extraordinary assemblage of models made from rice flour, clay, glass, shells, cork and wire, telling the story of the Old and New Testaments. Margarida Isabel Narcisa was the daughter of a wealthy family who entered a convent. In 1832, the king closed all the convents, so she moved into a house with her brother. In 1835, she began the now revered construction devoted to São João, only ceasing to add to it in 1858. For years it remained hidden in the Mother Church, but is now on show in the restored house she shared with her brother.

Museu Etnográfica de Vila Franca do Campo (*Rua Visconde Botelho, Vila Franca do Campo;* \ *296 539 118;* ⊕ *09.00–12.30 & 14.00–17.30 Tue–Fri, 14.00– 17.00 Sat & Sun*) An excellent museum in the renovated 19th-century house of an orange merchant, and in 1900, the first house to have electric light.

The museums of Ribeira Chã (⊕ *09.00–12.00 & 13.00–16.30 Mon–Fri; admission price nominal*) This charming elevated south-coast village between Lagoa and Vila Franca has three places of interest: the modern church in the village centre, immediately to the right of it the museum displaying models of various religious festivals held in the village, including the Cavalhadas de S Pedro, a horseback procession held on 29 June. Exhibited also is a replication of the way the *imperador* displays the crown and sceptre as part of the Espírito Santo Festival (see page 38). The museum was the idea and initiative of a long-serving parish priest whose statue is outside, and includes many photographs and items such as wedding dresses and old school textbooks donated by the parishioners, and the priest's own collection of coins.

Close by is the **Casa Museu Maria dos Anjos Melo**, once the home of a lady (1909–92) who as a child emigrated to the US and returned when 17 years old and taught English in the village, marrying a local stonemason. She bequeathed her house to the parish on her death and the priest had the idea of making it a museum. The house has not been changed, and reveals the very simple bygone way of living typical of the Azores.

A short downhill walk takes you to the **agricultural museum,** another excellent local initiative. Cultivated in the garden are yams, woad, oranges, flax and other early crops together with traditional medicinal herbs. In the farm building is a series of model nativities cleverly made by schoolchildren from corn cob husks, pine cones, tiles or wire wool. There are gourds once used as swimming aids, wine barrel cleaners, and a nice section on Dragon's Blood; it was grown in Flores for export as a dye to Germany, and it seems Azoreans diluted it with *aguardente* and egg yolk for treating back pain, and the girls used the pure sap to paint their nails. Another interesting exhibit is the manufacture of pastel balls for export to Flanders, the *goma e rezinhas,* a mix of pastel and beeswax; during the 16th and 17th centuries, Ribeira Chã had 700 people working on pastel. In the grounds are several wooden buildings with fitted artefacts: a typical bar, shop, shoemaker, barber, a weaving shed, carpenter's shop, and homemade toys, among others.

Museu de Trigo (Wheat Museum) (*Located by the Ribeira dos Bispos, between the ridges of Lomba do Loução & Lomba do Alcaide; www.cm-povoacao.pt; ⊕ 10.30–12.00 & 12.30–18.00 Tue–Sun*) Signposted off the main road as you leave Povoação on the Nordeste road, this splendid watermill has been skilfully restored in a glorious setting of pastures and hedgerows. It is a triumph of restoration and capture of a past culture, and highly recommended. Tea and local biscuits are served.

Museu do Tabaco (*Estrada Regional de S Pedro, Maia;* ☎ *296 442 905;* ⊕ *09.00–13.00 & 14.00–17.00 Mon–Fri, 10.00–16.00 Sat*) Especially on São Miguel, until relatively recently one would see large open-sided drying sheds laden with tobacco leaves. Now much rarer, the Azores still produces cigarettes, Coroa and Robusto Estrela cigars and the smaller and thinner Pérolas curubas.

Microbe Observatory of the Azores (*Antigo Chalé de Misturas, Caldeiras, Furnas;* ☎ *296 584 765; http://omic.centrosciencia.azores.gov.pt/;* ⊕ *Jul & Aug 10.00–17.00 Wed–Fri, 14.30–18.00 Sat & Sun; Sep–Jun 10.00–17.00 Tue–Fri, 14.30–18.00 Sun*) An observatory in a heritage building promoting the importance of microbial life on earth, with an emphasis on the microbial diversity in the Azores thermal springs. Exhibits explain what micro-oraganisms look like, where they live and what size they are, whether there is life inside the fumaroles and many other related topics and visitor activities. Adds a fascinating dimension to fumarole watching!

Museu do Nordeste (*Rua D Maria do Rosário;* ⊕ *10.00–12.30 & 14.00–17.30 Mon–Fri; admission price nominal*) Displays of local cultural traditions and skills in an interesting old building.

WALKING Three walks are described in detail in this book, starting on page 115. The Azores Tourism Authority's website currently details 28 waymarked trails for São Miguel together with their degree of difficulty, distance and time. Restored, some have again suffered nature's savagery and are currently, possibly permanently, closed; another warning to check a trail's status before setting out! Dividing the island into three sections, the following should be open.

In the west
Serra Devassa Medium difficulty, 4.4km, 2 hours. A circular walk from near Lagoa do Canário passing through the island's 'Lake District'.

Vista do Rei–Sete Cidades Easy, 7km, 2 hours. Begins at the well-known tourist viewpoint of Vista do Rei, goes round the western edge of the caldera, and drops down to Sete Cidades village.

Mata do Canário–Sete Cidades Easy, 11km, 3 hours. The route goes round the eastern and northern sides of the caldera down to Sete Cidades village.

Fonte do Sapateiro Medium, 3.8km, 1½ hours. Ascending from the village of Ginetes up to the caldera ridge of Sete Cidades; from here you can either walk to the viewpoint of Vista do Rei or down to Sete Cidades village.

Rocha da Relva Easy, 4.5km, 2½ hours. Just west of the airport, this walk begins from the car park giving access to Rocha da Relva, a small settlement on one of the few *fajãs* of São Miguel, perfect for growing grapes and other produce.

In the centre, between Lagoa and Ribeira Quente: south side
Pico do Ferro–Caldeira da Lagoa das Furnas Medium difficulty, 2km, 45 minutes. Starting from the Pico do Ferro viewpoint high above the Furnas Lake, it descends to the hot springs by the lakeside. Crossing a watercourse can be very slippery. Good for plants and birds, one could simply cover a first section.

Lagoa das Furnas Easy, 9.2km, 2½ hours. A circular walk, starting in Furnas and going round the Furnas Lake.

Redondo Easy, 3.2km, 1 hour. Begins at a signboard on the R1-1 on the Furnas to Povoação regional road in an area known as Redondo and follows a historic narrow path down to Ribeira Quente once used by fishermen taking their catch to sell in other villages.

Praia–Lagoa do Fogo Medium difficulty, 12km, 4 hours. Begins from a side road off the main south-coast road between Ribeira Chã and Vila Franca and ascends to Lagoa do Fogo.

Monte Escuro–Vila Franca do Campo Medium difficulty, 13.5km, 4 hours. Begins from Monte Escuro, at 889m, northeast of Lagoa do Fogo, and after views of the lake descends to Vila Franca via the Nossa Senhora da Paz chapel. This walk links with that of Vila Franca to Praia da Amora.

In the centre, between Lagoa and Ribeira Quente: north side
Praia da Viola Difficult, 5km, 2½ hours. Begins next to the church in Lomba da Maia, along Praia da Viola, and ends in Maia. Several old watermills and a waterfall can be seen *en route*. A walk of only a short distance, but at the end of the beach is a difficult rocky section best not attempted when the sea is rough, after which are more watermills, and a slippery ascent.

Percurso do Chá Medium difficulty, 5km, 2 hours. A circular trail from near the Vista dos Barcos in Porto Formoso, taking in the Porto Formoso tea factory and tea plantation.

Salto do Cabrito Easy, 3.5km, 1 hour. Begins next to the Pico Vermelho geothermal power station and finishes at the calderas or hot springs near Ribeira Grande.

In the east, east of Ribeira Quente
Moinhos da Ribeira Funda Medium, 3km, 1½ hours. Short circular walk beginning and ending in Ribeira Funda (Fenais da Ajuda), with a vertiginous stretch. This one links with the walk of Praia da Viola. Can be done alone as a circular walk or linking with Praia da Viola and ending in Maia.

Trilho do Agrião Medum difficulty, 8.4km, 3 hours. Begins in Povoação and follows the south coast to Ribeira Quente.

Ribeira–Faial da Terra Medium difficulty, 6km, 2 hours. From Água Retorta Forest Reserve, the route passes over some slippery bridges down via Sanguinho, to end in Faial da Terra. Take care as the bridges are very slippery and can be dangerous.

Faial da Terra–Salto do Prego Medium difficulty, 4.7km, 1½ hours. A circular route via the Salto do Prego waterfall and the small settlement of Sanguinho.

Lombo Gordo Easy, 4km, 1 hour. This route comes out near the church in Água Retorta.

Lomba da Fazenda Easy, 7.5km, 2 hours. A circular route from the Nossa Senhora da Conceição church via watermills, a bathing zone, a garden of endemic plant species, and recreation areas.

Pico da Vara (1,103m) – São Miguel's highest point Especially for the following two walks you will need good settled weather; in places it is boggy, and a white-out will give problems finding the way, and of course no wonderful views.

Povoação–Pico da Vara Difficult, 15.2km, 5 hours. This walk begins from Povoação and ends on Pico da Vara. From the summit trig point you can descend to the north-coast villages of Algarvia (7km) or Lomba da Fazenda (8km), or return to Povoação (15.2km).

Algarvia–Pico da Vara Difficult, 7km, 5 hours. From the village of Algarvia on the north coast to Pico da Vara, either return the same way, or go down to Lomba da Fazenda (8km) or Povoação (15km).

BIRDS AND FLOWERS The most famous rarity of São Miguel is the much-promoted Azorean bullfinch, found only in the native shrubbery of the **Serra da Tronqueira Nature Reserve**. There are now thought to be upwards of 1,000 individuals and they may be seen from along the unsurfaced road between Povoação and Nordeste. As a gardener, I have some sympathy for the early farmers who shot it almost out of existence to protect their crops from its infamous depredations. Here one may also find the Azorean woodpigeon. This mountainous area with its deep ravines and watercourses is densely covered with laurisilva or Macaronesian evergreen forest and the endemic species include laurel, holly, juniper, Portugal laurel and bilberry together with ferns. Make a point of visiting the Priolo Centre and its easy walking trail – see page 74.

Lagoa do Fogo Nature Reserve provides the most accessible site for endemic plants and even if not tempted by the path descending to the lake through this vegetation, exploration around the viewpoint can be rewarding enough. Juniper, laurel, frangula and erica shelter native hypericum and euphorbia and a patient search will reveal several more endemics. You cannot fail to hear the Atlantic yellow-legged gulls.

Sete Cidades and its varied sheltered habitats of fields and gardens can be productive for birds, while the lake offers respite for migrant species and in autumn occasional American vagrants.

The varied habitats around the village of **Mosteiros** are often rewarding, with migrating passerines in the cultivated areas and, on the lava beach, turnstones, whimbrels, little egret, roseate terns, and less often, sandpipers. **Caloura** is good for the common and roseate tern which breed here.

WHALE WATCHING Off the south coast of São Miguel was once a profitable area when the islanders used to hunt whales and now, some three generations or so since the last whales were killed, they are again swimming past the killing shores. Some companies offer straight whale watching, others combine it with a sea cruise along to Vila Franca and back, others to Ribeira Quente with a stop for lunch in a noted restaurant. Often your hotel can advise you what is on offer during your stay, or in summer simply walk along the seafront and quayside to find operators' kiosks.

For further details on whale watching, see pages 64–6.

SWIMMING I repeat, the Azores are not a beach destination. On the north coast swimming can be dangerous as there are many currents and hazards; you will see local people swimming, but they know where the dangers are. Use only obviously developed swimming areas. All beaches are black sand.

Ponta Delgada At the eastern end of the harbour promenade, harbour swimming and in summer a complex of pools with full services.

Lagoa Originally this was a long, popular 150m stretch of irregular coastline, but the old complex was virtually destroyed during the winter storms of 1997. A new complex has been built with greater protection against storm damage with two pools, both heated to 24°C in winter. The largest is a four-lane, 25m pool; the second is for children. There is also an ocean swimming area surrounded on three sides by lava – swimming is dependent on tides and strength of the sea. Sunbathing area, diving boards and slides complete the picture, together with a snack bar. EU Blue Flag designation.

Vila Franca do Campo Two beaches, Praia de Água de Alto and Praia da Francesa, known also as Vinha d'Areia, can be found here. Here also is the Aquapark, with pools and slides. The Ilhéu da Vila Franca, an islet just offshore, has a naturally protected swimming area and is also good for scuba diving and snorkelling; note that this is a protected nature area and there is concern that increasing visitor numbers are damaging the habitat and daily visitor numbers are limited.

São Roque Here are two beaches: Milicias or Areal Grande, and Areal Pequeno. Supporting facilities are available. Very popular, a short drive from Ponta Delgada.

Caloura Fishing harbour, natural pool, no beach.

Água de Alto A long stretch of sand between two promontories, by the Hotel Bahia Palace.

Ribeira Quente A fishing village, at the far end of which beneath steep cliffs is the Praia do Fogo. All facilities are on offer, and in summer there are several open-air restaurants. An extremely popular area.

Ribeira Grande Municipal swimming pools are available on the new esplanade.

Praia de Santa Barbara, near Ribeira Grande Facilities include good parking, toilets with showers, and a restaurant with sea view. Excellent surfing, used for competitions.

GOLF There are two courses on São Miguel, one at Fenais da Luz just a few kilometres north of Ponta Delgada, the other near Furnas in the east of the island. The prices are the same for both courses:

Green fee (18 holes) €80	Golf cart (9 holes) €27
Green fee (9 holes) €49	Trolley €6
Set of clubs (18 holes) €40	Driving range (50 balls) €6
Set of clubs (9 holes) €25	Driving range (all day) €10
Golf cart (18 holes) €35	

There is a strict dress code. Shirts must have a collar and sleeves; jeans and tracksuits cannot be worn on the course or in clubhouse facilities. Soft spikes are mandatory.

16 Oct–15 Mar ⊕ 08.00–18.00 (Furnas 09.00–18.00)
18 holes ⊕ until 14.00, nine holes until 16.00

16 Mar–15 Oct ⊕ 08.00–20.00 (Furnas 09.00–19.00)
18 holes ⊕ until 15.00, nine holes until 17.00

✓ **Golfe da Batalha** Office address: Rua do Bom Jesus, Aflitos, 9545-234 Fenais da Luz; ☎296 498 559/560 (clubhouse); e info@azoresgolfislands. com; www.azoresgolfislands. Designed by Cameron Powell Associates & built in 1996 with long fairways, large flowing greens & sinuously contoured bunkers, the course is a combination of links & woodland course with views over the sea on the first 9 holes, & superb landscapes on the second 9. Par 72. To play, there is a required maximum handicap: men 28; ladies 36. Main competitions: SATA Air Açores Azores Open, VCC; International Pro-Am. The clubhouse has a restaurant with a stunning view, open to non-players.

✓ **Golfe das Furnas** Office address: Rua do Bom Jesus, Aflitos, 9545-234 Fenais da Luz; ☎296 498

559/584 651 (course); e info@azoresgolfislands. com; www.azoresgolfislands.com. Designed by MacKenzie Ross (who also built the Estoril course near Lisbon & restored the Scottish Turnberry courses) & built in 1939 with 9 holes, it was extended in 1990 by Cameron Powell Associates to the full 18-hole course, par 70, & 6,232m long. Required maximum handicap: men 28; ladies 36. It is an intimate course set in a glorious landscape with always verdant grass, forest & tree ferns. At 500m altitude, clouds & mist can often swirl around the course & present a different kind of challenge to the golfer. About 15 mins' drive from Furnas or 1hr from Ponta Delgada; for a truly relaxing holiday stay at the Terra Nostra Garden Hotel & either taxi or drive to the course.

GARDENS During the middle years of the 19th century, at least three great gardens were developed in Ponta Delgada, and their owners vied with each other to have the latest introductions and the rarest plants. They are within walking distance of the town centre.

Jardim António Borges [102 B2] (⊕ *09.00–19.00 daily; summer to 20.00, entrance from Av Antero de Quental or Rua Antonio Borges; admission free*) Begun in 1858 by the affluent landowner António Borges, this 3ha garden remains by far the most ornate, or rather fanciful, of the gardens. Now a public garden managed by the municipality, there remain the great fern ravine with its romantic bridge, and the small lakes and various watercourses can readily be detected, although some are now dry. Boating and garden parties must have been huge fun. Most of the original planting has long gone but a great buttress-rooted *Ficus macrophylla*, and a huge *Albizia* sp are worth seeing. Although kept clean, the garden has seen better times, and I feel that today many trees are awaiting death to relieve them of their misery.

Jardim José do Canto [102 D1] (*www.jardimjosedocanto.com*; ⊕ *May–Oct 09.00–18.00 daily; Nov–Apr 10.00–17.00 daily; modest entry charge*) José do Canto was probably the most knowledgeable gardener of his time and, from the mid 1800s, began to build a plant collection that over the next 50 years would

total several thousand species. Not only did he compile lists of the species he wanted to acquire, he even kept a long list of the plants he did not want to grow! The garden of more than 5ha was considered one of the finest private botanical gardens in Europe. Much of the design and planting was supervised by English gardeners. The garden remains in private ownership, is next door to the Sant'Ana Palace, and is now the grounds of the Pensão Casa do Jardim. Without doubt the finest specimen trees in the Azores are to be found here, in maturity a noble memorial to the man who worked so hard to introduce them. Look especially for Australian Moreton Bay figs (*Ficus macrophylla*), honeymyrtle (*Melaleuca decora*) and Kauri pine (*Agathis robusta*), *Araucaria columnaris* from New Caledonia, the Japanese Kusamaki tree (*Podocarpus macrophyllus*) and Chinese camphorwood (*Cinnamomum camphora*).

The Presidential Palace or Sant'Ana Palace [102 C1] (296 301 100; e *presidencia.palacios@azores.gov.pt; garden open to the public when not in official use, but always check with the tourist office for current times; admission price nominal. Guided tours can be booked*). Now the office of the President of the Autonomous Region of the Azores, it is one of the best maintained gardens in the Azores. The house was once a family home of the Correia family who commissioned the English architect David Mocatta to build it in 1846. With three wings, it is in a neoclassical style with sculpture and statuary on the front elevation. Inside, in the main entrance and stairway, there are paintings by the Lisbon artist Ernesto Ferreira Condeixa commemorating the royal visit of King Don Carlos and Queen Dona Amélia in 1901. In the first-floor dining room an *azulejo* panel depicts the 1831 Liberal victory over the Absolutists at Ladeira da Velha, on the north coast east of Ribeira Grande. The 7.5ha garden is principally attributed to the work of two gardeners: Peter Wallace from Chatsworth for the general design; and, later, the Belgian François Gabriel who notably introduced many camellia cultivars. With the original layout little changed, it is a good example of 19th-century Victorian garden design. There are a number of mature trees, an attempt at a garden of native Azorean plants, and an impressive long *allée* of box trees. For the sharp-eyed, there are interesting shrubs to discover.

Ponta Delgada City Park [103 G1] (08.00–22.00; *located to the north of the city's historic centre, off the road to Capelas, the Caminho da Lavada, entrance near the park's club house; admission free*) This is a new public park of 18ha begun in 2007 and completed in 2011 with the construction of a club house with bar and restaurant next to a golf driving range. Soil contouring has been added, to reduce traffic noise from the busy radial road and create a sense of privacy. The defining pathways and their secondary paths, the traditional stone walls creating enclosed walkways like the rural *canadas* separating farm fields, the long pergola of granite pillars, expansive grass areas with groups of endemic and indigenous plants, others of ornamental shrubs, and of course many trees promise a most inviting future.

Arruda Açores pineapple plantation [103 H1] (*Rua Dr Augusto Arruda, Fajã de Baixo, 9500 Ponta Delgada;* 296 384 438; *Jun–Sep 09.00–20.00; Oct–May 09.00–18.00*) Admission is free to see the greenhouses and includes tasting of pineapple liqueur and delicious pineapple boiled sweets. There are pineapple fruits for sale, loose and in presentation boxes, plus various handicrafts. This was an orange farm in the 19th century, when the garden was first planted. With the demise of the orange trade towards the end of the century, the farm adapted and went over to pineapple production under glass, and remarkably set out at the same time to be a tourist attraction. There is a belvedere which was used as a lookout for the arrival of the orange boats.

Terra Nostra Garden, Furnas (See page 86) (*www.parqueterranostra.com;* ⊕ *Apr–Oct 10.00–19.00; Oct–Jan 10.00–17.00; admission €5*)

Beatriz do Canto Park, Furnas (⊕ *Aug 09.00–18.00 daily*) Once known as Myrtle Park because it lies on the banks of the Ribeira das Myrtas that flows through the village. Begun in the mid 19th century and funded by a group of property owners from Ponta Delgada who spent their summers in the valley, the English gardener George Brown dammed the stream to create a lake, and created lawns and walkways. Completed around 1862, it was also intended to include five summer residences for the members of the partnership, but this collapsed and only Ernesto do Canto built his chalet. Designed by the French architect A Hugé in 1866, it is a most charming building with ornate embellishments and balconies, its pink-washed walls fitting enticingly into the mature garden. Privately owned, it has been a long tradition to open the garden during August.

RECREATIONAL FOREST RESERVES (see also page 69)

Pinhal da Paz Located midway between Ponta Delgada and Fenais da Luz in the north, from Ponta Delgada take the EN4-1a to Capelas and turn right at Carreira village and follow the signs. This is a 49ha woodland garden developed on poor land of rocky outcrops and volcanic residues. Used once for grazing goats and sheep, in the mid 1900s it was planted by the grandson of plantsman Jose do Canto with ornamental trees and flowering shrubs including camellias and azaleas. Secured by the Regional Government 30 years ago, in the last few years it has been replanted and small themed gardens added, along with a forest study centre. Quite a few native species occur naturally throughout the reserve. So close to the city, it is a perfect place to spend easy hours walking in delightful woodland, especially in the less frequented northern areas.

Woodlands of Canário On the way to Sete Cidades, and a walk of 15 minutes to the Miradouro do Canário, one of the finest views in all the Azores (see page 107).

Chã da Macela Along the road from Lagoa to Lagoa do Fogo, turn off at the sign to Remédios, and continue as far as Cinco Caminhos, where the forest reserve is signposted. The 28ha range from 350m to 550m and at the reserve's highest point is the Macela *miradouro* from where on a clear day one gets a fine view of the island. Apart from Cryptomerias, there is a fair mix of trees, and away from the play area and other amenities, the reserve has large areas of relative wilderness along with fine scenery.

Cancelo do Cinzeiro From the R1-1, take the forest road to Pico Bartolomeu from between Nordeste and Lomba da Pedreira. In 10ha of around 550m altitude there are forests and meadows, plus children's and picnic areas and playing fields. Significantly there are pockets of natural native laurel forest and a collection of endemics, along with a resident population of Azores woodpigeons and a breeding population of little shearwaters.

Nordeste Nursery On the outskirts of the town, this 4ha nursery was one of the first forestry stations in the Azores, created in 1955, and houses the forestry services headquarters. The nursery's original function was to raise trees for local residents and afforestation of common land; a range of species are still propagated, but now, in addition, native species are also raised for the Tronqueira Mountains to expand the habitat of the *priolo* (see also page 74).

AROUND THE ISLAND

PONTA DELGADA This is the largest town in the Azores, with a university established in 1975. The fastest and easiest way to get to know Ponta Delgada is to take the Lagarta Trolley (a toy train) (*www.lagarta.net*) or follow on foot my *Town trail*; see below.

The Lagarta stop is at the western end of Avenida Infante Dom Henrique, opposite São Brás Fort. Between May and October five different circuits are offered at different times: heritage, historical, beach, gardens and outskirts (⏀ *09.00–23.00*). In winter, the choice is down to three routes (⏀ *09.00–19.00*). A commentary is given in English, and the fare is €5.

Town trail The town trail on the following pages should take about two hours, excluding the Carlos Machado Museum (see page 92).

We begin the walk at the tourist information office on the main promenade by the harbour [102 D4], the Avenida Infante Dom Henrique. The tourism department sells its own guide booklets to all the islands, illustrated with splendid photographs. Various other brochures and maps are also available free, as are the bus timetables for São Miguel.

Upon leaving, turn left and left again around the corner where in the square, **Praça Gonçalo Velho Cabral**, you will find the three arches of the original (1783)

PINEAPPLES

Pineapples were introduced as a replacement crop for oranges around 1850, and became so successful that after ten years they were being exported to northern Europe, including England where they featured in royal banquets. The Azores are not warm enough for their outdoor cultivation, and there were some 3,000 glasshouses producing yearly about 2,000 tonnes of fruit. With the high capital costs of new greenhouses, it is doubtful if this crop will continue when existing houses need to be replaced. The main growing area is in Fajã de Baixo on the edge of Ponta Delgada, also in Lagoa and Vila Franca do Campo. It takes two years to produce a ripe fruit with an average weight of 1.5–2kg. Earlier, heather, ferns and moss were taken from the mountains and made into a thick growing bed but nowadays, to protect the mountain vegetation, leafy branches of pittosporum and other shrubs are used. As these decay they give off heat, and in a closed or carefully ventilated glasshouse this is sufficient for the plants to thrive. Old stems are used for propagation, which take six months to produce young plants. These are planted out to grow on for another 12 months, at which stage ivy and other vegetation is burned in old oil drums to create a dense smoke. This triggers the plants to flower all at the same time, and in six months they are ready for harvesting. Without 'smoking', flowering would occur intermittently and it would take much longer before the crop could be cleared and the cycle begun again.

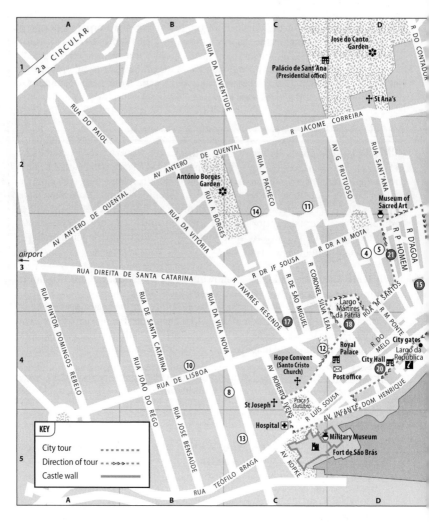

gates to the city [102 D4] which once stood by the old harbour wall. The modern statue commemorates the man after whom the square is named, supposedly the discoverer of São Miguel and Santa Maria.

Ponta Delgada had become important as a trading port, and in the 18th and early 19th centuries it was especially significant for the export of oranges. On several of the houses you will see square attic-like structures on the roof; here a servant would be stationed to watch for and give early warning of the approach of an orange schooner. This gave the grower or merchant valuable extra hours to harvest the fruit as it had to be picked fresh to travel well. Ships had to moor offshore and lighters (transportation barges) conveyed passengers and cargo from shore to ship. The harbour then was very small, and the square where you are now standing was the harbour. The bank on the east side and the buildings adjacent all have many internal arches which once fronted the sea. Land reclamation has pushed the sea back and allowed the new bank and other buildings, as well as the main promenade road, to be built in 1947.

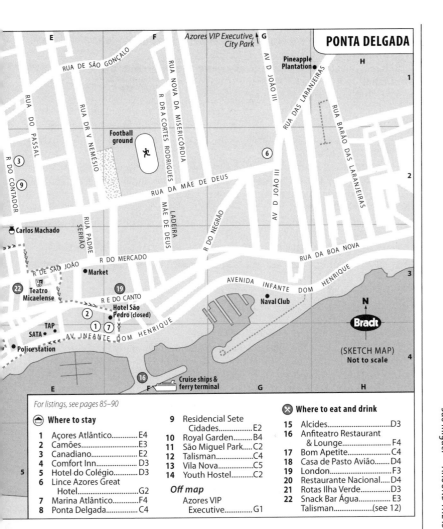

Azores VIP Executive, City Park

Pineapple Plantation

RUA DE SÃO GONÇALO

RUA NOVA DA MISERICÓRDIA

RUA DR A CORTES RODRIGUES

RUA DO PASSAL

RUA DR V NEMÉSIO

AV D JOÃO III

RUA DAS LARANJEIRAS

RUA BARÃO DAS LARANJEIRAS

Football ground

R DO CONTADOR

Carlos Machado

RUA DA MÃE DE DEUS

LADEIRA

MÃE DE DEUS

R DO NEGRÃO

AV D JOÃO III

RUA DA BOA NOVA

RUA PADRE SERRÃO

R DO MERCADO

Market

R DE SÃO JOÃO

AVENIDA INFANTE DOM HENRIQUE

Teatro Micaelense

R E DO CANTO

Hotel São Pedro (closed)

Naval Club

N

TAP
SATA

AV INFANTE DOM HENRIQUE

Bradt

Police station

(SKETCH MAP)
Not to scale

Cruise ships & ferry terminal

E   F   G   H

For listings, see pages 85–90

Where to stay

1 Açores Atlântico.............. E4
2 Camões..............................E3
3 Canadiano......................... E2
4 Comfort Inn.................... D3
5 Hotel do Colégio............D3
6 Lince Azores Great
     Hotel................................G2
7 Marina Atlântico..............F4
8 Ponta Delgada................. C4
9 Residencial Sete
     Cidades.................. E2
10 Royal Garden........... B4
11 São Miguel Park..... C2
12 Talisman................... C4
13 Vila Nova.................. C5
14 Youth Hostel............C2

Off map
Azores VIP
  Executive..............G1

Where to eat and drink

15 Alcides...............................D3
16 Anfiteatro Restaurant
     & Lounge.......................... F4
17 Bom Apetite...................... C4
18 Casa de Pasto Avião........ D4
19 London...............................F3
20 Restaurante Nacional.....D4
21 Rotas Ilha Verde.............. D3
22 Snack Bar Água.................E3
     Talisman...................(see 12)

Cross the square, and stand with your back to the Parish Church of São Sebastião. You are now facing a run of buildings that once fronted the sea. The city gates originally joined these. On your left, facing the Church of São Sebastião, is a tiny entrance to the **Café Mascote** (previously known as the Café Chesterfield); go into the old part, No 66, and see the arched roof while enjoying a coffee. This was once part of the original colonnade at the harbour's edge. Murals in the café show what it all looked like.

Exit the café and turn right and then right again down a small side street. On the left at the end is the police station, formerly the customs house. Take the little turning on the right about halfway along to go to the rear of the Café Mascote. Again you will see some arches in the outside wall, part of the colonnade at the edge of the harbour.

Return the same way as you came, to the **Church of São Sebastião**. This began as a very small chapel built to fulfil a vow made during the plague of 1523–31; in the 18th century, it was greatly added to in the Baroque style and the interior was decorated with ornate woodcarving. The exotic timbers used, especially jacaranda, reflect imports from the Brazilian colonies.

Retrace your steps towards the city gates and turn right, to see the **Câmara Municipal** or town hall. Originally it was the residence of one of the wealthy families and only at the beginning of the 20th century was it converted. The bell tower dates from 1724 and houses the oldest bell (16th century) in the Azores. Look in at the ground-floor entrance between the steps; here there is often a temporary exhibition of local interest. The statue in front of the building is of St Michael, patron saint of the island.

Continue past the town hall taking the road on your left, **Rua de Santa Luzia**. At the end, on the left, is the old post office. Leave the square, the Praça Vasco da Gama, and continue along the main promenade towards the **Forte de São Brás** at the end of the present-day harbour. Looking back provides a pleasing view of the continuity of architecture along the waterfront and by the post office. Please avert your eyes from the intrusive tower block at the far eastern end.

You will see a small floating deck at the harbour edge and café tables; this is the **Cais de Sardinha**, and was where sardines used to be landed. Continue along the *avenida*, past the present-day customs house, and see a corner building with a circular tower, the local headquarters of the Ministry of Defence. The 16th-century Forte de São Brás was built to defend the village against corsairs and pirates, including some from England. Enlarged in the 19th century, it is now the army headquarters and military museum (see page 92).

Opposite the fort is the square of **Praça 5 Outubro** (formerly the Campo de São Francisco), the traditional site for festivals and overlooked by the fine, green-washed, former Franciscan monastery. On the far side of the square, parallel with the seafront, is the **Convent and Chapel of Nossa Senhora da Esperança** (Our Lady of Hope) [102 C4], completed in 1541 and occupied by the nuns of the order of St Francis. The chapel is decorated with magnificent 18th-century tiles and gilding and is associated with the worship of the Christ of the Miracles. There is also an image of Ecce Homo, a statue that came to the Azores in the 16th century. The sculptor is unknown, but it came from Paris to the convent that existed at that time in Caloura. To protect the statue against frequent pirate attacks, the nuns left the coastal convent and took it with them to the newly built Nossa Senhora da Esperança. Some 150 years later a young girl called Teresa da Anunciada (1658–1738), from a rich family in Ribeira Grande, devoted herself to the nunnery and especially to the worship of this image. News of her devotion and fame of the miracles granted carried to all the islands and even as far as mainland Portugal. Subsequent emigration spread the worship of the Christ of the Miracles, and now pilgrims come from Azorean communities overseas to join the annual festival. The image may be seen between 17.30 and 18.30 every evening when a nun opens the internal gates to allow visitors in to see it, as well as the vestments and treasures. There is also a splendid ceiling and Baroque ornamentation. Once a year the image is taken on procession through the city, passing along the narrow roads carpeted with fresh flowers in geometrical designs.

Outside, in front of the chapel, there is a statue to Madre Teresa da Anunciada. Behind, at the first seat, the poet and political activist Antero de Quental shot himself in 1891, aged 29. The church to the left of the convent, **São José**, was part of the Lady of Conception convent and in the 16th century took 60 years to build. The façade is 18th century. Inside, it has a fine ceiling and much 18th-century decorative art. It is the major church of the old village and parish of São José.

From the square and by the convent, the pedestrianised road leading off is and has always been called the central road or **Rua Direita**, although today it is not central. Pass along the convent buildings and you come to green metal gates. Here you will find the side entrance to view the Ecce Homo.

Continue along the Rua Direita which becomes the Rua Marques de Praia e Monfort, where even now traditional shops are still to be found. On the right you will come to the **Royal Palace** [102 D4], once belonging to the marquis and now under reconstruction, opposite the Hotel Talisman. Walk past the palace and then look back and you will see on the roof an observation tower looking in all four directions. This was for defence. The car park was once part of the garden. It was the Marquis de Praia who in 1843 purchased the land in Furnas and began the great expansion of the Terra Nostra garden. Keep straight, passing the little garden square dedicated to the writer and orator Padre Sena de Freitas, and take the next road on the left, up the **Rua Comandante Jaime de Sousa**. Note one of the largest lookout towers on a private residence. You come to **Largo Mártires da Pátria** (Martyrs' Square) [102 D4] at the far side of which is a secondary school, originally the grand home of the wealthy 'Fonte Bela', so nicknamed because of his many water installations on the island. He was one of the first and most important of the orange growers and the largest landowner. The blue and white building on the left, to the west, is the old government or **Parliament House** of the autonomous region. Note the church with its ornate Manueline façade.

Take the **Travessa de Conceição** and then turn left into the Rua Machado dos Santos. A very small chapel at the top of a short flight of basalt steps is the **Chapel of Santa Luzia**, dated 1584. Luzia was the daughter of a rich family and was losing her sight; she promised that if she could keep her sight she would build a chapel in gratitude.

Turn left into the **Rua Carvalho Araújo**; at the far end you will see the splendidly ornate early 17th-century Baroque **Igreja do Colégio**. Following the expulsion of the Jesuits the church remained open for worship, but after a tenuous period in the early 19th century was used for storage and eventually abandoned. Acquired by the regional government, they began renovations in 1993 and in 2004 it opened as a museum and houses the Carlos Machado Museum's collection of sacred art. By the early 18th century in Ponta Delgada there were three religious communities (Franciscans, Augustinians and Jesuits), four nunneries, three sanctuaries for lay females and 28 churches. There were over 650 people in religious orders plus others totalling about 1,200 – one in eight adults of the Ponta Delgada population, with probably about a third of the population benefiting economically from the religious foundations. Enjoy the many wrought-iron balconies as you walk up this street. Next to the convent is the memorial garden to the São Miguel-born poet Antero de Quental (1842–91), with its elegant Art Deco sculpture, *Emotion and Reason*.

From the convent go eastwards along Rua Dr Aristides da Mota and Rua Dr G P Falcão and keep going until the narrow road opens out and you see a large building to the right surrounded by a tall whitewashed wall enclosing a garden. This is the **Carlos Machado Museum** [103 E3] (see page 92); turn right and follow the wall round to the entrance. If you have time, once the museum is restored, do make a visit; meanwhile the **Núcleo de Santa Bárbara** (see page 92) is close by.

Out of the museum turn left and right down the hill and, at the first crossroads, turn left. You will see on the right the tall **Teatro Micaelense** [103 E3]. This was originally the site of a military fortress, destroyed by fire in the early 1900s. The theatre was opened in May 1917, and is modelled on the Coliseum in Lisbon. It has been recently restored and seats 1,500. If you want to visit the **market** [103 E3] selling fresh fruit, vegetables, flowers, meat, fish, cheese and handicrafts, continue along the Rua Mercado for about 100m and you'll find it on the right-hand side of the road.

THE SOCIETY OF JESUS

Familiarly known as Jesuits, they were founded by the Spaniard Ignatius Loyola and six other young friends, and given Papal approval in 1540. It was just before the Counter-Reformation, a movement to counter the influence of Protestantism and reform the Catholic Church. With vows of poverty and chastity, they established schools throughout Europe with rigorous standards, in contrast to the clergy's generally poor education at the time, and sent missionaries worldwide to promote the Catholic faith and convert non-Christians. Today they form one of the largest single religious orders in the Catholic Church.

In 1549 King Dom João III of Portugal invited Jesuits to Brazil as missionaries and educationists. They quickly realised children were more responsive than adults so they built schools to teach Portuguese, literacy and religion and, because the children liked to sing, were among the first to use music in education in Brazil.

In 1553 the first Jesuit school opened in Portugal, in Lisbon, and in 1559 the University of Évora was founded, educating both clergy and laity. In 1570 they arrived in the Azores, first in Angra do Heroísmo and within weeks to São Miguel. By the 18th century theirs was the only organised network of education in the country; it was free of charge and open to all social classes. In addition they also undertook sacerdotal ministries, taught catechism, engaged in charitable works, visited hospitals, prisons, etc. Their influence at court was considerable, not only for their culture but also because many Jesuit priests were official confessors of the royal family.

As missionaries they played an important role, both in the east in China and Japan, and in Brazil. They became very influential in the country's early history, and helped found several cities including Rio de Janeiro and São Paulo. However, social justice was also one of their concerns, and they strongly opposed the enslavement of native Indians by the colonial powers in South America, and especially in Portuguese Brazil, and formed Christian Native-American city-states (Portuguese Reduções). This proved very controversial in Europe, and especially in Spain and Portugal where they were seen as interfering with the government's commercial colonial enterprises. This became one of the reasons for their later suppression.

The dominance of the Jesuits created envies and jealousies within certain sections of the civil society and in other religious orders. The powerful minister of King Joseph, the Marquis of Pombal, was a great defender of the 'Enlightenment' and was anxious to modernise the country but was hampered by past ignorance and resistance from the traditional aristocracy. A dubious assassination plot against the king gave Pombal the chance to destroy the Duke of Aveiro and the powerful Tavora family and weaken the nobility.

He then attacked sections of the Church, the Jesuit confessors of the royal family and later closed their schools and monasteries, confiscated their colonial possessions and ultimately expelled them in 1759 from Portuguese territory. He replaced their education with state education under his control, brought in science and mathematics and allowed the spread of French philosophy through which, together with social reforms, he sought economic development.

There are also very clean public lavatories, and a snack bar. Afterwards, retrace your steps to the theatre.

Walk down the hill and turn left into the **Rua Misericórdia** and you will come to the **city library** on your left with the red gates at the top of the steps. Take the right fork along to the old **Hotel São Pedro** [103 F3]; this was once the residence of Thomas Hickling, built 1799–1812, in Georgian style. Hickling was the wealthy Bostonian who built a summer house at Furnas and began what later became the Terra Nostra Park. Opposite on elevated ground is a church, the main **Church of the Parish of São Pedro**. Climb the steps for a good view out to sea. Ponta Delgada has over the years absorbed the surrounding villages and today has three parishes, two of which we have now met, and the central parish of São Sebastião.

From here walk down to the seafront and continue right along the promenade to return to the tourist office.

THE WESTERN PART OF THE ISLAND

Lagoa do Canário On the way to Sete Cidades from Ponta Delgada you will notice a forestry services sign to this lake on your right after you have passed a lovely old stone aqueduct. An unsurfaced narrow road lined with azaleas leads down to a car park, where there are picnic tables and barbecues. There are several things to see here. As you drove in you will have passed a small lake on your left down among the trees. Not only is this a lovely spot; around the lake is a very healthy community of royal fern, *Osmunda regalis*. From the car park another wide road leads you further on between the cryptomeria forest; it is a 15-minute walk to one of the finest *miradouros* (viewpoints) in all the Azores, a truly stunning view of the Sete Cidades lakes and village. As you return to the car park, on your left is a small track leading down; this takes you to a deep, very narrow ravine filled with a gurgling stream, tree ferns, several endemic plants and many ornamental azaleas. It is cool and moist, and wonderful for ferns and mosses.

Sete Cidades Mythology provides a romantic history. Once long ago in the kingdom of the Seven Cities, there was a king. He had a very pretty daughter who loved the countryside and happily roamed the fields, the little valleys and the surrounding hills. One day she came across a handsome shepherd boy tending his animals, and they shyly spoke. As the days went by she saw him again, and then again, and slowly romance blossomed and they fell deeply in love. Unfortunately, her father came to hear of this romance and was furious, because he intended his daughter to marry a neighbouring prince who was heir to a large kingdom. He forbade his daughter ever to see her shepherd boy again, but she pleaded so well that he agreed they could meet for one last time. At the final parting, they both cried so much two lakes were formed, one blue from the princess's eyes, the other green from those of the shepherd boy, and although they were parted forever, their tears have remained united.

Inevitably you will stop at the main viewpoint, the **Vista do Rei**, named from King Carlos's visit in 1901, where you can see both lakes of tears. The circumference of the caldera is roughly 12km.

The raffish traveller Thomas Ashe, describing his travels on São Miguel in 1813, wrote that the banks were planted with hemp or flax, which was cured in the lakes. There were only half-a-dozen houses in the valley where the hemp growers lived, and manufacturing was done by the village of Bretanha and neighbouring villages; some 50,000 yards was used domestically and more for export. The surrounding hillsides with their trees in little groves and bowers and the long winding valleys 'made them pre-eminently beautiful, and particularly favourable for romantic leisure and tender passions'.

The northwest coast along to Capelas Out beyond the airport the whole of this coastline is very pretty, and there are some especially lovely stretches of road running beneath tall, elegant plane trees with grass banks solid with blue agapanthus and topped with blue hydrangeas. At **Ponta da Ferraria** you can view the *fajã* from the road at the top of the cliff. In the rocky parts by the sea there are thermally heated natural pools. The old bath house is where a doctor would visit twice a week, descending by donkey along a little trail where now the road winds down. The level track leading from the sea was used by horse-drawn water carts to carry water to the bath house, used by patrons who could not afford to travel to Furnas. **Bretanha** is a pretty area originally settled by the French from Brittany; in the village is a restored windmill. Pass through **Remédios** and come to **Santa Bárbara**, where there is a very good restaurant, the **Cavalo Branco**, with regional food; take the first street right up a steep hill after the sign. They do a set regional meal which provides a taste of many good dishes, and is presented as a long sequence of small servings. In summer reservations are essential (❨ 296 298 365). The **Miradouro Santo António** overlooks small fields, the village and the sea beyond. Finally you come to the large village of **Capelas**, which once was an important whaling centre with a factory for processing the animals. Don't forget the **Museu M J Melo** (see page 92). Just beyond the village is the **Solar do Conde**, which is an old manor house with a formal garden. Here there is another excellent restaurant with a really good ambience – it's well worth travelling to (❨ 296 298 997).

THE EASTERN PART OF THE ISLAND: RIBEIRA GRANDE, NORDESTE, POVOAÇÃO AND FURNAS

Ribeira Grande The fast-flowing stream that now runs along the side of the very nice-looking town square and past one of the prettiest town halls anywhere originally attracted early settlers to build their watermills here. In 1507, it received its town charter. In France during the second half of the 17th century Colbert, Louis XIV's Minister of Finance, gave considerable support to numerous industries to boost economic development, but the subsequent religious intolerance made many skilled workers emigrate. With the arrival of French workers, linen and wool weaving brought great prosperity to Ribeira Grande in the 18th and early 19th centuries. Today it is expanding with light industrial development, but still manages to keep tucked away much of its old charm. Visit the main church of **Nossa Senhora da Estrela** to see the sacristy and its paintings of the Flemish School. The *misericórdia* church, the **Church of Espírito Santo**, in the main square, has one of the best Baroque façades in the Azores; curiously it has two doors. The **Ethnographic Museum** (see page 93) (*Rua São Vicente*) is located in one of the little backstreets nearby, and is excellent. You should certainly drive or walk to the sea, for a grand promenade has begun to be constructed with the completed first phase including a swimming pool, esplanade and excellent Alabote Restaurant (*Rua East Providence;* ❨ 296 473 526; *www.alabote.net*). Later phases will be built as money becomes available. As you leave the village you pass a fountain enclosed in the road, partly buried by lava from the eruption in 1563 that destroyed the village.

   Cerâmica Micaelense (*42 Rua do Rosário;* ❨ 296 472 600; ⊕ 08.00–18.00 *Mon–Fri*) on the road out to Furnas is a ceramic workshop making excellent tiles.

Numerous original and ambitious designs are displayed in their showrooms and around the workshops, and they will make any design to your order: pictures of your garden, your house, figurative, abstract; no end of fun.

Caldeiras and Lombadas Valley A 5km drive inland from Ribeira Grande, this tiny spa village of large old houses surrounds a central square where there is a hot spring and a thermal pond. Now a little tired, but slowly improving, it must have been delightfully romantic in its social heyday; the Restaurante Caldeiras (⊕ 10.00– 01.00 Tue–Sun) offers typical Azorean dishes. The road continues to Lombadas and takes you into really wild country along a narrow cobbled road, slippery when wet. At the head of the valley was a small hut where a mineral water spring came out. This was formerly the main source of bottled mineral water on the island, coming from a length of domestic garden hose whose further end disappeared somewhere under the heather on the adjacent hillside. I watched just three men washing, filling and capping the bottles; the whole enterprise was charming and the water delicious. A landslide several years ago wrecked it, but hopefully one day Lombadas water will again go into a bottle. From here you must either return towards Ribeira Grande and continue east along the north coast, or take the mountain road over the Cumeira Massif to the south coast.

Geothermal plants From the area around Ribeira Grande you will have seen steam rising in two or three places from the green hillsides heading up to the mountains. As you drive up to Lagoa do Fogo on the cross-island road to Lagoa, one of them is very close: the complex of silver-painted structures is part of the geothermal energy supply to the island (see page 23).

Caldeira Velha This is a strange place hidden among trees down a side turning a few kilometres along the main road crossing the island from Ribeira Grande to Lagoa. There is a small warm-water waterfall which runs into a small artificial pool; there are plenty of iron deposits and sulphurous smells, and it is a popular place to bathe. There are changing facilities and lavatories, and picnic tables beneath the trees.

Lagoa do Fogo Also along the same road to Lagoa is this well-named fire lake. It is a caldera with a lake at the bottom. The caldera walls are steep, but there is a path to the bottom; it is a protected area and several endemic plant species can be seen here. On a day when there are clouds and a strong wind blowing it is good fun to stand at the viewpoint near the edge of the crater and watch the clouds pour in and then get sucked up out again.

Miradouro de Santa Iria This is one of the loveliest viewpoints along the north coast. In summer on a balmy night you can stand here for ages listening to the cry of Cory's shearwaters as they swoop around the cliff below you and, at the same time, become intoxicated by the perfume of the Himalayan ginger lilies. If you have just arrived in the Azores and are transferring to your hotel in Furnas, always ask your driver to stop here; the pressures of the big city fall away and after just five minutes of these scents and sounds you already feel at peace and rejuvenated.

Porto Formoso and São Brás You are advised not to do this at weekends in summer because so many people come here and parking is a nightmare. Rather than continue along the main road, take the smaller road leading off down to the coast. At the T-junction turn right to drive slowly through a typical village to find a good fish restaurant, the **Cantinho do Cais** (*Rua Ramal, São Brás;* ✎ *296 442 631*). Find also the Praia dos Moinhos, where you will find fishing boats pulled up on a small sandy beach. An old watermill has been converted into a simple restaurant, **O Moinho** (✎ *296 442 110;* ⊕ *daily*). Note that the bay is sunlit only in the morning, the hill behind casting it into shadow later in the day.

Gorreana tea estate (*Plantações de Chá Gorreana, Gorreana, 9635 Maia, São Miguel;* ✎ *296 442 349; www.azores.net/gorreana; the factory is open to visitors 08.00–17.00 Mon–Fri; there is a small shop & fresh tea is served*) The first records of tea growing in the archipelago date from towards the end of the 18th century, although it is thought to have been known before then because of the Portuguese ships passing through on their return from Asia. It was the demise of the production of oranges and their export that stimulated the development of new crops, including tea. The Gorreana estate was founded in 1883 and is now one of the last of several estates that once thrived on São Miguel; 50ha remain, producing some 30 tonnes of tea annually. The first plants were introduced in 1874, grown from seeds brought directly from China. By 1883, these were producing their first crop and the drink proved so popular further varieties were brought from India. To manure the shrubs, lupins, which can fix nitrogen in the soil, were grown around them. Tea plants have thrived so well in the Azores that an especially aromatic variety has developed. The leaves, or rather the young shoot tips, are harvested between April and September by a simple machine operated by three or four men that straddles the rows of bushes; previously they were hand-plucked by women and girls. The leaves are then processed in the usual way in what are now old but beautifully engineered machines, and finally sorted and packed by hand. The distinctive packets are exported to the other islands, continental Portugal, Germany and Azorean communities in North America. In Germany an association has been formed – the Friends of Azorean Tea, and cuttings for propagation have been sent to Tregothnan Estate in Cornwall for their plantation.

Chá Porto Formoso (⊕ *10.00–17.00 Mon–Sat*) A second small estate nearby, towards São Brás, which also has a visitor centre, shows an interesting video of tea production and has a charming tea room and lovely view.

Maia This is a small fishing village where the large pink building houses a theatre, meeting hall and other community facilities.

Fenais da Ajuda If you have time, drive down to the village and past the main church until you come to a much simpler, smaller, church which was the first one to be built in the village in the early 19th century. Behind is a cemetery, at the far end of which is a splendid view along the coast to Maia and Ponta do Cintrão in the middle distance, and way beyond to the Ponta da Bretanha, which is the far northwest tip of the island.

Miradouro do Salto Farinha Clearly signposted from the road, this is another good place for a view. After heavy rain the 40m waterfall flows briskly and becomes a twin fall. You can walk down the path to the valley bottom and to the sea.

Ribeira dos Caldeirões, just before Achada You cannot miss this charming valley as you drive along the main road, with its lovely tree ferns, watermill, and in February the heavenly scent of all the pittosporum trees in flower. In 1986, severe floods destroyed most of Nordeste's watermills. More than 100 once existed; now only seven remain. Three have been acquired by the municipality to help restore the natural park area of Ribeira dos Caldeirões and to preserve the area's heritage and connect with a past traditional way of life. One mill has been restored as a working museum, and there is a café.

Santo António To see the local weaving, take the road going up, opposite the church.

Ribeira do Guilherme Just before you get to Nordeste, look out for the signpost on your left. There is a camping site below, and a picnic site. Also from above, you will see the semi-natural swimming pool by the side of the river where it joins the sea. To see watermills, follow the sign marked *Zone Balnear*. There is also a most charming garden laid out parallel with a stream feeding a watermill.

Nordeste Nordeste is so far from the rest of the island, and until the end of the 19th century was further isolated by poor roads, that boat used to be the preferred means of travel. It has always been a charming, sleepy little place that few tourists ever reached, but now this princess has been kissed by progress and is slowly awakening, with a new restaurant and other small developments, and most recently a fast road connecting Nordeste to Ponta Delgada. The town centre is dominated by the 18th-century church, and on one occasion I happened across a wedding, just after the service. Near the altar the bride and groom and all their guests were gathered drinking champagne and the choir above was singing merry songs, a very happy scene.

Located below the left side of the church is a small **museum** (🕐 *09.30–12.30 & 13.30–16.30 Mon–Fri*) with old ceramics from Lagoa and Vila Franca, early clothes, weaving and other items pertaining to the area. There is a **tourist information office** nearby (🕐 *10.00–12.00 & 14.00–16.00 Mon–Fri*).

Where to eat Restaurante Tronqueira (📞 *296 488 292*) is a modern restaurant with large windows looking into the surrounding garden. The **Parque Florestal** offers an attractive picnic area beneath cryptomeria trees, adjacent to neat rows of tree seedlings and formal hedges.

Serra da Tronqueira Here you have a choice, either to continue along the main road which is very pretty indeed with lovely *miradouros* and views of the coast, or to turn off from Nordeste and experience the Serra da Tronqueira.

This road runs through the mountains from Nordeste to Povoação, about 20km. It is unsurfaced and can be badly affected by heavy rain at any time of the year. However, should it have been recently graded and in good condition it is a wonderful drive on a clear day. If the clouds are low you will not see anything so do not waste your time. You can deviate and take the side turning 8km to Pico Bartolomeu, at the summit of which is a radio mast. In spite of the height it is a relatively limited view, but it is wild country with a mix of plantation cryptomeria and native forest. To the south you look over Água Retorta. Continue towards Povoação, and you reach a *miradouro* where you have a close direct view of Pico da Vara, the highest point of São Miguel at 1,103m. Covering the hills and valleys is the largest remnant of native vegetation, now a protected area; it is from this *miradouro* that I watched the rare Azorean bullfinch (*priolo*) flitting in and out of the dense foliage.

The Priolo Environmental Centre is only a 15-minute drive from Nordeste in the same direction and is an area well worth visiting for a glimpse of the wilderness, its trails and picnic site; see page 74 for details.

Viewpoints of the east coast There are several *miradouros* and picnic sites along this road, and they are constantly being improved and added to. The Nordeste Municipality has always taken a great pride in these, and deservedly so.

Ponta do Arnel provides a dramatic view down upon the lighthouse, the first to be built, in 1876.

Ponta do Sossego, the Place of Quietude, is a beautifully gardened belvedere offering splendid views of the steep coastline. The garden is on different levels, with delightful paths amid flowering hydrangeas, hibiscus, azaleas, camellias, palms and summer annuals.

Ponta da Madrugada is one of my favourites; on a sunny day the contrast between the bright colours of the flowers, the rich green grass and the deep blue sea is wonderfully vivid. Around 25 ago, when Azores tourism was really in its infancy and few tourists explored this road, we used to have a picnic lunch at this viewpoint. The head waiter would come with a colleague in a van from the Terra Nostra Hotel and set it all up on one of the tables. It would be a Lucullan affair, with several courses and linen napkins; and formally dressed waiters wearing white gloves would pour the wines. Alas, no more. The coast between Faial da Terra and Ponta do Arnel is a Special Protected Area; it is an important nesting site for shearwater and common tern, and there are some endemic plants and invertebrates.

Povoação This was the first settlement on São Miguel, and now has a pretty little town square and old streets leading down to the harbour. The church of Nossa Senhora do Rosário, built in the 15th century but restored in the 19th century and again recently, is thought to have been the first building of worship on the island. Don't forget the Wheat Museum (see page 93).

Ribeira Quente The valley down which you approach the village is very green and on the way you will pass beneath two tunnels where there is a waterfall. There is a new, long seafront and if you drive to the end there is a good black-sand beach with all amenities. Maybe one of the locals will tell you where the thermal area is; here, at low tide, the sea is very warm. You will notice considerable redevelopment for tourism and of the old harbour. Offering excellent seafood are several restaurants; in summer, with outside tables, they are very popular. The village physically divides into two: by the harbour and then by the church and beach. As you go along the seafront from the harbour to the beach area you will pass the Núcleo Museológico de Pesca Artesanal, part of one of Ribeira Quente's two schools. Exhibits include a typical fishing boat, nets and equipment used for local small-scale fishing.

Furnas If you approach from the north along the main road you will see a turning off to your right signposted **Pico do Ferro**. This is a fine viewpoint over the Furnas Valley, and helps get your bearings once down in the valley. Along with the view of Sete Cidades, this village in its huge caldera is among the best-known images of the Azores, and especially of São Miguel. Two places appear in all the brochures: the hot springs with their bubbling water and burping mud, and the Terra Nostra garden. Popular as a spa in the 19th century, Furnas attracted patients from as far as England. Sadly the spa building, which dates from the mid 19th century, is being turned into a hotel and threatens to be a gross intrusion. The municipal garden in front was laid out in 1940. The largest, noisiest and perhaps most fearful of the many hot springs or fumaroles is named *Pêro Botelho*, a 16th-century nickname for the devil. Around the calderas area some 22 different mineral waters emerge from the ground, the best-tasting from fountains, the lesser ones out of simple plumbers' pipes. At the edge of the village is a forest services' immaculately maintained tree nursery and trout farm; visitors welcome. The local large flat soft rolls called *bolos levedos* are made in Furnas and are delicious, especially in the Café Atlântico when filled with cheese and ham and toasted.

There are several large summer homes built by grandees in the 19th century, some with once lovely gardens. Terra Nostra garden, belonging to the Terra Nostra Garden Hotel, has a long history; it is open to non-residents, for whom there is an entrance charge (see page 86). Another most charming 19th-century garden is the Beatriz do Canto Park on the Rua de Santana that was earlier called Myrtle Park, from the Ribeira das Murtas stream that flowed nearby. It was made as a public park to further beautify Furnas by a partnership of philanthropic wealthy property owners from Ponta Delgada who spent their summer months in Furnas, and designed by the English gardener George Brown in 1862. The stream was dammed to create a lake, and lawns and walkways created many pleasant aspects. Five summer residences were included for the partners, but the partnership collapsed and only one was built, for Ernesto do Canto. This was inherited by Beatriz do Canto (1902–88), but it was hit by terrible floods and took many years to restore, through which she insisted on keeping the park open during August. This practice continues, from 09.00 to 18.00 daily, and the park is now named in her memory. During the rest of the year glimpses may be had of the gardens from the road.

Furnas Lake This is São Miguel's second-largest lake at almost 2km². On the far side from the road, and signposted, are the calderas, where for generations people have come to cook the famous *cozido nas caldeiras*. Holes are made about 1m deep in the hot earth into which a container is lowered filled with different meats, sausage and some vegetables, mostly kale, cabbage and potatoes. It is all left to cook gently for around seven hours. Cooked slowly, and so evenly, all the flavours and delicious juices are retained, although those with timid appetites can find it a little daunting. Across the lake you can see a pseudo-Gothic chapel dedicated to Our Lady of Victories built by José do Canto, one of the Azores' great gardeners. It is a family vault and he and his wife are buried there. Nearby is a private garden largely devoted to camellias; sleeping for years, it has a melancholy charm. You may visit the garden with the owner's permission, but beware: the paths can be very slippery. In early spring the magnolias and camellias give the impression they are in their native wild forest.

Furnas Monitoring & Research Centre (✆ 296 206 745; ⊕ 15 May–15 Sep 10.00–18.00 daily; 16 Sep–14 May 09.00–17.00 Tue–Sun) Located by Furnas Lake along from the chapel, it is accessed from either walking in from the main car park by the regional road (ten minutes) or by taking the trail following the lakeside from the area of hot springs (40 minutes). Attracting much press comment and praise, this very modern building was designed by the Portuguese architects Aires Mateus and Associates; its form was inspired by the landscape, and uses building materials traditional to the island.

Owing to the extensive conversion of woodland to pasture for cows and the subsequent fertilisers applied, the nitrogen run-off into the lake has caused eutrophication, an algae and phytoplankton bloom causing the death of animal life from oxygen starvation. The research centre is monitoring the various actions taken

At the end of December 1839, Joseph and Henry Bullar spent a winter in the Azores and later published in London a detailed account of their travels. Here is their description of a thermal bath at Furnas, or the 'Baden-Baden of St Michael' as they named it.

After looking at the calderas, we took our bath, and it was certainly never my good fortune before to bathe in an invigorating warm bath. It produced a feeling of strength instead of lassitude, and the skin seemed not alone to have been cleansed and rendered most agreeably smooth, but to have been actually renewed.

While bathing, our man cooked eggs for us in one of the small boiling springs, and we afterwards went to the iron-spring for a draught [of mineral water]. This flows from a stone spout into a hollow stone basin, and trickles down a bank into a stream below: it has a strong but not disagreeable iron flavour, effervesces slightly, and is extremely grateful and refreshing. The bath and the spring seemed the two things best suited to the outside and inside of man, on first rising from his bed; natural luxuries when in health, natural remedies when sick – luxuries without after-pain, remedies without misery in taking them – both which evils seem to be inseparable from the luxuries and the remedies of our own invention. Most invalids feel that before-breakfast existence is burdensome; but this bath and draught of liquid iron were as breakfast in producing serenity and happiness, and were more of a breakfast in giving warmth and briskness, and a feeling of health, as of the flowing of younger blood through the veins …

to recover the quality of the lake, by the removal of grazing animals, converting old pastures to productive legumes, establishing native flora on watersheds and other projects. Much is being learned about the life histories and requirements of individual plant species from the process of propagation and establishment of new native forest (laurisilva), and trials are underway to select from the native blueberry, *Vaccinium cylindraceum*, one that produces improved fruit for possible commercial use.

The centre houses an impressive exhibition about the Furnas ecosystem, the problems it faces, and the restoration projects. With a video presentation, exhibits, and knowledgeable personnel to further explain, the visitor can gain many insights into numerous aspects of the life of this region.

Vila Franca do Campo Located on a fertile plain or 'campo', Vila Franca was once a duty-free zone whose residents were exempt from paying taxes. It was also the island's first capital. There is good swimming and a large programme of tourist development is happening, including an aquarium theme park, a marina near Vinha d'Areia, health centre and Clube Naval expansion. There is a harbour with small fishing boats and there are fish restaurants – try the Praia Café, Lugar da Vinha d'Areia (⊕ *12.00–15.00 & 19.00–22.00 Tue–Sun*) – and good local cakes called *Queijadas da Vila*. Among many buildings of historical architectural merit is the Matriz, the Church of São Miguel Arcanjo or St Michael the Archangel. Completed in 1537, it has an impressive façade built completely of basalt, with a carving of Christ on the cross. On the edge of the town by a pretty little public garden is the old church and convent of São Francisco, dating from 1525; it is now a hotel. Don't forget the museum (see page 93).

Just off the beach is the **Ilhéu da Vila**, the remains of an old volcano where the sea has breached the crater wall creating a protected swimming area. Extremely popular with local people, it is accessed by a regular boat service between June and September. The island is also a nature reserve, and there is a conflict of interest between conservation and recreation, and a daily quota of visitors has been set.

If you have time, it is well worth driving up to the **Chapel of Nossa Senhora da Paz**, which can be seen from Vila Franca high on the hillside behind the town. From here there is a splendid panorama of Vila Franca and its surrounding pineapple glasshouses, and of the green landscape spreading down to and along the coast.

Lagoa Lagoa has long been the centre of São Miguel's pottery industry, which began in the 19th century. Crockery, pots, bowls, vases and other items in traditional designs and colours are made here and visitors are welcome to tour the factory, showrooms and museum of Cerâmica Vieira, founded in 1862. The old town's harbour was once busy with exports of woad and wheat.

Caloura This is a pretty area with a tiny fishing harbour and a natural swimming pool at the end of the breakwater, surrounded by old vineyards, each with its own stone wall. In the past few years substantial new homes have been built and it is now obviously a very desirable place to live; for the property-curious, it is interesting to see how a severe, stony landscape can be transformed. There is also a charming little convent by the sea, dating from the 16th century, now privately owned.

WALKS

Right from the early years of walking holidays in the Azores there existed the walks around Sete Cidades, the walk up to Lagoa do Fogo and the circuit of Furnas Lake. Two favourites from that time were the cliffside walk from Gaiteira along to Ribeira Quente, and from Furnas up over the rim of the caldera and down to Ribeira Quente. Sadly these two were destroyed in the tragic flash flood and landslides that swept down upon part of the village of Ribeira Quente in 1997. Restored, they have again suffered nature's savagery and are again closed – another warning to check a trail's status before setting out!

Three walks are described in this chapter: two that I pioneered and that have stood the test of time; the third around Furnas Lake, because the options can be done spontaneously and you may not have acquired the official guide brochure.

SETE CIDADES (*Time: about 4½hrs; distance: about 13km. See map on page 116*) There are numerous choices when it comes to exploring this area for there are several roads going down into the caldera and to the village of Sete Cidades, and there are various roads leading from the caldera rim down to villages along the coast. You will doubtless find various published descriptions of these. I think the walk described here is best, since, in one route, you have the most magnificent caldera views which constantly change as you progress along the rim, and the end of the day offers the contrast of approaching the sea with fine views of Mosteiros and the chance to see what living on a *fajã* is like. Even on a national holiday, at most you will meet a farmer or two attending their cows and maybe another walker.

Footpath conditions are easy, more or less level, with some steep pitches at both the start and finish.

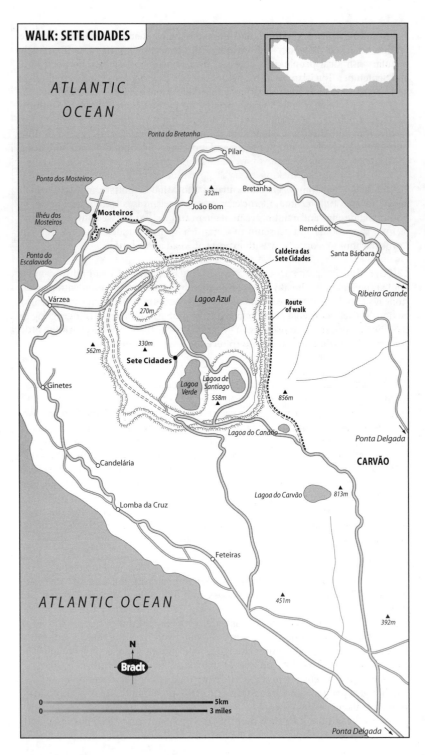

WALK: SETE CIDADES

ATLANTIC
OCEAN

Ponta da Bretanha

Pilar

Ponta dos Mosteiros

332m

Bretanha

João Bom

Ilhéu dos
Mosteiros

Mosteiros

Remédios

Caldeira das
Sete Cidades

Santa Bárbara

Ponta do
Escalavado

Várzea

Lagoa Azul

Route
of walk

Ribeira Grande

270m

330m

562m

Sete Cidades

Ginetes

Lagoa
Verde

Lagoa de
Santiago

558m

856m

Ponta Delgada

Lagoa do Canário

CARVÃO

Candelária

Lagoa do Carvão

813m

Lomba da Cruz

Feteiras

451m

392m

N

Bradt

0   5km
0   3 miles

ATLANTIC OCEAN

Ponta Delgada

If the weather is very windy it can be very unpleasant, and if there is low cloud, do wait for another day since you will miss all the wonderful views. Half the fun is identifying all the landmarks.

Take a taxi to the area known as Carvão. Approaching from Ponta Delgada go past the Miradouro de Carvão, past the sign on your left to Lagoas dos Empadadas and then take the second asphalt-surfaced turning on your right. This soon curves round in front of an old and rather beautiful stone aqueduct and then into cryptomeria forest. Stop at the first unsurfaced farm track on your left – it is on a bend in the road.

You begin the walk here, slowly ascending through the forest and upon emerging come to a cement road making a very steep ascent up to the caldera, finishing by a building. You may be lucky and have an enthusiastic taxi driver prepared to risk damaging his car; mine had never been there before and insisted on driving all the way to the top where there is a level turning area. He ran to the caldera edge and was dumbstruck by the stupendous view; it is so much more dramatic than from the usual viewing place at Vista do Rei. On a clear day with no wind this has to be the finest view in all the Azores.

From here you simply follow the farm road going anticlockwise around the caldera rim; it soon forks and you bear round to the left. Continue ignoring all roads and tracks leading off from the main road around the caldera. In about two hours you reach a *miradouro* with some picnic tables and a road descending off on your right.

Continue on round the caldera and in about another 30 minutes you see the Ilhéu dos Mosteiros just off the coast, and near here you are above a tunnel that runs from the blue lake out of the caldera above Mosteiros. The track descends a little to come to a junction by a large smooth face of grey tuff with names carved into it. Two roads go down on your right, one either side of the bluff; take the second of these. The road you were following continues on round the caldera.

You now descend, at times between high walls of tuff and, lower down, reeds, to reach an asphalt road after 20 minutes. Cross this and continue down on the track and within two minutes come to a T-junction. Turn left, and the road forks either side of a fountain bearing the sign 'Rua Direita Pico de Mafra'. Take the left fork and follow this steeply down to the houses and continue on quickly to come to a *miradouro* giving a splendid view over Mosteiros, its white houses contrasting with the black lava and blue sea. To go down to Mosteiros take the small concrete road going steeply down on the right, about 50m below the Espírito Santo chapel. From Mosteiros you may get a bus back to Ponta Delgada, or phone for a taxi.

LAGOA DO FOGO (*Time: about 5hrs; distance: about 14km. See map on page 118*) This moderately difficult walk starts from Ribeira da Praia on the south coast; the route is uphill most of the way, the steepest part at the beginning up a farm track. This has now been surfaced so you can drive up this first section. The return is by the same way to either Ribeira da Praia, where you could leave your car, or to Água de Alto, where there is a small bar from which to telephone for a taxi. The lake is at the bottom of a large crater. The walk begins almost down at sea level and climbs up through dramatic scenery to the lake, an ascent of some 600m. By the lakeside on a sunny day it makes a different place to picnic and, in summer, locals like to swim. If, however, upon reaching the lake you get pouring rain and dense mist, it is very atmospheric, but can be very cold.

Take a bus or taxi to **Ribeira da Praia**. If you have a car, then there are places nearby where you can park. You have two options: if you have time, use the old

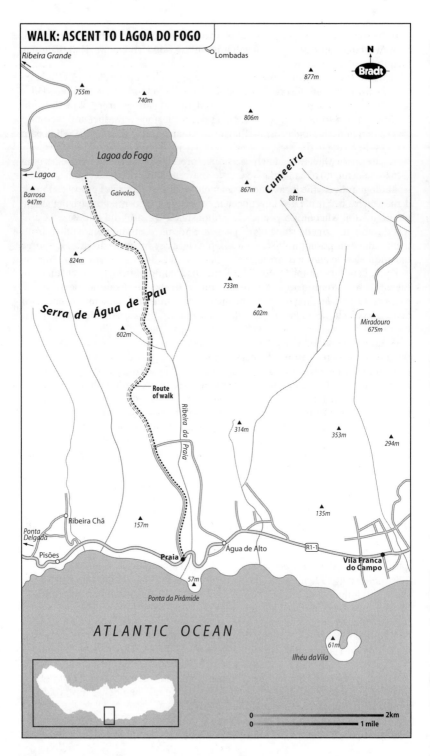

WALK: ASCENT TO LAGOA DO FOGO

N

Bradt

Ribeira Grande

Lombadas

877m

755m

740m

806m

Lagoa do Fogo

Lagoa

Gaivolas

867m

Cumeeira

881m

Barrosa
947m

824m

Serra de Água de Pau

602m

733m

602m

Miradouro
675m

Route
of walk

Ribeira da Praia

314m

353m

294m

135m

Ribeira Chã

157m

Ponta
Delgada

Pisões

Praia

Água de Alto

R1-1

Vila Franca
do Campo

57m

Ponta da Pirâmide

ATLANTIC OCEAN

61m

Ilhéu da Vila

0   2km
0   1 mile

road. Otherwise from Ponta Delgada take the expressway and follow the signs to Vila Franca do Campo, then leave the expressway at the sign Água de Pau (Nascente) e Água d'Alto. At the roundabout, take the second exit signed to Água d'Alto/Ribª Chã, and you will find the old road with access to the trail. The walk begins just before the bridge crossing the Ribeira da Praia and at the road sign saying 'Praia'. There is a farm track (now tarmac) ascending steeply which should be signposted to Lagoa do Fogo. Take this, and shortly another track goes off on your left; ignore this and continue, passing a stone building on your right and then through a cutting in the rock, emerging into a field of vines. Shortly there are lovely views out to sea providing an excuse to stop and recover your breath. The track then divides and you take the left fork.

Continue always by the main track and ignore smaller side tracks until you reach a cattle trough. Turn right and, ignoring all the tracks coming in from the left, continue until you come to some ruined houses on your right. From here there is a fine view over Vila do Campo and the islet Ilhéu da Vila. This islet is the result of a secondary eruption on the outer flank of the caldera that occurred beneath the sea some 4,000 years ago. The seawater caused an explosive (Surtseyan) eruption creating a rounded deposit of tuff with a central crater, the wall of which has been breached by erosion. Go past the ruined houses and a little further on you will find the route is marked with cement arrow posts. You will come to the *levada*, or watercourse; follow the trail alongside this carefully – it is broken in places. At the end of the *levada* simply follow the track until you reach the lake, passing hills of black scoriae and dark vegetation.

Return the way you came; do not be tempted to take the wide 'road' as the owners object to walkers crossing their land. If, however, you do not have a car, you can walk down to Água de Alto, where there is a bar from which you can phone for a taxi, or walk along the main road into Vila Franca; when you get to the end of the *levada* and have passed the ruined houses and begun to lose height, watch out for a wide road coming in from the left. Take this and you soon come to a stream crossing over the road. Cross by the stepping stones. The old electricity generating works were installed here in 1903. Follow the stone path on the other side and after a short ascent the track forks. Take the right fork and after another short climb the track levels out and follows the ridge down. The Ribeira da Praia is on your right, where you look down upon the waterfalls, the water tank and the length of the *ribeira* out to sea. If you look behind you to the hill above, there is a building with a small tower – it is another generating station. By a stone water trough the path joins another and you go on down the hill to come out on the main road into Água de Alto.

AROUND LAGOA DAS FURNAS The walks to Furnas Lake can easily be varied according to the time you have and how far you want to walk. Don't forget to allow time to visit the Furnas Monitoring & Research Centre – see page 113. See also the map on page 120.

Option (a) (*Time: about 2hrs; distance: about 5km*) The easiest option is to take a taxi from Furnas to the chapel of Nossa Senhora das Vitórias at the far side of the lake, and then walk back along the lake edge at the side of the main road to Furnas, downhill all the way, reversing the descriptions below under option (b).

Options (b), (c) and (d) The following walks begin at the pretty petrol station with its *azulejos*, near the Teatro das Furnas, just a short distance from the Terra Nostra Garden Hotel. At the garage the main road bears round to the left and a

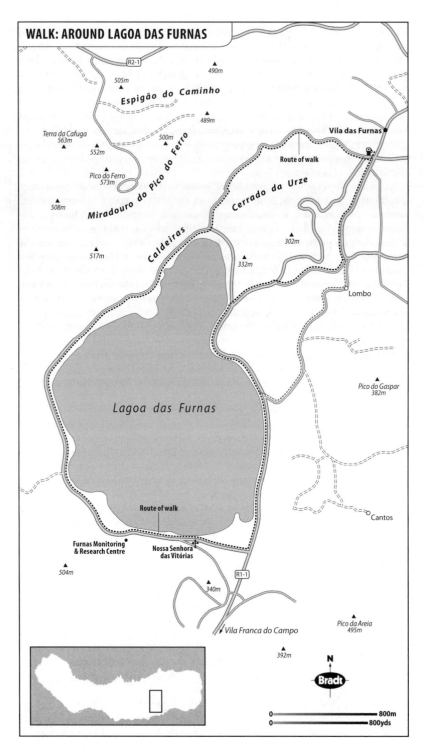

WALK: AROUND LAGOA DAS FURNAS

R2-1

505m

490m

Espigão do Caminho

489m

Terra da Cafuga
563m

500m

Vila das Furnas

Route of walk

552m

Miradouro do Pico do Ferro

Pico do Ferro
573m

Cerrado da Urze

508m

302m

Caldeiras

517m

332m

Lombo

Pico do Gaspar
382m

Lagoa das Furnas

Route of walk

Cantos

Furnas Monitoring
& Research Centre

Nossa Senhora
das Vitórias

504m

R1-1

340m

Vila Franca do Campo

Pico da Areia
495m

392m

N

Bradt

0   800m
0   800yds

cement road leads off very steeply up the hill. Take the cement road. Regrettably there has been an asphalt outbreak and what was a simple farm track is now surfaced, but there is virtually no traffic and the scenery remains as lovely as ever. Keep to the main route until it bears strongly round to the left with a good track on your right going steeply up into the shade of a belt of trees towards the top of the ridge. From here the road very quickly goes down the other side to the lake. You will smell sulphur and may notice steam coming from fissures in the banks. Now you have a choice of how long a walk you want to make; approximate times are given from the petrol station.

Option (b) (*Time: about 3½hrs; distance: about 11km*) To walk around the lake, turn right and pass the cooking area of the famous **Furnas Cozido**, and straight ahead come to a gateway. Simply continue along this track, first along a small stream, following more or less the edge of the lake. You will have noticed an old house by the water on the far side, and a chapel. These once belonged to the family of José do Canto, who created here yet another fine garden. There are many fine old camellias, some magnolias and a fern gully, but alien species have invaded and it is interesting to imagine how beautiful it must have been more than a century ago. Access is available only with the owner's permission. The road continues to join the main south-coast road from Ponta Delgada, which has so far been left in its original cobbled state. Turn left to complete your circuit of the lake, but some distance after the road has left the lake on its descent into Furnas you come to a low wall painted white on your right running alongside the road. Where it begins there is a wide asphalted track going steeply down. If you take this it is a short cut into the village.

Option (c) (*Time: about 2hrs, starting from the Furnas garage; distance: about 5km*) For the fastest return to Furnas, leave the lake in a clockwise direction to join the main road into Furnas. Take the short cut described above.

Option (d) (*Time: about 4hrs, starting from the Furnas garage; distance: about 12km*) As for option (b) but after you have left the chapel and are walking along the main road and before it starts to drop down towards Furnas, you will see a road off to your right, cut through the scoriae hillside. Follow this to enter a very pretty area with a domed hill, the Pico do Gaspar. Take the road round to your left in a clockwise direction, and take the road going off on your left that goes steeply uphill. When you emerge from the cryptomeria trees at the top of the hill, the road turns steeply down to your left. Before following this, just walk ahead for a short distance to get a beautiful view of Furnas. The steep road down to Furnas takes about 15 minutes, but be very careful because it is very easy to slip on the loose stones.

Rui Medeiros – Local Guide
Private Tours to discover the beauty, nature
& culture of the Azores Islands
www.azoresprivatetours.com

The 5 self-contained cozy cottages of Quinta dos Curubas overlooking
Vila Franca on São Miguel offer a comfortable stay in rural surroundings.
Whale watching and other excursions/activities can be arranged.

Information & Reservations: geral@quintadoscurubas.com
+351 96 17 39 880 or +351 96 251 51 89
www.quintadoscurubas.com

4

Santa Maria

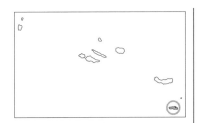

Santa Maria sees itself as the sun island, claiming that, being a little further south and east than all the other islands, it receives more sun and sea temperatures are higher. Statistics support this, and certainly it has been very sunny on every visit I have made. Where the airport is located and sheep graze the surrounding land, the area is flat and relatively arid. This changes rapidly on the approach to the central peak of Pico Alto, the highest point at 590m. Here once more is the typical Azorean green forest with cryptomeria trees and pittosporum mixed in places with native shrubs. Then comes the eastern half and its idyllic, picturesque, tranquil, verdant landscapes of woodland and pastures. These may be sprinkled with glimmering white traditional houses that are either scattered, in little clusters or in small villages. In places there are no buildings at all, or perhaps just a time-weathered basalt shelter tucked away in a corner of a field. There are dramatic coastlines, proud headlands and sheltered bays, and a novelty for the Azores: white sand. This island supplies the potters on São Miguel with some of their clay, and from deposits at Santana and Figueral came the lime to whitewash all the archipelago's houses.

To hire a car and meander along almost empty winding roads through such glorious countryside, stopping for views and parking the car at the end of a farm road and just exploring to the sound of birdsong, makes for a wonderful three or four days' holiday. High sea cliffs provide precipitous views and you can drop down to the coast at Maia and São Lourenço for sea swimming in manmade pools with their own natural wave machine. In contrast, the dry, flat western sector of the island is an altogether different landscape. Between exploring these environments you have the white sandy beach at Praia Formosa, and the sea pools at Anjos in which to relax. Other places of interest include the little chapel at Anjos associated with Columbus's first landfall on his return from the Americas and the quite remarkable stone terraced vineyards at Maia, an extraordinary work of such great skill and energy you are left wondering at the effort humankind is prepared to make to produce wine! And the amazing red soils and almost desert landscape of Paul da Serra.

BACKGROUND

GEOLOGY Although Santa Maria has not suffered any earthquakes during historical times and has no fumaroles or hot springs, and its original volcanic structures are partially eroded or completely destroyed, the island has features unique in the archipelago.

It has many outcrops of sedimentary rocks including limestones, conglomerates and sandstones, often with abundant and diversified fossil content. It is the only island where several major outcrops of pillow lavas can be seen, sometimes in well-preserved layered sequences. Pillow lava is hot fluid magma that erupts underwater

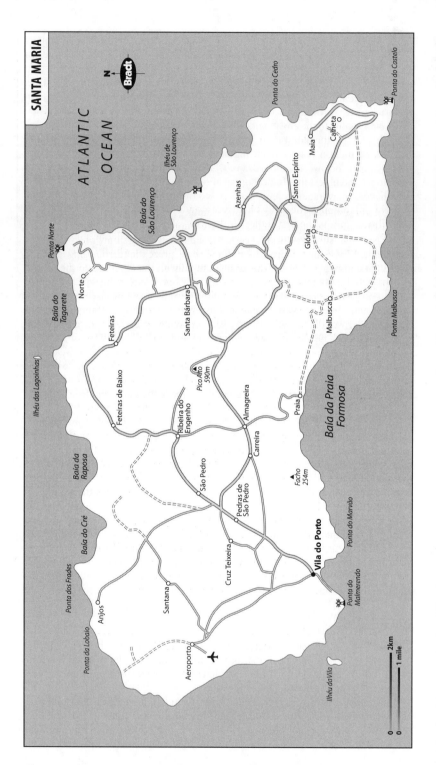

SANTA MARIA

ATLANTIC OCEAN

124

rather like toothpaste coming out of a tube, which then rapidly cools upon contact with the water and forms heaps of pillow or cushion-like structures up to around 1m across. Finally, being volcanic in origin as with all the other islands, it offers its own interesting volcanic structures and landscapes. Not only known for its sunnier climate, its beaches are also more like those typically associated with seaside resorts rather than the black gritty volcanic beaches largely found elsewhere in the archipelago. Their light colour is due to the erosion of carbonated rocks, ie: sedimentary limestone.

Santa Maria is the oldest island of the Azores and emerged from the sea around eight to ten million years ago, having been built up from basaltic eruptions from about 2,000m below current sea levels. That some lava flows include layers of sandstones and limestones indicates that at some point the island subsided. Erosion and changes in average sea level has exposed these marine sediments intercalated with volcanic outputs. The oldest basalts are around Vila do Porto – very appropriate, since this town was the first settled in the Azores. Following closely are the lavas from Pico Alto, which is one of a series of peaks that together define a north–south alignment separating a distinct quite flat area in the west which is very dry and poor in vegetation. To the east is a younger mountainous and hilly area very much greener with higher rainfall.

Outcrops of fossil-bearing marine sediments can be seen on the north coast and cliffs of Baía do Cré and Baía da Raposa, just east of Anjos, and along the south coast between Vila do Porto and Baía da Praia Formosa. The Barreiro das Feneca or Red Desert, east of Anjos and Monte Gordo, reminds one of the vast red landscapes of central Australia. It is an arid area of Pliocene (5.2 to 1.64 million years ago) sediments composed of clay minerals on top of a lava flow from the Pico Alto complex. The soils and vegetation, however, developed in a cover of very thin pyroclasts (small fragmentic rocks and ash) coming from the most recent explosive eruptions. The resultant altered clay is red owing to the oxidation of the volcanic products through the alternating warm and humid and contrasting dry periods of the Pliocene. Wind erosion has levelled the areas where there is no vegetation cover. The Barreiro da Malbusca, in the south between Malbusca and Ponta da Malbusca, is an old elevated beach, where nodules of manganese typical of an ocean floor can be found. Nodule minerals derive from the interaction of hot, upwelling, metal-bearing solutions at a plate boundary with organic sediments and grow very slowly; a centimetre can take well over a million years.

HISTORY Santa Maria is generally considered the first island of the archipelago to be discovered by the Portuguese, sometime between 1427 and 1432, and is so named because it was sighted on the Feast of the Assumption of Our Lady. It was also subsequently the first island to be settled. The initial settlement was made in 1439 by people mainly from the Algarve and Alentejo, on the northwest coast at a place named Praia do Lobos, just west of what is now Anjos, by the Ribeira do Capitão. This river is now called Ribeira de Santana. However, between 1460 and 1474, Vila do Porto became the principal administration centre of the island. Exports were woad and urzela for dyeing. In the 16th century, land in the west was developed for wheat. Santa Maria became a commercial satellite of São Miguel and sent to the larger island wheat, orchil, pottery clay and cheese. Needless to say, during the 16th and 17th centuries, French, Turkish and Moorish pirates attacked and destroyed the settlements many times. By the 19th century, demand for Santa Maria's exports had dwindled and emigration increased. It was the American wartime airbase built in 1944 that brought real change, and later it became an international airport for transatlantic flights; in 1977, it received its first visit from Concorde. Currently it is an air-traffic-control centre for the north Atlantic. The population has dropped considerably owing to emigration: in the 1960s, it had around 14,000 inhabitants; now it is down to some 6,000.

GETTING AROUND

There is a very limited island bus service on weekdays linking some of the villages, mainly for bringing people into Vila do Porto in the mornings and returning them late afternoon, which is of little help to the visitor. My experience is the drivers do not expect tourists as passengers so if you are alone at a bus stop they tend to drive past and not stop. You can use a taxi, but this is an island best explored with a self-drive car.

For travel to Santa Maria, see pages 47 and 53.

WHERE TO STAY

There are now three conventional hotels: one in town and two about 35–40 minutes' walk outside Vila do Porto. If you have a car, then this is not a problem, otherwise I would recommend staying in town. There is also some rural accommodation. For location of towns, see map page 124.

Hotel Colombo (88 rooms) Cruz Teixera, Vila do Porto; ☎296 820 200; e santamaria@colombo-hotel.com; www.colombo-hotel.com. Facilities include a restaurant, bar, coffee shop, pool, gym, Turkish bath, jacuzzi, massage & children's room with inflatables, PlayStation, ping-pong, etc. There is also bicycle hire. The building is an awful intrusion into the landscape, but it is a comfortable hotel. €€€€

Hotel Praia de Lobos (34 rooms) Rua M Assunção, Praia de Lobos, Vila do Porto; ☎296 882 286; www.hotelpraiadelobos.com. Good-sized rooms, very light & airy in a building sympathetic to local architecture; bar, convenient location in Vila do Porto. €

Hotel Santa Maria (50 rooms) Rua da Horta, Vila do Porto; ☎296 820 660; e reservas@ hotelsanta-maria.com. Built on the site of the old wartime officers' mess near the airport, this hotel has the advantage of all being on ground-floor level, each room with access to a large garden & a short walk to the pool & tennis courts. The bedroom floors are tiled & this strikes cold and uninviting in winter, but could be an advantage in summer because this part of Santa Maria can be hot. Facilities include a restaurant & bar. €

The Tourism Authority lists three addresses offering rural accommodation, including:

Casa São Pedro (4 rooms) Termo da Igreja, São Pedro; ☎296 884 044; e garajau@ virtualazores.com. This is a rebuilt family-owned manor house on the São Pedro road 3.5km from Vila do Porto. On the upper floor leading from an inner covered courtyard are en-suite rooms: 2 twins, 2 doubles. There is a guest lounge with TV, garden & pool, & horses for experienced riders. Their excellent restaurant, Rosa Alta, is 100m distant. €€

YOUTH HOSTEL
Rua Frei Gonçalo Velho, Vila do Porto; ☎296 883 592; e santamaria@pousadasjuvacores.com. Brand new & just 800m from the port.

CAMPING
Å **Praia Formosa** Near the sea; all facilities; restaurant nearby in village.

✖ WHERE TO EAT

VILA DO PORTO
✖ **Central Pub** Rua Dr Luís Bettencourt; ✆296 882 513. Does pizza & all things Italian, as well as the usual fare.

✖ **Clube Naval** ⏱ winter evenings. Down by the harbour, & has a bar. Also out on the quay, new developments include snack bars.

✖ **Restaurante Garrouchada** Rua Dr Luís Bettencourt; ✆296 883 038

✖ **Restaurante Os Marienses** Rua Cotovelo; ✆296 882 478

✖ **Restaurant Pipas Churrasqueira** Rua da Olivença; ✆296 882 000; ⏱ 09.00–midnight daily. Local cuisine.

ROSA ALTA
✖ **Pub Candeia Restaurante** ✆296 884 804. Near Cruz Teixeira. Recommended.

SÃO PEDRO
✖ **Restaurante Rosa Alta** ✆296 884 990. Located 3.5km from Vila do Porto. Excellent, with a lighter, very different menu from anywhere else on Santa Maria, plus a good selection of wines. Has a small comfortable bar for *aperitivos* & coffee.

PRAIA FORMOSA
✖ **Beach Parque** Snacks & bar, with a disco in summer.

SÃO LOURENÇO
✖ **Snack Bar O Ilhéu** ✆296 884 383; ⏱ Apr–Oct until 04.00 daily; winter Sat & Sun only

OTHER PRACTICALITIES

Emergency ✆112
Police Vila do Porto; ✆296 883 000
Hospital ✆296 820 100
Tourist information ✆296 886 355
(information office at the airport)

SATA Air Açores Rua Dr Luís Bettencourt, 9580-529 Vila do Porto; ✆296 886 501/2
Airport ✆296 886 504
Airport information ✆296 820 020/886 335

WHAT TO SEE AND DO

MUSEUMS
Dalberto Pombo Environmental Interpretation Centre (*Rua Teófilo Braga, Vila do Porto;* ✆ *296 206 790;* ⏱ *15 Jun–15 Sep 10.00–13.00 & 14.00–18.00 daily; other months 14.00–17.30 Tue–Sat. Guided tours at set times*) Founded on the collections of the naturalist Dalberto Pombo, a pioneer in the study of Santa Maria's biological and geological diversity, there are exhibits on butterflies, insects, birds and marine fossils.

FESTIVALS ON SANTA MARIA

Festas de Santo António Santo Espírito; 2nd week of Jun
Festas de São João Vila do Porto; last week of Jun
Maja Folk world music; 1st week of Jul
Blues Festival 2nd week of Jul
Festa do Sagrado Coração de Jesus Santa Bárbara; 1st week of Aug
Festa de Nossa Senhora da Assunção Vila do Porto; middle of Aug
Festival Maré de Agosto Praia Formosa; 3rd week of Aug
Festa das Vindimas São Lourenço; 1st week of Sep. *Grape harvest.*
Festa de Nossa Senhora da Anunciação Vila do Porto; 3rd week of Sep

4

Museu de Santa Maria (✎ *296 884 844;* ⊕ *10.00–12.00 & 14.00–17.00 Tue–Fri; 1 May–30 Sep also 14.00–17.30 Sat & Sun*) The island's Ethnographic Museum, located behind the church in Santo Espírito, is well worth seeing. Exhibits include early Santa Maria pottery, period household items, costumes and ethnographic items. This can be combined with a visit to the craft co-operative, Cooperativa de Artesanto de Santa Maria, for some of their delicious handmade biscuits (see *Around the Island*, page 131), since both are in the village of Santo Espírito.

WALKING There are three official trails:

Pico Alto–Anjos Medium difficulty, 14km, 4 hours. A super walk, the longest of the official trails, beginning in forest on the highest point of the island, down to red desert and to the hot, dry northwest coast. Remember to take water with you, double the amount you would normally carry because in the sun the second half of the walk can be very dehydrating.

Santo Espírito–Maia Medium difficulty, 6.8km, 3 hours. Beginning in Santo Espírito, the route takes you through woodland, pastures and vineyards passing several village artefacts and finally down to the sea at the southeast corner of Ponta do Castelo.

Entre a Serra e o Mar (Between the mountains and the sea) Medium difficulty, 9.5km, 2½ hours. A circular walk starting from the parish church in Santa Bárbara past typical houses, rural landscapes and good views. The Pôr do Sol café greets your return.

A relatively unknown walk from **Vila do Porto to the beach of Praia Formosa** is not waymarked, but is fairly straightforward, follows well-used tracks and offers terrific views from cliffs high above the sea. Parts are so lovely that visitors have been known to dally all day along its route and I am sure this will become an official trail. For further details, see page 131.

BIRDS AND FLOWERS Being the least visited by ornithologists, the island has few records, but it is home to a subspecies of goldcrest that is endemic to Santa Maria. One of the most interesting sites is the small islet of **Ilhéu da Vila** just off Vila do Porto, which can be viewed from the shore or better still a small boat. There are petrels and shearwaters, roseate and common terns and it is thought from earlier records to be the only breeding site in Europe for the sooty tern. Other islets good for birds and observable from land include **Lagoinhas** near Tagerete Bay, part of the North Coast Protected Landscape Area.

Ponta do Costelo on the southeastern corner and its designated area of 300ha combines a coastal strip of steep cliffs 200m high with an immediate offshore marine area. Known for shearwaters and Madeiran storm petrels, it is also a passage point for bottlenose dolphin and loggerhead turtle. The cliffs and stony beaches support endemic plants including herbaceous spurge, spurrey, lotus, tolpis and azorina. The *miradouro* makes an excellent place from which to look for whales.

SWIMMING
Praia da Formosa With its white-sand beach, this place is very popular in summer. There is an area marked off for surfboards and changing facilities with showers; snack bars and ice creams.

Anjos There are two pools, sunbathing areas, changing rooms and showers, and a snack bar (🕐 *summer 10.00–22.00; from Apr/May–Oct/Nov according to the season's weather*).

Maia Facilities include a sea swimming pool with changing rooms and showers, and two bars: Bar Prazeres da Maia has a restaurant and is open during the summer while the Flor da Maria at the farthest end of the bay is open all year.

São Lourenço In addition to a sea swimming pool with changing rooms and showers, and a snack bar, there are also small white beaches between the rocks.

RECREATIONAL FOREST RESERVES
Fortinhas Forest Reserve Santo Espírito. Located in the centre of Santa Maria on the western slope of Pico Alto, and noted for its tall trees which provide a cool ambience amid beautiful rural scenery. There are pleasant walks between the trees, tree ferns, azaleas and camellias; barbecue facilities and picnic shelters.

Valverde Forest Reserve A well-used and much-developed park at the edge of Vila do Porto, its 4ha are dominated by eucalyptus and cupressus trees. There is a deer enclosure.

AROUND THE ISLAND

As you travel around the island note the different house chimneys, especially the squarish ones topped with tall slender round chimney pots. Some of the parishes have their houses painted in the same colour: Santo Espírito, green; Santa Bárbara, blue; Almagreira, red; São Pedro, yellow; and Vila do Porto, tile coloured.

VILA DO PORTO Known originally simply as Porto, it became Vila do Porto in the 16th century when it was given its charter, the first town in the Azores to have this status. What is left of the old town runs uphill from the fort overlooking the harbour, now a modern port. The façades of the old grand houses give an idea of what it must have been like, together with the tiny cottages in the streets behind. All these are protected but sadly many owners of the large houses left for Lisbon in the 1950s and records have been lost, so by default their houses became very run down. They are now being redeveloped. As you walk down from town (along the Rua Teófilo Braga), look out on your left for the façade of the 15th-century building that supposedly belonged to Governor João Soares de Sousa. It may be recognised by its Gothic windows. Nearby houses have interestingly carved lintels and other details. The **Fort of São Brás** was built in the 17th century and of course provides a good view out to sea; with the cannon in position it is a fertile place to imagine early events. If you are staying at the Hotel Praia de Lobos then a stroll down to the fort after dinner is a pleasant ending to the day. In summer the cooling evening contrasts with the still-warm stones and makes a different but parallel smell to rain on sun-scorched earth. If you have time, take the old cobbled road down to the port and continue right round to the end of the *mole* (breakwater); there is a splendid view of the fort.

The modern part of the town, which starts roughly around the beginning of the Rua Teófilo Braga, is a linear development which looks as if it will go on growing longer. All the usual small shops are here including several small-scale supermarkets, and a market, just by the Hotel Praia de Lobos. The square in front of the town hall

4

might give it some future focus. If the **Câmara Municipal** is open, do step inside for a peep as it is a grand building. It was the first Franciscan monastery to be founded in the islands by the monks who came with the settlers; it grew wealthy, was looted, then rebuilt, then finally converted into a town hall. This is a history repeated throughout the islands, the converted uses also being hospitals and charities.

At the opposite end of the town there is a **forestry park** with a children's play area, picnic tables and washrooms beneath pine trees. There is also a small, sterile aviary and some alert-looking deer. A belvedere offers a view of Vila do Porto and the immediate countryside.

THE AIRPORT No, not quite, but the area surrounding it! This is limestone country and was once the most productive wheat area. Now the modern civilian airport takes a large percentage of the land, while beyond the boundary remains of the wartime airfield linger in the form of old Nissen huts and concrete slabs. There is also the big radio station, and much new housing greatly in need of tree planting to soften it. The old officers' mess was the only hotel on Santa Maria until recently; it burned down a few years ago, and has been rebuilt. Now the farmland is down to cattle that are thought by the locals to be better eating than those on the higher pastures, and Romney Marsh sheep, farmed for wool, and originally imported from England. If you leave the airport road and take the minor road to Santana you pass through this utterly different countryside; in the height of summer when all is brown and the sun blazes down it can seem quite hostile, but in October/November to May it is green. From Santana the road continues and joins the main road down to Anjos, but before it does you pass through an area of acacia forest which shows a splendid example of wind pruning.

SÃO PEDRO This small village near Vila do Porto is noted for its *mata-mouras*, literally 'moor killers'. These are pits in the ground once used to hide grain and other desirables from pillaging pirates.

ANJOS Once a tiny fishing village, Anjos then became a centre for tuna; now the factory is closed. The little bay has recently been very nicely developed for swimming. The island of São Miguel, 52 nautical miles away, can be seen on the horizon. On the roadside above is a picnic site with barbecue facilities.

The village is historically very significant as the first landfall of Christopher Columbus on his return from the Americas. A modern statue commemorates the quincentenary of this event (1493–1993). The Chapel of Nossa Senhora dos Anjos is possibly the first place of worship built in the Azores, being 15th century and rebuilt in the 17th century and again restored at the end of the 20th century. The small chapel has a triptych (recently restored) representing the Holy Family, St Cosmas and St Damian which, according to tradition, is from Gonçalo Velho's caravel. The iron rod displayed on the pulpit was a weapon used by pirates. On the outside wall is built a porch dedicated to the Holy Ghost; bread is distributed from here on the feast day.

SANTA BÁRBARA This is among the prettiest parishes of the island; in July/August the roadsides are flaming with orange-red montbretias and yellow gingers and there are photo opportunities every 200m. There is wonderful silence apart from the occasional crowing of a cockerel.

SÃO LOURENÇO BAY On the northeast coast, the bay is well worth visiting for the spectacular descent by road down the cliff face. On the way down, stop at the

Miradouro do Espigão for a splendid bird's-eye view of the bay and its cliffside vineyards. There are swimming facilities.

SANTO ESPÍRITO A pretty village surrounded by pastures and green hills. The **Church of Nossa Senhora da Purificação** is well worth visiting and must rate among the best kept of all parish churches. Go inside and be welcomed by the scent of wax-polished floors and pews with a gilt chapel reflecting sunshine from the windows. Originally constructed in the 16th century and beautifully restored in 1966, it is 17th-century Baroque with stone ornamentation on the front façade. It is also noted to be the church linked to the first Holy Ghost festivals in the Azores. The **museum** is located behind the church. For handicrafts, the local **Cooperativa da Artesanato de Santa Maria** sells delicious bread and *biscoitos* from its own bakery, and from several looms traditional woven items. Find it about 400m into the village from the church, past the games area and almost opposite the school. There is a snack bar in the village.

MAIA Many of the houses are now holiday homes, but there are still fishing boats on the quay of the tiny harbour. It is the stone terracing for grapevines that is truly amazing. Walls enclose areas just a few metres square and these reach up the cliffside almost until it becomes vertical. At intervals there are very narrow stairways between the vine enclosures running in straight lines up the cliff face to provide access. A book of photographs of the stones of Maia is for sale at the Santo Espírito Museum. The wine, purely for local consumption, is *vinho de cheiro*, plus a very pleasant sweet *aperitivo*. There are swimming facilities plus a restaurant and a bar.

PICO ALTO The side road up to the highest point of the island, at 590m, leaves the main road between Almagreira and Santo Espírito where it forks to Santa Bárbara. Here the landscape is utterly different from anywhere else on Santa Maria, as you ascend through dense cryptomeria plantations to arrive at a tiny summit with fine views and where some native plants can be found. There is a memorial to those who were killed when an Italian passenger jet clipped the summit as it was preparing to land.

PRAIA FORMOSA In a wide bay at the foot of steep cliffs is a very clean, pale sandy beach with rock pools at the eastern end, and it is the best-known swimming beach. Commercial development is really quite limited compared with a similar situation elsewhere in the world, and the road, with parking, runs along behind the beach. Vineyards tumble down the hillside to meet it. There is a small apartment hotel and campsites. In the close-by village there is a restaurant. At the western end are the remains of the 16th–17th-century Fort of São João Baptista, which the sea has almost demolished. In summer the cliffs here, normally dark with pittosporum and myrica trees, are marked with 4m-tall yellow flower spikes of agave.

WALK

VILA DO PORTO TO THE BEACH OF PRAIA FORMOSA (*Time: 2½hrs; distance: 11km*) Walk always with the sea to your right.

Starting in the Fort de São Brás, face the little church and round to the left you will see a low stone wall. Until recently there was an abattoir here, and landscaping the site should by now be finished. On the other side of the low wall you should see or be able to pick up a well-trodden path taking you down and across the Ribeira

Grande and diagonally up the opposite side. On the shore you will see some old machinery and ramps, the Calhao da Ropa; this was where the Caterpillar machines were brought ashore for the construction of the wartime airport. Inland, higher up the *ribeira*, are the remains of old watermills. Continue on the track that goes round in front of the wind turbines. As you pass the turbines, you see a volcanic hill ahead, the Facho de Vila, that is being slowly demolished for rocks and gravel for building materials.

As the main track bears left, take the smaller track off to your right to walk on the seaward side of the mountain. If you miss the path it does not matter because the main track simply goes round the hill on the landward side. Follow this grassy road between two stone walls and soon you will see Praia Formosa with its sandy beach and above, just before the bay, the Miradouro da Macela. It is made of black stone and is a little difficult to see against the hillside. This is your next objective. The track joins a main dirt road with some concrete farm buildings; you continue right. Look out on your left in the field for an old stone construction; this is an old *barro*, or kiln, used for firing roof tiles and other ceramics. The road takes you to a swooping valley with brilliant white houses: the village of Fonte do Mourato. When you come to a small track off to the right, take this to come to the main asphalt road just above the *miradouro*. Go down this road a short way to another asphalt road going off to the right which takes you straight down to the sea and past the ruins of an old fort fast losing a final battle against the sea, and so along to the seaside amenities of Praia Formosa.

Part Three

CENTRAL GROUP

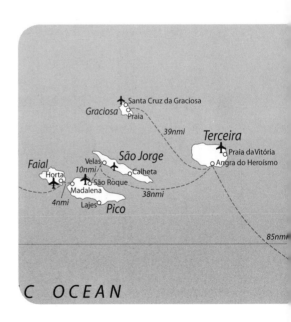

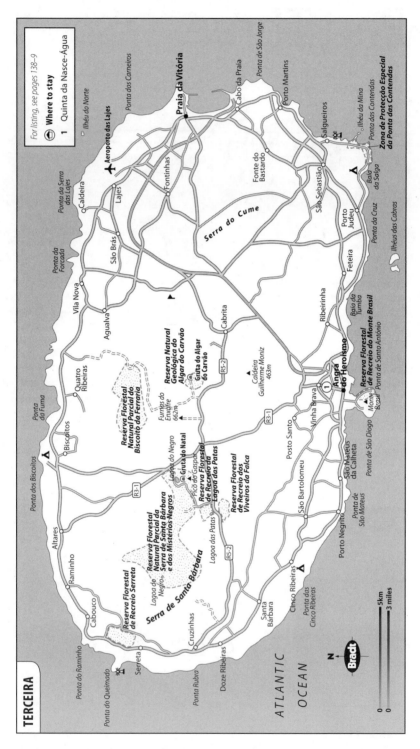

TERCEIRA

For listing, see pages 138–9

Where to stay
1 Quinta da Nasce-Água

Zona de Protecção Especial da Ponta das Contendas

Aeroporto das Lajes

Praia da Vitória

Serra do Cume

Reserva Natural Geológica do Algar do Carvão
Gruta do Algar do Carvão

Caldeira Guilherme Moniz 463m

Furnas do Enxofre 662m

Reserva Florestal Natural Parcial do Biscoito da Ferraria

Reserva Florestal Natural Parcial da Serra de Santa Bárbara e dos Mistérios Negros

Reserva Florestal de Recreio da Lagoa das Patas

Reserva Florestal de Recreio dos Viveiros da Falca

Reserva Florestal de Recreio Serreta

Serra de Santa Bárbara

Gruta do Natal

Pico do Gaspar

Lagoa do Negro

Lagoa das Patas

Lagoa do Negros

Reserva Florestal de Recreio do Monte Brasil
Monte Brasil

Angra do Heroísmo

Ponta dos Biscoitos
Ponta da Fuma
Quatro Ribeiras
Biscoitos
Altares
Raminho
Cabouço
Serreta
Ponta do Raminho
Ponta do Queimado
Ponta Rubra
Santa Bárbara
Doze Ribeiras
Cruzinhas
Ponta das Cinco Ribeiras
Cinco Ribeiras
São Bartolomeu
Porto Negrito
Ponta de São Mateus
São Mateus da Calheta
São Mateus
Ponta de São Diogo
Vinha Brava
Ponta de Santo António
Posto Santo

Agualva
Vila Nova
Ponta da Forcada
São Brás
Caldeira
Lajes
Fontinhas
Ponta da Serra das Lajes
Ilhéu do Norte
Ponta dos Carneiros
Ponta de São Jorge
Porto Martins
Cabo da Praia
Ponta da Praia
Salgueiros
Ilhéu da Mina
Ponta das Contendas
Baía da Solga
São Sebastião
Porto Judeu
Ponta da Cruz
Feteira
Ribeirinha
Cabrita
Fonte do Bastardo
Ilhéus das Cabras
Baía da Tumba

ATLANTIC OCEAN

N

Bradt

R3-1
R5-2
R5-2
R3-1

0   5km
0   3 miles

above Capelhinos on Faial was the site of the 1957–58 eruption and now hosts a widely acclaimed visitor centre
(SS) page 191

left The bubbling hot springs and mud pools of Furnas draw many visitors to taste some of the 22 different mineral waters
(SS) pages 112–13

below The famous crater lakes on the west of São Miguel, timeless, and glorious to explore
(AMA/S) page 107

above   Cafés and restaurants along the marina at Ponta Delgada are popular at night and often have live entertainment (SS) pages 101–7

left   The 19th-century Nossa Senhora da Conceição at Santa Cruz das Flores is one of the most substantial buildings in the town (SS) page 228

below   An important stop-over for yachts crossing the Atlantic, Horta's picturesque seafront and harbour give fabulous views of the Monte de Guia promontory (MH/S) pages 193–7

above Involved patterns of carefully laid flowers, chopped conifers and coloured wood shavings prepare the way for the Nossa Senhora de Piedada procession at Ponta Garça, São Miguel (SS) pages 90–1

left Introduced in the 18th century, tea is still produced commercially on São Miguel and is much sought by connoisseurs (SS) page 110

below *Cozido nas caldeiras* is a delicious stew, prepared using vegetables and several different meats and gently cooked in the ground for about seven hours (SS) page 113

above left	The *tourada à corda* is the Portuguese version of bullfighting, but the bull is not harmed (SS) page 40
above right	Bread is distributed to the poor during the festival of Espírito Santo (JD/D) pages 38–9
right	For a different swimming experience try the iron-rich warm-water pool at Terra Nostra garden (GB/D) page 86
below	Religious processions take place in many villages and towns throughout the islands and draw large crowds (SS) pages 90–1

above Yellow pimpernel, found in damp grassland in the mountains, is one of some 60 plant species that are endemic to the Azores (SS) page 260

left Steep sea cliffs are important nesting sites for Cory's shearwater (SS) page 10

below Exotic tropical rhododendrons from the mountains of Malesia thrive in the sheltered garden of Terra Nostra (CC) page 86

above left   Only swans ripple the water and disturb the tranquillity of the heritage gardens of Terra Nostra (CC) page 86

above right   Almost extinct, numbers of the rare Azorean bullfinch are now increasing thanks to intensive conservation work and protected habitats
(YB/S) pages 10 and 96

right   There are no native land mammals on the archipelago, but cattle were introduced in the 15th century
(SS) page 18

below   The sperm whale is the largest of all toothed whales: males can measure up to **20m** (SS) pages 12–15

archipelago° choice

EXPLORE THE
AZORES

Walking Holidays

Discover the natural beauty, from crater lakes to spectacular coastal walks

Whales & Dolphins

The Azores is one of the premier whale & dolphin watching sites in the world

Family Holidays

Fascinating sealife & a wealth of activities that will be enjoyed by all the family

Step into your own
tailor made adventure

YOUR HOLIDAY.
YOUR ADVENTURE.

5

Terceira

Terceira is best known for two things: the international airport and American airbase at Lajes and the historic UNESCO World Heritage Site of Angra do Heroísmo. This is unfair because, like all the other islands, there is much else waiting to be discovered for those not in a hurry. There are lovely villages, really wild country in the centre, volcanic caverns, vineyards, comfortable places to stay and a golf course. It is an ideal island on which to hire a car and explore at your own speed.

It is easy to spend a whole day seeing the historic buildings of Angra do Heroísmo together with the fort opposite and the whole of Monte Brasil. The drive around the beautiful west coast looking in at villages and charming museums is another joy and, if you choose to linger, a day is easily spent. The wild centre is a must, too; more or less in the middle of the island is the region known as Terra Brava, the Wild Land, and aptly named because of the bewilderingly broken country and dense vegetation in places. The island's highest point is Santa Bárbara, at 1,021m, in the west, and almost every day the summit is hidden in cloud. Its upper 300m is covered with typical scrub vegetation of juniper, erica, ling and bramble. On the northwest side of Santa Bárbara is the Serreta Forest, a mix of planted cryptomeria and eucalyptus and large patches of remnant native vegetation with endemic Azorean species. It is a good area for birds. Praia da Vitória is another town to explore, smaller and very different but no less charming, and if there is time seek out the view from the top of the Serra do Cume across the whole of the eastern part of the island. Between May and September some 220 Azorean bullfights will take place on the island so there is a fair chance you will experience one – remember, the bull is not killed or even wounded; it is the young men who run the risk of damage.

BACKGROUND

GEOLOGY The oldest part of Terceira, composed of basalts from the last million years, is below sea level, plunging down more than 1,500m deep to the seabed; it comprises 90% of the island. The remaining tenth is much younger. Like São Miguel, Terceira is made from four volcanoes, the oldest being Cinco Picos which covers much of the southeast, a stratovolcano that was once a steep-sided cone made of layers of lava. Its collapsed caldera is the largest in the Azores, about 7km across, and was formed some 300,000 years ago but it is now considerably eroded. The Serra do Cume in the northeast is the largest remnant, and the Serra da Ribeirinha is all that is left of the opposite rim, and between the two is the largest flat area in the whole of the Azores, disturbed only by five younger cinder cones in the crater bottom, the 'Cinco Picos'.

Behind Angra do Heroísmo is Guilherme Moniz Volcano, another stratovolcano with a collapsed caldera. The crater's south edge forms the Serra do Morião crescent which is still obvious and forms the hills seen looking north from Angra. In contrast, the north side of the crater has been completely destroyed by eruptions of the neighbouring Pico Alto Volcano, whose lava flowed into the Guilherme Moniz crater, a rare occurrence of lava forming the floor of another volcano. The vertical cave called Algar do Carvão was formed around the same time, about 2,000 years ago. Pico Alto was also responsible for the grey, acidic rock and the more than 60 domes seen to its north behind Quatro Ribeiras and Lajes. Domes form when lava is very viscous and does not easily flow, and so accumulates in the vent.

Around 23,000 years ago, present-day Angra was covered by a Plinian eruption, a powerful explosion of gas, steam, ash and pumice followed by avalanches of hot gas, ash and rock debris. Associated with this were two later Surtseyan volcanoes, when seawater entered the vent to mix with the rising magma and the resulting steam caused the magma to shatter into fine fragments. These two formed Monte Brasil, creating the historically significant bay and associated anchorage and, just to the east, off the coast opposite Feteira village, the now much-eroded Ilhéus das Cabras.

In the west is the Santa Bárbara stratovolcano, about 12km in diameter at sea level, with a caldera that collapsed 25,000 years ago and collapsed further forming a smaller caldera inside some 18,000 years ago. This volcano's oldest eruptions suggest that there were many lava flows with cinder cones and spatter, cinder-sized lava fragments that are still molten when they hit the ground and therefore flatten, forming 'cowpats'; these can meld together and make steep-sided mounds, mostly less than 10m high. The latest eruptions over the last few thousand years on the flanks of Santa Bárbara are associated with trachyte flows, a pale greyish acidic rock whose molten viscosity can form rugged lava flows and domes, in this case more than 85 domes.

Between Santa Bárbara and Pico Alto activity along the Terceira Rift (see page 7) created cinder cones and lava flows. Flows from Pico Gordo, located by the main road between Angra and Altares, reached the north coast to form the jagged black reefs of the Ponta dos Biscoitos and, now exploited, the Biscoitos vineyards. Along the same road, by the crossroad to Doze Ribeiras, the cone of Bagacina typifies the cinder cones, and between the two, near Lagoa do Negro, is a spatter cone.

In historical times, two eruptions occurred in 1761. The first created the Mistério Negro, near Pico do Gaspar, and the second, a few days later, a collection of cinder cones including Pico do Fogo, just to the east of Lagoa do Negro. The main Angra–Altares road runs conveniently between the two. In 1998 there was a submarine eruption 10km west of Terceira in a small area known as the 'Serreta High'. Surface signs were plumes of smoke coming from floating lava debris as it cooled. The basalt magma is rich in gases that are trapped inside, creating 'balloons' which float upwards towards the ocean's surface. As they rise the gases inside expand and cause the 'balloons' to explode. The debris floats on the surface for about 15 minutes and sinks when seawater enters as it cools. When great volumes of gas rise to the surface the sea becomes pale green, and it is very dangerous for boats, since they could easily sink. This surface evidence is not continuous, and its absence reflects quieter periods of submarine activity. The earliest eruptions detected were at 400m below sea level, and the magma subsequently has risen to 180m.

HISTORY Originally known as the Island of Jesus Christ, the island was later named Terceira or Third Island since it was the third island to be 'discovered'; it is also the third in size. The first settlers in about 1460 were led by a Fleming, Jácome de Bruges, with the first settlements around Porto Judeu and Praia da Vitória. Like the other islands, farming became of paramount importance with cereals and woad the prime crops. For centuries it was the most important island because of its sheltered harbour, protected by Monte Brasil. In 1534, Angra was the first settlement in all the Azores to be formally designated a town and the same year Pope Paul III made it the seat of the bishopric. Terceira was a stronghold of resistance to the Spanish authorities when they annexed Portugal in 1580, holding out for the Portuguese claimant, Dom Antonio, who was being helped by the French. It was the last Portuguese territory to submit to Spanish rule, when the Spaniards defeated the French fleet at Terceira in 1582, overrunning the island the following year and inflicting a terrible retribution. As a consequence of the later 16th- and 17th-century Spanish exploitation of the New World, the island's harbour became even more important. Ships bringing back gold and silver at this time assembled off Terceira to form a convoy for escort to Cadiz, to reduce the danger of attack by pirates from the north African coast. Later in the 17th century, this practice ceased and the island's economy plummeted, followed by emigration to Brazil. After Portuguese liberation in 1640, the islands became a staging post for British trading ships, until the opening of the Suez Canal in 1863. Oranges also came to the rescue and their export led to renewed prosperity, but as in the other islands their demise led once more to further emigration.

Along with São Miguel, Terceira played an important role in the struggle of the Liberals and Absolutists; at one time Terceira was the only Liberal stronghold in all of Portugal. In 1829, the Absolutists attempted to land at what was then called Vila da Praia and their defeat was marked by the new name of Praia da Vitória. In 1832, it was from Terceira and São Miguel that the Liberal forces from the Azores left for northern Portugal in their fight against the Absolutists. In 1766, the government of the Azores had been unified and based in Angra, which remained the capital of all the Azores until 1833 when the islands were divided into three districts. For a short time that year it was also the capital of Portugal when King Pedro IV was in residence – commemorated by the change of name to Angra do Heroísmo.

Lajes airport was constructed in 1943, for the Battle of the Atlantic and as a transit point for airborne troops flying to Europe, and today contributes to NATO's strategic role. It has three runways, the largest 3,600m long, and is used by both civil and military aircraft.

On New Year's Day 1980, a severe earthquake inflicted substantial damage, affecting also Graciosa and São Jorge. Many of the important buildings in Angra do Heroísmo were badly damaged and have taken years to painstakingly restore. In 1983, Angra was declared a UNESCO Historic World Heritage Site.

GETTING AROUND

If you are without a car, and especially if you are making a short visit, then the best place to stay is Angra, because in addition to that city, you can visit Praia da Vitória which makes a pleasant excursion wrapped around a good lunch. Or, of course, stay in Praia da Vitória, which is near the airport, and visit Angra. There is a regular on-the-hour bus service between 07.00 and 19.00 from the main square in Angra to Praia da Vitória which takes less than an hour and is a pretty drive around the southeast corner of the island. The bus stops opposite the fire station. Walk back in the direction from which the bus came and you soon come to a big junction; turn left and you are in town along the Rua de Jesus. The return bus is from the same stop, leaving again on the hour, between 06.00 and 19.00. Charles Darwin, when the *Beagle* put in at Angra for a brief visit on the journey home in September 1836, also made the excursion to Praia, on horseback.

There are also less frequent buses to Biscoitos leaving from in front of the public garden, departing at 07.45, 10.30 and 13.00 Monday to Friday, returning at 13.00,

14.30 and 17.30; the route goes round the coast and takes 1½ hours. It is, however, an island much better enjoyed if you have your own transport.

For travel to Terceira, see *Getting there and away*, page 47, and *Getting around*, pages 52–4.

 WHERE TO STAY

The main hotels are in Angra, and in Praia da Vitória which is just five minutes' drive from the airport. In Angra there is a city hotel conveniently on the main square, a small one by the harbour, a five-star near the marina and two neighbouring resort hotels about 20 minutes' walk along a busy main road west of town. Then there are numerous *residenciais* and some manor houses within driving distance. For location of listings see maps, pages 145 and 153.

HOTELS
Angra do Heroísmo

🏠 **Pousada São Sebastião** (28 rooms) Forte de São Sebastião; e guest@pousadas.pt; www. pousadas.pt. Formerly the Castelo de São Sebastião dating from 1555, overlooking the Bay of Angra; pool, terrace restaurant. €€€€€€

🏠 **Hotel Angra Marina** Porto das Pipas; ☎295 204 700; e reservations@angramarinahotel.com; www.angramarinahotel.com. The recently built first & only 5-star hotel in the Azores overlooks the marina; all rooms have a sea view. Indoor & outdoor pools, spa & private shuttle to the golf course. €€€€€€

🏠 **Hotel Terceira Mar** (139 rooms) Portões de São Pedro, São Pedro; ☎295 402 280; e terceiramarhotel@bensaude.pt; www.bensaude. pt. By the sea in a bay, 20 mins' walk to the centre of Angra. Restaurant, bar, gymnasium, & splendid outdoor pool next to the sea, tennis courts, jacuzzi, Turkish bath, sauna, massage, hairdressers. Very comfortable. €€€€€

🏠 **Angra Garden Hotel** (120 rooms) Praça da Restauração; ☎295 206 600; e angrahotel@ mail.telepac.pt; www.angrahotel.com. Restaurant, bar, lounge, health club, sauna, indoor pool, gymnasium, private parking. On the town's main square it is perfectly sited for the exploration of Angra. Rooms to the rear are quiet, overlooking one of the best public gardens in the Azores. €€€€

🏠 **Hotel do Caracol** (100 rooms) Estrada Regional, Silveira; ☎295 402 600; e hotel@

hoteldocaracol.com; www.hoteldocaracol.com. At the western end of Angra, about 30 mins' walk from the centre, with views across the small bay to Monte Brasil & out to sea. Restaurant & bars, health centres & spa, massage, therapy treatments, anti-stress programmes, sauna, jacuzzi, 2 gymnasia, squash, adults & children's outdoor pools, indoor heated pool. Sea bathing with access by ladder, & by the old boat ramp. €€€€

🏠 **Hotel Beira Mar** (23 rooms) Largo Miguel Corte Real; ☎295 215 188; e reservas@ hotelbeiramar.com; www.hotelbeiramar.com. Excellent restaurant. Located by the harbour, which could be noisy in summer. €

Praia da Vitória

🏠 **Hotel Apartamentos Praia Marina** (268 apts) Av Beira Mar/Largo José S Ribeiro Santa Cruz; ☎295 540 055; e reservas@ hotelpraiamarina.com; www.hotelpraiamarina. com. Overlooking the beach. Allergy-free rooms & apartments with equipped kitchenettes. €€

🏠 **Hotel Varandas do Atlântico** (30 spacious rooms) Rua da Alfândega; ☎295 540 050; e reservas.verandas@mail.telepac.pt; www. hotelvarandas.com. In front of the beach, 50m from the main square & the marina, 5 mins' drive from the airport. Some rooms balconied, some with connecting rooms for children. Excellent service, & a good alternative to staying in Angra. €€

MANOR HOUSES
🏠 **Quinta da Nasce-Água** [map page 134] (10 rooms) Lugar da Nasce Água – Vinha Brava, 9700-236 Angra do Heroísmo; ☎295 628 501.

Some of the rooms are in the house, some in adjacent cottages. A gracious house set amid rolling hills & pastures, with a charming formal garden, there is a 20m 3-level swimming pool, & tennis court, Turkish bath & golf training. A short taxi ride takes you to the centre of Angra, or every 30 mins there is a public bus or it's about 20–30 mins' walk. Dinner by arrangement. €€€€€

🏠 **Quinta de Nossa Senhora das Mercês** (6 rooms, 1 suite, 1 self-catering house) Caminho de Baixo, São Mateus, 9700-559 Angra do Heroísmo; ☎ 295 642 588; e geral@quintadasmerces.com; www. quintadasmerces.com. Between Angra & São Mateus it is a short drive to either town. The farm goes back to the 16th century, & the manor house together with its chapel was built in the 17th century. Set between the sea & woodland it has various common rooms, breakfast & dining room, library, games room & an inner courtyard. Outdoor pool & tennis court in a remarkable stone-walled enclosure with an all-weather artificial grass surface. There are 4 rooms with private garden, 2 with a sea view & 1 suite, Turkish bath, jacuzzi, gymnasium & woodland walks. Also a self-catering house with 2 bedrooms, kitchen & living room. Dinner available upon request 24hrs in advance. Probably the top manor house in all the islands, favoured by a reigning monarch (albeit the whole house), it is a place for a special occasion. €€€€

YOUTH HOSTEL
🏠 **Pousada de Juventide de Angra do Heroísmo** (70 beds) Negrito, São Mateus; ☎ 295 642 095; e pja.angra@oninet.pt. Also has 1 family

🏠 **Quinta do Martelo** (10 rooms) Canada do Martelo, São Mateus da Calheta, just west of Angra; ☎ 295 642 842; e quintamartelo@mail. telepac.pt; www.acores.com/quintadomartelo. Not a sophisticated manor house but a private & remarkable crafts centre, once an orange farm. The numerous outbuildings have been set up as a series of workshops including blacksmith/farrier, tinsmith, carpenter, joiner, cooper, cobbler, basket maker, weaver, broom maker, & even a barber's shop. It is a good historical exposition of the everyday life of a rural homestead. There is a restaurant with a splendid ambience, providing traditional & festive meals cooked on wood-burning stoves with home-baked bread. The owners' idea is to give their guests a feel for the atmosphere of a rural house on Terceira while providing comfortable accommodation. Less traditional are the swimming pool, tennis court, gymnasium & sauna, but they also have traditional Azorean games. Not a luxury stay, but a very interesting one & utterly different. Each room has a bathroom, all are differently furnished, & accommodation is provided in 2 houses. Rates include car hire with unlimited kilometres. €€€

room with bathroom. About 25km west of Angra, near the sea. €

CAMPING
🅰 **Baía de Salga** Near Porto Judeu; ☎ 295 905 451. Good facilities including electricity. Sea swimming. Closed in winter. Popular, necessary to book in high summer.

🅰 **Biscoitos** Good site with amenities.
🅰 **Cinco Ribeiros** On the southwest coast; ☎ 295 907 200. All-year campsite on grass beneath tamarisk trees. Full amenities, including laundry.

✖ WHERE TO EAT

There are many restaurants and much competition so choice is generally wider on Terceira than the other islands. Too many to list, those given below are just a few pointers. Don't forget the restaurants in the main hotels; on a lovely summer evening, try the *pousada*. Some village restaurants are also mentioned under the car tours described later in this chapter. For location of towns and listings see maps, pages 134 and 145.

ANGRA DO HEROÍSMO
✖ **Adega Lusitânica** Rua de São Pedro 63–65; on the road between Angra & the 2 resort hotels; ☎ 295 212 301

✖ **Beira Mar** By the harbour; ☎ 295 642 392

SÃO MATEUS
A short drive from Angra, or an even shorter one from the two resort hotels.

✗ **Adega São Mateus** Opposite the church;
📞295 642 345
✗ **Quinta do Martelo** Cantinho; 📞295 642 842.
Good Azorean food in a typical farmhouse setting; reservations advisable.

ALTARES
✗ **Restaurante Caneta** 📞295 989 162. It is tight on the right-hand side of the road with a not very obvious sign, on the corner of the Canada José Romeira. The small bar entrance leads to a charming garden area & upstairs is the restaurant. Recommended.

SÃO SEBASTIÃO
In the southeast, about a 15-min taxi ride from either Angra or Praia.

✗ **Os Moinhos** Rua Arrebalde, 9700-610 Vila de Sâo Sebastião; 📞295 904 508; ⊕ Nov–Mar closed Tue. Restaurant with terrific ambience in a converted watermill. Charcoal-grilled meat & fish, an excellent *alcatra*, & make sure you keep room for the *sobremesas*, delicious desserts including a chocolate mousse to travel for; finally a wine list, the best I have seen in the Azores. Prices are sensible, yet service comes with panache, & if the downstairs restaurant is busy the owner will open an intimate upstairs room for that special dinner. In winter, wood-burning fires. If you are staying in Angra or Praia, then it is well worth the 15-min taxi ride, but better reserve a table. Widely considered as probably the finest restaurant in the Azores.

OTHER PRACTICALITIES

Emergency 📞112
Police [145 E2] Praça Dr Sousa Junior, Angra;
📞295 212 022
Hospital [145 E1] 📞295 212 121
Tourist information [145 D3] 📞800 296 296
SATA Air Açores [145 D2] Rua da Esperança, Angra; 📞295 212 016

TAP Air Portugal [145 C2] Rua da Sé, Angra;
📞295 216 489
Airport information 📞295 540 047; lost & found, 📞295 540 032

FESTIVALS ON TERCEIRA

The Holy Ghost Festival held on the eighth Sunday after Easter takes place not only in Praia da Vitória but also all over the island in villages wherever the crown of the Holy Ghost is held, either in church or in a private house. The Vine and Wine Festival in Biscoitos on the first weekend of September marks the grape harvest and also offers traditional foods. There are also many more, smaller celebrations held all over the island for saints' days and secular events. Praia da Vitória has a nine-day gastronomic festival over two weeks in early August.

Carnaval all over the island; last week of Feb
10 Bodos Praia; May. *First event of the Holy Ghost Festival.*
Espírito Santo different parts of the island; May to Sep
Touradas á corda throughout the island; May to end of Oct
Angrarock Jun. *Rock Festival; see www.angrarock.com*
São João all over the island; 24 Jun
Festa de Sanjoaninas Angra; Jun. *Includes many cultural activities & evening entertainments.*
Festas da Praia Praia; 4–10 Aug. *Commemorates Praia's designation as a city; food fair with Spanish regions represented, bull running, concerts & exhibitions.*
Festival de Folclore, Gastronomia a Etnografia Angra; Aug
Angrajazz; 1st week in Oct. *Jazz Festival; see www.angrajazz.com*

WHAT TO SEE AND DO

MUSEUMS
Angra do Heroísmo
Museu de Angra do Heroísmo [145 E2] (*Ladeira de São Francisco;* ⏰ *10.00–12.00 & 14.00–17.00 Tue–Fri, additionally May–Sep 14.00–17.30 Sat & Sun*) Housed in the old Convent of São Francisco, once the headquarters of the Franciscan order of the Azores, the building itself is well worth the visit. Furniture and military exhibits are included in the permanent displays and there are frequently changing exhibitions.

Os Montanheiros [145 E1] (*Sociedade de Exploração Espeleológica, Rua da Rocha 6/8;* ☎ *295 212 992; www.montanheiros.com;* ⏰ *summer 10.00–16.00 Mon–Fri; winter 09.00–12.30 & 13.30–17.00 Mon–Fri*) The geological museum and headquarters of this very enthusiastic and active society; to view are topographical models of the islands, photographs and rock specimens.

Around the island
Museu do Vinho dos Biscoitos (*www.Casaagricolabrum.com;* ⏰ *10.00–12.00 & 13.30–16.00 Tue–Sun, Apr–Sep until 17.30 Tue–Sun; closed during the 3rd week of Sep during the grape harvest; admission free*) Good small private museum showing most interesting details of the family business and wine production going back over 100 years. There are small demonstration vineyards, and other fruit orchards.

Quinta do Martelo (*Centro Etnográfica e Gastronómico, Canada do Martelo, Cantinho, São Mateus;* ☎ *295 642 842;* e *quintamartelo@mail.telepac.pt; www.acores. com/quintadomartelo*) This is a private museum and restaurant just west of Angra with an excellent exposition of the traditional way of living. Open only to residents, and diners upon request. Telephone booking essential.

WALKING There are five official trails:

Mistérios Negros Difficult, 5km, 2½ hours. A circular walk from the Gruta do Natal, beside Lagoa do Negro. You will see plenty of native plants before you get to a difficult stretch over some recent lava deposits.

Baías da Agualva Easy, 4km, 2 hours. With a bit of road walking at the end this can be a circular walk between Agualva and Quatro Ribeiras in the middle of the north coast, offering good birdwatching.

Serreta–Lagoinha Medium difficulty, 7km, 2½ hours. A circular walk including the lake of Lagoinha, and plenty of native flora. Care is needed at some steep places.

Monte Brasil Easy, 7.5km, 2½ hours. Beginning and ending at the Relvão park, by the Spanish fort.

Relheiras de São Brás Easy, 5km, 2 hours. A circular route from the picnic area in São Brás, near Lajes airport, revealing old oxcart tracks, evocative of earlier times.

On Terceira feedback suggests one should keep a wary eye open for bulls; these are not typical farm animals, but those raised for the Tourada à Corda. The **Mountaineering Society** offers a guided walk between March and October from

09.30 to around 17.00 on Sundays. Walks are announced a month in advance with details available from the Montanheiros Museum (*www.montanheiros.com*); you will need to be reasonably fit and with transport to get to the start of the walk.

BIRDS AND FLOWERS A mix of bird hides and urban recreation is to be found near the town centre of Praia da Vitória. The coastline here was once the largest coastal wetland in the Azores, but when the town expanded most was destroyed. Now only a small area remains, the Ponds of Praia or Paúl Environmental Park, but they have recently been cleverly improved and are certainly effective as an urban landscape enhanced by habitats for waders, several species of waterbirds, herons, egrets and terns.

The best-known site among dedicated birders is a rather grotty disused quarry at **Cabo da Praia** that supplied the stone for the harbour at close-by Praia da Vitória in the 1980s. If you are visiting for the birds and not the scenery then it is regarded by many as the best place in Europe for spotting western Nearctic and Palearctic waders as well as ducks, egrets and seabirds; it is also an important breeding site of the Kentish plover. However, one informant tells me that it is necessary to visit the quarry at the correct time since tidal times are important to your chances of success. The special thing about this quarry is that it was dug to a depth where the sea seeps through fissures in the rock and enters from underground. Water does not come over the cliffs from the sea just 100m away, but the twice-daily sluicing in rhythm with the tide has created a remarkable wetland habitat. Protected from the wind and excellent for waders, species usually seen only in Africa and North America seem to be able to find this quarry so if you visit two to five weeks either side of mid-September and go during the two- to three-hour period either side of low tide you could be rewarded with very interesting sightings. As yet, it has no protected status, and the salt plants, weeds and grasses will add quite a few species to a holiday plant list.

To salve your aesthetic sense drop down to the Special Protected Area of **Ponta das Contendas** and the **Baía das Mós**, the southeast corner of Terceira. Originally there was a 500m-long peninsula created by lava flow and through erosion and chemical change it is now discontinuous, the furthest point being Ilhéu da Mina. Many species of both resident and migratory birds may be seen, but it is botanically uninspiring.

As compensation, botanists will be pleased that **Lagoa do Negro** and the surrounding **Mistérios Negros** is mentioned here for their benefit alone. West of centre, this remarkable volcanic area has formed a swamp and other special ecosystems rich in mosses and lichens; of special interest are the bog-lovers *Littorella uniflora* and *Isoetes azorica*. However, if birders continue on towards **Pico Alto**, 808m high with a collapsed caldera, woodcock and snipe might make a change from their usual observational menu.

SWIMMING Around the coast there is a mix of semi-natural rock pools and artificial pools, many with WC and changing rooms open in summer. The long sand beach at **Praia da Vitória** is popular, as is the smaller one on the other side of the marina. In **Angra** there is a small beach near the marina with facilities, a beach with a long history, for it was used for careening ships.

Silveira By the Hotel do Caracol at the western end of Angra, with a public bathing area in the deep inlet protected by Monte Brasil.

Negrito With harbour swimming facilities, changing rooms and a small café/bar.

Ponta das Cinco Ribeiros Harbour swimming, changing rooms and a small café/bar. Campsite nearby.

Biscoitos Natural rock pools amid interesting volcanic rock formations; changing facilities available.

Baía das Quatro Ribeiras Natural swimming pool, changing facilities and nearby campsite.

Porto Martins Near the harbour. A natural swimming pool, like a conventional pool but with a wave machine! There are changing rooms and a restaurant.

Salgueiros Sea swimming with changing facilities.

Baía de Salga Near Porto Judeu. Sea swimming with changing facilities. Campsite nearby.

GOLF
✓ **Club de Golf da Ilha Terceira** Fajãs Agualva, 9760 Praia da Vitória; ✆ 295 902 444/299; e reservas@terceiragolf.com; www.terceiragolf. com; closed Mon, email for tee-off times; green fees for non-members: daily pass €30; set of clubs inc trolley €20; clubhouse with restaurant open to non-members, small pro shop. Designed by Cameron & Powell & opened in 1954 at 350m above sea level, it is set in another Azorean landscape of tall trees, lakes, colourful azaleas & hydrangeas & with its wide fairways is reckoned to be the easiest of the 3 Azores courses. 18 holes, par 72. Handicap requirements: men 28; ladies 36. There is also a driving range & golf lessons are available.

GARDENS The Duque da Terceira Garden is a charming historical urban space with some interesting plants, located in the centre of Angra (see pages 69 and 146 for details).

RECREATIONAL FOREST RESERVES Monte Brasil, the volcanic peninsula overlooking Angra do Heroísmo (see page 147), and Serreta Forest (see page 150).

AROUND THE ISLAND

The programmes suggested below take a total of three days, but can certainly be done in less time. Alternatively, you can easily select your own itinerary from the notes. Angra do Heroísmo is a must and will take you a morning. You could then spend the afternoon and early evening on Monte Brasil. Travelling slowly around the west coast to Biscoitos will never fail to delight, passing through small villages and past many houses, their whitewashed exteriors sparkling in the sun, even when the hills of the interior are covered with cloud. Including the museums and a reasonable lunch this will take an easy day. If the skies are clear or the clouds are not too low then a day could be spent exploring the wild hinterland, with many old volcanic cones and extensive areas of broken and tumbled land covered in grasses, mosses or tree heathers. This gives the opportunity to judge which day to do what, according to the weather. Since almost every visitor goes to Angra, the two car tours begin from the city.

ANGRA DO HEROÍSMO Given the setting and Renaissance urban planning, it is difficult not to slip back through time to the period when Angra was the centre of the Atlantic universe. Trading and treasure ships gathered and passed through here from both the East Indies and the New World, and the town grew ever more prosperous. It was central, too, to the Azores archipelago until usurped by Ponta Delgada. Ban the cars, change the shop windows, clamber into period costume, and all you need is a pirate ship to come sailing into the bay! Well, perhaps not quite, but it is fun to wander around at night when the streets are empty, and allow the imagination to fly.

The Duke of Cumberland's flotilla of English corsairs sank the Spanish galleon *Nuestra-Señora de Guia* off Terceira in 1589, an example of just one of almost 900 ships recorded lost from various causes in the Azores in the past 500 years. In the Bay of Angra alone there are some 80 shipwrecks, the deepest lying in 60m of water, the oldest from 1543. Angra provided the safest haven but, when storms blew in from the southeast, it became a dangerous dead end and disastrous for those ships too slow or unable to leave in time. It seems there are few doubloons to be found because any treasure was recovered soon after the shipwreck since such losses would severely impact upon the Portuguese and Spanish economies. These wrecks, however, represent the most marvellous sites of marine archaeology, time capsules because of the suddenness of their demise. There is now an underwater wreck trail.

Although no-one wants to live in a theme park, what a stimulating centre Angra could become for the study and interpretation of a most exciting and vivid period of history. The exploration, exploitation and colonial expansion of new lands and the maritime consequences of politics and war on mainland Europe could become a major visitor site like the new one at Faial's Capelinhos.

Angra city tour During summer several of the buildings are open to visitors. Begin at the centre of the city in the **Praça Velha** [145 D2], the most attractively paved square with a Renaissance influence. At the western end and built in the 19th century is the **town hall** [145 D2], which is open to visitors and has one of the largest and finest great halls in the whole of Portugal. Leave the square by the Rua Direita and almost immediately on your right is the balconied house of the **Count of Vilaflor** [145 D2], later Duke of Terceira, commander of the Liberal armies and leader of the Liberal army at the Battle of Praia in 1829. The visual unity of the front elevation is satisfying, but I do not think the count would have approved of the condom dispenser on the wall along from his front door! The house is open to visitors. The Rua Direita is Angra's first main street and leads from the harbour directly to the main square and to the governor's house a little beyond.

At the lower end of the Rua Direita on the left is the dominating 18th-century **Misericórdia church** [145 D3]. The first hospital in the Azores was built on this site in 1492, supported by the Brotherhood of the Holy Spirit; one of the founders was João Vaz Corte-Real, Governor of Angra, who is thought to have been the first to discover Newfoundland. The present building dates from the 18th century, built by an association of the earlier brotherhood and a charitable institution, the Misericórdia. Badly damaged in the 1980 earthquake, it is again open to visitors. Further round the harbour wall the small sandy beach was once the site of the shipyards that supported the early trading ships. The new yachting marina, begun in 2000, is seen by many as an ugly intrusion and violation of a historical patrimony, and when the constant metallic rattling from the masts of berthed yachts disturbs the night air historical reverie can be difficult.

Walk round until you come to the blue-and-white-painted building behind which is a flight of stairs taking you to the upper road. Take the Rua Carreira Cavalos, the Way of the Horses, so named because a festival devoted to the horse

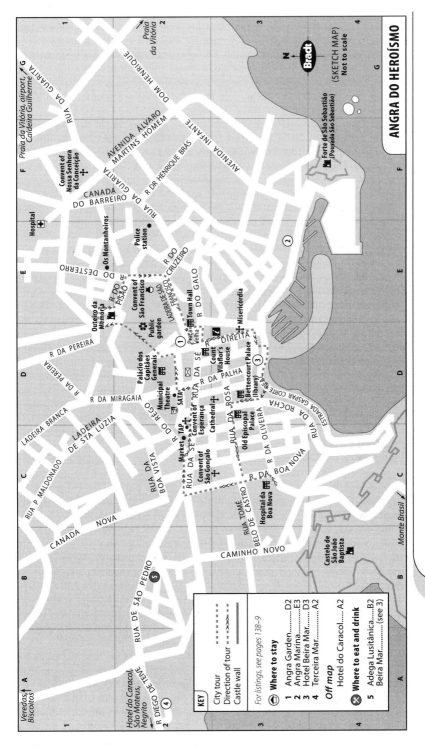

ANGRA DO HEROÍSMO

(SKETCH MAP)
Not to scale

KEY

- - - - - - City tour
- >>>>> - Direction of tour
━━━━━ Castle wall

For listings, see pages 138–9

① Where to stay

1 Angra Garden	D2
2 Angra Marina	E3
3 Hotel Beira Mar	D3
4 Terceira Mar	A2

Off map

Hotel do Caracol.....A2

✕ Where to eat and drink

5 Adega Lusitânica	B2
Beira Mar	(see 3)

was held here; at the far end on the right-hand corner is the **Bettencourt Palace** [145 D3]. Built at the turn of the 18th century, it has a fine portico above which is the Bettencourt family coat of arms. It is now a public library and open to visitors. On the other corner is the **old Episcopal Palace** [145 D3], with little remaining of the original dating from 1544. If you are interested in embroidery, before you turn right, go along the Rua da Rocha, past the **Montanheiros Museum**, and find the showroom **Açorbordadas** (⊕ *09.00–18.00 Mon–Fri, 14.30–18.00 Sun*).

After the Bettencourt Palace go along the Rua da Rosa and at the end you are outside the walls of the massive **Convent of São Gonçalo** [145 C3], founded in 1545 for the nuns of the Order of St Clare. It is Angra's oldest and the largest in the Azores. The small side door should be unlocked, and it is well worth entering. There are figured choir stalls, 18th-century Portuguese tiles, a 17th-century silver crucifix, paintings and an ornamental ceiling.

Turn left at the crossroads along the Rua da Boa Nova to quickly find the **Hospital da Boa Nova** [145 C3], a military hospital built by the Spanish for the soldiers stationed in the castle.

Retrace your steps and continue straight along the Rua Gonçalo Cabral passing the modern sports centre on your left. At the main road turn right along the Rua da Sé to come to the cathedral church of Angra, **Santíssimo Salvador da Sé** [145 D3], founded in 1570. Of interest are the 16th-century painted panels, the Indo-Portuguese-style lectern made in the Azores of Brazilian jacaranda wood and whale ivory, and the altar's early 18th-century silver antependium made on Terceira. The church was finished in 1618 while Angra was under Spanish dominance, and its craftsmanship is influenced by Flemish, local and Spanish Baroque styles. There is also a museum of religious objects.

Continue down the road, taking the first turning off left to find the splendid **Palácio dos Capitães Generais** [145 D2]. The original building was a Jesuit college, and the island's governor had it modified during the second half of the 18th century and made into a palace. Two kings have stayed here: King Pedro IV in 1832, and King Carlos I in 1901. The interior is richly decorated and is open to visitors (⊕ *10.00–12.00 & 15.00–17.00 Mon–Fri*).

Nearby you will see the entrance to a public garden, the **Duque da Terceira Gardens** [145 D2]. Initiated in 1862 as an experimental garden for agricultural development, it 20 years later also provided space for public use, which became a garden that was enlarged in 1888. This garden was developed by a Belgian, Francisco J D Gabriel, who began his early horticultural career in a Liège nursery before coming to the Azores aged 18 to work on São Miguel. He managed the garden for 15 years, until his death in 1897. A wonderful urban period garden of the late 19th century, it was noted in its heyday for its many exotic ornamental species. In February/March the magnolias are at their best and, of course, never get damaged by spring frosts. If you walk through the garden you can climb the steps that take you steeply up to **Outeiro da Memória** [145 E1], the Memorial Hill.

This was the site of the first fort built in the Azores around 1474; the obelisk was erected in 1846 in memory of King Pedro IV. The reward for making the climb is the fine view over Angra and across to Monte Brasil.

Go out of the garden and take the small road off on the right, the Rua do Pisão. Once there was a stream flowing in this area, and early in the town's development this was put into an open conduit and served for some 500 years the industries that sprang up alongside: watermills, tanneries and other enterprises. The narrow winding streets here are fun to explore and at the bottom you come to the **City Museum**, housed in the **Convent of São Francisco** [145 E2]; the entrance is off the Ladeiro de

São Francisco, the road running up from the main square beside the public garden. The building alone is well worth seeing, and the museum offers permanent displays about the Azores and temporary exhibits. After, you can simply walk down the hill to the square where this walk began, or go up the hill, the Rua da Guarita, to see the impressive exterior of the 17th-century **Convent of Nossa Senhora da Conceição** [145 F1], built in the 16th century with 17th- and 18th-century alterations. According to the contemporary account by Edward Boid, when in 1832 King Pedro gathered his supporters in Angra prior to his invasion of Portugal, the monasteries were converted to military barracks but officers left the convents untouched: conventual infamy was shocking and the Conceição convent became the most fashionable resort of faithless husbands and amorous celibates, with the nuns in amorous communication through the grated windows and 'the grass was worn away under every window of this convent by the frequency of these communications'.

MONTE BRASIL [map page 148] During the Spanish occupation Sir Francis Drake unsuccessfully attacked Angra and eight years later, in 1597, the Earl of Essex with around 100 ships failed to seize a fleet of Spanish treasure galleons anchored in the bay. To defend the harbour against such attacks and at the same time secure control of Angra, King Filipe II constructed the Fort of São Filipe at the foot of Monte Brasil, later given its more familiar name of **São João Baptista**. The exterior wall is 4km long and some 400 artillery pieces defended it. Three other smaller forts along the coast, including that of São Sebastião, provided crossfire so completing the defence. Inside the fortress is the **Igreja de São João Baptista**, commemorating the restoration of Portuguese sovereignty in 1640 and the governor's palace.

If you are in a hurry, then drive or take a taxi up to **Pico das Cruzinhas** to enjoy the view of Angra. You can clearly see the old historical core; look for the last-century pyramid erected on the first fort to be built, then below the governor's palace, the Santissimo Salvador da Sé church, then down to the harbour at the bottom of the Rua Direita to the Misericórdia church. To the right on higher ground is the conspicuous Convent of São Francisco; to the left is the Convent of São Gonçalo, close to the large modern indoor sports complex. Note also the 17th-century Castelo de São Sebastião that once protected the eastern approaches, now a *pousada*. To the left, westwards, is an area known as Caminho de Baixo where the rich people of Angra once had their summer houses. Behind you on the grass mounds are British gun emplacements from World War II. The tall stone cross and the surrounding wall again incorporating the cross is a typical monument that the Portuguese built wherever they landed and claimed new lands; this one was erected in 1946 commemorating the five centuries of settlement in the Azores.

Here you can spend a very enjoyable full day exploring this old volcanic hill on foot, walking easily from the centre of Angra, or from Pico das Cruzinhas. You can also incorporate a guided visit of the Fort of São João Baptista, starting daily on the hour during summer.

Following the surfaced road, these are some of the walks you can do. The first signposted side road will take you to the little chapel of **St Antonio** at the end of the asphalt road. From here to the end of the unsurfaced track it takes about 45 minutes to walk there and back; you will have good views of Angra and views eastwards of the south coast. Alternatively, from near the chapel, you can take the signposted trail as described in the Tourism Authority's trails booklet.

Return to the main road and continue until you reach the rim of the caldera. The caldera itself is used by the military and you are not allowed to go down. Look for the signpost to the **Vigia da Baleia**; it takes about an hour to walk there and back.

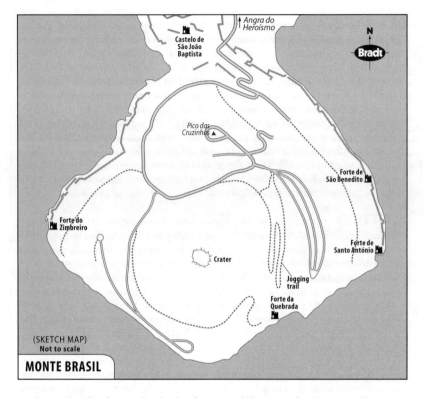

It is a good walk often in the shade of trees, and the reward is a commanding view seaward; if you have binoculars and the time, try your hand at whale watching. You can also walk in the other direction up to **Pico do Zimbreiro**, Juniper Peak, on the west side of the caldera. The junipers have long gone, but endemic laurel and heather remain.

When you return to the main road continue round the caldera until you come to another large track on your right. There is a children's play area, picnic tables and a WC. From here it is another very pleasant walk up to **Pico do Facho**, Signal Peak, the highest point of Monte Brasil at 205m. For four centuries it was a semaphore station; the lookout used large and small flags to signal the number of vessels approaching and from which direction.

THE WEST-COAST TOUR: ANGRA DO HEROÍSMO TO BISCOITOS

São Mateus Just two miles west of Angra is this pretty village and harbour, one of the most important fishing harbours in the Azores. Between 16.00 and 17.00 the boats land their catches to sell on the quayside. The colourful little boats create a cheerful scene and there is a small fort overlooking the harbour. Take time, too, to explore the nearby backstreets. There are two good fish restaurants.

Negrito This is a small village with an old fort by the harbour, with swimming facilities and a small café/bar. An old small trying area has been preserved where in basalt are the fireplaces and pots for reducing the whale blubber. On the nearby headland is Terceira's youth hostel. As you continue, you should be able to see São Jorge on the horizon.

Cinco Ribeiras Soon on your right is Azulart, Estrada Dr Marcelino Moules, the **ceramics studio** of Aurelia Rocha (℡ 295 907 034; http://azores.home.sapo.pt/ azulart_cinco_ribeiras-terceira.htm). Her pots are all wheel-thrown and in stoneware are traditional Terceiran designs, and in earthenware traditional shapes and designs of the Azores. All are hand painted, and commissions are accepted. Reflecting the enterprise needed for life on an island in mid-Atlantic, she has built her own kilns. Ceramics in the early days on Terceira used clay imported from England, shipped over in the empty sailing boats coming for the orange crop, and clay is still imported from the continent as the island clay from Santa Maria does not take glazing and can be used only for *alcatra* pots and similar that do not need a glaze.

Further on, on the left, is the **Canada do Pilar**, a narrow road between houses going down to the coast. The small factory making *vaquinha* cheese (🕐 08.00–22.00 *Mon–Fri, 15.00–22.00 Sat & Sun*) is along here, where you can sample and buy the three cheeses made and enjoy a coffee and the delicious traditional small cake of Terceira, made by a lady in the village. *Queijo vaquinha* is the traditional cheese. It is made with salt only on the outside and sold in small blocks like butter. O Ilha cheese, the cheese of the island, has the salt incorporated into the milk, and *queijo vaquinha picante* has red peppers added. The dairy does not make any butter, so all the milk, not separates, goes into the cheese. Cheese was first made on Terceira in 1912, and *vaquinha* translates as 'small cow'.

At the end of the road you get to **Ponta das Cinco Ribeiras**, a harbour with swimming facilities, also the remains of a small fort that the sea has almost washed away. Close by is a camping site under trees with electricity and amenities.

Rather than return to the main road, you can continue parallel with the sea following always the asphalt road. It is a very pretty drive through a landscape of stone-walled fields and pastures, and eventually you will come to Pézinho da Senhora, a recently developed parking area with picnic tables and barbecue facilities, and an old-style oven for people to use who no longer have them in their modern houses. There is also a bullring, and the red-painted boards with white circles are the only means of defence from the bull! The arena is also used for music and folklore events.

From the picnic area take the road going inland and the left fork to quickly come to a little chapel with white tiles, with an adjacent large house on the Largo Nossa Senhora da Ajuda. There were no springs in this area, so water was at a premium. To the left of the large house is a small cistern; you will see steps going up to a small door. Look inside and you can see where a bucket can be lowered into the water, stored from rainfall falling onto the roof. The name Pézinho da Senhora comes from a rock in the river that has the imprint of a girl's foot; follow the steps down on the right of the chapel and you will see a small grotto, where the *senhora* is supposed to have appeared. The large house next to the church, originally a small priest's house but later enlarged, was for pilgrims to stay visiting these miraculous places, an equivalent to a *Romeiro* house on São Miguel.

Continue on the asphalt road to come into Santa Bárbara. If you missed all this, you can pick it up turning from the main road signposted to Largo Nossa Senhora da Ajuda, opposite the Mercado Bárbarense.

Santa Bárbara As you continue around the coast you come to the farming community of Santa Bárbara, with its white-painted houses so startlingly bright in the sunshine. The Spanish colonial influence in the architecture of the parish church suggests the 16th century. Inside there is a 17th-century organ from the Convent of Nossa Senhora da Conceição in Angra and the furniture in the vestry is made from jacaranda and other tropical hardwoods. You can find beautiful New-World woods used in often unexpected places, brought to the Azores as ballast. Near the church is a café and a 19th-century *império*.

Doze Ribeiras Some 200m before the church on the right-hand side of the road look out for the oldest house; there is no sign. In front of the stone building is a large tank for rainwater with a half-dome catchment roof; on the roof there is a washing tub and pots used for bread making. There is an oxcart, a windmill that would have ground *burra de milho* or donkey corn, used for feeding farm animals; note the sheets of zinc on the corn store to keep the rats away. In summer there are folk-dance performances. Nearly all the adjacent small houses were built with the help of the Portuguese military for the elderly unable to afford to rebuild after the disastrous earthquake in 1980. Houses are painted annually for the Holy Ghost or summer festivities.

Serra de Santa Bárbara Beyond Doze Ribeiras take the right-hand R5-2 turning inland, eastward, to the impressive volcanic area behind Santa Bárbara. Look on the left-hand side of the road for a signpost to Serra de Santa Bárbara; take this side road (5km) to go to the top of the mountain where, if the weather is clear, you may see the most beautiful views of Terceira Island. Return to the main road and turn right to rejoin the main road running along the coast.

Serreta This is a small village with its important Church of Our Mother of Miracles where promises are made by people from all over the island. Beyond the village you will come to a sign to a *farol* or lighthouse which makes a nice walk, or you can continue to Raminho and take the trail back to the lighthouse. It was off this stretch of coast that the undersea Serreta Volcano was recently active, and the volcanic bombs could be seen coming to the surface. Roughly midway between Serreta and Rominha lies the much-visited Serreta Forest Recreational Reserve; of some 15ha, it provides numerous trails to picnic areas. The *Chafariz da Pomba* or Dove fountain is the focus for the feast of Nossa Senhora da Serreta from 13 to 18 September, peaking on *Serreta Monday* with afternoon bullfights.

Raminho The signposted Miradouro do Raminho is a substantial viewpoint looking along the coast and is a good place for seabirds, with WC, parking and picnic tables beneath the trees. There is also a *vigia* (a simple lookout shelter) for spying whales. In the distance on a clear day you can see São Jorge and Graciosa.

Altares The local **museum** (⊕ *14.00–17.00 Wed–Sun*) is just past the blue-and-white church. This is a small village with an excellent restaurant, the Restaurante Caneta (for further information, see page 140). You will see a hill on the coast called Pico de Altares (on maps called Matias Simão) with a monument at its summit. This was once a *vigia*. If you have time, climb to the top (153m) for the view along the coast.

Biscoitos This area was always intriguing because of its volcanic origins and black lava; *biscoito* means 'biscuit'. This came from the last eruption in 1761, when lava flowed down from the area around Pico do Gaspar. It was also known for its *Verdelho* wines, and is again becoming recognised in the Azores for its wine production and wine museum. Francisco Maria Brum (1860–1928) first began making wine over 100 years ago and was the first to graft grapes after the disastrous

Phylloxera outbreak that decimated the vines. The years between 1910 and 1960 saw the maximum production. The family make white wines including a special small production of only 500 litres. However, by the time it is put into bottles only 400 litres are left, so it goes into half-bottles to provide 800 for sale! The museum is on your left as you turn into Biscoitos village.

At the end of the village there is a small roundabout; turn left towards the sea to view the vineyards, the tiny walled enclosures called *curraletas*. There are also natural rock pools for swimming. Turn east to continue parallel with the sea. Near the harbour are changing facilities for more natural swimming pools. Left of the harbour is an unsurfaced track leading westwards along the coast; this is a pleasant walk above the rocks. Turn left to rejoin the main road and when you again come to the wine museum turn right to take the main road inland to Angra. In July and August this road is made spectacular with all the flowering hydrangeas.

THE WILD HINTERLAND TOUR, WITH PRAIA DA VITÓRIA Setting out from Angra, take the R3-1 road heading across the interior of the island for Biscoitos. At the crossroads near Pico do Gaspar turn left to take the R5-2 leading to Doze Ribeiras; this road is called the Estrela dos Ribeiros. Continue until the road off to your left, signposted to São Bartolomeu; take this to reach a forestry park with picnic tables beside a lovely clear and sparkling stream beneath lofty cryptomeria trees. There is also a forest nursery here.

Returning to the Doze Ribeiras road, turn left and continue as before for a short distance to the turning off on your right to Lagoa do Negro; it goes across to the R3-1. This is a beautiful road, particularly in July and August when much of its length is lined with hydrangeas. First passing pastures, you soon enter wild country with native vegetation, especially the area called **Mistério Negro**, an extensive area of black cinders thrown out by the last major eruption on Terceira in 1761. You will find the Lagoa do Negro on your right, and opposite is a stone house by the road. This is the entrance to the cave, the **Gruta do Natal** (⊕ *20 Mar–31 May 15.00–17.30; Jun 14.30–17.45; Jul–Aug 14.00–18.00; Sep 14.30–17.45; 1 Oct–17 Oct 15.00–17.30; admission adult €8*), a 697m-long, branched lava tube with stalactite- and stalagmite-like structures.

Continue on the same road until you come to a major junction. Turn right to go to Angra (left goes to Altares, opposite to Biscoitos). Just before you get to the crossroads you came to earlier, take a left turning to an area for car parking where there is a *tentadeiro*, an area where bulls are selected for the bullfight. On summer mornings you are likely to find plenty of activity here.

Now continue on the main road to the crossroads. At the crossroads, turn left towards Cabrito. If you would like a sharp reminder that you are on a volcanic island, then take the wide road you soon come to on your left signposted to Furnas do Enxofre; this road ends in a turning area. The route can be slippery so take care. A small path leads in about 15 minutes' walk to several small caves. Do not enter these or be tempted to explore them – the gases emitted are very dangerous. You will find the ground quite hot, and steam emissions have often turned the grass brown. The area is a geological protected zone. This was the first of the two excursions Charles Darwin made on Terceira when the *Beagle* put into Angra on their homeward voyage.

Return to the main road and continue, taking a turning on your left, signposted to Algar do Carvão. The **caves** (⊕ *31 Mar–31 May 15.00–17.30; Jun 14.30–17.45; Jul & Aug 14.00–18.00; Sep 14.30–17.45; Oct 15.00–17.30; admission adult €8*) are a huge lava tube about 100m long, the remains of an eruption some 2,000 years ago; there are stalactites and stalagmites, formed by silica. Opposite is the Caldeira do Guilherme Moniz, a primary volcano with a crater perimeter of 15km that is among the largest in the archipelago.

As you return from the caves, look for the turning to Agualva, now off on your right. This is a really good drive passing a tumultuous volcanic landscape covered with native vegetation. Growing along the Ribeira Agualva are the most impressive tree ferns.

From Agualva, follow the main road along to Vila Nova and Lajes, and to Praia da Vitória.

Praia da Vitória In contrast with other towns in the archipelago, Praia always feels open and bright. It has an attractive main square and a long pedestrianised shopping street. The extensive lowlands of this eastern half of the island produced large quantities of wheat, and the wealth created is reflected in many fine houses in the town. At first called simply Praia, it gained town status in 1640. In 1581, after bombarding Angra, a Spanish fleet of ten ships was reconnoitring the Terceira coast and anchored in Salga Bay, in the southeastern corner. They were seen and the alarm given but by the time the Portuguese arrived 1,000 Castillians had landed and were already bent on destruction. After a morning's fierce but indecisive fighting an Augustinian friar had the idea to drive cattle at the enemy. Over 1,000 animals were stampeded at the Spaniards, who fell back in disarray and were either killed or drowned on the shore. Thus ended the Battle of Salga. Again battle came to Praia in 1829, when the town, supporting the Liberal cause, successfully resisted an attempted landing by an Absolutist fleet of 21 ships. In commemoration, the town was called Praia da Vitória in 1837. The nearby Lajes airport now covers much of what were the great wheatfields of earlier days.

In the main square, the **Praça Francisco Ornelas da Câmara**, is the Liberty Statue, erected on the first centenary of the 1829 battle won by the Liberals in homage to the heroes. Overlooking the square is the attractive town hall, and further along on the Rua de São Paulo is the parish church, the **Santa Cruz church**. This was founded by one of the first settlers and has a 15th-century Gothic doorway and a 16th-century Manueline side doorway. Inside there are fine carvings, rich gilt ornamentation and various works of art. Further along on the same road on the left is the house where the writer **Vitorino Nemésio** (1901–78) was born. He held several senior academic posts in Lisbon and was a novelist, poet and scholar and also a popular television personality; his novel of 19th-century life on Faial and Pico, *Stormy Seas*, is in English translation.

In the opposite direction, towards the far end of the main pedestrianised Rua de Jesus, is the town market, built in the final quarter of the 19th century. Alternatively, in the opposite direction, take the Rua da Alfândega which leads down to the beach and along to the new marina.

Porto Martins The area was once covered in vineyards, of which there are still some small traces, but now there are many new houses, summer houses for people in Praia da Vitória. Near the harbour is a natural swimming pool and a restaurant.

Salgueiros Take the minor road to Ponta das Contendas, passing a field of *Strelitzia reginae*, the bird of paradise flower, grown for cut decoration. From the headland there are views of the three rocks, the Três Marias, which are a protected bird sanctuary.

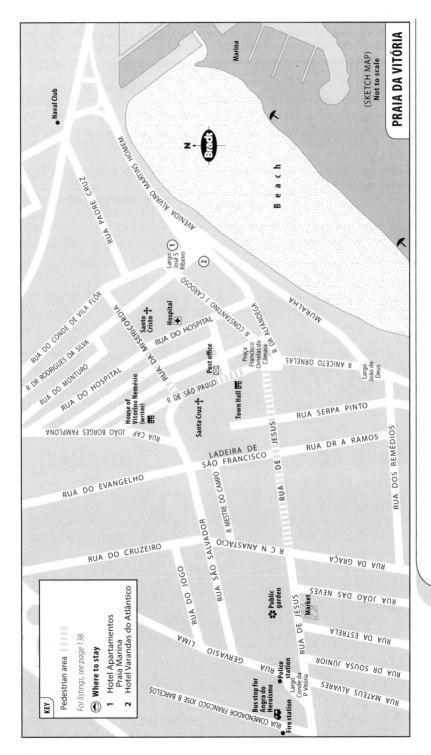

PRAIA DA VITÓRIA

(SKETCH MAP)
Not to scale

KEY

Pedestrian area

For listings, see page 138

Where to stay

1 Hotel Apartamentos
  Praia Marina
2 Hotel Varandas do Atlântico

Naval Club

Marina

Beach

RUA PADRE CRUZ

AVENIDA ALVARO MARTINS HOMEM

RUA DO CONDE DE VILA FLOR

R DR RODRIGUES DA SILVA

RUA DO MONTURO

RUA DO HOSPITAL

RUA CAP JOÃO BORGES PAMPLONA

House of
Vitorino Nemésio
(writer)

Santo
Cristo

Hospital

RUA DO HOSPITAL

RUA DA MISERICÓRDIA

R CONSTANTINO J CARDOSO

Largo
José S
Ribeiro

Post office

Praça
Francisco
Ornelas da
Câmara

R DA ALFÂNDEGA

R ANICETO ORNELAS

Largo
João de
Deus

MURALHA

R DE SÃO PAULO

Santa Cruz

Town Hall

RUA SERPA PINTO

LADEIRA DE
SÃO FRANCISCO

RUA DR A RAMOS

RUA DE JESUS

RUA DO EVANGELHO

R MESTRE DO CAMPO

RUA DOS REMÉDIOS

RUA DO CRUZEIRO

R C N ANASTÁCIO

RUA SÃO SALVADOR

RUA DO JOGO

GERVASIO LIMA

Public
garden

Market

RUA DA GRAÇA

RUA JOÃO DAS NEVES

RUA DE JESUS

RUA DA ESTRELA

RUA DR SOUSA JUNIOR

RUA MATEUS ALVARES

Bus stop for
Angra do
Heroísmo

Police
station

Fire station

Largo
Conde da
P Vitória

RUA COMENDADOR FRANCISCO JOSE B BARCELOS

São Sebastião The 15th-century parish church has interesting internal features including frescoes on the walls and unusual ceilings, and in the facing square is a monument to the Battle of Salga. Note also the nearby *império* with its depictions of food and hydrangeas. (See also *Where to eat*, page 140.)

Porto Judeu This is a small fishing village, a happy place to visit because of its simplicity. **Restaurante Snack-Bar Rocha**, Caminho da Esperança, is next to the infants' school on the main road (✆ 295 905 185; ☉ *until midnight daily*). It is especially noted for octopus cooked in red wine (*polvo guisado*).

Serra do Cume If you have time, it is worth making the side trip to drive along this elongated hill top; the highest point is 545m. The view is of small, rich green fields enclosed by stone walls and hydrangeas, and the harbour of Praia with breakwaters appearing like a crab with two claws. Behind is a view of the largest flat area in the whole of the Azores, lying between the Serra do Cume and the Serra da Ribeirinha northeast of Angra.

6

Graciosa

The general opinion is that Graciosa, meaning 'gracious', is the most relaxed of all the islands. Most certainly it is where I would choose to stay in all the world if ever strife and tribulation became too great and I needed to recuperate. I can record little change in the 30 years since my first visit. A roughly oval-shaped island lying southeast/northwest and the least humid of the archipelago, Graciosa's highest point is Pico Timão at only 398m. As a result, villages are distributed more or less equally across the countryside, and not located only around the coast. The pace is slow, men can still be seen travelling in pony traps or riding donkeys along the roads, there are good eateries, the walking is easy and everyone recognises the visitor second time round. The scenery is picturesque, an idyll of pastures and enclosures, little clusters of whitewashed houses around village churches, occasional windmills with their distinctive red, onion-shaped domes – there were once 36 – and all surrounded by a glittering blue sea. Like rare wine, it is an island to be enjoyed slowly. It is also, perhaps, a window into what the world could be like with fewer inhabitants.

Of greatest attraction is the Furna do Enxofre, the cavern at the bottom of the caldera, first seriously explored in 1879 by Prince Albert of Monaco. The winery of Terra do Conde should not be missed, nor the Ethnographic Museum, both in Santa Cruz. Otherwise, just relax and enjoy being on Graciosa. The entire island is a UNESCO Biosphere Reserve.

BACKGROUND

GEOLOGY Graciosa can be considered as having two main regions. The first is a mountainous zone comprising the Caldeira Volcano, the Serra das Fontes and the Dormida and Branca *serras*. The second region, the northwest plateau, is generally flat and low; it is characterised by several cinder cones and associated lava flows now weathered enough for lava-walled vineyards, pastures and arable fields to thrive.

Starting from 1,500m below sea level, the oldest emerged rocks, at around 6,000 years old, are the stacks of horizontal flows forming the base of the Serra das Fontes. The Serra Dormida and Serra Branca date from around 350,000 and 270,000 years ago respectively. These uplands are steeply scarped, probably formed by faulting.

The Caldeira Volcano started to build 50,000 years ago with violent eruptions caused by water mixing with magma and creating tuff deposits of ash and rock fragments, such as at Ponta da Restinga and Carapacho. During the course of several thousand years, many powerful explosions of gas, steam, ash and pumice took place, alternated with less explosive eruptions producing lava flows or highly dangerous avalanches of hot gas and rock fragments which together built the stratovolcano – a fairly steep-sided cone of layered lava fragments and flows and other emissions. On its flanks other eruptions formed the cinder cone Labeiro

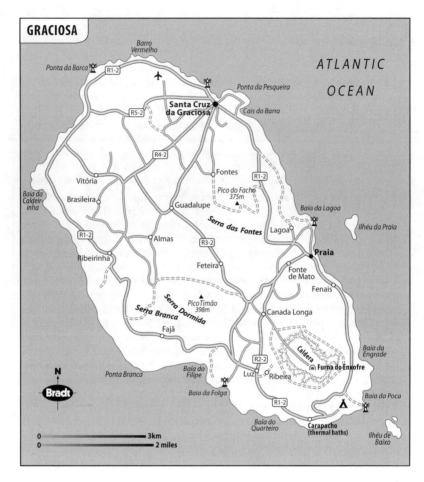

Barro
Vermelho

Ponta da Barca

R1-2

Ponta da Pesqueira

**Santa Cruz
da Graciosa**

Cais da Barra

R5-2

ATLANTIC

OCEAN

R4-2

Fontes

R1-2

Pico do Facho
375m

Baía da Lagoa

Ilhéu da Praia

Vitória

Baía da
Caldeir-
inha

Brasileira

Guadalupe

Serra das Fontes

Lagoa

Praia

R1-2

Almas

R3-2

Fonte
de Mato

Ribeirinha

Feteira

Fenais

Serra Dormida

Pico Timão
398m

Canada Longa

Serra Branca

Baía da
Engrade

Fajã

N

Bradt

Ponta Branca

Baía do
Filipe

R2-2

Luz

Caldera

Furna do Enxofre

Ribeira

Baía da
Poca

Baía da Folga

R1-2

Baía do
Quarteiro

Carapacho
(thermal baths)

Ilhéu de
Baixo

0 ————— 3km
0 ————— 2 miles

do Moro that dominates Praia and also, among others, what are now the eroded remnants of two offshore islets: the Ilhéu da Praia and Ilhéu de Baixo. The volcano's crater dates back 12,000 years and had a lava lake that might have overflowed from the shallow northwest flank and branched eastwards to the sea near Praia and west to Baía da Folga. The well-known Furna do Enxofre is a chimney or vertical vent left as the magma drained when still liquid. The associated cavern has two main fumaroles and an underground lake 22.5m deep below sea level.

The last eruption was 2,000 years ago, by Pico Timão at the end of the Serra Dormida. Its lava flow left a very rough broken surface known as *aa* lava (from the Hawaiian word), with a total length of 4km by 1km wide reaching the sea in the area of Arrochela, just north of Praia. In historical times an earthquake damaged Praia and Luz in 1730, and the Terceira earthquake of 1980 devastated Carapacho and Luz.

HISTORY There had always been a strong relationship between Graciosa and Terceira and so doubtless it was sailors from Terceira who first discovered the island and encroached upon it. The leading settler and man responsible for clearing tracts of vegetation was one Vasco Gil Sodré who came originally from Montemor-o-Velho in Portugal along with his family and household retinue and established himself at Carapacho. He was not, however, given the governorship; this went to Christopher Columbus's brother-in-law. It is thought many of the first settlers came from the Beiras and Minho regions of Portugal and from Flanders.

Graciosa soon proved very suitable for the cultivation of cereals and vines, and well within a century of first settlement was already exporting wheat, barley, wine and brandy. These exports were first shipped to Terceira, the economic and administrative centre that also had the harbour frequented by large ships. Needless to say the wealth this generated attracted pirates, and some 13 forts were built to protect the island and its women. Grain had to be stored in hidden underground chambers. These crops remained dominant for very many years, but now, apart from grapes, like the rest of the islands, beef and dairy products are the main farming outputs. Fishing has become difficult in recent years because of the decline in fish stocks.

At one time the population numbered around 14,000 inhabitants, but emigration reduced this substantially and again there was a considerable exodus in the 1950s. At first only one member of a family was allowed to leave, but this was relaxed by 1959. The population is now about 4,400 and has stabilised; today mothers go out to work and families are small.

Graciosa proudly claims visits from three historical figures. Firstly Chateaubriand stopped over when fleeing to America from the French Revolution, afterwards to become known for his political writings as secretary to Cardinal Fesch and in 1822, ambassador to London. In 1814, the poet Almeida Garrett wrote some of his earliest poetry during his stay with an uncle on the island, and lastly the hydrographer Prince Albert of Monaco visited in 1879, and descended the Furna do Enxofre cave at the bottom of the caldera.

GETTING AROUND

There are buses to every village but, for the tourist, the times are often not very convenient. A printed timetable is available from the tourist information office, or the bus company in Rua Boa Vista. Your hotel should also have details. The best way to use the buses is to make the outward journey by bus from Santa Cruz, and return by taxi. Taxis are available in Santa Cruz (about 12), Luz (two) and Praia (two), and any bar will telephone for one. The distances are not great and therefore taxis are not expensive. For travel to Graciosa, see page 53. For location of towns, see map opposite.

WHERE TO STAY

HOTELS Three *residenciais* are within an easy ten-minute walking distance of the main square in Santa Cruz, and a new hotel is a pleasant 30 minutes' distant.

Graciosa Resort and Business Hotel (46 rooms, 6 villas with rooftop patios) ☎295 730 500; e info@graciosa.hotel.com; www.graciosahotel.com. Overlooking the pretty bay of Cais da Barra & surrounded by old vineyards that in part have been restored & incorporated into the hotel's grounds. Restaurant & good pool. €€€

Residencial Ilha Graciosa (15 rooms) Av Mousinho de Albuquerque, 9880-320 Santa Cruz da Graciosa; ☎295 712 675/6; e gracitur@grwonline.com. A simple but well-restored manor house with a comfortable lounge & bar with a lovely old basalt wine press. Small garden courtyard. €

Residencial Santa Cruz (18 rooms) Largo Barão de Guadalupe, 9880-344 Santa Cruz da Graciosa; ☎295 712 345. Only 100m from the sea, & close to town. €

RURAL ACCOMMODATION

⌂ **Casa das Faias** (8 rooms) Rua Infante D Henrique, Santa Cruz; ☏ 295 732 766; e casadasfaias@sapo.pt; www.gracipescas.com. In Praia, 100m from the marina, 200m from the beach. €

⌂ **Moinho de Pedra** (4 apts) Estrada do Aeroporta, Santa Cruz; ☏ 295 712 501; e info@ moinho-de-pedra.pt; www.moinho-de-pedra.pt.

A converted typical windmill of Graciosa in Praia, 200m from the beach. €

⌂ **Quinta dos Frutos** (4 rooms) Rua Dr Manuel Correia Lobão Frutos, near the village of Vitória, 500m from Guadalupe; ☏ 295 712 557; e quintadosfrutos@sapo.pt; www.quintadosfrutos. no.sap.pt. Traditional basalt farm buildings set in a large orchard. €

CAMPING

Ⓧ **Carapacho** ☏ 295 712 959. A lovely small site on 3 levels with sea views & sheltered by trees. Showers, toilets, electricity, stone barbecue. Go first to the Dolphin Snack Bar to register.

Carapacho Spa is immediately adjacent, as is the sea swimming pool.

Ⓧ **Praia** Above the town with a sea view.

✕ WHERE TO EAT

The Graciosa Resort Hotel has a good restaurant, and with the Quinta das Grutas these two new venues now give some much-needed sophistication. Although most of the accommodation is in Santa Cruz, almost all the better restaurants are out of town. However, a taxi to and from each is not expensive and takes only minutes. Fish is excellent, but fresh, crisply cooked vegetables seem even more of a rarity on this island. Islanders living in Santa Cruz like to get out at weekends in summer, so the restaurants can be busy.

SANTA CRUZ

✕ **Clube Naval da Graciosa** Cais da Barra; ☺ summer at about 16.30 until closing time daily, depending on customers; winter, earlier every evening. This is a basic facility with a straightforward menu. It is very pleasant on a summer evening to walk along the coast to the ruined building that you can see in the distance & return to the club for a beer.

✕ **Costa do Sol Restaurante** Largo da Calheta; ☏ 295 712 694. A bit bleak.

✕ **Snack Bar Santa Cruz** Rua da Boa Vista. Specialities are *frango no churrasco* (a kind of barbecued chicken) & *alcatra peixe e carne* (a very slow-cooked stew). A tiny place, very friendly, with very good prices, & they serve a large mixed salad! Fun & recommended.

BAÍA DA FOLGA

✕ **Restaurante Estrela do Mar** Folga; ☏ 295 712 560; ☺ year-round 07.00–midnight Tue–Sun. Very simple small restaurant near the harbour. Great atmosphere, very casual, good fish & lobster. On summer weekends it is advisable to book.

PRAIA

✕ **Panificação Graciosense** In the street behind the beach; ☏ 295 712 589. Tables outside, but in the back of the front bar is a super restaurant with a nice atmosphere. Menu with lots of fresh fish & seafood, & sells Pedras Brancas, the VLQPRD island wine to accompany your meal. In the bar are all the island's special pastries, plus a lot of other calorific temptations.

CARAPACHO

✕ **Dolphin** Just above the campsite; ☏ 295 712 014. Modern, simple & good, both the restaurant & an open terrace with a wide sea view. Fish always very fresh. Very busy on summer weekends.

RIBEIRINHA

✕ **Quinta das Grutas** ☏ 295 712 334. New, in a delightfully rural situation with good ambience, serving typical regional food with sophistication. Bread freshly baked in traditional wood-fired oven. Proprietor has lived in Austria.

NIGHTLIFE

There is very little nightlife, and what there is is mainly found in Santa Cruz. On summer evenings many islanders gather in the spacious centre of town to stroll and talk until after midnight. There are several bars, some of which have small discos – identified by their music. Near the airport is a discotheque-pub, the **Vila Sacramento**, open in the evening at weekends. It has seating beneath trees in a garden, and the dance area inside. One constant pleasure comes from just sitting on a wall above the harbour and listening to the sea, especially if there is moonlight.

SHOPPING

Graciosa wines, of course, and also Graciosa cheese are this island's specialities. *Queijadas da Graciosa*, small cakes, are delicious with an espresso coffee and are rather like a treacle tart mix in a crisp, thin pastry cup. With ingredients of flour, sugar, eggs, milk, butter and *canela e sal* (cinnamon and salt), they make a fantastic energy source when descending calderas. The little factory making them, together with another speciality only to order for weddings, is in Praia and visitors are welcome.

OTHER PRACTICALITIES

Emergency ☎112
Police Santa Cruz; ☎295 712 527
Resident doctor ☎295 712 525/294

Post office Av Mouzinha Albuquerque, Santa Cruz; Rua Rodrigues Sampaia, Praia
SATA Air Açores Santa Cruz; ☎295 712 456
Airport information ☎295 712 457/8

WHAT TO SEE AND DO

MUSEUMS By the old harbour in **Santa Cruz** is another splendid **Museum of the Azores** (☎ *295 712 429;* ⊕ *09.00–12.30 & 14.00–17.30 Mon–Fri; Jun–Aug also 14.00–17.00 Sat & Sun*), established back in 1983 and housed in a late 19th-century traditional building of a wealthy family that they used for storing corn and for making wine. Here you will find, in several rooms devoted to times past, furnished family rooms, various antiques and paintings, the tools of several important trades

---

FESTIVALS ON GRACIOSA

As with all the other islands there are small festivals throughout the summer but two are of especial interest for the visitor. When the **Espírito Santo** or **Holy Ghost** celebration takes place one can enjoy participating in the island's hospitality, taking the special bread and local wine. This occurs widely over the island, but especially in Santa Cruz, Luz, Guadalupe and Praia (São Mateus). The **Festival of Santo Cristo** is celebrated with boat races, *touradas* or bullfights, plus cultural and musical happenings. Santa Cruz really decorates itself for the celebration, and becomes wonderfully busy with visitors from the other islands as well as North American emigrants.

Carnaval Easter
Espírito Santo 7th Sun after Easter
Santo Cristo early Aug

and all the gear to make wine in the old way. In the road opposite, fronting the sea at No 65, is an annexe signed *Barracão das canoas* where there is a whaling boat and exhibits to do with whaling; because this is so simply done and in a shed by the harbour you get the feeling that if a rocket were to be fired a crew would come rushing down to launch the boat.

At Rochela, in **Vila da Praia**, just up from the beach, is the **Núcleo Marítimo** displaying items to do with fishing and whaling. At **Fontes**, a short drive from Santa Cruz, is a restored working windmill, standing resplendent in the landscape with its white base and bright red cupola. On the road to the **caldera** in a low basalt building with paintwork of traditional Graciosa green is the **Tenda do Ferreiro**, a museum devoted to the work of the blacksmith.

The opening hours of the main museum in Santa Cruz are detailed on page 159. The other museum branches are open in summer only, or by request for a small group. In winter, when there are few visitors to the island, the museum concentrates its services at the island's schools.

WALKING There are three official trails:

Around the caldera and Furna do Enxofre Easy, 9km, 3 hours. See map on
page 163. A torch is recommended. Take a picnic and you can happily spend most of the day exploring this route. A taxi (about €10) from Santa Cruz into the caldera and down to the entrance to the cavern is the easiest way to start this walk, and you can easily time your visit between 11.00 and 14.00, the best period for when the sunlight enters. From the visitor centre, walk back up the road and through the tunnel, and down the road to take the first turning off on the left. This gives access to the intermittently tarmac-surfaced road that runs round the outside of the caldera which you should follow in a clockwise direction. On the way you will pass a small *furna* or cavern, the Furna do Abel, and signposted is the lavatube Furna Maria Encantada; this is some 60m long and was probably formed when the lava lake that was inside the caldera reached its highest point.

Serra Branca–Praia Easy, 7km, 2½ hours. Crosses the island from west to east,
with good views across the island.

Baía da Folga Easy, 2km, 1 hour. Quite fun to do after a good meal at the little
restaurant in Folga.

BIRDS AND FLOWERS With little high ground and almost everywhere farmed, not many naturalists in the past have studied the island. However, it was while on Graciosa some years ago I concluded ornithologists had a pretty easy time as I watched a most handsome yacht sail by close inshore with half-a-dozen pairs of binoculars trained on the low cliffs below me; I later discovered they were a research team engaged upon a long-term study of the roseate tern.

The basalt islet of **Ilhéu da Praia** is a Special Protected Area of 11ha and is said to have one of the richest and most diverse concentrations of seabirds in the Azores with many migratory species. It is a little more than 1km out from Praia. Breeding colonies have declined through human disturbance so while it is nice to know they are there, it is best they are left in peace. However, from the opposite shore or the harbour quay it is easy to observe the action with a good telescope. Another possible area in the far southeast is the Special Protected Area of the **Ilhéu de Baixo** and adjacent rocky shoreline.

Disappointed wildflower enthusiasts will just have to resort to applied botany – the grape vine and its products.

SWIMMING Santa Cruz has a public open-air swimming pool with all facilities at the near end of the harbour quay.

There are natural and manmade rock pools at **Barro Vermelho**, with showers and changing facilities, at most 2km from Santa Cruz, and the area is backed with tamarisk trees which makes it nicer. **Praia** is Graciosa's only beach and is very popular, although the sand can sometimes disappear after a winter storm. There are changing rooms and showers, and a counter selling ice creams, etc; across the road is a café/bar with a restaurant deeper inside (see page 158). Carapacho has good access to protected sea swimming.

Carapacho Spa (⊕ *May–Sep*) Located in Luz and not long ago renovated, this spa now has 16 individual immersion rooms and a medical consulting room. In addition to a purely indulgent and relaxing soak of 15 minutes (maximum recommended time), on offer are courses of treatment under medical supervision for rheumatism and skin disorders. A spa since 1750, the water temperature varies between 35˚C and 40˚C. There is a natural rock pool nearby, and it is altogether a very popular place in summer.

BOAT TRIPS Built in the early part of the last century, the *Estefânia Gorreia* played an important part in Graciosa's economy during the whaling period when it went out supporting the small boats, towing the whales back to shore. The last whales were caught in 1974. At Cais da Barra, by the Clube Naval, you can see the slipway, and next to it the trying area. The large buildings nearby are all to do with whaling. The boat also played an important role in emergencies, taking people to the hospital in Terceira before the time of the air services. Beautifully restored, it sometimes makes trips round the island; check at Club Navale for further details. Other opportunities for boat trips, kayaking, whale watching, fishing, diving, walking tours and birdwatching are provided by:

Gracipescas Rua Serpa Pinto, Santa Cruz; ☏295 712 001; e turismo@gracipescas.com; www.gracipescas.com

Nautigraciosa 11 Rua do Corpo Santo, Santa Cruz; ☏295 732 811; edivingraciosa@gmail.com

AROUND THE ISLAND

FULL-DAY TOUR (*about €100 for a whole day, €60 for half a day, or by the hour at around €18*) A day tour by taxi will take in, among other places, the caldera and Furna do Enxofre, the view of Santa Cruz from Serra da Ajuda, Praia, the lighthouse at Ponta da Restinga, Carapacho, the Serra Branca, Porta Afonso (the track is too rough for cars and you will have to walk) and the lighthouse at Farol da Ponta da Barça, with its whale-like rock formation. If you like to swim, I suggest you arrange with your driver a morning itinerary starting at 09.00 and, if the building works are completed, stopping at Carapacho around 12.30. As soon as you arrive book your lunch for say 14.00 at the Dolphin Restaurant (see page 158), then have a swim and a shower or try the spa. You can arrange to be collected at 16.00 and continue the tour with a stop at Praia for coffee and the museum, to return to Santa Cruz around 17.00–17.30. If you don't want to swim, then take your midday break at Folga and enjoy exploring the harbour and its surrounds and isolation, before continuing again at 15.30 to Praia.

SANTA CRUZ DA GRACIOSA The town focuses on the main square of cobbles laid beneath large metrosideros trees, elms and araucarias, and a large water tank, originally used for watering cattle accessed by a sloping cobbled road. There are several small bars and cafés nearby, and some shops. The shops are rather scattered and are not always obvious, which is inconvenient if you need something in a hurry, but a most charming and welcome contrast to the ubiquitous commercial form. The taxi rank is in the square, with a line of telephones each housed in a little model windmill. Roads leading off are often lined with grand town houses and domestic buildings with interesting wrought-iron balconies and other architectural detail.

The tiny harbour with its simple quay and a semi-natural swimming pool has an early charm; above is a narrow cobbled street and pairs of seats in the wall. It is on a small and intimate scale. Further round is a modern quay, built in the 1960s, and recently enlarged quays and marina. Graciosa's own **Terra do Conde winery** is adjacent to the Residencial Ilha Graciosa, open for tasting and sales.

On the hill above, the **Monte da Ajuda**, are three chapels: São João, São Salvador and Nossa Senhora da Ajuda, all floodlit at night. The last can be likened to a castle; it is 16th century and has 18th-century *azulejos*. All three are usually closed, but sometimes, if anyone is around to ask, a key may be found. There is a surfaced road to the top where a splendid view can be had of the whole town. A little below the chapels is a small bullring, used during festivities in August; a stepped path leads down and continues on into town.

If you take the coastal road from the square leading to Praia, Rua Infante D Henrique, and walk for about ten minutes you will come to a large building on your right that was until recently a noisy power station. On the same Rua Infante D Henrique is the **Associacão de Artesãos da Ilha Graciosa**; you will see a silver nameplate on the building. The entrance is towards the end of the side passage. Here you will find the women working, and a display of their completed work and items for sale. It is open weekdays during normal business hours.

Take the turning to the left down to the old harbour, the **Cais da Barra**. It is a pretty bay with several small boats moored during the summer. Here you will find the Clube Naval building and maybe refreshments. You will soon realise this is on the site of an old fort, **Forte de Santa Catarina**, which dates from the period before 1800, and there are old rusty cannons still threatening the ghosts of long-dead pirates. Peer over the wall and in the black lava you will discern an old ramp where the whales were once hauled ashore. On the headland beyond (reached by the farm track along the coast) are the remains of a large building and defensive walls, which the sea is slowly undermining. This was once a Jewish settlement, the **Forte Deis Judeus**, and there is a tiny cemetery in black basalt engraved 'Cemetario Judaica' nearby. This coastal stroll makes for a good after-dinner perambulation for those staying at the Graciosa Resort Hotel, otherwise the walk back along the asphalt road following the coast is a pleasant return walk into town.

PRAIA Praia is a fishing port with a high sea wall, and an arched gateway leading from the beach through the wall into a long street with a café/bar (see *Where to eat*, page 158). The usual cobbled square is in the road behind, before the **Church of São Mateus**, rebuilt in the 19th century; inside there are Flemish images of St Matthew and St Peter and a *pietà*, all 16th century. A second eatery is to be found a short way up the ascending road to the right as you exit from the beach. The beach itself is almost white sand and very popular, with a café and other amenities. In the near distance is the modern **Negra Quay**, the island's main port.

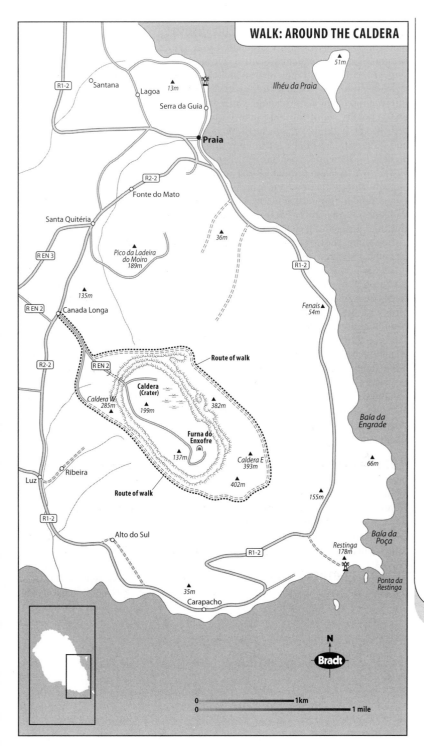

R1-2
Santana
Lagoa
13m
Serra da Guia
Praia

Ilhéu da Praia
51m

R2-2
Fonte do Mato

Santa Quitéria

R EN 3

Pico da Ladeira
do Moiro
189m

36m

R1-2

135m

R EN 2
Canada Longa

Fenais 54m

R2-2
R EN 2

Route of walk

**Caldera
(Crater)**

Caldera W.
285m

199m

382m

*Baía da
Engrade*

**Furna do
Enxofre**

137m

Caldera E
393m

66m

402m

Luz
Ribeira

Route of walk

155m

R1-2

*Baía da
Poça*

Alto do Sul

Restinga
178m

R1-2

*Ponta da
Restinga*

35m

Carapacho

N

Bradt

0 — 1km
0 — 1 mile

AROUND THE CALDERA AND FURNA DO ENXOFRE As you enter the caldera from the tunnel, made in 1953, a dramatic landscape confronts you. Small meadows are grazed by cows and all around cryptomeria forest climbs the steeply enclosing slopes towards the sky. The road soon forks, to the left down to a picnic site, to the right down to the entrance of the Furna do Enxofre. The visitor centre provides information about the volcanology of Graciosa, especially the caldera and cavern, and generally about the Biosphere Reserve classification (↖ 295 714 009; ⊕ 16 Sep–30 Apr 14.00–17.30 Tue–Sat; 1 May–14 Jun 09.30–17.30 Tue–Fri, 14.00–17.30 Sat; 15 Jun–15 Sep 10.00–18.00 daily. Guided tours 16 Sep–30 Apr 14.30 & 15.30; 1 May–15 Sep 11.30, 15.00, 16.30). For walkers there is a short cut through the woods, which leaves through a gap in the wall on the left-hand side at the only hairpin bend in the road and which descends quite steeply to the entrance kiosk. Please note the gas emissions are closely monitored and sometimes it may be too dangerous to visit; more likely in winter. Unfortunately there is no way of knowing this until you get to the entrance.

In summer the best time to visit is between 11.00 and 14.00 when sunlight enters. Descend a concrete spiral staircase of 184 steps to the cave floor. This was officially opened on 30 July 1939, a great improvement over the rope ladder used on the first descent by Prince Albert of Monaco 60 years earlier. It seems that it was built to enable farmers to get water for their animals. The narrow opening allows a few ferns and mosses to grow. A little into the cave is a small gently bubbling mud pool, sounding rather sinister in the darkness. The ropes preventing further descent into the cavern result from the deaths of two visiting sailors some years ago who were overcome by an unexpected emission of sulphurous fumes deeper inside the cave. There is a lake, and at one time a rowing boat enabled further exploration when the lake was 130m across and 15m deep. In recent years the lake has gone down 11m, and there is speculation there may be an underground connection with the thermal area of Carapacho. The floor of the lake is below sea level.

After leaving the cavern, a day can be spent very happily exploring and enjoying the peace of the caldera.

ILHÉU DA BALEIA If you walk out of Santa Cruz along the north coast you first pass what was once the main vine-growing area and a stretch of coastline that is a popular bathing area among the rocks near the few houses of **Barro Vermelho**. Beyond this you come to **Ponta da Barca**, with its lighthouse, about 5km from town. Close to the shore is a rocky islet that looks, with a little imagination, like a whale; there may be some seabirds as well. It is a walk along the road, but there is little traffic; in summer the best time to do this is in the cool of the evening.

VIEW OF THE OTHER ISLANDS The best and most readily accessible view is from the main road as it skirts the Serra Branca following the south coast between Luz and Ribeirinha. Pico, São Jorge, Faial and Terceira can all be seen on a clear day.

São Jorge

Town of Velas so beautiful
Leaning on the sea side
More beautiful I have yet to see
Not kissed by the moonlight

Oh, island of infinite grace
Far away from you, thinking with
    obsessive thoughts
My longing has no end

In my beating heart
The days: eternity
In the heart separation…
being more 'cold' in the friendship,

is more 'warm' the absence to be alone…
when the sweetest is the missing
the heart is more crucified.

Anselmo da Silveira, Angra, November 1949.
On an *azulejo* in the town garden, Velas.

A friend of mine in Velas greets his visitors with 'Welcome to São Jorge, my island with 10,000 people and over 20,000 cattle'. Known widely beyond its shores for its delicious, strong, Cheddar-like cheese, São Jorge's many other attributes are far less recognised. Every visitor will react in his or her own way to each island they see, but to me São Jorge is an island of mystery. Perhaps because, before ever setting foot, I saw it first across the channel from Pico, a long cliff wall rising from the sea and invariably disappearing into cloud or mist. I also caught glimpses from Graciosa, Terceira and Faial. Finally, one summer, I went across in a small boat from São Roque to Velas and watched with fascination as the slow voyage gave diminishing detail of Pico's coast behind me and an increasing but narrowing view ahead of São Jorge and of the little port and main town of Velas. Approaching the harbour I could not but be aware of the huge presence of Pico Mountain behind me now that I was distant from it, its sharp cone at the forefront of the island, the high plateau behind like a girl's long hair in the wind or like the carved figure on the prow of an ancient sailing ship. Trying to look in opposite directions at the same time, Velas harbour became prettier with every chug of the engine. Tying up at the quay, the imposing gateway and walls dating from the time of pirates promised quiet pleasure. While my bag was whipped away in a truck to the hotel some little distance away, I walked the few metres into town; narrow streets, small shops, the main church, some manor houses, a little square or two, the sound of voices coming from tiny bars. Clouds hung heavily upon the uplands beyond, concealing them in spite of my coming closer. Perhaps tomorrow the clouds would repent and reveal all.

    Even on dull days there is an intense pleasure to be derived from walking along little-used farm roads in utter, total silence with stone walls, hedgerows, cows and occasional trees giving depth to the stage. In sunshine and with a deep-blue sea beyond, the cliff paths are magnificent for scenery, combining landscape grandeur

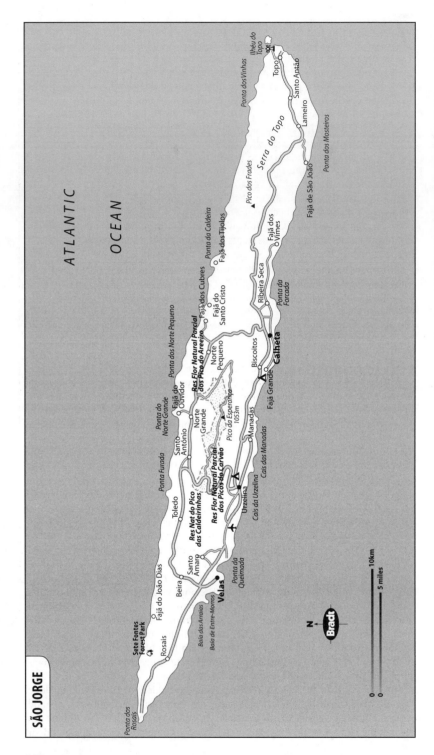

SÃO JORGE

ATLANTIC
OCEAN

Ponta dos Rosais

Sete Fontes Forest Park
Rosais
Fajã do João Dias
Ponta dos Rosais

Beira
Santo Amaro

Baía dos Arraiais
Baía de Entre-Morros

Velas
Ponta da Queimada

Toledo
Ponta Furada

Res Nat do Pico das Caldeirinhas

Santo António
Ponta do Norte Grande
Fajã do Ouvidor

Norte Grande

Res Flor Natural Parcial dos Picos do Carvão

Pico da Esperança
1053m

Urzelina
Cais da Urzelina

Manadas
Cais das Manadas

Fajã Grande

Ponta dos Norte Pequeno

Res Flor Natural Parcial dos Pico do Areeiro

Fajã dos Cubres

Norte Pequeno

Biscoitos

Calheta

Fajã do Santo Cristo

Ponta da Caldeira
Fajã dos Tijolos

Ribeira Seca

Ponta da Forcada

Fajã dos Vimes

Pico dos Frades

Serra do Topo

Ponta dos Mosteiros

Fajã de São João

Lameiro

Santo Antão

Ponta dos Vinhas

Topo
Ilhéu do Topo

N

Bradt

0   5 miles
0   10km

166

and intimate vignettes together with unexpected human interest while steep descents to *fajãs* on tiny tracks give a tender appreciation of the hardships of the islanders.

Although it is an island with good walks, graded unsurfaced roads have in recent years ramified throughout the island and in reasonable weather allow the motorist to explore many of the previously hidden beauties of the island. The best of these are shown on the latest maps prepared by the tourist offices, and there are other newer ones not shown. Many very happy days can be had exploring these back roads as well as the little-trafficked main roads from which side roads lead into small, often charming villages.

On a full moon the island comes into its own; the channel across to Pico reflects and shimmers, while the great black unequal-sided triangle of Pico massively provides the theatre setting. In Velas, drop down to Neto's Bar by the harbour, and on the tiny terrace, if you are lucky, thrill to the haunting mew of Cory's shearwaters as they fly just above your head in the dark.

By car, São Jorge is an island on which to spend slow days relaxing, stopping to explore the accessible little settlements along the coast, and to enjoy the scenery. The *fajãs*, while not unique to São Jorge, are a very special feature of this island and their microclimates and settlements are most rewarding to explore. There are numerous viewpoints, the two ports of Velas and Calheta, lovely sites for picnics, and opportunities to make easy short walks. In Brown's guidebook of 1926, he laconically says: 'The Lisbon steamers touch alternately every fortnight. There are no carriage roads.' Now there are plenty to take you to lovely places. One can also take the ferry and visit Pico and Faial islands; see page 53 for details.

BACKGROUND

GEOLOGY São Jorge is cigar-shaped, 56km long and at most 8km wide. A long ridge running along its length characterises the island, arising abruptly from the sea and ascending to Pico da Esperança (1,053m) at about the centre. The average height of this central ridge is 700m. The coasts are very steep, in places over 400m and almost vertical, particularly on the north side. Much of the land surface is above 300m and villages are at much higher altitudes than anywhere else in the Azores, so that they can be nearer the fields.

Different from all the other Azores islands, São Jorge originated from fissures, cracks or faults so deep in the Earth's crust that magma may rise to the surface. From these, lava usually erupts with little or no gaseous explosions and so mostly produces lava flows; however, they can also erupt explosively, forming cinder cones. There are no stratovolcanoes like on Pico or on Faial, nor are there any big calderas or craters. Initially, though, these fissural eruptions, some 1,000m down on the sea floor, would have been very explosive as the hot magma met the seawater, but as the island built up above the sea, the thermal shocks ceased.

The island has a northwest–southeast orientation which reflects the regional plate tectonics and fault lines. Two areas make up the island, separated by a fault line cutting obliquely across the middle, which is now covered with recent volcanic emissions. Wearing deeply into this fracture is the Ribeira Seca creek, just east of Calheta.

The Topo complex is the island's oldest, up to 600,000 years old, but the relief of this eastern side is more difficult to interpret and it is harder to identify the volcanic features and lava flows because it is so eroded. The younger areas to the west of the Ribeira Seca fault mirror the same eruption style of Topo; lava flows and explosive eruptions, leaving cinder cones. The wide spine of the central and western region comprises the Manadas complex and the Rosais complex, at around 24,000 and 30,000 years old respectively. From fissures lava welled out and piled up to thicknesses of over 500m, burying older cinder cones under newer flows. The glorious walk or drive along the island's spine passes the cones of the youngest eruptions from just a few thousand years ago.

The sheer cliffs of the coast are probably due to faulting. The *fajãs*, for which São Jorge is so well known, are caused in two ways: detritus *fajãs* are gravity deposits produced by landslides caused by erosion of the base of the cliff such as Fajã dos Cubres, while lava *fajãs* are created by lava flowing over the cliffs into the sea making a platform, as with Fajã do Ouvidor. São Jorge has 46 in all – 30 on the north coast and 16 on the south – but many were abandoned following the 1980 earthquake and now only the larger and safer ones are inhabited. They are much valued for their microclimate and the cultivation of vegetables and fruit.

During historical times there have been several eruptions, the first in 1580, east of Velas, whose lava flows formed the Ponta da Queimada. It also emitted hot gas and ash that spread quickly close to the ground, burning those unfortunate enough to be caught, and killing many cattle. In 1808 came the infamous eruptions at Urzelina that continued for six weeks, with 13 large cinder cones exploding over several days together with lava flows. This was followed by avalanches of hot gas and stones that extended over Urzelina as a dense black cloud. Terrified villagers cowering in the church were protected, but endured the sound of falling debris on the roof. Not long after came a lava flow half-burying the church, still graphically to be seen in the village today. The survivors said they had seen a vision of hell.

HISTORY Topo, at the island's far eastern extremity, was settled by a Flemish nobleman, Van der Hagen, who had first been made Captain of Flores, but this was so remote no-one wanted to settle there and he asked the king if instead he could have São Jorge. Velas was founded around the middle of the 15th century and developed sufficiently within 50 years to be given its town charter, with an economy based on exporting wool and archil, a lichen used for dyeing, and growing wheat and grapes. Three centuries later, oranges became an important export crop, with schooners coming to Urzelina from England to load the boxes of fruit. As with some of the other islands, the lack of a good harbour meant isolation until the airport was built. The principal products are now cattle and, most importantly, cheese. Three large factories now make the famous São Jorge cheese. Like all the other islands, São Jorge suffered from the predations of pirates; it also suffered earthquakes and two major volcanic eruptions, in 1580 and 1808.

GETTING AROUND

There is a limited bus service which brings passengers into Velas from the villages in the morning, returning in the evening. However, it should be possible to do some touring, giving you time in Calheta and Rosais. Buses leave from Rua Miguel Bombarda, next to the police station, but you must check for the latest times.

VELAS–CALHETA On Wednesdays and Fridays a bus leaves Velas at 08.30 and via the north coast arrives at Calheta at 09.30. The return bus leaves Calheta at 15.30, arriving in Velas at 16.30.

VELAS–ROSAIS On Monday through to Friday a bus leaves Velas at 09.45 and arrives at Rosais church at 10.15, returning at 14.45, arriving in Velas 15.15. You can ask the driver to put you down at the road leading to Sete Fontes Forest Park, to save you walking back from the church. For the return, it is better to get the bus at the church.

If you want to make a tour of the island by taxi, or use taxis to access the walks, then it is better to book it through the local travel agency, who will ensure you have a driver to explain things, and who will know the walks. Taxi prices start at around €60 for a half-day tour, €120 for a full day going down to Topo. If you are travelling alone or as a couple in summer it is possible to join with others and share a minibus: contact Aquarius, Rua Infante D Henrique, Velas (✆ 295 432 006).

For travel to São Jorge, see page 53. For location of Velas listings see map, page 174, and for location of other towns see map, page 166.

 ## WHERE TO STAY

VELAS

⌂ Cantinho das Buganvilias Resort
(19 apts) Rua Padre Auguste Teixeira, Queimada; ✆ 295 432 271; e cantinhodasbuganvilias@ gmail.co; www.cantinhodasbuganvilias.com. Beautiful coastal location 5km from Velas &1.5km from the airport. Spacious modern apartments with lots of light, but the positions of some & large windows may compromise privacy. Pool, fitness centre, children's area, bar, restaurant. €€€–€€€€

⌂ Hotel São Jorge (58 rooms) Rua Dr Machado
Pires, Velas; ✆ 295 430 100; e hotelsaojorge@ clix.pt; www.acores.com/hotels.jorge. In a good situation overlooking the sea & across the channel to Pico & a few mins' walk from the centre of town. Rooms have balconies & AC. Swimming pool, bar, breakfast room, but no restaurant; room rates include airport transfers. €€€

⌂ Quinta de São Pedro (1 house, 3 apts
& 3 suites) About 800m from Velas; ✆ 295 432 189; e quinta.saopedro@sapo.pt; www. quintadesaopedro.com. This property, dating from the 17th century, has been comfortably fitted out, providing 2-person apartments, 4-person suites & a 2-person rustic house, all with ocean views to Pico & Faial. Garden, pool, games room, tourism support & airport transfers. €€€

⌂ Casa do António (8 rooms) Rua Infante
D Henrique, 9800-554 Velas; ✆ 295 432 006; e antonio@viagensaquarius.com; www. viagensaquarius.com. This is a wonderfully eccentric & personal well-designed, well-built new extension to an old building so there are quirky stairs & corners & the whole thing comes together in a mock Art-Deco style. A really fun

place & right by the harbour with, in summer, Cory's shearwaters whipping by overhead to their nesting sites in the nearby cliff face. The owner/ designer has put considerable thought into making guests comfortable, & the rooms are all en suite. There is a breakfast room (with excellent varied breakfast), & a small elevated garden. €€

⌂ Quinta do Canavial (4 rooms in main house,
7 apts in annexe) Lugar do Canavial, Velas; ✆ 295 412 981; e quintacanavial@hotmail.com; www. quintadocanavial.com. Overlooking the bay of Entre-Moros on the edge of Velas, this is an old manor house in a garden setting. Pool, restaurant serving evening meals on request, courtesy transport. €€

⌂ Residencial Livramento Casa de Hospedes
(12 rooms) Av do Livramento, Velas; ✆ 295 430 020. Near the fire station. €

⌂ Residencial Neto (23 rooms) Rua Cons Dr
José Pereira, Velas; ✆ 295 412 338. Close to the harbour. With TV, bar & small seawater swimming pool. €

CALHETA

⌂ Residencial Solmar (8 rooms) Rua
Domingos d'Oliveira 4, 9850-036 Calheta; ✆ 295 416 120. €

CAMPING

𝝠 Fajã Grande Calheta; ✆ 295 416 324. Close
to the sea, there is a good natural rock pool with European Blue Flag status. The campsite is supervised 24hrs, with all facilities, including a children's playpark, & tents can be hired. There are also bungalows for 4 people. It is very attractive with a pergola & belvedere, a great place to sit & watch the sunset. To find the campsite take a steep

7

cement road down to the sea; there is no signpost. Shops are very limited; there is no bakery, but there is a kiosk & a snack bar.

Å Urzelina camping ground ✆ 295 414 401. All amenities & resident warden. Swimming pool & natural rock pools. Close by are 3 restaurants, grocery, bakery & coffee shop as well as several windmills.

Å Velas ✆ 295 432 002. São Jorge's main town now has a new camping site, located near the football ground in the Baía de Entre os Morros about 15 mins' walk from town & providing free transport to & from the harbour. It has a freshwater swimming pool & tents, with sleeping bags for hire.

✖ WHERE TO EAT

This is difficult because it seems that more than on any other island, the restaurants keep changing, with some closing and new ones opening. There is also the lovely story from some years ago of several hundred visitors arriving by ferry for the day to attend a festival who found all the restaurants closed because their owners were also attending the festival! However, in Velas, always reliable over many years and open every day, but sadly now in winter only as a bar, is the **Restaurante Velense** [174 F2] down by the harbour, adjacent to the tourist office. Velas is a nice tiny place to explore, and you will find enough choice of places to eat.

If you want to eat outside Velas, then here are some ideas, otherwise ask at your hotel or keep a lookout as you travel around. For location of towns see map, page 166.

SANTO AMARO
✖ **Fornos de Lava** Travessa de S Tiago, Santo Amaro, not far from Velas; ✆ 295 432 415. A delightfully rural place, with luxuriant views over pastures; the owners are really trying hard &, a true novelty for the Azores, they grow their own vegetables & herbs for the restaurant.

FAJÃ DE SANTO AMARO
✖ **A Quinta** 100m from the airport, on the main road; ✆ 295 430 240. In a stone building: serves a normal menu & also traditional food, but for this in winter advance warning is required. Operated by the local school of tourism, so student staff are nervous but usually efficient.

URZELINA
✖ **Restaurante Urzelina** Estrada Regional, on the main road ✆ 295 414 016; ⊕ 05.00–midnight Thu–Tue (meals 12.00–15.00 & 19.00–22.00)

FAJÃ DO OUVIDOR
✖ **Café Amilcar** Close to the harbour; ✆ 295 417 448; ⊕ year-round daily. This simple café offers good fish – the owner is also a fisherman.

CALHETA
✖ **Os Amigos** Ponta de São Lourenço, in Calheta near the museum; ✆ 295 416 421. Café restaurant. Good food & service, sea view.

RIBEIRA SECA
✖ **Café – Ponto de Encantra** ✆ 295 416 240; ⊕ 07.30–midnight Wed–Mon. Located at Canada dos Vales, on the main road just before Ribeira Seca, this place does a buffet meal *Almoço e Jantar* (lunch & dinner). An inviting restaurant with views across to Pico.

NIGHTLIFE

☆ **Discotec Zodiac** Not far from the Hotel São Jorge; ✆ 295 412 677; ⊕ Sat & Sun. This is the main option.

☆ **Tamanco's Bar** 1 block on from Discotec Zodiac is this bar with live music at weekends.

Otherwise there are several small pavement cafés where you can listen to the shearwaters.

OTHER PRACTICALITIES

Emergency ✆112
Police [174 F2] Velas; ✆295 412 339
Hospital [174 E3] Velas; ✆295 412 122
Tourist information office [174 F2] Rua
Conselheiro Dr José Pereira, Velas; ✆295 412 440;
⊕ 09.00–12.30 & 14.00–17.30 Mon–Fri

SATA Air Açores Rua de Santo André, Velas;
✆295 412 125
Airport information ✆295 412 395

WHAT TO SEE AND DO

MUSEUMS
Sacred Art Museum [174 F2] (⊕ *09.00–12.00 & 14.00–17.30 Mon–Fri*) Housed
in an annex of the Matriz de São Jorge church, Velas. The opening hours do rather
depend on whether someone is working in the museum at the time. Exhibits
include sacred images, silver, censers and monstrances.

Francisco Lacerda Museum (⊕ *09.00–17.30 Mon–Fri*) Occupying a house
built in 1811 in Calheta, there is a permanent exhibition about the history and
ethnography of the island and a supporting library.

WALKING São Jorge has some memorable walks and several are long established
so fairly clear to follow. There are six official walks, and I describe three of my
favourites on pages 178–82.

FESTIVALS ON SÃO JORGE

Velas is making quite a local name for itself with the Semana Cultural or
week-long cultural festival held in early July to coincide with the annual
Horta–Velas–Horta yacht race, when numerous events are staged including
cultural conferences and exhibitions as well as more usual pop, rock and
folk music and bullfights. There is another in April. Also in July, in Calheta,
is the biennial festival with processions, cultural and sports events. The
dates of many festivals vary each year, so please check with the tourist
information office. There is also some criticism of the way these festivals
have developed, with too much imported rock music to the detriment of
traditional Azorean culture.

Festa de São Jorge Velas; week around 23 Apr
Espírito Santo Jun
Semana Cultural Velas; 1st week of Jul
Festa de São Tiago Ribeira Seca & Calheta; 4th week of Jul
Festa do Sant'Ana Velas; last week of Jul
Festival de Julho Calheta; 3rd week of Jul
Festa de N Sra Rosário Velas & Norte Pequeno; middle of Aug
Festa da Caldeira do Sr Santo Cristo Calheta; 1st week of Sep
Festa de N Sra das Dores Velas; 2nd/3rd week of Sep
Festa de N Sra das Neves Velas; 3rd week of Sep
Festa de N Sra Rosário Topo; 2nd week of Sep
Festa de Santa Catarina Calheta; last week of Nov

Serra do Topo, Caldeira de Santo Cristo, Cristo–Fajã dos Cubres Medium difficulty, 10km, 2½ hours. Down to and along the north coast.

Serra do Topo–Fajã dos Vimes Medium difficulty, 5km, 2½ hours. Mostly downhill, on the south coast.

Fajã de São João–Lourais–Fajã dos Vimes Medium difficulty, 10km, 3½ hours. Along the south-coast cliffs.

Pico do Pedro, Pico da Esperança–Fajã do Ouvidor Medium difficulty, 16.8km, 4 hours. Along the spine of the island.

Fajã de Além Medium difficulty, 6km, 3 hours. A circular walk down to the *fajã* from near the Santo António chapel, west of Norte Grande.

Trilho do Norte Pequeno Medium difficulty, 11km, 3 hours. A circular walk from Norte Pequeno descending the cliff face to the *fajã* settlements.

RECREATIONAL FOREST RESERVES
Sete Fontes Forest Park Signposted from the Velas to Rosais road. Here, at the Seven Fountains, the forestry department has laid out an attractive 12ha park with ornamental planting sheltered and shaded by trees. There are picnic tables, a barbecue area, and some animals. The surrounding countryside is a mixture of meadows and forestry. Many of the roads are unsurfaced, and a relaxing day can be spent exploring the area on foot (see also page 173).

Silveira Off the EN-2 main road, from Velas 5km beyond Calheta. This 10ha forest between 300m and 375m altitude on a steep south-facing hill is picturesquely crossed by several streams, once used to power watermills. There are numerous paths and shady walks, picnic areas, a deer enclosure, and some amusing exercise equipment. It is quite charming (see page 177).

BIRDS AND FLOWERS The most interesting areas are the famous *fajãs*. Best known is **Fajã dos Cubres** on the north coast east of Norte Pequeno, formed largely by the 1757 earthquake and subsequent erosion and with a biologically rich, very indented lagoon. Groundwater enters the lagoon but causeways built across it have created two habitats, essentially marine to the west and fresh water in the east. It is among the most important wetland habitats in the Azores. Growing among the pain-inflicting sharp rush, *Juncus acutus*, is goldenrod, *Solidago sempervirens*, or cubres after which the *fajã* is named. Wild celery, wild carrot, orache and the submerged herb beaked tasselweed are among the varied plants. Eurasian coot and greenshank, snipe, terns and a long list of rarities can make this a rewarding site for birds, especially coming as it does at the end of a beautiful cliff walk (see page 181).

A little further eastwards along the coast is the **Fajã de Santo Cristo**. Its lagoon is well known for being the only place in the Azores where cockles are found, but these delicious molluscs are now protected. It is also one of the best places for surfing. This nature reserve has one of the largest populations of endemic scabious, *Scabiosa nitens*.

Ilhéu do Topo off the far eastern end of São Jorge is a Special Protected Area because of its birdlife. The islet has in excess of 2,000 Cory's shearwaters among its many breeding seabirds.

At the other island extremity, the high coastal cliffs at **Ponta dos Rosais** support an interesting vegetation that can only without difficulty and danger be glimpsed from a distance. It is an important site for migratory birds and is a passage point for whales, dolphin and turtles.

SWIMMING

Velas Artificial pool, and also natural rock pools near the Hotel São Jorge.

Urzelina Natural pools and harbour swimming with changing facilities. About 100m further on at **Portinhos** is another access to the sea with facilities and a grassy relaxation area.

Fajã Grande Natural rock pool with all facilities.

Fajã do Ouvidor Natural swimming pool with facilities near the harbour, including a restaurant.

AROUND THE ISLAND

São Jorge is an attenuated island so to travel everywhere takes a disproportionate amount of time. Many visitors are based in Velas and content themselves with seeing Rosais in the far west, and then a central circuit taking in both north and south coasts but not going further east than Calheta.

VELAS Velas, the main town of São Jorge, remains very small, and the old part around the pretty harbour has been generally well cared for and is most charming. The narrow backstreets, some fine houses with their wrought-iron balconies, the little shops, and the inviting, intriguing and imposing 18th-century gateway, or **Portão do Mar** [174 G2], all go to make a pleasing whole. You will even find a boat or two parked on the road along with the cars. Some of the little streets have been very prettily pedestrianised, and paved in the traditional manner of small black setts with designs in white depicting activities of the island. One street is now a pretty shopping area, with hanging baskets filled with flowers, a good cake shop at one end and the attractive town square at the other, and a fine replica now replaces the time-battered classic old bandstand. At a little distance the unmistakable and very modern community building declares Velas is really part of the 21st century; inside is the public library, meeting rooms and a splendid 220-seat theatre. There is an imposing parish church, the **Church of São Jorge** [174 F2] no less, which has been built and modified from the 17th century and of particular note is the carved wooden retable. The 17th-century **Church of Nossa Senhora da Conceição** [174 E3] was a former Franciscan monastery and is now cared for by nuns and well worth seeing. Tucked away in one of the small streets is a museum of sacred art, showing Indo-Portuguese items and silver altar vessels. Built upon a *fajã*, the harbour and old town is beautifully set against surrounding high cliffs, and the new marina complements it.

ROSAIS Rosais itself is a very linear village running along the road, but this is also the name given to the whole of the end of the island west of Velas. After you pass through the village you will come to the signposted Miradouro Pica da Velho, and at 493m this gives a commanding view over this part of the island. The viewpoint is generously planted with camellias, hydrangeas, azaleas and agapanthus so it is also very pretty when they flower; it is part of the Sete Fontes Recreational Reserve.

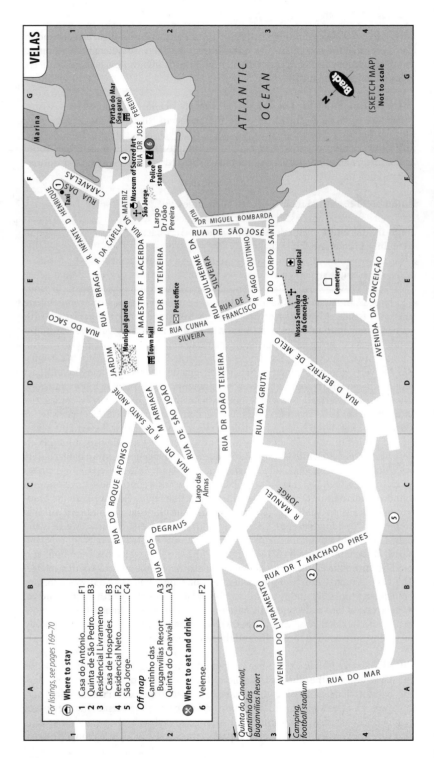

VELAS

For listings, see pages 169–70

Where to stay

1 Casa do António.............F1
2 Quinta de São Pedro........B3
3 Residencial Livramento
   Casa de Hospedes..........B3
4 Residencial Neto............F2
5 São Jorge...................C4

Off map

Cantinho das
Buganvilias Resort...........A3
Quinta do Canavial............A3

Where to eat and drink

6 Velense....................F2

ATLANTIC

OCEAN

(SKETCH MAP)
Not to scale

Marina

Portão do Mar
(Sea gate)

RUA DR JOSÉ PEREIRA

Museum of Sacred Art

Police
station

São Jorge

Largo
Dr João
Pereira

RUA DAS CARAVELAS

D HENRIQUE

R INFANTE D

RUA T BRAGA

R DA CAPELA

RUA DA MATRIZ

R MAESTRO F LACERDA

RUA DR M TEIXEIRA

RUA DR MIGUEL BOMBARDA

RUA DE SÃO JOSÉ

RUA GUILHERME DA SILVEIRA

RUA DE S FRANCISCO

R GAGO COUTINHO

R DO CORPO SANTO

Hospital

Nossa Senhora
da Conceição

Cemetery

AVENIDA DA CONCEIÇÃO

RUA D BEATRIZ DE MELO

RUA DA GRUTA

RUA DR JOÃO TEIXEIRA

RUA DE SÃO JOÃO

RUA DR M ARRIAGA

RUA DR A DE SANTO ANDRE

RUA DO ROQUE AFONSO

RUA DOS DEGRAUS

Largo das
Almas

R MANUEL JORGE

RUA DR T MACHADO PIRES

AVENIDA DO LIVRAMENTO

AVENIDA DA CONCEIÇÃO

RUA DO MAR

Quinta do Canavial,
Cantinho das
Buganvilias Resort

Camping,
football stadium

RUA DO SACO

JARDIM

Municipal garden

Town Hall

Post office

RUA CUNHA SILVEIRA

Taxi

174

FAROL DOS ROSAIS This lighthouse is at the far western end of the island, and is also the end of the road. It is now abandoned, after the earthquake of 1980 made the cliffs unstable. Be very careful if you walk near the lighthouse as there are deep holes in the ground.

THE CENTRAL PART OF THE ISLAND BETWEEN VELAS AND CALHETA Leaving Velas, take the road to the north coast signposted to Norte Grande, and go first through **Beira**, and continuing on the north road you pass through **Toledo**, now just a tiny village, which was probably first settled by Spanish immigrants soon after King Philip of Spain invaded Portugal. The settlement of **Santo António** was destroyed in the earthquake of 1980, and rebuilt.

Norte Grande–Velas Norte Grande is the largest village in the north. Do visit the church, Nossa Senhora das Neves, Our Lady of the Snows, dated 1762; it has a quiet and beautiful interior with splendid *azulejos* and modern stained-glass windows. Note the weathervane in the shape of a fish; this is peculiar to São Jorge and is the symbol adopted by early Christians. Take the road steeply descending by the side of the church and signposted to **Fajã do Ouvidor**. Stop first at the *miradouro* for a fine view of the village below; on a clear day you can see Graciosa and to your right, further along the coast, Fajã da Ribeira da Areia. Go down to the *fajã* where there is a small harbour and a natural swimming pool. From the harbour yams were once exported to Graciosa in exchange for clay roof tiles. There are waterfalls along the coast; if you are enjoying a gloriously sunny day and a period without rain, bad luck! You will not see much. Come instead when it is raining in torrents and you will see good waterfalls. The lava here came from what is now called Pico da Esperança, 1,053m, which you can see high above you, but the eruption is lost in pre-history. There are two short walks you can do here over the lava, taking the path next to the house with the new conspicuous stone driveway.

In the middle of the next village, **Ribeira da Areia**, there is a stone sign pointing the way down to Fajã da Ribeira da Areia; it takes about 45 minutes to descend, somewhat longer to climb back up. It makes you appreciate just how isolated some of these communities were and still are.

Move on to the large village of **Norte Pequeno** where the road turns south to Calheta. Look out for the asphalt road signposted down to Fajã dos Cubres; from the top there is probably one of the finest views of the coast. The *fajã* beyond is

DECORATIVE PAVING

Decorative paving has long been a feature of Moorish Spain and Portugal, although today it is the latter where it is most popular. It first appeared in the Azores in 1825, when the governor had it laid in front of his residence in Horta. The idea soon spread but most of the present paving dates from the 1940s. The black stones are, of course, basalt from abundant local sources but the white are limestone and have to be imported. A full container load costs around €4,000. On mainland Portugal the situation is reversed, and white dominates. A knapping-hammer is used to shape the individual stones which are then laid on a thick layer of sand and dry cement, with the gaps filled with dry sand. It is always fascinating to watch the paviors at work as they apply their considerable skill in a seemingly most nonchalant manner to give great charm to the archipelago's streets.

Fajã da Caldeira de Santo Cristo, another isolated settlement with its nearest road an hour's walk from the road ending below you. Its lagoon is well known for being the only place in the Azores where cockles are found; these delicious molluscs are now protected, but harvested in strictly limited numbers. It is also one of the best places for surfing.

Cross the island to Calheta, but before you get there take the main road left signposted to Topo and then go down to **Ribeira Seca**. On the skyline above you will see five wind turbines generating 20% of the island's energy requirement. The road is very pretty, lined with flowering azaleas, hydrangeas, escallonia and tibouchina shrubs. Near the church is a large private house covered with painted tiles, and a 17m-tall chimney inspired by the Royal Palace at Sintra. It was built in 1905, in French colonial style, by Gaspar de Silva, a Hawaiian emigrant who returned very wealthy – the current epidemic of pretentious new building would seem to be nothing new! Another house belonging to him with the same kind of exterior tiles may be seen in the centre of Velas. Francesco Lacerdo, the Azores' greatest composer and friend of Claude Debussy, was born here in 1869 and later lived in Urzelina.

Go along the lower road into **Calheta**, in size second only to Velas. Calheta developed as a town, but Velas has the better harbour and so became the principal town, later reinforced by the construction of its nearby airport. There remains a healthy rivalry. Calheta is on Fajã Grande, one of the flat coastal plains around the island. There is a recently extended busy harbour, with its small fishing fleet, near which may be seen an old tuna factory. There are public toilets, a post office and a café/bar serving light meals. There is also the Francisco Lacerda Museum (see page 171). The tourist information office ($\oplus$ *Mon–Fri*) is next to the municipal offices.

Continuing on the lower road from Calheta you pass through **Fajã Grande** itself, whereupon leaving on the left is a blue-and-white-painted factory that cans tuna fish in an old style; the brand name is Santa Catarina and is held to be among the best; production is seasonal and come winter the shops quickly sell out.

Following the main road back to Velas, you will come to **Manadas** (meaning 'a group of cows') where you must stop to see the 18th-century parish church dedicated to Santa Bárbara. It is very small and in a most beautiful setting by the sea adjacent to the ruined remains of a fort that once defended the little harbour. This gem of Azorean Baroque is the finest in the archipelago, and the interior has remained almost unchanged for many generations. There are splendid tiles telling the story of Santa Bárbara, a rich gilt carved altar and a cedarwood ceiling. Legend has it that in 1485, a sailor, Joaquim António da Silveira, found an image of Santa Bárbara in a wooden box off the coast of São Jorge and thought a church in her honour should be built. Work started in 1510, but it was later enlarged to its present form in about 1770, and of the original there remains a window and a font. The church may be locked, but someone in the nearby houses just past the bottom of the hill on the right will know who has the key!

At **Terreiros** is a small harbour with picnic tables and two restaurants. **Urzelina** suffered tremendously in the eruption of 1808 when the lava flowed down and buried everything except the church tower and this remains today as a monument to the buried village. Many of the villagers sheltered inside the church and were either buried or suffocated. It is on the right, close to the main road, surrounded by a pretty little garden. Overlooking the small harbour is a seating area with two commemorative stones. The first concerns a former harbour master. A British schooner, the *Tamar Queen*, anchored offshore and was boarded by the harbour master Amaro Soares but bad weather quickly blew up and the ship set sail for England. Sadly, Senhor Soares was murdered, and the crew later punished. The second gives the names of early settlers. Immediately above the harbour are the remains of an old Portuguese fort, now a summer café/bar. On the harbour's other side is a house with a large tile picture on its wall; this was once a temporary store for oranges before they were exported to England. There are some manor houses in the village that reflected the wealth of the orange farmers. Urzelina gets its name from the lichen that was such an important export in the early days after settlement. A small ethnographic museum by the harbour is open in summer.

Ribeira do Nabo is a small village beyond Urzelina where the Cooperativa Artesanto Sra da Encarnação offers a good range of nicely handmade goods including knitted pullovers, appliqué, macramé, ceramics, items in wood, jams and many other things. Before you reach the airport at Queimada there is a road going down to the sea and a very primitive landing place called Cais da Queimada. In summer there used to be a boat that ferried between here and Velas, long before construction of the new marina. The blackened stone tower that looks as if it might once have been a windmill is an old lime kiln. The best thing though is the sea-level view of Velas, worth seeing if you travel by air and do not come or go by the ferry.

THE EASTERN PART OF THE ISLAND To reach Fajã dos Vimes, going down from the main road to Topo, is a most beautiful drive though luxuriant forests of largely acacia, the high humidity offering shelter for ferns and mosses. Stop at the Miradouro dos Vimes; 300m below is Fajã Fragueira and in the distance your immediate destination of Fajã dos Vimes. As you further descend note two old watermills and the overhead wires still used today for transporting forage and fuelwood to the houses way below. In the village, find the Café Nunes; here they make arabica coffee from beans grown in the village. The plants produce two crops a year. Close by is the small weaving centre where the famous woollen bedspreads are woven. Made with natural colours and traditional designs and looms, and wool imported from Santa Maria and mainland Portugal, they are not only collectors' items, but also a great pleasure to use. Sadly, there are now only two people weaving and it takes a week and a half to make a double bedspread. These cost around €500. Other people also make them, and they can be found in the shops in Velas. Towards the cliff you will see growing many pollarded willows that are used for basket making; *vimes* means 'withy' or 'osier'. From the end of the village there is an obvious footpath eastwards to make the short walk to Fajã dos Bodes and its watermill.

Return to the main road and continue eastwards; if you have time, drop down to Fajã de São João with its mixed orchards enjoying the microclimate, the watermills and dragon trees. Back on the main road, you will pass extensive areas of pasture to come to Santo Antão and finally Topo with its lighthouse. Just off the end is the Ilhéu do Topo, a strictly protected sanctuary for birds. The very first settlement on São Jorge was at Topo, but the Serra do Topo so separated the people from the rest of the island that it was easier to go by boat to Terceira for their supplies rather than travel by land.

On the way back to Velas, above Fajã dos Vimes, you will see a surfaced road going off on your right by the side of the turbine parks. This ranks highly among the many beautiful roads of the Azores, as it winds along through a gentle landscape of small pastures surrounded by hedges, especially lovely in July and August when the hydrangeas are flowering. It is not a long drive, so do stop along the way and enjoy late-afternoon shadows and the tranquillity. You will come to a junction. Turn left to Silveira; if you turned right you would go to Norte Pequeno. Soon you will see signs marking the way to the Silveira Recreational Forest Park, a beautifully green

7

semi-gardened area to stroll around. Should you arrive earlier in the day, then it is a cool place to enjoy a picnic (see page 172).

WALKS

Given reasonable weather the coastal walk, Loural to Fajã de São João, and the walk across to the north coast, down to Fajã da Caldeira de Santo Cristo and along the coast to Fajã dos Cubres, are the finest and just being up on the route of my first walk, Caldeirinhas to Norte Grande, with its ever-changing views, never ceases to inspire.

CALDEIRINHAS TO NORTE GRANDE (*Time: about 5hrs; distance: 15km*) The walking is easy, with a gradual ascent followed by a long descent all the time along a wide, well-made, unsurfaced road that follows the spine of the island. At up to some 1,000m altitude, this walk should be made in good weather otherwise mist will certainly obscure the views, and these are truly magnificent on a clear day. In winter, it is a photographer's dream. It can be very atmospheric if mist engulfs you. This happens, but take care, especially in winter, for then these high places are deserted; only in the summer months are cattle brought up to graze and people are about.

Ask your taxi to put you down at Caldeirinhas. This is just to the east of Pico das Caldeirinhas, on the road that crosses the island from Urzelina to Santo António, where the unsurfaced farm road begins, signposted to Pico da Esperança.

Cross the cattle grid at the beginning of the black dirt road, and just keep walking! The road later changes to softer coloured, less threatening, red stones. The large volcano of black scoriae – you can see that some has been quarried for building use – is the one that so tragically erupted in 1808 and destroyed Urzelina. As you move on past this rather sobering place the road snakes between different small peaks and gives you constantly changing views. Look out for Graciosa Island on your left, and then Pico on your right, and for the villages down on the coast; you will soon see Urzelina with its small harbour and blue-green swimming pool, and Norte Grande on the opposite north coast. When you reach the base of Pico da Esperança there is a path to the summit should you feel tempted to climb it; at 1,053m it is the highest point of São Jorge.

Following the road round its base the most fabulous view awaits: the rest of the length of the spine of São Jorge and all its grassy calderas. It is an amazing landscape, and has to be seen to be believed. In the far distance are the wind turbines above Ribeira Seca and to their right you should just be able to make out the tiny white church of Loural, and to the left Norte Pequeno. Continue along the spine, and when a dirt road comes in from your right, this leads down to Manadas. You could of course take this road, and end your walk on the south coast; it takes about 1½ hours to descend, but do carry on and then, as you start to leave the island's spine and begin to descend to the north coast, the road winds down through an amazing dwarf forest of endemic juniper and tree heathers. On a clear day you can see Terceira and Graciosa. When you get to where the road forks, ignore the right-hand fork which leads down to Norte Pequeno. At the next fork the right-hand road is marked with a green signpost to Norte Pequeno. Ignore this and continue until you come to another road going down to your right, signposted this time to Norte Grande. Drivers must take this to drop down to the main road, then turn left to the village. Walkers have the privileged option of avoiding a 2km walk along the main road by ignoring this turn-off and following the road you are on straight ahead over a cattle grid. In about 2km you will come to a road going down on your right. Take this to come into Norte Grande, where you can get a taxi.

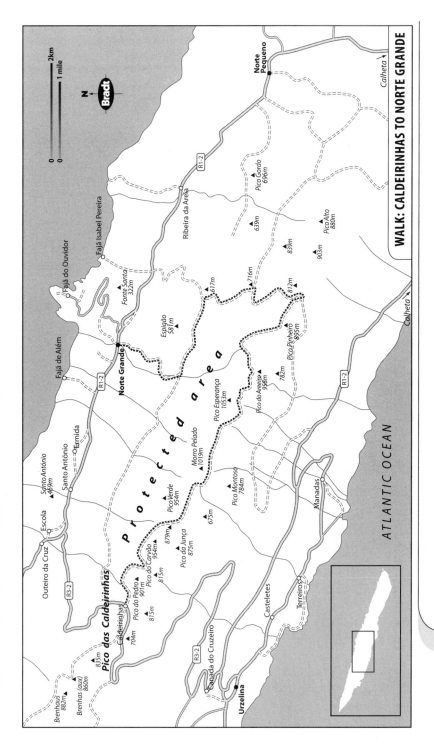

ATLANTIC OCEAN

WALK: CALDEIRINHAS TO NORTE GRANDE

Norte
Pequeno

Pico Gordo
696m

639m

Pico Alto
880m

839m

903m

Calheta

Ribeira da Areia

R1-2

617m

716m

812m

Fajã Isabel Pereira

Fonte Santa
322m

Espigão
581m

Pico Pinheiro
895m

782m

Pico do Areeiro
956m

Calheta

Fajã do Ouvidor

Fajã de Além

Norte Grande

Pico Esperança
1053m

R1-2

R1-2

Santo António
469m

Ermida

Santo António

Morro Pelado
1019m

Pico Verde
954m

675m

Pico Montoso
784m

Manadas

Escola

Outeiro da Cruz

Pico do Pedro
901m

879m

Pico da Junça
875m

Casteletes

Terreiros

R2-2

815m

Pico do Carvão
954m

815m

Canada do Cruzeiro

Caldeirinhas

704m

Pico das Caldeirinhas

835m

R3-2

Urzelina

Brenhas
882m

Brenhas (aux)
860m

Protected area

N

Bradt

0   1 mile
0   2km

WALKS: SOUTH COAST TO FAJÃ DE SÃO JOÃO; NORTH COAST TO FAJÃ DOS CUBRES

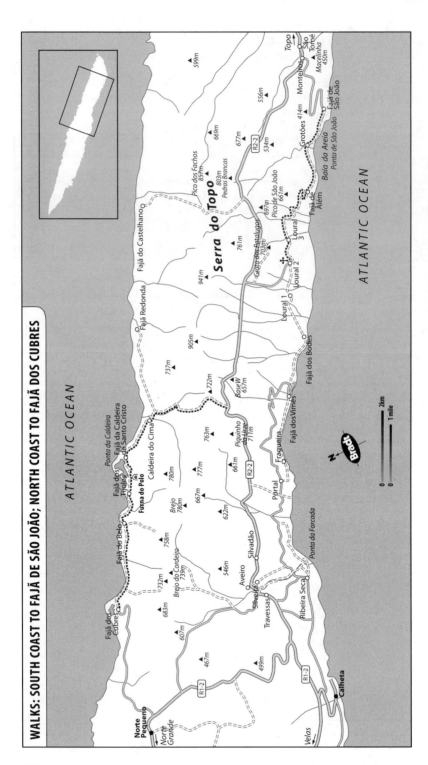

SOUTH COAST TO FAJÃ DE SÃO JOÃO (*Time: about 2hrs, & about 1hr to drive back to Velas; distance: 7km*) Not only a good walk, this path also reveals something of the simple life of the farmer using these steep slopes to produce crops or pasture animals. In summer this is best done in the late afternoon, so that as you walk into Fajã de São João you can watch the sun beginning to set behind Pico. It is almost all downhill and the path can be difficult when wet.

You can either ask your driver to meet you at a pre-arranged time at the end of the walk in Fajã de São João, or you can walk 5km up the asphalt road into São Tomé, which is a small village on the main road with a bar from where you can telephone for a taxi.

If you are driving yourself, go to **Loural** and begin the walk from the church. Follow the farm road for about 700m and you come to farmhouses and a little stream.

The other option is to take a taxi to the place on the main road near the old cheese factory above Loural, where a grassy farm track 3m wide between two low stone walls sets off downhill for 100m or so, then veers round to the left. The drivers know it. It is about 1.5km after the sign to Lourais; Lourais is the plural of Loural because there are three Lourals! Follow the farm trail and soon on your left you can hear a stream flowing with its banks covered by tall shrubs, remnants of the laurisilva forest that would once have covered these hills. Rounding the bluff, there is the sea, and a lovely view of the church at Loural. Head on down the path to where you come to farmhouses and a little stream. Thanks to overgenerous EU money, you will see the newly asphalted road leading up to Loural church.

From this point continue on the farm road winding down the hill and when you come to a turning off to the left by a cattle trough take this and go down an old paved donkey trail.

In 15 minutes you pass a waterfall, and then caves enlarged with small boulders used as shelters for a horse, or a couple of cows and even a pig. Continue, and the village of Fajã de São João comes into view at the foot of a high cliff. You pass small stone houses where their owners live for two or three months twice a year: in the winter to grow their beans and potatoes and again in September and October to make their wine. Then just above the beach pass a stone watermill and you are in the village.

NORTH COAST TO FAJÃ DOS CUBRES (*Time: about 2hrs down to Caldeira de Santo Cristo & 1hr to the end of the walk in Fajã dos Cubres; it takes about 1hr to drive back to Velas; distance: 10km*) It is magnificent country and you will want to stay and enjoy the ever-changing views, and the contrast between the high grasslands where you begin the walk and the fascinating villages at sea level, in their microclimate.

This walk begins above Fajã dos Vimes on the Topo road, at a point about midway between Ribeira dos Vimes and Ribeira do Capadinho. Ask your driver to take you to the *canada* or old trail leading down to Fajã da Caldeira de Santo Cristo. It begins on the other side of the road from a concrete shelter, now well signposted at the start of the walk, about 5km on from **Silveira**. Arrange for a taxi to collect you at the end of the walk from **Fajã dos Cubres**.

The old stone track climbs for a short distance and very soon you have left the south coast behind and at around 700m altitude you look down over the Caldeira do Cima to the north coast. The land falls away before you and you are atop an amphitheatre enclosed by hills. About 20 minutes into the walk you come to a ridge between two ravines. The path, now narrow, starts winding down through a mixture of grazed grassland, juniper and tree heather. There are several gates along the path, with self-closing devices made from gnarled tree stems that look as though they have come straight from a children's book of illustrated fairy tales.

About 45 minutes into the walk you come to a fork in the path and you bear round to the left. In another 20 minutes you are down to a tumbling brook, and a good place for a picnic with somewhere to cool a bottle of wine. Almost immediately another stream comes down from the right with a small bridge over it.

Ten minutes later you reach two watermills by the side of a larger stream, and a splendid grassy bridge crossing it. Note the large plants of New Zealand flax, *Phormium tenax*, growing around the mill houses, once used for tying the flour sacks. Continuing, you will come to a view looking down into the Fajã da Caldeira de Santo Cristo and its lagoon; the path follows the cliff. Another 20 minutes and you are by the church.

This must be one of the most isolated villages in the Azores, and having got down to it you have now to leave as do the villagers. This is by a clearly worn track running along the coast. In half an hour you pass the remaining buildings of Fajã do Belo and in another 40 minutes you reach Fajã dos Cubres.

8

Faial

Known as the Blue Island because of its abundant hydrangeas, Faial is quite spectacular when they are blooming from mid-July through August. My taxi driver said he had calculated there are 56km of hydrangea hedges. Some years ago a letter appeared in *The Times* London newspaper bemoaning the abundant hydrangeas in the Azores and appealing for something else to be planted!

Much of the landscape is pasture, although there is now some forest; at one time the tree cover was so depleted that wood for fuel was imported from Pico. At the time of settlement the island was luxuriously forested, including an abundance of what the Portuguese called *faya*, and so named the island Fayal. The plant was later collected by Kew's first paid plant hunter Robert Masson in 1777, who introduced it to the gardens where it was scientifically named *Myrica faya*.

Although the island is dominated by its central caldera and nearby highest point of 1,043m, the visitor is not really aware of this, travelling around the island past its pretty villages, lush pastures and vigorous hedgerows.

Picturesque Horta has long been a major port of the Azores and it is really this town that has dominated the island; today its marina is a major tourist attraction and the harbour has the largest maritime painting collection in the world. More than 1,400 yachts put in each year for supplies and repairs as they make the Atlantic crossing and in summer this influx of mostly young visitors certainly enlivens the evenings, especially between May and July.

History is everywhere among the streets and old buildings, and always across the channel is the great cone of Pico. Sometimes it is totally clear of cloud, seeming arrogantly to challenge the elements to renew their erosive attacks. More often, it is adorned with a fast-changing wardrobe of clouds, engulfing its summit, encircling its midriff, or clothing it from apex to base, and obscuring it from our sight but not our consciousness; you never tire of glancing across the channel. In winter with its uppermost quarter briefly dusted with snow and fronted with a travel-brochure blue sea the mountain is breathtakingly beautiful.

Horta, the only town, will take at least a half day to explore, easily a full day with the museums. Seeing the highlights of the rest of the island can be done on a half-day taxi tour. The view into the caldera, green and a nature reserve, and the reverse view down to Horta, across the channel to Pico Island and up to its volcano summit with São Jorge beyond, make it well worth a drive up. Then there is Capelinhos, the site of the major 1957 eruption which added another 2km² to Faial; the half-buried lighthouse and village houses, slowly becoming exposed once more by wind erosion from their smothering of ash, bear witness to the human drama. All of this is now enhanced by the recently opened interpretative centre spectacularly built below ground in the fallout from the eruption, for which you should allow 1½ to two hours. Recently there have been many new developments and Faial now offers

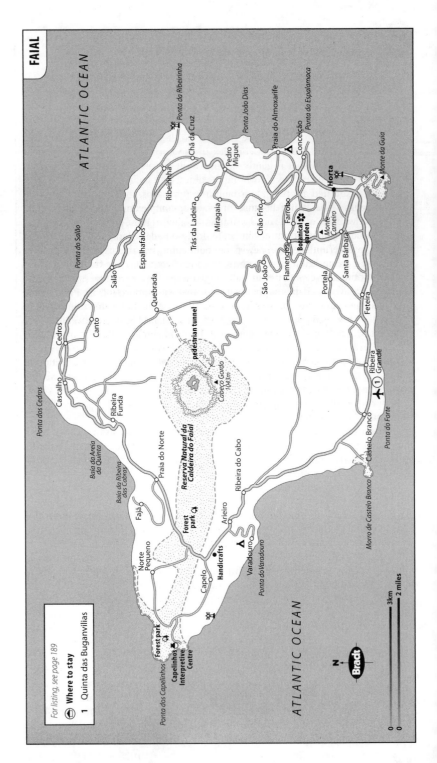

FAIAL

ATLANTIC OCEAN

ATLANTIC OCEAN

For listing, see page 189

Where to stay

1 Quinta das Buganvilias

Ponta dos Cedros

Ponta do Salão

Baía da Areia da Quinta

Baía da Ribeira dos Cabras

Ponta dos Capelinhos

Ponta do Varadouro

Morro de Castelo Branco

Ponta do Forte

Ponta da Espalamaca

Monte da Guia

Ponta João Dias

Ponta do Ribeirinha

Cascalho

Cedros

Canto

Salão

Espalhafalos

Quebrada

Ribeira Funda

Praia do Norte

Fajã

Norte Pequeno

Capelo

Varadouro

Arieiro

Ribeira do Cabo

Forest park

Capelinhos Interpretive Centre

Handicrafts

Forest park

Reserva Natural da Caldeira do Faial

Cabeço Gordo 1043m

pedestrian tunnel

Ribeirinha

Chã da Cruz

Pedro Miguel

Trás da Ladeira

Miragaia

Chão Frio

São João

Flamengos

Farrobo

Botanical garden

Monte Carneiro

Santa Bárbara

Portela

Feteira

Ribeira Grande

Castelo Branco

Conceição

Praia do Almoxarife

Horta

N

Bradt

3km

2 miles

0

0

184

a good range of interests and activities including well-marked walking trails, with another museum and an aquarium at Porto Pim planned.

BACKGROUND

GEOLOGY Faial is the nearest island to the Mid-Atlantic Ridge, some 100km to the west, and grew up on its flanks from a depth of 1,500m from the same northwest–southeast-aligned fissures that gave rise to Pico. It was formed by four volcanic complexes. First, the Ribeirinha complex in the northeast of the island, part of a shield volcano (one that is gently sloping, built of very fluid basaltic lava from many closely spaced vents) and forming the oldest rocks of Faial at around 700,000 years ago. Associated are two major fault lines or scarps, to the north and to the south of Pedro Miguel village. Second, the Cedros complex in the north and linked to the development of the central Caldeira Volcano; Horta Formation, the third stage of Faial's construction, began around 11,000 years ago, with what at first were Surtseyan eruptions when seawater could enter the vent, mix with the rising magma, and create steam causing the magma to shatter into fine fragments. Once the vents were above water, eruptions changed to more moderate types. Monte Queimado and Monte da Guia, which protect what is now Horta harbour, date from this period. Monte da Guia, consisting of thin layers of yellowish ash, often compacted or welded into tuff, erupted in shallow water whereas the burnt cinders of adjacent Monte Queimado erupted on dry land. Finally, there is the Capelo Formation, the most recent complex. The Capelo Peninsula grew westwards from a series of eruptions on land, remaining evidence being the alignment of domes starting from near the Caldeira Volcano that are a continuum of the Pedro Miguel Fault. Only two eruptions at the very end of the peninsula occurred underwater: these were Costa da Nua and the latest, Capelinhos. The Ilhéus dos Capelinhos were evidence of an earlier eruption, but they were destroyed by the Capelinhos eruption. In historical times, the Cabeço do Fogo (*cabeço* meaning 'head') and Picarito erupted in 1672; they caused seven months of intermittent earthquakes spreading ash over the island and lava flows which buried houses and farmland in and around Praia do Norte and formed the present Zona do Mistério. It is assumed some of the four systems may have been active simultaneously.

The Caldeira Volcano that today dominates the island began as a stratovolcano, a steep-sided cone with a medium or low basaltic explosive activity forming bedded layers of lava fragments and flows. Some 16,000 years ago, this eruptive pattern changed to a mainly explosive acidic form, producing a pale viscous acidic rock which often formed rugged lava flows and domes. During this later period the Caldeira Volcano erupted at least 14 times, one of them coinciding with the opening of the caldera 1,000 years ago. This was a Plinian eruption, a highly dramatic and powerful explosion of gas, steam, ash and pumice rising kilometres into the air, together with pyroclastic flows – avalanches of hot gas, ash and rock debris. The caldera is now 400m deep and 1,450m in diameter with almost vertical walls. The highest point of the island is Cabeço Gordo at 1,043m, a basaltic cinder cone on the side of the Caldeira Volcano.

Future events will most likely occur in connection with the Capelo Formation and the Caldeira Volcano. At a second level, the Horta platform might offer excitement, as might the faults of Pedro Miguel.

HISTORY Early maps present the island as *Insule de Ventura*, and the Portuguese discovered it in the first half of the 15th century and began settlement. Led by

Josse Van Huerter, a few Flemish settlers came to Faial in 1468, and just 20 years later their number had grown to 1,500. Establishing themselves first at Praia do Almoxarife, they soon moved inland to the Vale dos Flamengos, not far from Horta, and the parish still called Flamengos reflects this early settlement. The first two areas developed were at either end of what is now the main port and marina of Horta. The Azores have always played an important role in the history of the Atlantic. Laden Portuguese ships returning from the West Indies would seek protection from the many pirates awaiting them off the African coast. As both the new English settlements in North America and the West Indies and the Portuguese Empire grew, Horta became a busy sea port, then the only really safe anchorage in the Azores. Horta was not only trading but also victualling, supplying good fresh water and fresh vegetables, repairing ships and providing crews for East Indiamen, West Indiamen, codfishers, slavers, ships carrying wine, or sugar, or salt, or miscellaneous cargoes, and men-of-war. In addition, there has always been a great deal of inter-island trading, as well as between the islands and mainland Portugal.

Of course, it was not always peaceful; in 1583, the Spanish attacked and fought a battle for the Santa Cruz fortress. This still overlooks the harbour, but is now a hotel. During Spanish rule English privateers attacked several times; Sir Walter Raleigh razed Horta by fire, carried off the governor and either captured or destroyed all of a Spanish fleet home-bound from Mexico. A far more peaceful English visitor was Captain James Cook who, in 1775, checked his navigational instruments onshore before sailing off to explore the South Seas.

Early whaling fleets came to Horta for supplies, rest, to offload whale oil and recruit crews, anchoring in Porto Pim. Later, entrepreneurs developed warehouses and other facilities to further attract ships to Horta. Among these was American John Dabney who arrived at the beginning of the 1800s, and whose family influenced commerce for 100 years. Oranges and Pico wine were two important exports they handled, as well as whale products, whale fishing, ships' chandlery, and much else. Extremely successful, they lived life on a lavish scale, building several large houses, entertaining and exchanging latest news with ships' officers, and being generous benefactors to the islanders. The number of whalers increased, especially from New Bedford, which is now twinned with Horta. Work began in 1876 on the docks and sea wall to better protect the port so that steam ships could also call as well as sailing ships, and so bunkering services were added with much of the coal shipped out from Liverpool, England.

The world's first reliable transatlantic telegraph cable connection was laid in 1866, and more quickly followed during the next 50 years linking many regions of the world. In 1893, the first cable was laid linking Horta with Ponta Delgada and on to Carcavelos on the Arrabida coast south of Lisbon. This was operated by an English company, the Europe and Azores Telegraph Co, which eventually became, in 1934, part of Cable & Wireless.

These early telegraph cables had a relatively short operational range, and Horta's mid-Atlantic position was ideal for a relay station for transatlantic cables. It was also a good interchange location, and Deutsch-Atlantische Telegraphengesellschaft, founded in 1900, laid its first cable to link the USA and Germany via the Azores. Further cables followed, between Horta and Waterville in Ireland, Horta and Porthcurno in Cornwall and on to Mindelo in the Cape Verde Islands to connect with other cables to Africa and South America.

In the early 1900s, there were some 300 employees – British, Germans, Americans and Portuguese. The last cable connecting Horta was laid in 1928, the latest technology allowing simultaneous transmission of five messages in each direction, a total of 500 words per minute. Now Horta was one of the most important cable centres in the world. It was in 1969 that the last cable company left, superseded by new technology. Today something like 70–80% of telephone and data communications are made through submarine fibre-optic cables, the remainder via satellites. Modern systems can cross the Atlantic without the need for intermediate landing stations. The cables cross the Mid-Atlantic Ridge spaced well apart where there is a low occurrence of volcanic activity, and faults owing to seismic tremors are rare.

The 1893 cable linking the Azores with mainland Europe also meant the meteorological observations made in the Azores, so far out in the Atlantic, could be transmitted rapidly; this had a tremendous influence on the development of weather forecasting. In 1901, construction of the Prince Albert of Monaco Observatory began on the summit of Cabeço das Moças, above what is now the Faial Resort Hotel, and it is still in use today. Colloquially, *moça* means 'mistress', and the hill was thus named because it was where visiting sailors courted the town's young women.

The first transatlantic crossing by seaplane was made in 1919 by the American Albert C Read, who landed off Horta *en route*, to be followed by many others. In 1933, Charles Lindbergh flew to Horta seeking an acceptable year-round route for Pan-Am's seaplanes from America to Europe. Soon after Horta became the regular stopover for the Pan-Am clipper flights, to be followed by Lufthansa, Air France and Imperial Airways, now British Airways. However, there were disadvantages: the harbour was not large enough for landings and take-offs and the big flying boats had to use the open ocean, taxiing in and out of the harbour. Ocean swells could delay flights and in December 1939, four clippers were stranded for three weeks. This romantic era of travel ended with improved land-based aircraft and a runway constructed on Santa Maria.

Now the summer yachts crossing the Atlantic make the cosmopolitan life of Horta, and tourism generally is the new growth industry. Meanwhile, cattle and fishing continue in the background.

GETTING AROUND

There are public buses, but you will need to check the current timetable with the tourist office. They are infrequent and unfortunately of little help to the visitor and so it is better to ignore them. Most frustratingly, the new interpretative centre at Capelinhos is not well served; currently you can either get out there by or leave at around 12.30. If you get stuck, you will find local drivers amenable to hitchhikers.

The best way to see the island is to take a half-day taxi tour, which will cover more or less the same ground as described below under touring by self-drive car and will cost about €60. Allow about 30 minutes for the drive from the airport to Horta; the taxi fare is around €13 plus 20% at weekends and holidays.

One thing you can do which is fun, weekdays only, is to take the 11.45 bus going westwards from the stop close to the tourist information office. This will take you round the coast to Ribeira Funda, from where it continues clockwise in line with the coast back to Horta. The whole circuit takes two hours. When you board the bus, ask for a ticket to go right round the island; you get two tickets. It is a very pretty ride at any time, and on a really sunny day under a clear blue sky in early November the island is especially beautiful. First following the coast and a sparkling blue sea you get to Capelinhos, and a good view of the 1958 eruption site and the half-buried lighthouse. Twenty years ago the area was pretty well deserted, with damaged or destroyed houses lying abandoned or buried in ash. Now people are returning, and either restoring the old houses or building new ones and it is becoming very attractive. On to Praia do Norte and to Cedros, passing through some well-forested areas, it is then down to Ribeirinha before climbing up to Espalamaca, looking down to Praia do Almoxarife on your left, to Pico, and opposite, the splendid view of Horta.

For travel to Faial, see pages 47 and 52–4.

EXCURSIONS TO OTHER ISLANDS To travel to Pico by ferry, there are regular 30-minute sailings from Horta to Madalena throughout the year and in summer about every two hours starting at 07.15, with the latest returning at 21.30. In summer a day excursion to Velas on São Jorge is possible every day, leaving Horta at 08.00 arriving at Velas at 10.15, returning at 20.20 and arriving at Horta at 22.15, but this timetable changes and you need to check the Transmacor website (*www.transmacor. pt*). Similarly, on Mondays, Wednesdays, Fridays, Saturdays and Sundays there is a service leaving Horta at 07.15 via São Jorge to Angra do Heroísmo on Terceira arriving at 12.00, returning at 18.15, and arriving Horta at 22.50. Again, check the website for the latest information. For location of listings see map, pages 184 and 194.

 # WHERE TO STAY

HORTA

Pousada de Santa Cruz (26 rooms) Rua Vasco da Gama, 9900-017 Horta; ✆292 202 200; e recepcao.stacruz@pousada.pt; www.pousadas.pt. A 16th-century fort declared a national monument in 1947. Renovated to the high standards of Pousadas de Portugal, not all rooms have a sea view; the restaurant offers regional dishes, & there's also a bar with terrace & pool overlooking the harbour & views across to Pico. €€€€€

Faial Resort Hotel (143 rooms) Rua Consul Dabney, 9901-856 Horta; ✆292 207 400; e geral@faialhotel.com; www.fayalhotel.com. Bar, snack bar, lounge, shop, games room, beauty salon, conference rooms, indoor pool, fitness room. Going since 1973, with part occupying buildings once belonging to one of the cable companies, plus addition of new wings, all set in grounds with tennis courts & swimming pool. The restaurant in the main building has a stunning view looking across the channel to Pico. €€€€€

Hotel do Canal (103 rooms) Largo Dr Manuel de Arriaga, 9900-026 Horta; ✆292 202 120; e reserves@bensaude.pt; www.bensaude. pt. By the busy harbour. Restaurant, bars, winter garden, games room, fitness centre, sauna, jacuzzi, Turkish bath, hairdresser, conference room, garage. €€€€€

Hotel Horta (80 rooms, inc 4 suites) Rua Marcelino Lima, 9900-122 Horta; ✆292 208 200; e info@hotelhorta.com; www.hotelhorta.com. Nicely appointed hotel, all rooms with balconies & sea view; heated outdoor swimming pool in a garden setting; located near the Azorean General Assembly building immediately above the town centre, entailing a short uphill walk. Very quiet & one of the most civilised places to stay in the Azores. €€€€

Hospedaria Verdemar (12 apts) Rua Dr Melo E Simas; ✆292 200 3000; e verde.maracp@mail.telepac.pt; www.verdemar-azores.com. Spacious, modern, fully equipped self-catering apartments in private enclosed grounds above the town centre, with a short uphill walk. €€€

Residencial São Francisco (32 rooms) Rua Conselheiro Medeiros, 9900-144 Horta; ✆292 200 980; www.residencialsaofrancisco. net. Simple but comfortable rooms, in the centre of town so may be noisy. French spoken. Long established but now needs some refurbishment. €€

Vila Bélgica (3 rooms) Caminho Velho da Caldeira 13, 9900-089 Horta; ✆292 392 614; www. azoresvilabelgica.com. A charming bed & breakfast with views across to Pico.

The Tourism Association (*www.casasacorianas.com*) lists 13 inviting rural tourism establishments around the island, offering from two to ten rooms.

⌂ **Quinta das Buganvilias** (8 double rooms) Castelo Branco, by a bus stop on the EN1-1A, above the airport & 6 miles from Horta; ☎292 943 255; e qta-buganvilias@hotmail.com; www.

quintadasbuganvilias.com. An old family property, with the *quinta* converted into what is now a long-established guesthouse with a bar & lounge all in a garden & orchard setting of 5 acres. €€

CAMPING

Å **Praia do Almoxarife** ☎292 292 131. This valley is charming & the village has several good eating places, the small beach is nice, & there is a lovely view across to Pico, all within a 15min taxi drive from Horta or by local bus. The campsite is supervised 24hrs, with all facilities, & tents can be hired.

Å **Varadouro** Near swimming pools, amenities & restaurant.

✖ WHERE TO EAT

In Horta, there are quite a number of restaurants, and of course the main hotels are open to non-residents; the **Faial Resort Hotel** has a stunning view across to Pico from the restaurant, and **Hotel Horta**, rather out of sight but with a good restaurant, should not be out of mind. For location of listings see map, page 194. Four recommended places are:

✖ **Restaurante Kabem Todos** Rua Bombeiros Voluntários; ☎292 292 120; ⊕ 12.00–15.00 & 19.00–23.00 Mon–Sat. In the pink wedding-cake building to the left of the fire brigade station, in the market square (Praça da República). Obviously a triumph with the locals, so best to reserve a table. Sensibly priced. Heartily recommended.

⌨ **Café Porto Pim** On the road by the port & overlooking the bay. Another easily missed eatery; tables outside. Excellent for a snack lunch offering good soup & a welcome range of sandwiches.

✖ **Taberna de Pim** Rua Nova 3, by Porto Pim; ☎292 392 239; ⊕ 11.00–01.00 Tue–Sun. Small, nice atmosphere, food cooked to order.

⌨ **Casa Tea House** Rua São João, 2 streets above the main post office; ☎292 700 053; ⊕ 14.00–midnight Mon–Fri, until 02.00 Sat & Sun. Recently opened, this is a most attractive & enterprising venture. Super ambience, delightful garden & roof terrace with town views, the perfect place for a pot of tea; take your choice from Asia, Africa, South America, plus herbal,

flower & fruit teas. Also wicked cakes, snacks & sandwiches, including smoked salmon, goat's cheese & other offerings not freely available in the Azores. Plus coffee, wines & beers.

✖ **Canto da Doca** Rua Nova, Horta; ☎292 292 444. Located in the corner of the harbour, this offers a very different meal where you cook your own dinner of seafood or meat on a very hot lump of basalt. It is great fun, albeit noisy & rather expensive for the experience, but at least there are no complaints about the chef!

PORTO DO VARADOURO

✖ **Vista da Baía** On the way to Capelo; ☎292 945 140; ⊕ Thu–Tue. Serves the best barbecued chicken on the island at a very reasonable price, with great sunsets thrown in.

CEDROS

✖ **O Esconderijo** Rua Jean Alves; ☎292 946 505. A cosy little restaurant with good food as long as you can find it! Signposted from the main road in the centre of Cedros.

ENTERTAINMENT

CINEMA The theatre [194 C1] near the main square in Horta, with its ornate music hall-style rows of boxes and Art Deco ceiling, has recently been restored and offers a mix of Hollywood and art cinema, together with occasional orchestral and jazz music. See the website for their current film programme (*www.cineclube.org*).

OTHER PRACTICALITIES

Emergency ☎112
Police [194 B5] Largo Duque d'Avila e Bolama, Horta; ☎292 208 510
Hospital [194 A4] Estrada Princípe Alberto do Mónaco, Horta; ☎292 201 000
Post office [194 C2] Largo Duque d'Avila e Bolama, Horta; ☎292 200 770

SATA Air Açores [194 C3] Largo do Infante, Horta; ☎292 293 912; also at the airport ☎292 943 112
TAP Air Portugal [194 C4] Rua Vasco da Gama, Horta; ☎292 292 665
Airport information ☎292 943 111; lost and found ☎292 943 112

WHAT TO SEE AND DO

Wandering through the streets of Horta, enjoying the present and past harbours, and making a tour to see the caldera and the scene of the last eruption is what most visitors do. One thing you should not miss is the Capelinhos Interpretative Centre, an outstanding design concept packed with information about volcanoes. If you have a car, then there are little villages to explore, tempting places to stop from which to make your own short walks, and whale watching from the clifftops.

For pleasure boat and fun fishing trips, check with the tourist information office to see who might be offering what.

MUSEUMS
Horta
Museu da Horta [194 C2] (*Largo Duque d'Avila e Bolama*; ⊕ *10.00–12.30 & 14.00–17.30 Tue–Fri, 14.00–17.30 Sat & Sun*) Housed in a former Jesuit College, it is noted for its collection of fig wood sculptures, one of the island's traditional handicrafts.

FESTIVALS ON FAIAL

By far the busiest celebration is Sea Week at the beginning of August. Primarily a yachting regatta with whaling-boat races, the channel between Faial and Pico is a mass of fluttering sails. Different musical groups perform each evening, including bands from mainland Europe, local bands and folklore groups. There are exhibitions too, and the road along the seafront is closed, allowing thousands of people to promenade. On the first Sunday at the beginning of Sea Week the Festival of Nossa Senhor da Guia, Protector of the Fishermen, takes place with a procession from Porto Pim. The dates of many festivals vary each year, so please check with the tourist information office or www.marinasazores.com for the Sea Week.

Sports and Cultural week Horta; end of Apr
Festa de N Sra Angústias Horta; 6th Sun after Easter
Festa de São João da Caldeira Horta; 24 Jun
Sea Week Horta; 1st to 2nd Sun in Aug
Festa de N Sra Lurdes Feteira; last week in Aug
Festas do Espírito Santo From May until Sep, intermittently
Festa de N Sra Saúde Varadouro; 1st week Sep
December festival Horta; Dec

Casa Manuel de Arriaga [194 B3] (*Traversa de São Francisco, Horta;* ✆ *292 293 361;* e *museu.hort.info@azores.gov.pt;* ⏲ *10.00–12.30 & 14.00–17.30 Tue–Fri; 14.00–17.30 Sat & Sun*) Opened in 2011, this stimulating new museum is in the home of the first President of the Republic of Portugal, elected in 1911. A humanist and political intellectual, the museum celebrates his life, private ideals and Republican values. There are permanent and temporary exhibitions, library and other resources.

Museu Scrimshaw Café Sport [194 C4] (*Horta;* ⏲ *09.00–12.00 & 14.00–17.00 Mon–Sat*) A private collection of over 100 scrimshaw items.

Old Whaling Station of Porto Pim, or Centro do Mar [194 C6] (*Monte da Guia;* ✆ *292 292 140;* e *pnfaial.fabricadabaleia@azores.gov.p; www.oma.pt;* ⏲ *May–Sep 10.00–18.00 Mon–Fri, 15.00–19.00 Sat & Sun; Oct–Apr 10.00–17.30 Mon–Fri*) This new museum completes the story of whaling in the Azores. In addition to all the machinery *in situ*, there are videos to watch and guided tours by a very enthusiastic staff. Begun in 1943 with Norwegian-made equipment, the former whaling station processed sperm whale oil, bonemeal, and meatmeal for cattle feed and functioned for 30 years. Around the same time factories were also established in Capelas on São Miguel and Santa Cruz on Flores. In addition to the museum, in a different space, concerts, theatre, art exhibitions, conferences and ecology/marine workshops are held, plus a children's programme on environmental subjects. There is also a shop and bar. To get there either follow the road to Monte da Guia at the southern end of the harbour, or walk across the beach from Porto Pim.

Around the island

Capelinhos Interpretative Centre (*www.vulcaodoscapelinhos.org;* ⏲ *Jun–Sep 10.00–19.00 Tue–Fri, 11.00–18.00 Sat & Sun; Oct–May 09.30–16.30 Tue–Fri, 14.00–17.30 Sat & Sun; admission €10, 50% discount for over 65s*) The eight-month story of the destructive 1957/58 eruption is explained using an eight-minute holographic projection dramatically showing the stages of eruption. A series of galleries follow, illustrating the Azores microplate and how the islands began to form, highlighting some of the key elements of volcanology on each island, explaining the different sorts of eruption, and covering a variety of related topics. The centre is built underground, in the ash and debris that buried the nearby villages and half the nearby Capelinhos lighthouse; all that appears in the bare landscape is a very low raised circle that allows natural light to the main chamber below. The internal design creates a great feeling of space and swirling lines and is aesthetically both stimulating and pleasing. The final section is the lighthouse itself, and one can climb the 140 steps to the upper balcony for the view. The spiral ascent is steep and narrow, so be warned. Available is a very small explanatory brochure with excellent graphics, but I hope in time there will be more detailed publications about all the Azores' volcanoes and landforms, guides to one of the most exciting geological areas in Europe. The building was opened to coincide with the 50th anniversary of the eruption, and one should allow two hours to do justice to the presentation. There is a shop and a good café. Since it opened it has deservedly gained many national and international awards for its design and content.

Crafts school – Escola de Arteanato do Capelo (*Alto dos Cavacaos, Capelo;* ✆ *292 945 027;* ⏲ *Jul & Aug 09.00–19.00 Mon–Fri, 14.00–17.00 Sat & Sun; Jun & Sep 10.00–18.00 Mon–Fri, 14.00–18.00 Sat & Sun; Jan–May, Oct–Dec 10.00–17.00 Mon–Fri, 14.00–17.00 Sat & Sun*) Near Capelo, on the way to Capelinhos Volcano.

Here you can see artisans at work and a display of their products: fig pith and fish scale sculpture, lace, embroidery, corn dollies, basketry and much else.

WALKING There are four official walks:

Caldeira Medium difficulty, 8km, 2½ hours. A circuit of the crater starting at the caldera viewpoint; it is not signposted as the trail is well trodden, however, I suggest it is only attempted in settled weather with good visibility, not only so that you can enjoy the constantly changing views, but also because if the clouds or mist come down, you could take a wrong track. Note that the caldera is a nature reserve and descent is not permitted.

Rocha da Fajã Medium difficulty, 5.5km, 2½ hours. A circular walk out of Praia do Norte.

Capelo–Capelinhos Medium difficulty, 7km, 2½ hours. Beginning from the forest park at Capelo and taking in two optional ascents of volcanic cones, ending at the Capelinhos Interpretative Centre. It can be hot and dehydrating so take double your normal water supply.

Lombega–Morro de Castelo Branco Easy, 4km, 1½ hours. A circular walk from Lombega village to Morro de Castelo Branco, a headland noted for its birds and flora. Be aware that ascent of the headland itself is dangerous, and should not be attempted.

RECREATIONAL FOREST RESERVES
Capelo 80ha of woodland with numerous trails, including much of the walking trail from Capelo to Capelinhos Interpretative Centre. In the early days after settlement, woad was cultivated here, but the good land was lost when the 1672 eruption of Pico do Fogo covered all with lava and it became another area of Mistério. It is now a protected area, and in the woodlands on higher ground Azores endemics can be found. Picnic tables, etc, make this a very popular place on summer weekends.

BIRDS AND FLOWERS The **Caldeira do Faial Nature Reserve** is good for the smaller endemic or rarer plants and in the grassland by the footpaths and around the viewing area inside the tunnel *Lactuca watsoniana*, *Daboecia azorica*, *Thymus caespititius*, *Centaurium scilloides*, *Hypericum foliosum*, yellow pimpernel and more can be found. The two most common birds are chaffinch and blackcap. The new volcano at **Capelinhos** regularly has nesting common terns and the roseate tern has also been recorded. Waders and ducks put into the beach at **Porto Pim**, and at the back of the beach grow sea daffodils. The protected area of **Monte da Guia** supports several native plant species.

SWIMMING
Varadouro On the southwest coast, on the way to Capelinhos. Natural rock pools, changing facilities and occasional lifeguard. There was also a thermal bath here, but the spring stopped flowing after the 1988 earthquake; the hunt is now on to find where it is presently coming out.

Porto Pim The relatively long sandy beach in the bay with almost sand-coloured sand, was once the original harbour. Shallow water for some way out, so the water is warmer. Very popular, and on the edge of Horta town; there are facilities at the far end of the beach, towards the Centro do Mar.

Praia do Almoxarife Very small sandy beach, near the camping site. Some 15 minutes by taxi from Horta, with facilities and a restaurant nearby.

WHALE WATCHING AND UNDERWATER OBSERVATION Quayside cabins in front of the Café Sport house outlets for all sea-based activities. Locations of old *vigias* are signposted – look out for them, especially around Cedros. This is a splendid initiative, for they are the perfect places for a picnic and binoculars; it is amazing how many waves turn into dolphins by the end of a bottle of wine.

OceanEye (*Rua Dr Manuel Garcia Monteiro, Horta;* m *966 140 608;* e *info@ oceaneye.pt; www.oceaneye.pt*) The *Ana G* is a special 007 James Bond-style boat that provides a modern version of the glass-bottomed boat and allows easy underwater observation around the islands of Faial and Pico. Expect to see in their natural habitat fish and other marine creatures and geological features. The trips lasting 1½ to 1¾ hours (€30) have both a recreational and an educational role and highlight the conservation and biodiversity of this marine environment. Kept in Horta harbour, find the company's cabin on the quayside.

AROUND THE ISLAND

HORTA The island's only town is made up from two adjacent bays: one small and rounded, Baía do Porto Pim, the other larger and more open. The remains of a volcano crater divides them, the Monte da Guia, from which may be had splendid views of both. The smaller is intimate, and was an American whaling centre from the end of the 18th century and during the 19th century. As many as 400 ships have been recorded in the harbour. Even by the beginning of the last century, two-thirds of all sperm whales harpooned were caught off the Azores. The old whale factory and the slipway where whales were landed and hauled up for processing after being caught by the Azorean open boats is now an excellent museum. In the town itself there are some fine buildings, and there is a walk northwards along the esplanade out to a little park. Work is now finished on the new €35 million quay to complement the existing one dating from 1876 on the south side of the bay; it will take up to medium-sized cruise ships, and, again as in Ponta Delgada, cruise passengers are able to walk from their ship straight into town.

Audio tour An audio tour is now available from the ART (Tourism Regional Association) information kiosk located in Largo do Infante D Henrique, close to the marina. The Audio tour is in Portuguese, English and French and the equipment rental cost is €6. There are about 40 locations included, and it is still under development.

Town trail This conveniently divides into two walks, and we begin with the central and northern parts of town.

Central and northern Horta Start at the **Pousada de Santa Cruz** [194 C3], the castle built in 1567 to defend the harbour. Opposite the *castelo* is the tourist information office. Go right, passing the little garden on your right overlooking the marina and take the left fork along the Rua Conselheiro Medeiros at the side

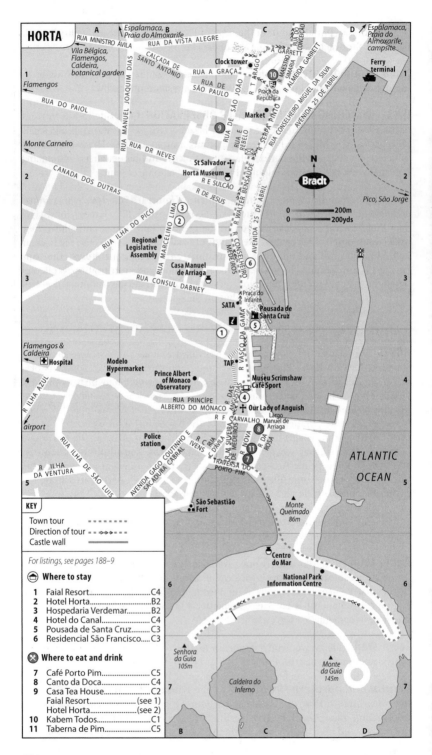

HORTA

A   ↗ Espalamaca, **B**   **C**   **D**   ↗ Espalamaca,
RUA MINISTRO ÁVILA   Praia do Almoxarife,   Praia do Almoxarife, campsite

Vila Bélgica,   CALÇADA DE   RUA DA VISTA ALEGRE
Flamengos,   SANTO ANTÓNIO   **Ferry**
Caldeira,   RUA DA GRAÇA   **Clock tower**   **terminal**
botanical garden

Flamengos   RUA DE   Praça da   **1**
  SÃO PAULO   República

RUA DO PAIOL   **Market**

Monte Carneiro

CANADA DOS DUTRAS   St Salvador   Pico, São Jorge
  Horta Museum   **2**
  R E SULCÃO   **Bradt**
  R DE JESUS   0   200m
  0   200yds

RUA ILHA DO PICO   Regional
  Legislative
  Assembly
  Casa Manuel
  de Arriaga   **3**
RUA CONSUL DABNEY

  Praça do
  Infante
SATA   Pousada de
  Santa Cruz

Flamengos &   TAP
Caldeira   Hospital   Modelo   Museu Scrimshaw
  Hypermarket   Café Sport   **4**
airport   Prince Albert   Our Lady of Anguish
  of Monaco   Largo
  Observatory   Manuel de
RUA PRINCÍPE   Arriaga
ALBERTO DO MÓNACO

Police   ATLANTIC
station   OCEAN
  TRAVESSA DO
  PORTO PIM

  São Sebastião   Monte
  Fort   Queimado
  86m

KEY

Town tour	- - - - - - -
Direction of tour	= ➤➤➤ =
Castle wall	— — — —

For listings, see pages 188–9

🛏 Where to stay

✖ Where to eat and drink

Centro
do Mar

National Park
Information Centre

Senhora
da Guia
105m   Monte
  da Guia
Caldeira do   145m
Inferno

of the pastel-green wedding cake of a building, charming with its wrought-iron balconies. One of its shops, round the corner facing the sea, is my favourite coffee bar with its Art Deco interior.

Soon on your left you will see towering above you the former convent of St Francis, built at the end of the 17th century; the original convent was destroyed by Essex and Raleigh in 1597. To its right is the charming St Francis church, built in 1696; scheduled for restoration, it is currently closed to visitors.

From the church continue eastward and you soon come on your left to the old Jesuit college, founded in 1719 for the training of missionaries to serve in the Portuguese colonies. It is now the **Museu de Horta** [194 C2], plus government offices. Although a small museum, it is well worth visiting. On display are some early maps of the Azores, recent secular paintings, an exhibition of remarkable models made with the soft inner tissue from fig stems by Euclides Rosa, who was from Faial, together with various other items. Examples from Horta's impressive collection of sacred art, including statuary of several centuries, are also exhibited. Some originate from Flanders but many were carved from cedarwood in the Azores. The Friends of Heart School in Angra made figures which were taken to the other islands and the figures come not only from churches and chapels no longer extant, but also private homes. Next door

HORTA'S VOLUNTARY FIRE SERVICE

In 1875, a house burned down and the governor was so angry that no-one came in time to extinguish it he offered a reward to the first eight men to come with a pump and a lesser sum to the first 12 men with buckets. This was how a rudimentary fire service began, and continued until 1912, when Horta's water supply was improved and the Associaçao Faialense de Bombeiros Voluntarios could be established. Church bells would sound the alarm and each district in Horta had its own signal; four bells for Angusuas, six for Matriz, eight for Conceição, until they were replaced by a siren in 1966.

Extinguishing shipboard fires was and still is their responsibility. Their payment for dealing with a fire on a World War I Italian troopship enabled the volunteers to purchase in 1930 their first two motorised fire engines. Shipboard fires were frequent between 1958 and 1968 because of the number of ships transporting fishmeal, which had a tendency to self-combust. Today's very professional association of *bombeiros* is one of more than 450 departments nationwide supervised by the Portuguese National Fire Authority, the SNB.

The firemen are still volunteers who give their time and risk their lives, thus continuing a long tradition. Horta has 54, all with understanding employers. Volunteering tends to run in families, sometimes three generations serving at the same time. They are called by the siren that continues to sound until enough firemen arrive to crew the engines. Volunteers can join the association from age 14 and remain until 60. Training is done on the island, often with imported specialists. The department is also involved in civil rescue service, and disaster simulations from fires to earthquakes and volcanic eruptions are undertaken twice a year. Volunteers also visit each school on the island at least once a year to teach the children how to respond in emergencies. The service is now funded by a combination of private, municipal and central government sources, supplemented by demonstrations and firefighting courses around the island to raise money. The fire department is also responsible for the ambulance service, whose crews are the only permanently paid members of staff.

8

is the **Church of São Salvador** [194 C2], the principal or Mother (*Matriz*) Church of Horta, begun in 1680 and completed in 1760.

Leaving the Horta Museum turn left and take the road along the right side of the post office, the Rua Serpa Pinto, to come to the marketplace on your left. Next to this is a little garden square, the **Praça da República** [194 C1]; on the diagonally opposite corner is another wedding cake of a building, this time pink, with splendid white balustrades. In earlier times houses painted pink were owned only by the aristocracy. Go up the road coming steeply into the square by this building. Take the first right, and you will see a clock tower at the top. This is the **Torre do Relógio** [194 C1] (clock tower), built in the early 18th century; it is a symbol of Azorean perseverance in the face of seismic forces which destroyed the 16th-century Mother Church. The adjacent public garden dating from 1857, the **Jardim de Florêncio Terra**, has fine dragon trees, while the massive building behind is the **Hospital da Misericórdia**, now empty and awaiting a new role. Leave this area by the road behind the clock, which you will find goes steeply down the Ladeira da Paiva. At the bottom go left to cross a small stream, the Ribeira da Conceição, near which Faial's first settlement was begun in the 15th century. You will see the small church, the **Igreja de Nossa Senhora da Conceição**, inscribed with the dates 1527, 1597, 1749, 1926 and 1933. This church has suffered a traumatic history. Originally built by the early settlers, it was destroyed during the first sacking of the town in 1597. A church built much later was destroyed in 1926. Its replacement was built in the Art-Deco style of the time and this in turn was damaged in 1941 by an explosion in a nearby army barracks. Following a major restoration, it is now pristine and most elegant. From here, either return along the roads through the town, or go south to the sea and return along the esplanade.

Southern Horta To explore the second, southern sector, again leave from the **Pousada de Santa Cruz** [194 C3]. This time turn left and walk down the road to pass the Café Sport. Some 20 years ago this was a small bar known to all sailors who called in at Horta, and a visitors' book was maintained which had many amusing entries. Now there is a shop and other enterprises including a museum of scrimshaw, and the guest book with all its early entries is posted on the internet; with good self-publicity the café is now known to a much wider circle around the world.

Proceed on and keep to the higher road and you will soon come on your left to the **Igreja de Nossa Senhora das Angústias** [194 C4], the Church of Our Lady of Anguish, just recently restored. Continue straight and you will soon reach **Porto Pim**, the original harbour of Horta. Note the defensive walls and the remains of the **Fort of São Sebastião** [194 B5], constructed during the 17th century as protection against pirates and other attackers. You should try to visit at night when the gateway is floodlit and very pretty. Construction of the new harbour began in 1876.

Take the road running behind the sea wall left of the gateway to access the beach. You will see the small houses of one of the oldest remaining parts of Horta, all nestling at the foot of **Monte Queimado** [194 C5]; *queimado* means 'burned', referring to the cinders. Walk along the beach to the far end to visit the old whale factory. This was built only about 50 years ago and there is an earlier factory dating from 1836 built originally for drying cod. It is now a museum and cultural centre, the Centro do Mar (see page 191), with occasional cultural events and exhibits to do with the sea. This small area is full of history, for you can find near the museum the point where the submarine cables came out to connect to relay stations, and also the ruins of a summer villa and its garden, once belonging to the influential Dabney family. A new museum devoted to the family and their role in the development of the island is under construction.

From the whale factory take the road that climbs to the summit of **Monte da Guia** [194 D7]. On the way you will pass a little chapel, dedicated to Senhora da Guia, also once used as a lookout for whales. The summit of Monte da Guia is 145m but it is closed to visitors. To return, follow the road all the way down and as you descend enjoy the splendid views of Porto Pim and Horta. Look also across Porto Pim Bay and to the hill behind, **Monte das Moças**, where you will see an observatory. The building dates from around 1901, and has been in use as a meteorological observatory since 1915. It was named **Prince Albert of Monaco Observatory** [194 B4] in 1923, a year after the prince's death. Just below this are the buildings and tennis courts of what is now the Faial Resort Hotel; previously these buildings were the residential compound belonging to the American Western Union Telegraph Co, built in the 1920s with reinforced concrete to withstand earth tremors. Hotel Faial opened in 1973, and has had new buildings added in recent years.

As you return to town and pass the harbour, pause to view the drawings and cartoons on the walls left by visiting yacht crews. This free outdoor art gallery exists because it is said to be bad luck to sail away without leaving your mark. Sadly, however, one or two have become memorials. Considerable care and time have clearly been taken by some artists, others are rushed scrawls, but all show a record of the many crews that have put in at Horta on their travels across the oceans.

JARDIM BOTÂNICO DO FAIAL

The garden was established to fulfil the following objectives:

- To conserve those Azorean species threatened with extinction through cultivation and propagation
- To build and maintain a collection of plants native to the Azores and Macaronesia
- To establish typical plant associations found at different altitudes
- To maintain a collection of native species for the interest of visitors

Because of its location the garden is able to grow species that are found at both sea level and at various altitudes in the mountains, and four altitudinal zones are represented. The coastal vegetation represented in the garden includes such Azorean endemic species as *Festuca petraea, Euphorbia azorica, Azorina vidalii* and the non-endemics found outside the Azores *Juncus acutus* and *Solidago sempervirens. Erica scoparia* ssp. *azorica* and *Myrica faya* are also growing in this zone, although they merge with the next, intermediate zone. This second zone is not very clearly defined in nature and in addition to the two previous species also includes *Picconia azorica*. The third zone represents the vegetation found in the higher altitudes of the islands' mountains, above 600m. Here are found *Ilex perado* ssp. *azorica, Vaccinium cylidraceum, Juniperus brevifolia, Erica scoparia* ssp. *azorica* and *Laurus arizorica*, species typical of the laurisilva forest unique to Macaronesia. For those species that demand wind shelter, shade or more humidity, comprising a fourth zone or category, an artificial ravine was made where can be grown such rarities as *Lactuca watsoniana* and *Sanicula azorica*. (See *Appendix 2*, page 254, for more information on species.)

There is also a visitor centre with photographs and some explanation about the different ecosystems. It is very much a developing garden and there are new areas and projects being added all the time.

PRAIA DO ALMOXARIFE Just the other side of the ridge immediately to the north of Horta is one of the prettiest valleys on the island. Long settled, the houses have charming gardens and in the past few years several restaurants have opened. There is a small sandy beach with changing facilities, and the camping site is nearby. It is a relaxing place from which to enjoy a fine view of Pico. You can walk back, first up the surfaced road to the top of the ridge. Here you will see a trodden path leading down to the old northern sector of Horta, but only do this if there is not much traffic about. A bus runs to Praia do Almoxarife from the stop at the northern end of the Horta marina at 07.15, 12.45 and 18.15 Monday to Friday, returning at 07.30, 13.00 and 18.30.

THE BOTANIC GARDEN AT FLAMENGOS (⊕ *15 Jun–15 Sep 10.00–13.00, 14.00– 18.00 Mon–Fri, 10.00–18.00 Sat & Sun; 16 Sep–14 Jun 09.30–13.00, 14.00–17.30 Tue–Fri, 14.00–17.30 Sat*) This is in the grounds of the Quinta de São Lourenço, with an extensive area of old gardens sheltered by magnificent hedges to protect them from the salt-laden winds. Established in 1989, the small botanic garden, the Jardim Botânico do Faial, is devoted to the endemic and indigenous plants of the archipelago, and is most attractively designed with gentle hills and a ravine filled with ferns. Here some of the more showy species such as *Thymus caespititius*, the native thyme, *Azorina vidalii*, the native campanula, dramatic *Euphorbia stygiana* and the most desirable shrub of all, the endemic bilberry *Vaccinium cylindraceum*, can be enjoyed in season. In addition, if you (understandably) have been struggling to identify all the different evergreen shrubs native to the islands, here is an excellent opportunity to study them close at hand and compare them; they have labels!

CAPELINHOS This is the site of the 1957 eruption and it is fascinating to see how it is, years later, with a few hardy pioneering plants trying to establish themselves, and the effects of wind erosion. Come here on a blustery day and you see the fine particles blowing on the wind and indeed feel them stinging your face. The stunning new visitor centre explains it all (see page 191). It is worth walking or driving down to see the small fishing harbour below Capelinhos. Also near the village is the forest park which is a pleasant place to walk.

CAR TOUR Faial is small, and this itinerary provides a fascinating half-day tour. If you can, take a picnic to enjoy in the forest park at Capelinhos.

Horta–Espalamaca–Ribeira Funda–Praia do Norte–Capelinhos–Castelo Branco–Horta
Leave **Horta** and begin by driving up to the ridge that overlooks the town from the north and stop at the belvedere **Espalamaca**. Here you have a fine view over Horta, the harbour, and of fields nudging their way up to the houses, so quickly does town end and countryside begin. Along the ridge of Espalamaca are several windmills and, neatly nestling in its valley, **Flamengos** village. Turn around and look down upon a pretty valley and Praia do Almoxarife.

Take the EN1-2a, which will lead to the caldera, and the little **Chapel of São João** is your next stop, after a cool drive beneath cryptomeria trees. São João is at the junction, where you have a view down over meadows to Horta across the channel to Pico. In early summer the hedgerows here are bedecked with tiny double red roses, coinciding with the Festa do São João in June.

Turn right in front of the chapel (EN 2-2a) and drive up to the **Caldera** along a narrowing road lined with tall hydrangeas. You will pass a road off to your right

Earthquakes began on 16 September 1957 and on 27 September, the sea began to boil near the Capelinhos rocks. On 29 September, explosions began and cinders were thrown into the air. By 1 October, cinders were thrown 600m high, the eruption cloud rose to 6,000m and an islet began to form round the crater. By 7 October, there was a cone-shaped island 60m high and 640m across, but already the sea was destroying it. Two days later it was 100m tall and over 700m across in the shape of a horseshoe, opening to southward. The sea entered this break so that the vent of the volcano was underwater, causing very violent explosions and fragmenting the new lava into ash and cinders. By 30 October, the sea had washed away the entire island.

In early November, eruptions began again and by the middle of the month a new island was linked to Faial by a narrow bar of black ash. Eruptions continued through the winter and by March 1958, more than 2km² of land had been added. During the following months lava flowed into the ocean, and, with the vent protected from the sea, incandescent lava was thrown up most spectacularly more than 500m, continuing intermittently until 24 October. In one period of 36 hours over 300 earth tremors were registered, shaking the whole island. In total some 300 houses were destroyed and almost every house on the west side of Faial was damaged; 2,000 people were rehoused. Crops were destroyed and a 5m layer of ash and rocks buried houses and many of the fields around the villages of Capelo and Norte Pequeno. Wind erosion is now slowly exposing these once more. The eruption changed the lives of many islanders when hundreds emigrated to the USA and Canada.

leading to Quebrada and Ribeira Funda on the north coast. There are wonderful views across to Pico and São Jorge. The road ends by a **tunnel**, at an altitude of 900m. The tunnel is very short, so walk through and view the caldera which is now a nature reserve, with very restricted access. The large crater is 400m deep and 1,450m in diameter. The common native shrubs are juniper and erica. Above the tunnel on the caldera's rim is the Oratory of São João. On a clear day Pico, São Jorge and Graciosa can be seen; almost due west from the summit is a line of cinder cones marking the fracture along which eruptions have occurred in recent geological time. To the east you can make out the impressive Pedro Miguel Graben, where the earth's crust has been displaced downwards between faults on either side of it. From the German *graben*, meaning 'trench', and orientated WNW–ESE, it is a major volcanic feature of the island.

Drive back down to the turn-off previously mentioned, now on your left, leading to **Ribeira Funda**. For flowers, this is one of the prettiest roads, and during July and August the hydrangeas are at their best. There are good views from two viewpoints along this road, and between trees and hydrangeas there are glimpses of villages and the sea beyond. Stop and enjoy, too, the glorious view over the Ribeira das Cabras and note the extensive lava beds before coming to **Praia do Norte**.

Praia do Norte is a good place to stop for coffee before going to **Capelinhos**, held to be one of the most interesting volcanic sites in Europe.

Continue more or less parallel with the coast on the EN1-1a to **Castelo Branco** where there is a fine view of the coastline before proceeding to **Feteira**. You will often see this place mentioned in brochures. Lying between the airport and Horta, it is a length of coast with contorted lava rocks and rock arches of some curiosity.

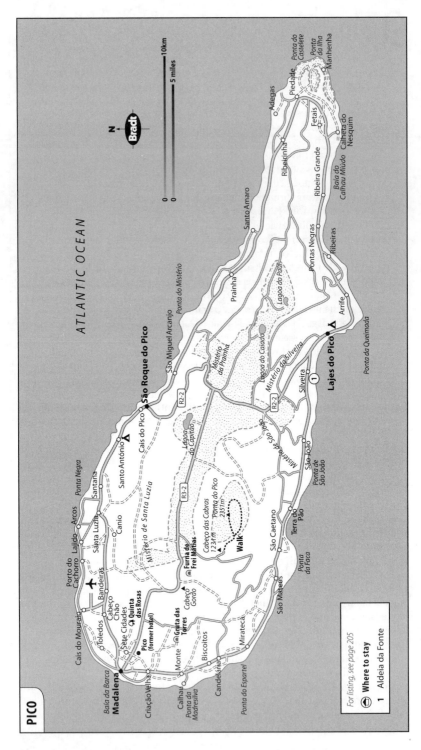

PICO

ATLANTIC OCEAN

N

Bradt

0   5 miles
0   10km

Baía da Barca
Madalena
Cais do Mourato
Toledos
Porto do Cachorro
Lajido
Arcos
Santa Luzia
Santana
Ponta Negra
Canto
Mistério de Santa Luzia
São Miguel Arcanjo
Santo António
São Roque do Pico
Cais do Pico
Ponta do Mistério
Santo Amaro
Prainha
Ponta do Mistério
Criação Velha
Ponta da Madresilva
Calhau
Cabeço Chão
Sete Cidades
Pico (former hotel)
Gruta das Torres
Monte
Cabeço Gordo
Quinta das Rosas
Furna de Frei Matias
Mistério de São João
Lagoa do Capitão
R3-2
R2-2
Lagoa do Caiado
Mistério da Prainha
Lagoa do Paúl
Ribeirinha
Adegas
Ponta do Costelete
Piedade
Ponta da Ilha
Manhenha
Fetais
Biscoitos
Candelária
Mirateca
Ponta do Espartel
São Mateus
Ponta da Faca
São Caetano
Terra do Pão
Mistério da Silveira
Cabeço das Cabras 1234m
Ponta do Pico 2351m
Walk
São João
Ponta de São João
Silveira
Arrife
Lagoa do Paúl
Ribeira Grande
Ribeiras
Pontas Negras
Baía do Calhau Miúdo
Calheta do Nesquim
Lajes do Pico
Ponta Queimada

For listing, see page 205

Where to stay

1   Aldeia da Fonte

9

Pico

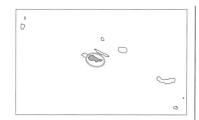

Pico is to most visitors Pico Mountain itself, a remarkable, steep-sided, dormant volcanic cone rising to 2,351m, and Portugal's highest mountain. Certainly this peak and the numerous black lava flows in different parts of the island make Pico the most distinctive of all in the archipelago. The finest views are to be had looking across the channel head-on from Faial, or the long side view from São Jorge; on the island itself, I love the view of the summit from Lajes. In the western end of the island you are always aware of Pico's overshadowing presence, whether dense clouds hang just above Madalena's rooftops obscuring everything above 40m, or the sky is at its bluest and all is revealed. The mountain always looks over your shoulder.

Of all the islands this is the most obviously volcanic, especially around Madalena and along the coast by the airport where the black stones have been gathered and made into tiny walled enclosures, square ones for vines, round ones for figs. Long ago, red and pink scrambling roses, the dark purple-blue trumpet flowers of the climbing ipomoea, and carpets of nasturtium escaped from cultivation, and now add wild colour for many weeks if not months of the year. Houses are of black stone, dressed around the windows, whitewash on the walls. Pico, with nearby Faial, was the centre for land-based open-boat whale hunting; some seven years after the last whale was killed boats again went to sea hunting whales, only this time just to watch, and again Pico has become one of the main centres.

The southern slopes of the island are more sheltered and less windy and so protective enclosures go high above the coastal villages. In contrast, the northern slopes are far more forested. Pittosporum and native myrica have invaded the lower slopes where there were once extensive vineyards among the stones, adding further large areas of tree cover. On the uplands most of the native vegetation has been cleared for cattle pasture, helped by subsidies from a then embryonic European Community – a dubious investment, since the resultant grass is very poor. However, there are pockets of native and endemic plants and hopefully current measures will be sufficient to save them; 1,500ha above the 1,200m contour are a designated protected zone. These remnants provide Pico with the most easily accessible areas of indigenous vegetation where you can begin to imagine just how the islands might have appeared to the very first settlers.

To explore the island's uplands by car, to find the lakes and other beautiful areas, just to stop and enjoy the grand scenery and the ever-changing cloud patterns around the mountain, is reason enough to come to Pico. But added to this are the cultural and historical interests and, for the experienced walker, the extraordinary experience of being on the summit of Pico where on a clear day the stupendous views embrace the sister islands of Faial, São Jorge, Graciosa and Terceira. Much closer, below, daughter cones and craters pockmark the plateau giving a tiny hint of what an extraordinary scene this must have been when it was most active. The mountain is only dormant; at the very summit on Piquinho, also called Pico Pequeno, the little peak that is a small cone in the summit crater, there are fumaroles, rocks are very warm to the touch and there is a smell of sulphur. Escaping gases and flowing hot magma when the surface lava was cooling have created caves and tube-like tunnels; several are known and named, but others are buried beneath vegetation or a thin tumble of rocks so great care is needed and it is essential not to wander from paths. The second-largest island in the Azores surely has something for everyone.

An island tour by car or taxi is a must, driving as high as the road reaches on Pico Mountain and down to sheltered areas by the sea, enjoying impressive landscapes and exploring villages and country life, while the coast has numerous headlands, some of which provide spectacular *miradouros*. The central mountain road running the length of the island offers endless interest, with side excursions off to small lakes and viewpoints. The museum in Lajes tells the fascinating story of whaling in the Azores and is another must, and the more adventurous can go whale watching and attempt the ascent of Pico. Pico was once famous for its fortified Verdelho wine and, in the last several years, new methods of cultivation and production are once again making saleable table wine. Originally the vines were grown in very small stone-wall enclosures to protect the plants from salt winds and to gain extra heat, and they are an extraordinary memorial to the tenacity and hard work of the earlier settlers. Extensive areas stretching along the western coast from just outside Madalena are so impressive that in 2002, UNESCO designated them a World Heritage Site. A visit to the winery followed by a tasting completes the picture.

BACKGROUND

GEOLOGY   Given that the channel between Pico and Faial is only 100m deep it is quite likely the two islands could be part of the same volcanic complex. Pico Mountain is 2,351m above sea level and rises 3,500m above the surrounding ocean floor.

The island of Pico can be viewed as three sections: the stratovolcano of Pico Mountain that dominates the western part of the island; Topo Volcano, a shield-like structure located on the southern part of the island above the town of Lajes do Pico; and the 29km-long westnorthwest–eastsoutheast-orientated plateau, the Planalto da Achada, located between the central part of the island and its eastern end and characterised by scoria and spatter cones and associated lava flows.

Pico Mountain began as a shield volcano, a broad and gently sloping volcano formed by repeated eruptions from a cluster of vents at different time intervals creating a large plinth some 16km wide at sea level and about 1,100m altitude. Extensive lava flows have completely covered the base of the volcano, thought to be around 240,000 years old. Most of the conspicuous cinder cones of the lower slopes originate on this shield, and are relatively recent.

The magnificent summit cone was created by eruptions from vents clustered closely together, forming a stratovolcano, a steeply sided cone of lava fragments and flows. Its development can be divided into three phases. The first was terminated by the formation of the older summit collapsed crater at 2,050m, presently 550m across and 25m deep. The second phase was the creation of Piquinho, the small lava cone 125m high in the larger crater, some 17,000 years ago. This, too, has a very small collapsed crater, which gives off occasional fumes from between warm rocks. The third phase included eruptions from the nested lava cone (Piquinho) 1,300 years ago, and from an eruptive fissure on the top of the stratovolcano. The larger crater was once much deeper, but has filled with *pahoehoe* lava discharged from Piquinho, a smooth lava usually formed from basalts emitted in a hot fluid state.

Wherever plants have so far failed to gain a foothold on the steep slopes, basaltic cinders, ash, small stones and scree dominate the landscape.

Topo Volcano rises 1,022m above sea level and 2,500m above the ocean bottom, and its oldest formation not under the sea has been dated at 250,000 years old. Topo is a basaltic shield volcano and has two subsidiary structures: Terra Chãs and Santa Bárbara, which some authors have interpreted as volcanic calderas. While the Santa Bárbara area does correspond to the remains of an old collapsed crater, or caldera, it has been suggested the Terra Chãs depression could be due to lateral movement of the flank driven by gravity and tectonic instability.

The **Planalto da Achada** is an elongated plateau occupying the central part of the island from Pico Mountain in the west to its eastern termination; as one very apt description has it, stretching out eastwards like a comet's tail. Numerous volcanic cones lie along the axis of the plateau with a general westnorthwest–eastsoutheast orientation. These are mostly made of cinders, with a wide range of size and shape. The largest cone has a diameter of 900m at its base and a height of 190m, while the smallest represent fissure eruptions building small spatter ramparts, ie: lava fragments spewed upwards as a fountain that are still molten when they hit the ground and thus form 'cowpats' which often weld together building ramparts or cones. Lavas issuing from sources along the plateau are mostly *aa*-flows, lavas with a very rough broken surface, and have cascaded down the steep slopes of the plateau either towards the north or south coast and then spread, sometimes into the sea such as to form the Ponta dos Biscoitos near Santa Bárbara, between Lajes and Ribeiras.

The plateau's oldest above-sea-level formation is 230,000 years old, which means the oldest sections of Pico Island are the Topo Volcano, followed by Pico Mountain.

Data shows 14 eruptions have occurred on Pico Island in the last 1,000 years and more than 35 in the last 2,000 years, with longer quiet periods on the Planalto da Achada than on Pico Mountain. Historic volcanism and carbon dating of lavas suggest that eruptions are not evenly distributed through time, but that events are separated by alternating short and long periods, and that peace reigns on average for 130 years. Since settlement, eruptions occurred in 1562, 1718 and 1720.

Visitors arriving on Pico soon hear about the **Mistérios**, extensive areas of sharp, broken and often forbidding black lava. These puzzled the first settlers arriving from 1466, who had yet to witness an eruption and experienced almost 100 years of volcanic tranquillity before they saw their first eruption in 1562. This eruption created the Cabeços do Mistério cinder cones and sent a basaltic lava flow into the sea to form the Ponta do Mistério, east of São Roque on the north coast. It must have been terrifying as the surrounding forests caught fire and sometimes as many as 40 glowing hot streams of lava illuminated the night, all over a period of two years. The 1718 eruption left an inheritance of several cinder cones and a lava flow that created Cachorro, near the present airport, a dramatic formation as though inspired by a punk hairstyle. At the same time, on the opposite south coast a lava flow destroyed the then village of São João and formed the headland of Ponta de São João. The 1720 eruption occurred just northeast of São João and created the Mistério da Silveira.

HISTORY The first houses are thought to have been built in Ribeiras, but real settlement began in the area of what is today Lajes, in about 1460, and was for many years the principal port and town. Later it was to develop as the centre of the whaling industry in the Azores. São Roque dates back to 1542, possibly because it is opposite Calheta on São Jorge, just 18km away. It is thought to have been first populated by people from Graciosa. Again, later, it was a whaling base with a large processing factory.

Until the latter half of the 19th century, wine production was a very important economic activity and the island's Pico Madeira wine was exported in substantial volume, to England, the US, and famously Russia. The vineyards, especially those along the west coast south from Madalena, were owned by some half-dozen families from Horta who came over for the summer to oversee the grape and wine production. Their large summer houses may still be seen today. Ever-increasing use of the important harbour on the adjacent island of Faial brought greater prosperity to that island and allowed the development of Horta, which in turn influenced the development of Madalena. Horta was the export centre for Pico's wine. Facing each other across the channel, the two towns have always been closely linked. In 1852, disease (*Oidium tuckeri*, a mildew) nearly destroyed the vines and 20 years later when the aphid insect Phylloxera struck the remaining vines were destroyed. This was the final blow to a very valuable export, for already the market had been declining. In the US the fashion for fortified wine was losing out to American-made whiskey, and the belief that wine was good for one's health was under question, along with increasing movements for total abstinence. Sadly, with the loss of the vines, exactly what was the Pico wine so extolled by the tsars is now a mystery. The Madeiran wine trade did, however, slowly recover, although minus the American market. This collapse of the wine trade brought terrific hardship to the islanders, for at the time of maximum wine production Pico's population was 32,000, and caused a massive emigration to Brazil and California. Those who could afford to paid their way onto passing ships, while the less fortunate embarked illegally on whaling ships serving a minimum contracted term of two years. With the vines gone, the families sold their large land holdings and so people were able to acquire small plots of their own. Later, returning islanders brought with them the American Isabela grape, which thrived, and so the smallholdings began producing a wine for local consumption known as Vinho de Cheiro, a low-alcohol partly fermented wine. Around this time, with skills gained from working on the American whalers, land-based whale hunting began from Pico, using small open boats. This soon spread to other islands, and whaling made a substantial contribution to the economy until world demand fell for the oil for lamps and machinery when cheaper synthetics became available. Many factories closed, while hunting continued on an ever-decreasing scale until the final whale was killed in 1984.

Today, like all the other islands, cattle and dairy produce drive the economy, despite the relatively poor quality of the land. In Madalena there is a tuna-fishing fleet, and tourism is increasing.

GETTING AROUND

There is a bus service which follows two routes: the north-coast Madalena–São Roque–Piedade, and the south-coast Madalena–Lajes–Ribeirinha, but the times are infrequent. To make a round-the-island tour from Madalena take the south-coast bus going to Ribeirinha at 10.00, arriving Piedade at 12.00, and the north-coast bus to Madalena leaving Piedade at either 13.30 arriving 15.15 or 17.45 arriving 19.40. From Lajes to Madalena the respective times are 06.45 arriving 08.00 and 13.55 arriving 15.15 and Madalena/Lajes 12.45 arriving 13.55 and 17.45 arriving 18.20. Check with the tourist office in case of any changes.

The island divides quite easily into a half-day car tour – Madalena–Santa Luzia–São Roque–Lagoa do Ciado–Lajes/Madalena or variations – and a full-day tour taking in most of the above plus going down to the little-visited far eastern end of the island. The price for a taxi is around €100 for a day, €60 for a half-day tour.

If you have a hire car, then there are three days of happy motoring ahead of you, taking two full days to explore the main road that encircles the island, and a third day up on the heights. With three days, you should have one day of good weather for the mountains! A half-day tour is detailed, a full-day tour is hinted at, and the mountains have limited roads and you simply follow your instinct and enjoy the supreme tranquillity.

For travel to Pico, see pages 47 and 52–4.

EXCURSIONS TO OTHER ISLANDS To go to Faial by ferry there are regular 30-minute sailings from Madalena to Horta throughout the year and in summer about every two hours starting at 08.15 with the latest returning at 20.45. In summer there are sailings every day to São Jorge, leaving Madalena at 08.30 or São Roque at 09.40, arriving at Velas at 10.15; to return, depart Velas at 21.10, arriving at São Roque 21.40 and Madalena 21.50. A day trip to Angra do Heroísmo on Terceira is also possible on Mondays, Wednesdays, Fridays, Saturdays and Sundays, departing Velas 09.20 and Calheta 10.00, and arriving at Angra 12.00. Return departs Angra at 18.15, arrives at Calheta 20.15 and Velas 20.55. These are subject to change and you need to check the Transmacor website (*www.transmacor.pt*).

WHERE TO STAY

There is one hotel in Madalena, two in Lajes, and one in nearby Silveira. Many of the private homes offering lodging have a meeting point to pick up guests for the first time, or will meet the ferry. Check with the tourist office for details of rural tourism accommodation and guesthouses. For location of listings see maps, pages 200 and 212.

Hotel Caravelas (69 rooms) Rua Conselheiro Terra Pinheiro, Madalena; 292 622 500; e geral@hotelcaravelas.net; www. hotelcaravelas.net. Modern city hotel very near the harbour. **€€€**

Hotel Apartamentos Aldeia da Fonte (family suites, suites & studios) Silveira, 9930 Lajes; 292 679 500; e info@ aldeiadafonte.com; www.aldeiadafonte.com. A series of basalt-built self-catering cottages & bedrooms 5 mins by car from Lajes, with a central restaurant & lounge bar in a charming garden/woodland setting on cliffs a few metres above the sea. A great effort has been made to integrate the buildings with the landscape. Offers a very wide range of leisure activities,

including whale watching & climbing Pico, & a series of self-guided walks from the hotel. Also available is 24hr private medical & nursing care for the elderly who want to escape the crowds & northern winters. Excellent restaurant. **€€**

Alojamento Bela Vista (16 rooms & apts) Rua do Saco, Lajes do Pico; 292 672 000. Close to the sea near the whalers' museum, & remodelled in 2007, providing rooms or self-catering apartments. **€**

Residencial Whale'come ao Pico Rua dos Baleeiros, Lajes do Pico; 292 672 010; e viallelle@espacotalassa.com; www. espacotalassa.com. Situated next to & run by the Espaco Talassa whale-watching base. **€**

SELF-CATERING
Baía da Barca (10 apts) Lugar da Barca, Madalena; 292 628 750; e reservas@ baiadabarca.com; www.baiadabarca.com. Just 0.7km from the ferry quay in Madalena is this well-designed & landscaped new complex of

self-contained luxury apartments, some with panoramic views of the sea. All have kitchenette & sitting room, some with a fireplace, outdoor pool, spa, bar, & breakfast included. **€€€€**

CAMPING

⚖ Lajes ☎292 679 700. At the far end of town within easy walking distance of all amenities.
⚖ Madalena 200m beyond the medical centre; showers & lavatories.
⚖ Santo António São Roque; m 917 815 902; e cms@mail.telepac.pt. Excellent 24hr supervised

sheltered site amid pine trees with all amenities, barbecue, tennis court, children's playpark, deer enclosure. Within 200m are restaurants, a disco & the sea. Close by are the Furnas pools & access to the sea.

✖ WHERE TO EAT

Pico has over 20 eateries, but I have yet to find any inspiring, with the exception of Hocus-Pocus in Silveira, which is really trying hard to lift the standard. The further east you go, the fewer there are. For location of listings see maps, pages 200 and 212.

MADALENA Most of the larger restaurants offer a self-service buffet at lunchtimes with a set price of around €9–10.

✖ Restaurante Marisqueira Ancoradouro ☎292 623 490. Rua João de Lima Whitton, Areia Larga, near the wine co-operative. Seafood & traditional dishes such as black pudding with pineapple, along with a view of the lights of Horta.

SILVEIRA
✖ Restaurante Hocus-Pocus ☎292 679 504. Belongs to the Aldeia da Fonte Hotel & offers a traditional menu, & also international & Chinese specialities. Nice ambience, good surroundings; definitely trying to do things differently. Recommended.
✖ O Lavrador Estrada Regional; ☎292 672 604

LAJES
✖ Restaurante Lagoa Largo São Pedro; ☎292 672 272. The menu includes shellfish.
✖ O Ritinha Av dos Baleeiros; ☎292 672 271

SÃO ROQUE
✖ Restaurante Avenida Rua das Poças; ☎292 648 230

SANTO ANTÓNIO
✖ O Rochedo Furna, near the swimming area; ☎292 642 666

PIEDADE
✖ Ponta da Ilha Manhenha; ☎292 666 708

PRAINHA
✖ Canto do Paço Rua do Ramal; ☎292 655 020; www.cantodopaco.com

OTHER PRACTICALITIES

Emergency ☎112
Police Lajes, Estrada Regional; ☎292 672 410; Madalena, Rua Secretário Teles Battencourt; ☎292 622 860; São Roque; ☎292 642 115
Health centres Lajes, Lg Vigário Gonçalo G Lemos; ☎292 679 400; Madalena, P Á Dr Caetano Mendonça; ☎292 628 800; São Roque, Rua do Cais; ☎292 648 070

Post office [map page 212] Lajes, Rua Gen Lacerda Machado; Madalena, Rua Visconde Leite Perry; São Roque, Rua do Cais
SATA Air Açores [map page 212] Rua D Maria da Glória Duarte, Madalena; ☎292 628 391
Airport information ☎292 622 414

WHAT TO SEE AND DO

Essential to Pico's past, and very much to the present because of the tourism that is keeping the island's history in the forefront of consciousness, are wine and whales. This means the extensive vineyards around the coast near Madalena and the wine museum and three very different whale museums. Then there is the landscape and of course all the little villages that can be visited on a car tour.

MUSEUMS
Museu dos Baleeiros (Whalers' Museum) (*Rua dos Baleeiros, Lajes;* \ *292 672 276;* ⊕ *May–Sep 09.30–12.30 & 14.00–17.30 Tue–Fri, 14.00–17.30 Sat & Sun; Oct–Apr 10.00–12.30 & 14.00–17.00 Tue–Fri, 14.00–17.30 Sat &Sun; closed Mon & bank holidays*) This is a fascinating exhibition about whaling as it was in the Azores until 1985. The exhibits are appropriately displayed in three original 19th-century boathouses plus ancillary areas. They include boats, tools and other artefacts, photographs, many good examples of scrimshaw, a blacksmith's workshop and much else, as well as a library well stocked with titles about whaling and cetaceans. Twenty years ago it was a tiny museum where you often had to get the key from a nearby house. Long-held ambitions for a museum to truly reflect the bravery and lifestyle of the Azores' whalers have now been realised and the displays are constantly being improved. The museum provides an essential experience for any visitor wishing to understand the role of whaling in the social and economic history of the islands.

Centre for the Arts and Marine Sciences (*Rua do Castelo on the outskirts of Lajes, coming from Madalena;* \ *292 679 330;* e *cacm-sibil@sapo.pt;* ⊕ *10.00–19.00 Mon–Fri*) A former whale-processing factory, in this large restored building can be seen some of the original processing machinery, video and multi-media presentations about cetaceans, a good bookshop, and a small snack bar. It also has facilities for exhibitions, research and teaching, and holds evening events.

Museu da Indústria Baleeira (*Rua do Poço, São Roque;* \ *292 622 147;* ⊕ *May–Sep 09.00–19.00 Tue–Fri, & 09.00–17.00 Sat & Sun & holidays; Oct–Apr 09.00–18.00 Tue–Fri*) Housed in the old whale factory that was built in 1946 and

---

FESTIVALS ON PICO

In July Madalena celebrates its patron saint, Santa Maria Madalena, with several days of cultural and musical events. Coinciding with the Festival of Our Lady of Lourdes is the week-long Semana dos Baleeiros or Week of the Whalers. This is celebrated every August in Lajes by a whaling boat regatta and with *fado* and other traditional music as well as modern concerts, an arts and crafts fair and other cultural events. São Roque celebrates Cais de Agosto at the end of July with music and guest bands, guided excursions on Pico Mountain, other guided walks, and exhibitions. Especially popular are the boat trips in restored whaleboats belonging to the São Roque Yacht Club. In the first or second week of September the Pico Wine Co-operative holds a grape festival with folk dancing and other events to celebrate the harvest.

Espírito Santo Lajes; 2nd week of Jun
Domingo do Espírito Santo Madalena; 2nd week of Jun
Espírito Santo Criação Velha; 2nd week of Jun
Terça-Feira do Espírito Santo Madalena; 2nd week of Jun
Festa de Santa Maria Madalena Madalena; last week of Jul
Cais de Agosto São Roque do Pico; last week of Jul
Festa do Sr Bom Jesus Milagroso São Mateus; 1st week of Aug
Festa de São João Pequenino São João; middle of Aug
Semana dos Baleeiros Lajes; 4th week of Aug

closed in 1984 to become a museum ten years later. The original US-manufactured machinery is well oiled as though it had only just finished working. You can begin to see what it must have been like when a huge sperm whale was brought in for processing; definitely missing is the smell, not even a lingering whiff, which would really have brought it to life. It is located near the harbour and Clube Naval.

Wine Museum (⏰ *09.00–12.20 & 13.30–17.00 Tue–Fri, 09.00–12.30 Sat & Sun; closed Mon; admission free*) About a 30-minute walk on the main road (Rua Carlos Dabney) from Madalena to the airport. Take the road off left just before you get to the buildings of a former hotel and you will come to the museum housed in an old Carmelite convent enclosed by a high stone wall and doors painted orange. Look out for the conspicuous tall araucaria and large metrosideros tree by the entrance. There are fascinating old photographs and early equipment. You can also taste and purchase Pico wines. A real bonus in the garden is a small grove of dragon trees and their seedlings, totalling around 70 stems. The largest individual tree has a canopy spread of about 16m and a stem diameter of 1m.

WINE

Cooperativa Vitivinícola (winery) (*Av Padre Nunes da Rosa, a short walk past the Madalena municipal swimming pool;* ☎ *292 622 262; www.picowines.net;* ⏰ *08.00–17.00 Mon–Fri*) Here you can see the production and bottling plants, and taste their Angelica and Lajido. Guided tours should be booked 24 hours in advance.

Moinho do Frade (⏰ *Jun–Sep 09.00–17.00 Tue–Sun; Apr, May, Oct 16.00–17.00 Sat, 09.00–10.30 Sun; Nov–Mar 09.00–10.00 & 14.00–15.00 Sun*) The historically important UNESCO World Heritage wine-growing area just south of Madalena starting at Criação Velha captures an important economic and social period of the Azores. This recently restored windmill provides a splendid elevated view over an extraordinary landscape.

Cachorro Adega (⏰ *summer only*) Near the airport, this is a small traditional *adega* (wine cellar) with local wine and liqueurs for tasting and purchase along with some handicrafts; it also serves coffee.

CAVES

Gruta das Torres (m *924 493 921;* ⏰ *1 Jan–14 Jun & 16 Sep–31 Dec 14.00–17.30 Tue–Sat, guided tours 14.30 & 16.00; 15 Jun–15 Sep 10.00–18.00 daily, guided tours 10.30, 12.00, 13.30, 15.00, 16.30; admission €7, family ticket €13*) A ten-minute drive south from Madalena, the cave is signposted near Criação Velha. Under the control of the Mountaineering Association (*Os Montanheiros Núcleo do Pico, Apartado 33, Lajes do Pico;* m *913 459 081;* e *Nucleodopico@montanheiros.com*), this lava cave is a fascinating volcanic phenomenon arising from lava flowing from the eruptions of Cabeço Brava and appears as a tunnel running through and emerging from an old lava flow. The principal tunnel is 4,480m long and mostly around 15m high. There are much smaller lateral secondary tunnels that show greater geological diversity. There is good public access and explanation and the entrance has been built of basalt rocks cleverly designed to blend into the landscape. The maximum tour group size is 12; an initial briefing is given, followed by a 450m walk, which all takes about an hour. Hard hats and lamps are provided, and you will need strong shoes.

The surfaces of lava flows often develop into two types which have been given the Hawaiian names of *aa* and *pahoehoe*. The *aa* is formed from the more viscous lava which soon congeals and does not travel far and the surface is a jumbled mass of angular and rugged rocks. A *pahoehoe* surface is formed from more fluid lava and frequently resemble huge coils of rope; as the lava cools it often produces a skin-like surface beneath which the lava is still liquid and as this continues to flow the smooth skin gets wrinkled and ropey. The image comes to mind of a dollop of hot jam on a plate to test the setting point from the wrinkles when pushed by the cook's finger. Occasionally this skin-like solidified crust gets attached to the sides of the channel and when the molten lava beneath drains away the crust is left suspended, thus forming an empty tunnel. Liquid lava dripping from the roof congeals into stalactites and other curious shapes and the tunnel may present numerous different manifestations of the lava flow. With time they can also develop secondary features such as stalagmites and stalactites of limonite, an iron mineral, or silica. This tunnel shows good examples of both lava types and is rich in geological forms. The temperature inside the tunnel is a constant 15°C throughout the year, and a high humidity is maintained by water filtering through the roof.

WALKING Pico has a huge potential for walking and so far has nine official trails, plus the ascent of Pico Mountain (for further details, see pages 216–17). There is some glorious countryside with a lot of hidden history and of course landscapes unique to Pico, especially among the forested land and on higher ground; drive up into the hills and stop wherever it is tempting to make a short walk. At the same time one has to be on guard for quickly descending cloud and mist, and not forget there are 81 known cavities in the lava and many holes well concealed beneath the moss, ferns and other vegetation, so keep to obvious paths.

Caminhos de Santa Luzia Medium difficulty, 10.5km, 3 hours. *Caminhos* means 'paths' or 'trails', and this walk follows old routes with interesting historical/ social artefacts and lava forms. It starts near Fetais, east of the airport, drops down to Lajido on the coast, then back up to Santa Luzia, followed by a circuit where you will see native plants.

Vinhas da Criação Velha Easy, 8km, 2 hours. Beginning at Porto do Calhau south of Madalena it follows more or less along the coast to Areia Larga through part of the wine-growing area. The trail is on lava and scoriae and on a hot dry day you will need to take double the normal water supply.

Lagoa do Capitão Medium difficulty, 9.2km, 3 hours. Beginning next to the lake and ending at Cais do Pico, with fine views of the island's north coast and in good visibility São Jorge and Graciosa, the route goes across pastures and through good native forest.

Ladeira dos Moinhos Easy, 3.4km, 1¼ hours. A circular walk beginning and ending in São Roque, passing on the way six watermills, some rebuilt, some in ruins, and an old threshing floor.

Caminho dos Burros Vertente Norte Medium difficulty, 11.2km, 3½ hours. This walk begins up on the central plateau, from the spinal road before Lagoa do Caiado in the Mistério da Prainha Forest Reserve, then descends towards the north coast and forks either to São Miguel Arcanjo or Baía das Canas.

Prainha do Norte Easy, 8km, 2½ hours. A short circular route beginning and ending in the public garden of the village. It passes old houses and beautiful stone bridges and down to Pico's only sandy beach and the Caso do Fio, a building used for the early transatlantic communications cable. Then following the coastline, reach a natural swimming pool in the rocks, and so back into the village.

Caminho das Voltas Easy, 6.3km, 2 hours. Begins at the Terra Alta viewpoint by the EN-1, between Ribeirinha and Santo Amaro, and ends in Santo Amaro following part of the old and once main trail to Ponta da Ilha. It passes old vineyards and small stone bridges, and an abandoned small butter factory, once more giving glimpses into the past.

Ponta da Ilha Difficult, 10km, 3 hours. At the far eastern tip of Pico, this walk starts at Portodo Calhau near Piedade, and ends at the Manhenha lighthouse, following the fishermen's path along the coast. *Pahoehoe* lava makes the going difficult underfoot. Between May and July part of the trail is closed due to nesting terns, and an alternative is marked.

Calheta do Nesquim Medium, 12km, 4 hours. A circular walk from the church in Calheta do Nesquim, a village with a long history of whaling. The route goes along the coast, climbs up through pastures and woodland to high points giving good views, and past a whale lookout.

RECREATIONAL FOREST RESERVES
Mistérios de São João Along the south-coast EN-1 between São Caetano and São João, this small area of 4.3ha is a narrow lava flow stretching down almost to the sea. Originally dominated by heather, it was planted in the 1960s with various conifers and now dominated by the Mediterranean maritime pine, *Pinus pinaster*. In recent years it has been adapted for leisure use, with trails, barbecues and picnic tables, exercise facilities, an observation tower for birdwatching and an interpretation centre for volcanism.

Prainha Along the northern EN-1 from São Roque to Piedade. Extensive recreation facilities beneath the pines including children's play area, a multi-sports facility with showers, deer enclosure, footpaths and some restored typical rural buildings.

BIRDS AND FLOWERS Pico offers the easiest access to remnant laurisilva forest and provided there is no thick fog, the road passing **Lagoa do Capitão** will reveal a good number of the typical Azorean species including superb specimens of the handsome *Euphorbia stygiana*. The various lakes in this highland area can attract ducks and waders. The harbours offer good opportunities for birding, especially Madalena; the recommended place is **Ponta do Arieiro**, just to the south, which also gives sight of two small islands. **Lajes** has a number of habitats beyond the harbour thanks to a large eroded lava flow that offers intertidal pools and marshland. Vitally, it helps protects the town from winter storms, but has suffered badly in recent years. It is rated one of Pico's best sites for shorebirds, herons, terns and rarities.

WHALE WATCHING Pico is one of the main islands associated with whale watching because Lajes is where it all began, and company shops and offices are easy to find in both Madalena and Lajes. Approved boat operators are listed on noticeboards by the quay. Similar services are also readily available across the channel in Horta on Faial, from where most of the larger more comfortable boats operate.

SWIMMING

Madalena Right in town, by the harbour, is one of the best swimming pools that looks really inviting, with space, sea views and Faial across the channel. There is also a good natural rock pool, where even with a good swell the surface is stable. There are changing facilities, showers, etc, and all for no charge. In summer there is a snack bar, but there is also a restaurant nearby. In midwinter, the locals were swimming in the harbour because the water there was warmer than the pool. There are numerous sea bathing areas around the island.

GARDENS

Quinta das Rosas (⏱ *Jun–Sep 08.00–20.00 daily, Oct–May 08.00–16.00 daily*) This was a private garden and evidently once beautiful and filled with plants, especially roses. It was bequeathed by its owner to the government and some interesting exotic plants remain, while efforts are being made to restore it. A visit will pass an hour or so if you have time to fill; it is about ten minutes by taxi from Madalena.

CAR TOURS

Car tour 1: Madalena–São Roque–Lajes–Madalena Madalena years ago was a little sleepy sort of place and because it had not been touched for ages had a pleasing air. With the new harbour, new hotel and other developments, it is still a sleepy place and viewed from the sea at a distance with Pico Mountain in the background it looks very picturesque.

Depart from **Madalena** and first take the main road to the airport at Bandeiras and from near the airport follow the road signs to **Porto do Cachorro** on the northern coast. The tiny harbour, really just a slipway, is set among a tumble of black lava. Find nearby the *rolas pipas*, the ramps made in the lava for rolling wine barrels to the sea. Lava here is contorted into many weird shapes and arches where the sea rushes in; in fact the sea has been rushing in rather effectively and the little cement pathway that once led the visitor safely through is being destroyed and you are now advised to keep your distance. The flat concrete building at the edge of the sea is for generating electricity from wave power. The black lava buildings are mostly *adegas*, places where village wine, the *vinho de cheiro*, is made and stored and in September it can be very jolly here. One of them is now a small museum and shop. You will find a sunken, grassy area and a larger stone house with a well in front that at one time served the nearby communities of both Santa Luzia and Bandeiras. Such wells, known as tide wells, were dug near the sea so that seawater entering it would be filtered and at least made brackish for general use and, in times of severe drought, drinking. Note also the typical stone and cement cisterns with their roofs sloping down to the centre to catch and store rainwater. Near the museum is the church, dated 1460.

Continue parallel with the coast, coming first to **Lajido** where there is another communal well, this time in the middle of the road. An old distillery, *adega* and manor house have been restored. You have been passing through an area of *mistério*, a tumble of lava from the 1718 eruption emanating some 900m up the side of Pico. The lava took two years to cool and prevented travel between São Roque and Madalena so that people were obliged to go by sea. Right by the roadside just before you get to **Arcos** you should be able to make out the wheel tracks of oxcarts in the lava flow. You will come to **Santa Luzia**, a traditional wine-producing

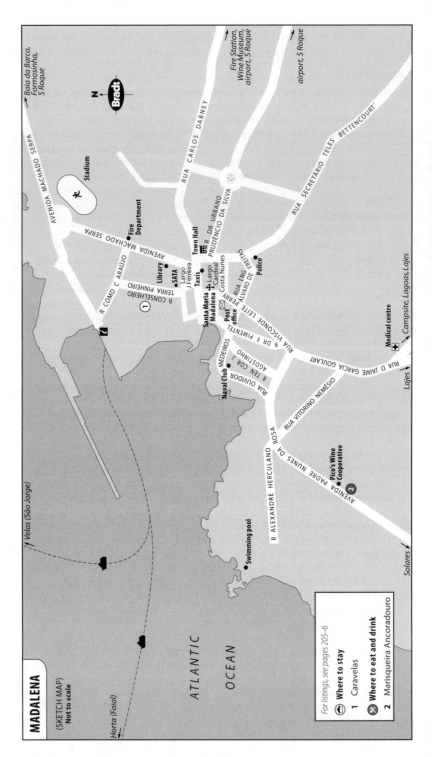

MADALENA

(SKETCH MAP)
Not to scale

N

Velas (São Jorge)

Horta (Faial)

ATLANTIC
OCEAN

Baia da Barca,
Formosinha,
S Roque

AVENIDA MACHADO SERPA

Stadium

Fire Station,
Wine Museum,
airport, S Roque

airport, S Roque

RUA CARLOS DABNEY

Fire
Department

AVENIDA MACHADO SERPA

Town Hall

R DR URBANO
PRUDENCIO DA SILVA

R COMD C ARAUJO

Library

SATA

TERRA PINHEIRO

R CONSELHEIRO

Largo
J Ferreira

Taxis

Largo
Cardeal
Costa Nunes

Santa Maria
Madalena

Post
office

RUA ENG
ALVARO DE FREITAS

Police

RUA SECRETARIO TELES BETTENCOURT

R Dr Medeiros

Campsite, Lagoas, Lajes

Medical centre

RUA D JAIME GARCIA GOULART

Lajes

RUA VISCONDE LEITE PERRY

R DR F PIMENTEL
MEDEIROS

R TEN COR J
AGOSTINHO

RUA OUVIDOR

Naval Club

RUA VITORINO NEMESIO

AVENIDA PADRE NUNES DA ROSA

R ALEXANDRE HERCULANO

Pico's Wine
Cooperative

2

Swimming pool

Solares

For listings, see pages 205–6

Where to stay
1   Caravelas

Where to eat and drink
2   Marisqueira Ancoradouro

212

Not surprisingly, the extraordinary appearance of this tree has ensured it a place in parks and large gardens wherever there is a suitable Mediterranean climate. However, in its native state it is classified as endangered. The tree is endemic to the Canary and Cape Verde islands, where already it is extinct on some individual islands, and there are just two surviving wild trees on Madeira, where it was once widespread in the arid lowland areas, especially on adjacent Porto Santo where it is incorporated into the town's coat of arms. So abundant was it on Porto Santo it seems that when the first settlers arrived they felled trees in large numbers without learning how to propagate them, and flooded the market with resin until the price dropped so low they ceased harvesting, thus inadvertently saving whatever trees remained. The fruits became famous for fattening pigs, but here, too, the tree is now extinct.

Bound to mythology, it would seem Hercules might have been the first plant hunter associated with it. His 11th and last Labour was to seek and bring back three golden apples from the Garden of the Hespérides, and after searching all the known world he is thought to have located the garden on an island beyond the Atlas Mountains. The garden was guarded by Landon, the hundred-headed dragon, and when Landon was killed his blood flowed out across the land and from it trees sprung up which we now know as dragon trees.

With the scientific name of *Dracaena draco*, this very slow-growing umbrella-shaped tree grows to a height of 15m or more, develops a hugely wide crown, and produces numerous branched inflorescences of small greenish-white sweetly scented flowers followed by 1cm-wide fleshy orange fruits. After each flowering, the tree then branches. Their trunks do not have annular rings like most other trees so to determine their age one has to know roughly how often they flower, once every ten to 15 years (maybe more frequently in the Azores), and count the number of branches. Once thought to live for very many hundreds of years, this has been revised downwards to 600 or so. It would be fun to determine the oldest specimen in the Azores, since they have been cultivated here for at least 500 years, and used as nail varnish as well as medicinally.

From the dragon tree comes dragon's blood, the sap of the tree that upon drying becomes a reddish resin, and in the Canary Islands this was used by the aboriginal Guanche to embalm their dead. Dragon's blood was widely known in ancient times, used as a dye and medicine, but this probably came from *Dracaena cinnabarini* on the island of Socotra, and from Somalia. Other plants produce resins also known as dragon's blood and *Daemonorops*, a palm, from Sumatra, is the main source of the dragon's blood varnish for violins.

That *Dracaena draco* is now an endangered species is probably due to habitat loss and other human influences, but before the Spanish invaded and colonised the Canary Islands, we are told a flightless bird related to the pigeon and about the size of a turkey used to feed upon the fruits of the dragon tree. It soon became extinct, and one theory is that the dragon trees there declined because the seeds had to pass through the bird's digestive system before they would germinate. If this is true, it would be interesting to know if anything eats the seeds in the Azores, because they certainly seem to germinate well in the garden of Pico's wine museum!

area, and then **Santana**. Some of the large, pretentious, and totally out-of-scale new houses intruding upon the landscape are summer holiday homes, some of their owners still working in North America.

Just past **Santo António** you come to an area called **Furnas**. Here the lava solidified as it flowed down and met the sea, and the smooth swirls of rock resemble congealed chocolate sauce. Continue to **São Roque** where there is a café in the centre of the village. If you want to visit the whale factory museum, before you get to São Roque look out for a house with green-painted shutters on your left; take the road off past it to go down to the harbour where you will find the museum near the Clube Naval. The club, incidentally, provides very good-value meals. If you miss this turn-off and get to the post office, you will need to go back about 200m.

From **São Roque** take the EN-3 signposted to Lajes and head for the mountains. There are glorious views behind you back to the coast as you climb. When the road stops climbing at around 700m the landscape is of rounded hills, pastures and remnants of the original forest that once covered much of the island. You will come to a junction with the EN-3 heading back to Madalena. Turn right, taking the EN-3 for about 2.5km to come to a small road off at 90° on your right leading to **Lagoa do Capitão**. This is just a small lake with a few isolated endemic junipers still withstanding the winds; walk anticlockwise round and follow the path leading off right uphill. Go behind the hill to be rewarded with a magnificent view of the whole length of São Jorge and, below, the coast of Pico around São Roque, something most visitors miss.

Retrace the way you came to rejoin the previous road, turning right in the direction of Lajes. Continue until you come to a narrow side road off to your left, signposted to **Lagoa do Caiado**. Drive down this road for a few hundred metres and here you will see some of the important native plant species, many of which are endemic, found only in the Azores. While botanically fascinating, do be very careful if you wander from the road because there are many deep hollows between the rocks under the covering of mosses for the unwary to fall into and possibly disappear!

Return to the main EN-3 road and descend to **Lajes**. It is a pretty drive; do allow time to take it slowly. Images that come to mind are of tall, stately cryptomeria trees, green meadows, hills, rounded hills, conical hills and glimpses through trees of hills going on higher up. Sunshine and shadow on the road; shining bright leaves; leaves of large-leaved gingers give a sub-tropical effect; and occasional camellia trees 5m tall are in full red bloom in January. Just before you get to Lajes on your right is the SIBIL whale-processing factory, now the Centre for the Arts and Marine Sciences (see page 207).

Lajes was the first settlement on the island and is well worth an hour's exploration. The 17th- and 18th-century houses offer interesting architectural details and the little chapel of São Pedro at the far end is a delight inside, built around 1460 by the first settlers. Regrettably it has been rendered with cement so that it could easily be mistaken for somebody's outbuilding; for centuries it had a thatched roof. Next to the Church of Our Lady of the Conception is the town hall, formerly a Franciscan convent. From the harbour there are fine views of Pico Mountain; the whalers' museum is also just by the harbour (see page 207).

As you drive back to Madalena following the coast, you will see in the woodlands around **Mistério de São João** inviting picnic areas built by the forest services. Then, before you reach Madalena, turn off the main road towards the coast to the village of **Criação Velha**. (If you have time, turn off before this and explore some of the coast and its settlements.) Criação Velha begins the wine-producing area along to the small port of **Areia Larga**, formerly used whenever bad weather closed nearby

Madalena. This UNESCO-recognised heritage area captures something of former times when Pico wine was in full production and would have been swarming with hundreds of workers. You will see clearly above all the stone walls the **Moinho do Frade**, a restored mill which provided an elevated view over the vineyards (see page 208). Continue round the coast coming to the wine co-operative on the outskirts of Madalena near the municipal swimming pool.

Car tour 2: Around the coast of the eastern part
With a whole day stretching ahead of you a tour of the eastern sector is really a journey of gentle exploration following the main road that encircles the island and dropping down to explore little places on the coast that appeal as and when you get to them. Guidance would spoil the fun, but there are just a couple of areas that you might not notice.

Calheta de Nesquim and Ponta da Ilha at the eastern tip
Coming from Lajes along the southern coast, drop down from the main road to Calheta de Nesquim following the steep winding cobbled road (very slippery when wet) and stop at the Church of São Sebastião. This is a typical Roman Catholic village church immediately overlooking the harbour, dated 1856; note the old whalebone door latch and handle. Return to the main road by the road you came down and when you come to conspicuous blue tourist signs take the first right to **Ponta da Ilha** and the immaculately kept lighthouse at the eastern tip of Pico. From here there is a fine view of the eastern sector of São Jorge and in the distance Terceira looking almost circular with a central plateau. Return to the main road and immediately take the tourist sign to **Parque Matos Souto** and the **Desenvolvimento Agrario**. Awaiting you at the end of the winding road is a delightful garden with shade trees and ornamental flowers, lily pond and picnic tables maintained by the forestry service. Even if you are not ready for your picnic, it is charming to visit.

Once more return to the main road and shortly you will come to **Piedade** where there is a bank and some shops. Along the very straight stretch of road following look out for a small viewing point of **Terra Alta**, a narrow concrete belvedere 330m atop the steep sea cliff; it provides a fine view across the channel of São Jorge while directly below you is a forest of pittosporum and a few native laurels trying to compete with the invader.

Take the turning down to **Santo Amaro** and stop in the square by the Church of Nossa Senhora do Carmo. About 100m along the road following the sea wall is the most charming crafts museum in a traditional house. Very original corn dollies, straw hats, embroidery, fish-scale flower pictures, weaving and other crafts are displayed, together with three rooms furnished in traditional manner. Another house is a craft workshop while a third is a small shop selling many crafts plus angelica liqueur and delicious fig jam. Near the slipway is the boatbuilding yard, the main centre for the whole of the Azores. Access to the sea at this point is very gentle, something so rare in the islands that this may be the reason boatbuilding began here. In the Rua António Maria Teixeira there is a **private museum** (☉ *09.00–18.00 Mon–Fri*) explaining the art of wooden boatbuilding and aspects of Azorean maritime history.

Stay on the lower road and continue to **Prainha** and the square and its cafés at the side of the church, with its little garden. From the main door of the church is a good view of São Jorge. Take the road that continues on behind the church which quickly turns steeply uphill to rejoin the main road and continue to São Roque. You will pass by the **Prainha Forest Park**, a splendidly laid-out picnic and recreation area beneath the trees, with good washroom facilities.

THE ASCENT OF PICO

The ascent of Pico Mountain, about 5km, can take between two and five hours, depending upon how fit you are and the weather conditions, but generally it takes about three hours up and three hours down. The descent can be harder than the ascent. First, you reach the crater rim, where it is a 30m sheer drop, so bear round to your right to go down to the crater floor. The crater is 500m across. There you have the diminutive Pico, Piquinho, a steep rock scramble of 100m, to make the summit, where you find warm rocks and fumaroles.

It is strongly recommended you go with an official guide, of whom there are almost 50, both men and women (✆ 292 623 524). Part of the voluntary Bombeiros service, guides are trained in mountain rescue and first aid. The fee is from €100 for up to four people, depending on the services required and if it is a night climb. At the refuge climbers must pay €3 if climbing with a guide, or €10 without. Taking a guide means you are their responsibility; without a guide you are responsible for yourself and if you get into trouble and need rescuing there is a very substantial fee to pay.

Beginning at Cabeço das Cabras at 1,231m it is an ascent of over 1,100m, about 5km, in part over loose stones and scoriae. There are marker posts at 100m intervals but in poor weather they are difficult to see and a satisfactory method of waymarking in Pico's conditions is still being worked on. It is not a technically difficult climb but you need to be a strong walker and capable of coping with fast-changing weather conditions. You will need boots or substantial shoes with a good gripping sole and layers of clothing including a windproof jacket and waterproofs. At Cabeço das Cabras at the end of the tarmac road is the reception building (⊕ Jun–Sep 24hrs – & sometimes during May if the weather is good). There is a briefing room, and photographs with explanations about Pico and its ecology, also a small bar with coffee and emergency-type snacks, and lavatories. Here you must sign in, as a strict record is kept of who is on the mountain. You will also be loaned a GPS, which is compulsory. The GPS gives a signal every ten minutes which is traced on a computer monitored by the rescue service. The above precautions are imposed because climbing Pico has become very popular and walkers do get into trouble. In 2011, 3,000 people climbed the mountain. Some people have been killed as the ground can be dangerous off the small footpath and the weather changes very quickly. Incautious visitors have had to be rescued by the Civil Protection Service and a cavalier attitude to the mountain is irresponsible. The best time is in June, July and August; later it gets very cold.

To watch the sunset and sunrise from the summit, start out at 02.00, or go up the evening before, between 17.00 and 19.00, and bivouac. The cave that was used for many years for this purpose is now closed since the 1998 earthquake. Winter climbing is for experienced mountaineers only, and registration is done at the fire station in Madalena, on the Estrada Regional to São Roque, about 20 minutes' walk from Madalena harbour.

However many mountains you might have climbed, to be on the top of Pico is to be 2,351m high in mid-Atlantic, and that is an experience to stay with you for life. To the south is Antarctica, 9,000 miles away and with nothing in between. In other directions and given luck with the clouds you should be able to see Faial, São Jorge, Graciosa and Terceira. In June and July the two native species of thyme and heath, *Thymus caespititius* and *Daboecia azorica*, are in full flower and the higher slopes are a spectacular pink and wine, a veritable rock garden of massed colour.

Before setting off it is wise to see what the day's weather is likely to be, for to make the ascent without the views would be terribly disappointing. Therefore make your decision by 08.00. Alternatively be bold and arrange to be taken up to the start of the climb by 02.00 so you can be high on the mountain, if not at the summit, for sunrise. The early morning light has a special quality and as the sun catches the lower daughter volcanic cones and slowly spreads up the mountainside to strike you, banishing the cold of dawn, it vindicates the decision to make the effort. The ultimate, of course, is to watch the sunset, then bivouac and wait for the sunrise. When I made the climb in June, Pico was surrounded by clouds and looked very unpromising. The next day dawned clear and was almost perfect, and the following day it rained torrents. As with all mountains, it is a mixture of luck and timing.

Part Four

WESTERN GROUP

Corvo
Vila do Corvo

Santa Cruz das Flores
Lajes

Flores

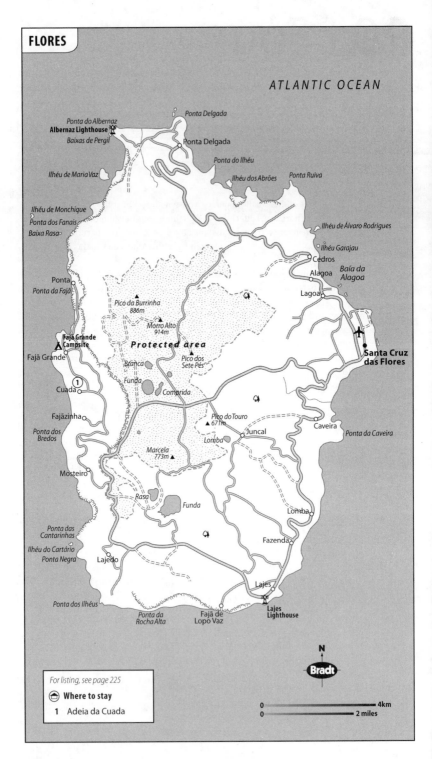

FLORES

ATLANTIC OCEAN

Ponta Delgada

Ponta do Albernaz
Albernaz Lighthouse
Baixas de Pergil

Ponta Delgada

Ponta do Ilhéu

Ilhéu de Maria Vaz

Ilhéu dos Abrões   *Ponta Ruiva*

Ilhéu de Monchique
Ponta dos Fanais
Baixa Rasa

Ilhéu de Álvaro Rodrigues

Ilhéu Garajau

Cedros

Alagoa   *Baía da Alagoa*

Ponta
Ponta da Fajã

Lagoa

Pico da Burrinha
886m

Morro Alto
914m

Fajã Grande Campsite
Fajã Grande

Protected area

Branca
Pico dos Sete Pés

Cuada

Funda

Comprida

Santa Cruz das Flores

Fajãzinha

Ponta dos Bredos

Pico do Touro
▲ 671m

Lomba

Juncal

Caveira   *Ponta da Caveira*

Mosteiro

Marcela
773m ▲

Rasa   Funda

Lomba

Ponta das Cantarinhas
Ilhéu do Cartário
Ponta Negra   Lajedo

Fazenda

Lajes

Ponta dos Ilhéus

Ponta da Rocha Alta   Fajã de Lopo Vaz

Lajes Lighthouse

N

Bradt

For listing, see page 225

🏨 **Where to stay**
1 Adeia da Cuada

0 ————————— 4km
0 ————————— 2 miles

220

10

Flores

> At night, in the silence of this small sanctuary, you can almost hear the sound of the sun falling against the horizon... afterwards, everything seems even more serene, but at the same time more intense, fragrant, inexplicably captivating, as if part of a poem.
>
> Quoted from the Aldeia da Cuada's brochure.

Not only have you now reached the westernmost island of the archipelago, you are also at the western extremity of Europe. Europe ends at Flores, the Isle of Flowers, on longitude 31° 15' W, and 1,380 miles from Lisbon. Given the island's small area, only 17km long and 12.5km wide, it is probably the most intensively rugged of the archipelago, with peaks, valleys, crater lakes, waterfalls and precipitous cliffs. Small pastures and arable fields all surrounded with hydrangea hedges or lichen-encrusted stone walls tie these together. Like Graciosa and Corvo, Flores is now a UNESCO Biosphere Reserve.

Although it is a long way from anywhere, Flores is an island of quite spectacular natural beauty and well worth the effort to reach. July and August are the peak times, June and September are busy, then tourism fades away. Come in winter, see no other tourists, enjoy sharp lighting, cloud effects, rainbows, storms, brilliant sunshine, wonderful conditions for photography – for in winter there is tremendous clarity – and simply escape from the madding crowds. Today, however, all too often the tourist is in a hurry to see everything and move on. Having invested travel time and fares to reach Flores, do stay at least three nights, even if you are not a walker; if you are, then think of five nights. If you want to visit nearby Corvo, you should allow an extra day. Ideally, you would spend a whole week. In winter, be tempted to rent an old restored comfortable cottage with wood-burning stove, bring books and CDs, and retreat for a month or three.

Whatever you do, make sure you have spare days in your itinerary to allow for cancelled flights due to bad weather. It is bad luck when flights are cancelled, but it can happen at any time of the year, especially in winter when Flores bears the brunt of the Atlantic winter gales. There is a lovely story about a consul in Flores who had never left the island and, in the mid 1800s, boarded a ship that had called to take on fresh provisions. The weather became too rough for the ship to remain at the anchorage and stood out to sea for safety; the wind became stronger and it was impossible for a small boat to go ashore. Being short of provisions, the ship sailed away with the consul to its intended destination, arriving a few days later in England!

The main highlights are the landscape and geological features: the peaks of Sete Pés, Burrinha, Marcela and Flores's highest point at 914m, Morro Alto, all best seen from the viewpoint overlooking the Fazenda da Santa Cruz Valley; the Rocha dos Bordões basalt pipes; the seven different lakes in the centre of the island; several waterfalls; sea cliffs 600m high; and, for navigators, the islet of Monchique used as one of the main reference points to check navigational aids when sailors relied upon astronomy. Everywhere the countryside is beautiful, and there is constant temptation to stop the car and quietly take in the atmosphere. For walkers, there is the ultimate in conversation stoppers: walking the length of Europe's westernmost coastline, eclipsed only by Greenland. In summer when the weather is settled, one of the finest ways to appreciate the island is to take a 3½-hour boat trip around the coast, part of which you will see anyway if you go to Corvo by boat.

This rugged island defiantly stands proud of the ocean, with many lengths of precipitous cliff challenging the sea to do its worst. In a few places the land descends less abruptly to meet the sea, resulting in ravines and narrow river mouths, and just occasionally the descent could almost be described as sharply gradual, for example in the northeast and the odd point of flat land in the east, convenient for the airport and main town of Santa Cruz. All the villages lie around the island's circumference, either close by the sea or perched upon the clifftops. Flores is unique among the Azores for being without a large caldera or dominated by long fissures. The chance of history made Flores the frontier post of Europe rather than of the US.

BACKGROUND

GEOLOGY Flores is the westernmost island of the Azores and with Corvo rests upon the North American Plate. Both islands are on a nine- to ten-million-year-old oceanic crust. Flores's volcanic build-up occurred in two phases: first a complex that formed the embryonic island mostly below sea level with the oldest rocks around 2.5 million years old and the youngest some 650,000 years old, which were partly emergent and influenced by sea-level changes. The second complex, all above sea level, was active between 670,000 and 3,000 years ago, and created a diverse geological landscape. It consisted of thick, sometimes very thick lava flows which alternated with lesser pyroclastic (rock and ash) deposits, with a final eruptive stage of considerable lava flows from two or three volcanic centres.

One of the special features of Flores is the 'Lake District', which includes Lagoa Funda, Negra, Comprida, Seca and Branca. These are *maars*, shallow, flat-floored craters caused by multiple explosive steam eruptions when rising magma comes into contact and interacts with groundwater or surface-derived water below the original ground surface. No cone is formed, and ejected material can form a low rim around the crater and the resulting depression often fills with rainwater. In all the tourist brochures are photographs of the Rocha dos Bordões, a fine example of columnar jointing located near the road between Mosteiro and Lajedo. These arise in the inner part of very thick lava flows when the hardening process proceeds relatively slowly to the flow's outer surface and sets up tensional stresses during contraction. Hardening along numerous parallel axes, usually perpendicular to the flow's surface, breaks the lava down into pentagonal or hexagonal prisms. Later weathering exposes them as 'basaltic organs', 'elephant roadways', and other suggestive forms. More familiar examples are Scotland's Fingal's Cave and Ireland's Giant's Causeway.

There have been no eruptions during historic times and geological evidence suggests the volcanoes are now extinct.

HISTORY The name Flores, meaning 'flowers', is thought to derive from the many yellow flowers of *Cubres* that adorned the sea cliffs at the time of Portuguese discovery. This is the local name for *Solidago sempervirens*, a North American species that might have been introduced, but has certainly been in the Azores for a very long time.

Diogo de Teive and his son João discovered the island around 1452, much later than the other two island groups. The first settlement was attempted by a Flemish nobleman Willem Van der Hagen at the bottom of the Ribeira da Cruz, a deep and dramatic valley with a small rocky beach giving access from the sea. They tried to grow woad for export but because of the island's isolation and lack of a good natural harbour this failed after a few years, and Van der Hagen retired to Topo on São Jorge. **Permanent settlement** began only in around 1504 with people mainly from Portugal, Terceira and Madeira together with slaves from Cape Verde, and supplemented by Spanish, German, English, Jewish and Moorish families. Possibly by 1515, Lajes was already a small town, and 30 years later so was Santa Cruz, and by the end of that century the parish of Ponta Delgada on the north coast was also well established. Contemporary accounts tell us the population of Flores was around 1,300, and conditions primitive. The houses were straw-thatched huts, the paths were muddy and so bad they could not be used by wheeled carts. Seldom did they get a boat visit from Terceira, and then only between March and September because of the winds.

However, the Azores were good hunting grounds for **pirates and corsairs** and in June 1587, five English vessels destroyed Lajes. The Spanish organised each year two major convoys called the *Flota* and the *Galeones* to protect ships bringing back bullion from South America. In 1591, a British squadron waited to intercept the *Flota* on its way back from Mexico. The British crews had suffered greatly from illness and were largely ashore when a Spanish fleet sent to the Azores to meet and protect the *Flota* hove into sight. The British rapidly embarked but one ship, the *Revenge*, was slow to escape and was cut off. Single-handed the ship, under the command of Sir Richard Grenville, a wealthy landowner and cousin of Sir Walter Raleigh, fought the entire Spanish fleet for 15 hours, sinking two enemy ships before surrendering; an action immortalised by Tennyson's poem, *The Revenge*, beginning 'At Flores in the Azores Sir Richard Grenville lay...'. Sir Richard was mortally wounded and buried ashore but, being Protestant, not in consecrated ground. About the end of World War II, a storm exposed near the shore the buried remains of a man much taller than the islanders, together with a big sword. Could this have been the long-lost grave of Sir Richard? If it was, the remains are again lost.

By 1770, the island was no more peaceful, for in that year two American privateers badly bombarded Lajes, but were eventually fought off with a cannon firing broken crockery, bottles and stones and finally a cannonball. However, by the end of the century the relationship changed, and the islanders ended by trading with the pirates to mutual advantage.

The early economic activity was survival; yams were the mainstay, plus potatoes and other vegetables together with fish and bread, with the export of woad and minor products such as archil (lichen) and dragon's blood, while sheep produced wool. There was also casual trade and repairs with those ships that by losing their longitude came to Flores by chance. By the middle of the 18th century, supplying whalers and other shipping provided an income to the island, which peaked around the middle of the 19th century with meat, fruit and vegetables being exchanged or sold for export to the other islands, Madeira and beyond. Reflecting the economy, the population also peaked at this time, and since then over the last 150 years has gradually declined, largely through emigration, from over 10,000 to the present total of around 3,800. Open-boat land-based **whaling** began in 1860 and reached its peak in the late 1930s; there followed construction early in the next decade of the whale factory in Santa Cruz and a second one in Lajes, but these were always handicapped by the lack of a good harbour. Whales killed by Corvo men were towed to Flores for processing, and the last whale killed in the Western Group was off Corvo in 1981.

Roads within the island were bad or non-existent for a very long time, and only in the 1950s did this begin to change. What really ended the isolation of the island was the building of an airport, port improvements and the opening of a French **meteorological observatory** and satellite-tracking station in the 1960s. The French have gone, made redundant through new technology, and the economy depends upon meat and tourism. Fishing is small and enough for the island, although in the peak of summer visitors it can barely meet demand.

GETTING AROUND

There are public buses, but they are infrequent and do not always operate every day so better to ignore them, although there is a published timetable available from the tourist office. If you get stuck, you will find local drivers amenable to hitchhikers.

Taxi hire for a day's sightseeing tour costs around €16 per hour from Santa Cruz. Most likely your driver will follow the route described under *What to see and do* (see page 226). The high-level tour described in *Itineraries* (see page 228) takes about four hours and the tour to Ponta Delgada on the north coast takes around two hours.

For travel to Flores, see page 53.

WHERE TO STAY

In Santa Cruz das Flores there are three conventional hotels and a small one that is part of a bar/restaurant. There is rural accommodation in Fajã Grande. In the peak summer months demand is such that you will have to book in advance. For location of listings in Santa Cruz das Flores see map, page 229; for all other listings see location of towns on map, page 220.

⌂ **Hotel das Flores** (26 rooms) Zona do Boqueirão, Santa Cruz das Flores; ☎ 292 590 420. Offers comfortable rooms, gymnasium, games room, outdoor pool & restaurant. On a headland with views of Corvo Island, adjacent to the former whaling station that will become a museum, 15 mins' walk into town. €€€

⌂ **Hotel Ocidental** (36 rooms) Av dos Baleeiros, 9970-306 Santa Cruz das Flores; ☎ 292 592 552; e hotelocidental@hotmail.com; www.hotelocidental.com. Good location, next to the sea. Many rooms have balconies & a splendid sea view. The hotel is tiled throughout & although spotlessly clean, it looks cheerless. Has a restaurant (⊕ Apr–Oct). Also offers diving & boat tours. €€

⌂ **Hotel Servi-Flor** (34 rooms) Bairro dos Franceses, 9970-305 Santa Cruz das Flores; ☎ 292 592 453; e hotelservi-flor@mail.telepac.pt; www.servi-flor.com. Converted from the old accommodation & restaurant building that once belonged to the French-operated communications relay station, & known as the 'French Hotel'. Rather

dark & gloomy, but well heated in winter. Bar, swimming pool, gymnasium & minigolf. Has a restaurant open throughout the year (*12.00–14.00 & 19.00–21.00*). €€

⌂ **Residência Argonauta** (5 rooms) Rua Senador José de Freitas, Fajã Grande, 9960-030 Lajes das Flores; ☎ 292 552 219; e info@argonauta-flores.com; www.argonauta-flores.com. This charmingly refurbished traditional & characterful house, over 300 years old, has retained many early features. There are 5 en-suite rooms in the main house with breakfast room & bar, and 2 self-catering units in a second old house. Its Italian owner, Pierluigi Bragaglia, is the author of a substantial guidebook (2009) to the history & walks on Flores, & offers advice on the walking routes & a guide service plus other guest services, including sea kayaking. €

⌂ **Residencial Vila Flores** (18 rooms) Travessa de São José, 9970-341 Santa Cruz das Flores; ☎ 292 592 190. In the centre of town, with integrated public bar & restaurant. €

SELF-CATERING
🏠 **Adeia da Cuada** (14 cottages) Cuada, 9960-070 Fajã Grande; 📞292 590 040; e aldeiacuada@ail.telepac.pt; www.aldeiacuada.com. On the west coast, 2km from Fajã Grande. This is rental accommodation without catering. Through emigration Cuada village became deserted. Now, 14 of the abandoned houses have been refurbished to a high standard, with fully equipped kitchen, TV, stereo, telephone & heated by wood-burning stoves, offering 1-, 2- & 6-bedroomed accommodation. Each has a small simple garden, pasture really, & access is by narrow paths between walls. It is charming, in a delightful pastoral setting near the sea. **€**

CAMPING
⋀ **Fajã Grande** A grazing field is prepared by the town hall each year for tents & is the only official campsite on Flores. This shares the facilities provided for the beach & in summer there is a restaurant. Nominal charge.

✖ WHERE TO EAT

The options are very limited, and best in summer. Almost all offer the basic Azorean fare without much variation in presentation. There are too many new snack bars opening and insufficient restaurants. They are mostly found in Santa Cruz where there are also several snack bars scattered around, some of which offer cooked meals, especially lunchtime. I recommend the **Buena Vista** (🕙 *11.00–21.30 Mon–Fri, until midnight Sat, until 18.00 Sun & in winter*) near the town swimming pool for a coffee/salads/snacks with views over the ocean. For location of listings in Santa Cruz das Flores see map, page 229; for all other listings see location of towns on map, page 220.

SANTA CRUZ
✖ **Restaurante Sereia** Rua Dr Amas da Silveira, leading down to the harbour; 📞292 592 220; 🕙 for dinner from 18.00 daily
✖ **Restaurante Baleia** Lugar do Boqueirao, by the old whale factory; 📞292 592 462. Has an ocean view.
✖ **Servi-Flor Restaurant** In the old French Hotel; 📞292 592 454
✖ **Café Rosa** Rua da Conceição; 📞292 592 162. Offers the cheapest all-in winter lunch.
✖ **Hotel Ocidental Restaurant** 📞292 590 100. Very popular in summer.
✖ **Hotel das Flores** Zona do Boqueirão; 📞292 590 421. Has a nice dining room/restaurant.

LAJES
✖ **Restaurant Beira Mar** Rua Porto; 📞292 593 153
✖ **Restaurante Estalagem Pousada** Av Emigrante; 📞292 593 547

✖ **Restaurante Porto Velho** Av Emigrante; 📞292 593 525; 🕙 until midnight daily
✖ **Restaurante Casa do Rei** Av Peixoto Pimentel; 📞292 593 262

FAJÃ GRANDE
✖ **Restaurante Zona Balnear** Zona Balnear da Fajã Grande, by the beach; 📞292 552 170. With seating outside it is a good place to watch the sunset.
✖ **Restaurante Casa da Vigia** Just up from the Argonauta; 📞292 552 217. A small restaurant with lots of atmosphere, dine indoors or in the enclosed garden; includes homemade pasta & vegetarian options; expensive but very enjoyable.

PONTA DELGADA
✖ **O Pescador** A small restaurant owned by a fisherman which deserves to draw visitors to this rather distant northern village & the attractive hinterland.

NIGHTLIFE

Lucino's Bar in the centre of Santa Cruz serves light meals and burgers. **Toste's Café**, behind the Hotel Ocidental, is a music pub with seating outside where people can dance until dawn in summer, at weekends in winter. The **Buena Vista Café**, above the swimming pool, occasionally has live music.

OTHER PRACTICALITIES

Emergency ✆112
Police Santa Cruz das Flores; ✆292 592 115; Lajes; ✆292 553 186
Resident doctor At the health centre in Santa Cruz; ✆292 592 316 (24hrs). There is no hospital on Flores & emergency cases are flown to Terceira.

Post office Rua Senador André Freitas; ⏲ 09.00–12.30 & 14.00–17.45 Mon–Fri
SATA Air Açores Rua Senador André Freitas, Santa Cruz das Flores; ✆292 592 425; airport; ✆292 592 411

WHAT TO SEE AND DO

MUSEUMS See *Santa Cruz das Flores*, page 228.

WALKING There are four official marked trails:

Ponta Delgada–Fajã Grande Medium difficulty, 12km, 3 hours.

Lajedo–Fajã Grande Medium difficulty, 10km, 2½ hours.

Fajã de Lopo Vaz Medium difficulty, 4km, 2 hours.

Miradouro das Lagoas–Poço do Bacalhau Medium difficulty, 7km, 3 hours.

The first two of these combined form what I call the west-coast walk. Starting at Ponta Delgada means one descends to Fajã Grande, but I would rather ascend

FESTIVALS ON FLORES

In July, the Emigrants Festival is Flores's biggest celebration, with music and folklore groups coming from other islands as well as Flores; there are exhibitions and various cultural events and a Carnival Ball.

Festa de N Sra Lourdes Santa Cruz; 2nd week of Feb
Festa do Espírito Santo throughout the island; end of May
Festa de São João Santa Cruz; 4th week of Jun
Festa de São Pedro Santa Cruz; end of Jun
Festas do Emigrante Lajes; middle of Jul
Festa do Sr Santo Cristo Lajes; 1st week of Aug
Festa de N Sra Guia Santa Cruz; 1st week of Aug
Festa de N Sra Milagres Lajes; middle of Aug
Festa da Santíssima Trindade Lajes; middle of Aug
Festa de N Sra Remédios Lajes; 3rd week of Aug
Festa do Espírito Santo da Praça Santa Cruz; 4th week of Aug
Festa de N Sra Saúde Lajes; 1st week of Sep
Festa do Bom Jesus Santa Cruz; 3rd week of Sep
Festa de N Sra Rosário Lajes; 4th week of Sep
Festa de N Sra Conceição Santa Cruz; 2nd week of Dec

from Fajã Grande since this path can be wet and slippery. Therefore I suggest starting from Lajedo and ending in Ponta Delgada as described on pages 233–9; this can be done either as a single entity or over two days. The third walk is an interesting down and back-up affair, also described on page 239. The fourth walk I have not followed but I think it is especially important to ensure this is attempted in reliably clear, settled weather since without good visibility it could be difficult to find the route. If one has a car, it might be quite fun to do a short out-and-back walk around the lakes.

In addition I have included an enjoyable walk from Fazendas and the Parque Florestal through mostly farmed countryside back to Santa Cruz, and four short walks for motorists.

Hopefully, more routes will be opened up which would then provide several days of magnificent walking and make the journey to Flores doubly rewarding. As it is, any stroll into the countryside within sight of the sea carries the added frisson of excitement on account of the distance from anywhere else – half the Atlantic before major landfall. Meanwhile, really keen walkers should consider staying at Residência Argonauta (see page 224), where guidance is available, and certainly buy their published guidebook to Flores (see page 267). Always check beforehand with the local tourist office if the trails are open.

BIRDS AND FLOWERS There are three protected zones: the extensive central area of lakes; the south coast from Lajes and along the west coast up as far as near Mosteiro; the northeast coast from Santa Cruz to the Albernaz lighthouse and down to include the Ilhéu de Maria Vaz. These include the islets where the largest European colonies of roseate tern nest. It is thought that with their potential for Nearctic land birds and storm-tossed American vagrants, the westernmost islands offer the greatest birding excitement. A noted area for the land birds, with its small fields and woodlands, is around **Fajã Grande**. The central area has considerable and complicated geological interest while its humid Atlantic climate of fogs, strong winds and high rainfall has created boggy habitats dominated by juniper and sphagnum moss and other parts good for laurisilva species. Resident birds include canary, goldcrest, chaffinch, blackcap and grey wagtail and the whole wetland complex is regarded as an important area for regular migratory birds and also for the common tern.

SWIMMING
Santa Cruz das Flores There is a great natural rock pool halfway between the Ocidental and Servi-Flor hotels with showers and the Buena Vista Café.

Fajã Grande Black-pebble beach and a quay for access, with facilities and a restaurant open in summer.

BOAT TRIPS On a small and remote island what is available is inevitably going to vary each year, but trips in summer around the Flores coastline make a fascinating excursion to see the rock formations and seabirds; you can also see islets and various caves, including the intriguing Gruta dos Incharéus below Caveira, 50m long and 25m wide. Boat owners might also arrange fishing trips. Check with the island's tourist information office in Santa Cruz (📞 292 592 369).

DAY TRIPS TO CORVO In summer there is a ferry service on Tuesday, Thursday and Saturday, and in winter on Tuesday and Saturday. The round trip costs €20 and takes 40 minutes to cover the 13-mile journey. See www.atlanticoline.pt for the latest information and times as there may well be more sailings. All crossings are subject to weather conditions on the day.

AROUND THE ISLAND

Santa Cruz das Flores is the town of main interest, and the other villages are mentioned under the car tours below.

SANTA CRUZ DAS FLORES This is the island's principal town and includes the airport, and an enjoyable exploration will take around three hours. The most striking building is certainly the 19th-century **Nossa Senhora da Conceição church**, of substantial, solid architecture made more imposing by two towers framing the front elevation. Equally substantial is the charming Baroque **Convento de São Boaventura**, now the **Flores Museum** (🕓 *09.00–12.00 & 14.00–17.00 Tue–Fri*). Begun in 1642 for the Franciscan Order, in 1734 it became a hospital and then later a school. Set around an internal cloister, the rooms display items to do with whaling, including scrimshaw, old hand-tools of various trades, linen and wool production and weaving, agricultural implements, and other ethnographic items. They have, too, a collection of religious statues plus jewellery and other objects concerned with the cult of the Holy Spirit. See also the **Church of São Boaventura** which is integral to the convent. Look for the Hispanic-Mexican influence in the chancel, the plant motifs and allegorical figures painted on the cedarwood ceiling, and a 16th-century Portuguese School *Annunciation*. Two British visitors, Joseph and Henry Bullar, described Santa Cruz in 1839: 'The streets are long and narrow, and fields intervene between the houses. There are no large private dwellings, the great majority being cottages of the poor. Above them all rises the church, which is one of the largest in the Azores...' The Franciscan monastery, an extensive building, has been sold, and is shut up.

Traditionally, visiting strangers were accommodated in the convents in rooms set aside for guests. The garden opposite the monastery contains a handsome well. Nearby is Pimental Mesquita's house, built in the 17th century for the then governor of Flores and Corvo, and now a public library. This is thought to be the oldest home on Flores and the first to have a tiled roof and glazed windows.

CAR TOURS I suggest you do the lakes area in the high country and the south and west coast in one day; in fact this is about a four-hour tour. Then another day drive up to the northeast corner, to Ponta Delgada, about a two-hour tour. If you have enough days on Flores, then time your journey to the lakes and high country when there is no fog. If the day is not clear but very windy this could be a good time, for often low clouds will be travelling quickly and you will get windows of clarity, often in spectacular light. Discuss this with your driver before you set off and go by his years of experience. There are plans to hard-surface the rough track that runs from near Comprida to join the main road between Cedros and Ponta Delgada in the far north, which if it happens would offer further route options.

Touring the high country together with the south and west Leave Santa Cruz by the Lajes road and take the first major turning off to your right, signposted to **Fajãzinha** and **Fajã Grande**. You will soon get marvellous views on your left of the Ribeira da Cruz as you ascend, followed by a view to your right of Fazenda Valley. Look out for the Miradouro Pico da Casinha; here you might

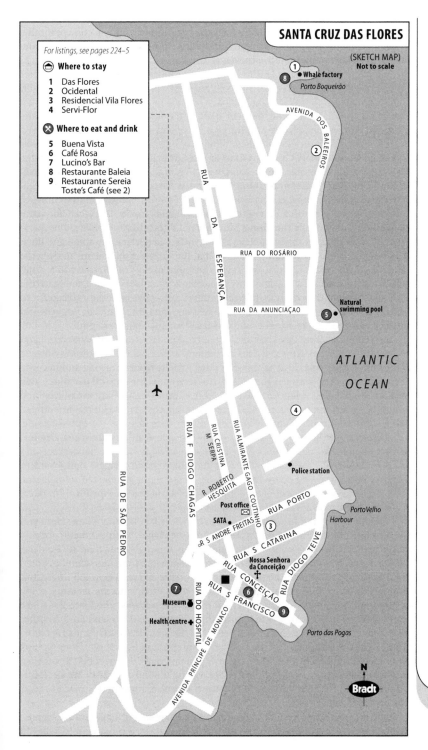

(SKETCH MAP)
Not to scale

For listings, see pages 224–5

Where to stay

1 Das Flores
2 Ocidental
3 Residencial Vila Flores
4 Servi-Flor

Where to eat and drink

5 Buena Vista
6 Café Rosa
7 Lucino's Bar
8 Restaurante Baleia
9 Restaurante Sereia
   Toste's Café (see 2)

Whale factory

Porto Boqueirão

AVENIDA DOS BALEIROS

RUA DA ESPERANÇA

RUA DO ROSÁRIO

RUA DA ANUNCIAÇÃO

Natural swimming pool

ATLANTIC OCEAN

RUA DE SÃO PEDRO

RUA F DIOGO CHAGAS

RUA CRISTINA M SERPA

RUA ALMIRANTE GAGO COUTINHO

R ROBERTO HESQUITA

Police station

Post office

SATA

R S ANDRE FREITAS

RUA PORTO

Porto Velho Harbour

RUA S CATARINA

Nossa Senhora da Conceição

RUA CONCEIÇÃO

RUA DIOGO TEIVE

RUA DO HOSPITAL

RUA S FRANCISCO

Museum

Health centre

AVENIDA PRINCIPE DE MONACO

Porto das Pogas

N

Bradt

notice steep grassy slopes with narrow terraces running along the contours; these were made by hand 50 or more years ago to make the pasture accessible for cows. Then the landscape becomes open wet grassland and trees and you pass through an area called Castanheiro. Continue to the next asphalt road intersection and after passing a little chapel (Our Lady of Flores) turn left. At the next junction turn right, following the sign to Caldeira da Lomba. Continue on, and ignore the turning left down to Caveira and quickly on your right is the first of the seven lakes, in the **Caldeira da Lomba**. It is surrounded by a large landscape of rounded, weathered cones looking like a series of headless shoulders. In winter the boggy tufted grasses and mosses reflect an emerald shimmer in the low light, darkened in places by the almost black-green of the rushes. This lake is 15m deep. From the lake you can look across hydrangea hedges to the south coast.

Follow the road on, ignoring a left turning down to Fazenda, and come to a junction. Ahead is a grand view of the **Boca da Baleia** – mouth of the whale. At the bottom of this huge valley is a group of forestry buildings and blocks of cryptomeria trees. Turn right, and as the road climbs you will see two lakes, one above the other. The top one is **Caldeira Rasa**, meaning 'flat', because, as you will see shortly, the lake is level with the road; it is 16m deep. The lower lake is **Caldeira Funda** of Lajes which means 'behind', named because it is at the back of Lajes. When you reach the next road junction, turn left and drive up to get a closer view of the two lakes. You will see Funda on your left and then Rasa on your right. At Lake Rasa you will find a turning place and two signs naming the lakes and giving their depths.

Turn round and retrace your route; pass the intersection you came from and continue straight on. You will cross a cement bridge and a sign identifying the **Ribeira Grande**, and come to the main road. Cross this main road and take the unsurfaced road opposite to go to **Caldeira Seca** on your right and to **Caldeira da Água Branca** on your left further up the hill. At the point where the unsurfaced road changes to asphalt is the **Caldeira Seca** on your right. Opposite you can see **Caldeira Comprida**, but a better view can be had from the opposite side. Continue on up the hill and shortly you'll come to **Caldeira da Água Branca**, with a depth of a mere 2m. Follow on until you come to a turning place and retrace your route to the junction. At the junction turn right, signposted to Lagoas. Very soon you come to a turn-off to the right, signposted to Caldeira. Take this and now you will get a better view of **Caldeira Comprida**, 17m deep. Caldeira and Lagoa are used interchangeably.

Continue on to the top of the road where there is a turning place. Here you see **Caldeira Funda**, at 108m, the island's deepest lake. Often the water appears black, and in the tourist literature you will increasingly see it called Caldeira Negra. However, in a certain light it also often appears in various shades of green and there is opposition to this name change! The highest mountain ahead of you with a radio/TV mast is Morro Alto, at 914m. Return to the junction at the bottom and turn right. Soon you reach a junction with an unsurfaced road on your right going up Morro Alto. Ignore this, continuing down and cross another bridge over the Ribeira Grande and on until you find the crossing to Fajãzinha and Fajã Grande off to your right. After the bridge and before the crossing look out on your right for a very narrow opening in the 'walls' with a cobbled pathway; this is the **Miradouro of Craveiro Lopes**, giving the most spectacular view over Fajãzinha and Ribeira Grande. Facing west, it is also a wonderful place to view the setting sun.

Take the next turning right to go down to **Fajãzinha** and **Fajã Grande**. Ignore the turning almost immediately on your left up to the radio masts; it is better to see this view on your way back up. Continue down, ignoring the road off to your left to Fajãzinha, and at the beginning of the bridge and on your right you will see a white-painted watermill, the **Moinho da Alagoa**. If you are lucky, the miller may be there and the mill working. You can also take a short walk here (see page 233).

After passing two bridges the road gently descends. Look out for a wide asphalt road off to your right – it is not signposted. Take this; it is an upper road around Fajã Grande. You will pass a rock-crushing enclosure on your left and the road descends through dense pittosporum and acacia trees, and then past many white stone walls enclosing small fields. These have now gone to pasture, but presumably in earlier times they grew vegetables and other crops. Continue down until you find a road going off sharply back to the right. Take this turning and at the bottom reach a junction where you will find a small bridge. Turn right to go to the village of **Ponta da Fajã**, but it is a cul-de-sac so you will have to return the same way. You can also make a short walk to the **Codfish Pool** – see page 233. It is also the start of the last stage of the west-coast walk to Ponta Delgada. Turn left to go to the bathing place and **Fajã Grande**. You will soon see the restaurant with its welcoming tables set out near the sea.

Looking north along the coast there is a good view of Ponta da Fajã with its high cliff backdrop and, out to sea, the **Ilhéu de Monchique**. When you leave the restaurant area and if there is not too much visitor traffic (it is a very popular area with the islanders so there could be many cars), drive on through the very narrow village main street to leave Fajã Grande and regain the road you came down on.

If you have time, go down to Fajãzinha, a very charming village where time seems to have stood still. Signposted by the village shop is the road to the Quejaria Tradicional, the tiny village cheese factory. You will find it at the end of a very narrow road so take a fun drive, passing many small houses and their productive gardens. Cheese is made all year round after 14.00; a soft cheese every day and a dry cheese when there is sufficient milk. Both are delicious. In the village you will also find the restaurant Pôr-do-Sol.

To leave, head back up towards the main road you came by and climb the hill, this time taking the turn-off to the right, and stop at the viewpoint **Miradouro da Fajãzinha** beneath the radio/TV mast to enjoy the superb aerial view of Fajãzinha and Fajã Grande. Continue on this road, descending parallel with the coast, and you will soon see the deserted village of **Caldeira**. Shortly afterwards you come to the village of **Mosteiro**, the white-painted houses and church running down the side of a ridge with its background of 'organ pipes', the Rocha dos Bordões. It is a charming scene, with the village surrounded by small fields enclosed by stone walls. The population numbers about 70.

Once you have passed the village you come to a T-junction where you turn right. Soon you get a good close view of the **Rocha dos Bordões**, and you can stop the car to better study the formation. The road continues on curving round beneath the rocks and soon the hillside above the road is covered in dense vegetation. There were once fields and pastures, all hedged with hydrangeas and you can still make out these boundary hedges in amongst all the aggressive invading growth of pittosporum, tree heather and myrica. The next village to come into view on your right is **Lajedo**; the road then curves away and you follow a straight stretch into **Lajes**.

Lajes has no real focus but you will see the church on your right surrounded by a cluster of buildings, so turn into the village and park near the church. From the front of the church is a good view down to the harbour. There is also a very clean public WC at the side of the belvedere. In the nearby Rua dos Pescadores is a well-signed handicrafts shop with the short and inconvenient opening times of 09.00–

11.00! To explore the harbour either walk down, or drive back to the main road and turn left soon to find a road off left signposted to the port. Park on the spare ground opposite the Beira Mar Café, and take the narrow road in front of the café. In a minute or two you will be at the beach, where there are picnic tables. There are several snack bars (see page 225). Tackling the last, short sector of this island tour, note as the road climbs beneath dense evergreen trees on the road between Fazenda and Lomba two privately owned watermills by the side of the road. The first on the right is the **Moinho do Rei** and the second, on the left in a bend, **Moinho do Brisita**. Then you pass the village of **Lomba**. Just after that is the small village of **Caveira** and you come into the **Ribeira das Cruz** and get a view to Santa Cruz. This *ribeira* you are crossing is dramatic with its broken topography and dense evergreen vegetation. Look down to the coast and see the small and sheltered **Fajã do Conde**, the site of the very first settlement on Flores. Minutes later you pass the first houses of **Santa Cruz**.

Touring Ponta Delgada and the northeast
Leave Santa Cruz from the northwest corner of the airstrip and quickly climb, getting views of the rugged coastline. Soon you are crossing ravines filled with evergreen pittosporum and myrica trees, and all is cool and humid. The pretty little village of **Fazenda de Santa Cruz** is unmistakable thanks to its conspicuously sited church. On the clifftop high above you will see the rooftops of Cedros village. Below, in the bay, are many rocks including the largest, Ilhéu Alagoa. Drive round the **Ribeira do Cascalho** passing the tiny settlement of **Alagoa** and ascend to **Cedros**; just before the top of the climb there is a viewpoint marked by a low stone wall giving a fine view to Alagoa and Santa Cruz. As you continue you will get constant views of Corvo to your right. Leaving Cedros the road travels inland, but gives you a fine view of Ponta Ruiva way below on its exposed *fajã*. After about 8km you will see **Ponta Delgada** village below you; this is the largest village on Flores. From above, the land looks flat but this is deceptive for when you descend to explore the village you will find there are plenty of steep hills. The road forks towards the bottom of the descent and by following the left fork you will get a good view of the tiny harbour.

Head back on the same road: turn right (it is signposted), to go to the **Farol do Albernaz**. This is a narrow asphalt track going to the lighthouse which was built in 1911 and is the most westerly navigational aid in Europe. There is a good view of the precipitous coast, and the large rock just off the boulder-strewn beach is the **Ilhéu de Maria Vaz**, while out to sea is the **Ilhéu de Monchique**, which can also be seen from Fajã Grande. Come back on the same road and this time continue going on straight into Ponta Delgada village until you reach the **Casa do Povo**. I suggest you will find it easier to park here, since the streets are very narrow, and exploration is better on foot. Don't forget the fisherman's restaurant O Pescador (see page 225). Return to Santa Cruz by the same main road, or, if you have plenty of time and light, you could take the road off on your right just over midway between Ponta Delgada and Cedros and go south through the centre of the island via the 'Lake District'.

WALKS

FOUR SHORT WALKS FOR MOTORISTS All can be done as part of the car tour as they are very short, but the fourth can be done as a separate expedition from Santa Cruz and fill a very pleasant couple of hours.

Short walk 1: Alagoa (*Time: about 20 mins*) From Santa Cruz take the road to the north towards Ponta Delgada and at Alagoa, between Lagoa and Cedros, leave your car by the main road where you see a large rock-crushing depot, and walk down the unsurfaced road starting by the notice declaring the area has special protection for wild birds. This leads you between the scattered houses and down to the beach. There are five islets in the bay and for centuries this was the island's only accessible natural harbour when a strong southwest wind was blowing.

Short walk 2: Moinho do Alagoa (*Time: 10–15 mins*) Not to be confused with the Alagoa above. You will see a stone-paved path starting 50m beyond the watermill. Follow this into the trees, keeping left and going uphill. The path ends at a place called Grota da Prainha, which is really just a watery glade beneath the trees, but on the way you will get closer views of the Ribeira Grande waterfall.

Short walk 3: Poço de Bacalhau (the Codfish Pool) (*Time: about 10 mins*) After you turn right to take the cul-de-sac to the village of Ponta da Fajã you will soon come to a small bridge over the pretty little Ribeira das Casas and its gurgling stream. There is a signposted footpath nearby; simply follow the stream past two old watermills. Finally you have to scramble over a stone wall to reach the pool and its waterfall.

Short walk 4: Parque Florestal, Fazenda de Santa Cruz (*Time: about 1½ hours*) Driving there, on leaving Santa Cruz take the north road passing Monte, and in Fazenda turn left in front of the bus shelter, just below the church. Go uphill past houses and ignore the right-hand turning to the church. Soon you come to a fork; go right for the park, and the dam. For a full description, see page 239.

LONGER WALKS
Flores west coast walk (*Time: about 7½hrs; total distance: about 22km*) By far the grandest walk to achieve is the west-coast walk. If you are fit this can be done in one day, but to really enjoy the experience it is better done at the speed of the Azores and spread over two days. It is not so strenuous walking but there are steep ascents and, more importantly, steep descents which can be slippery in wet conditions or when smooth cobbles are buried by soft juicy foliage. There is also some boulder-hopping to do and at least one stream to cross. After rain it will be muddy in places, and sometimes the path may be running with water. You should avoid this walk on very windy days, especially in winter. Otherwise it is straightforward and you will be rewarded by wonderful ever-changing views of coast and countryside, and experience walking a route that has been in use for 500 years.

Stage 1: Lajedo–Mosteiro–Fajãzinha–Fajã Grande (*Time: about 3½hrs; distance: 10km*) For a shorter walk arrange to meet your taxi in either of the villages *en route*. This first sector crosses a series of hills and river valleys and passes within sight of the Rocha dos Bordões, the famous basalt rock formation, as well as giving some excellent coastal views. It includes a long and steep descent into Fajãzinha. Take a taxi to the Church of Nossa Senhora dos Milagres in the centre of Lajedo, from Santa Cruz. Opposite the church is an *império* with brown-painted doors. Follow the road that goes steeply up on the right of this building, and then left. The road levels off and you continue to where it ends and a cement path comes up the hill and joins it. Continue straight and you are on the footpath. There is, or maybe was, a tourist notice marking the start of the walk, but it faces flat-on the full force

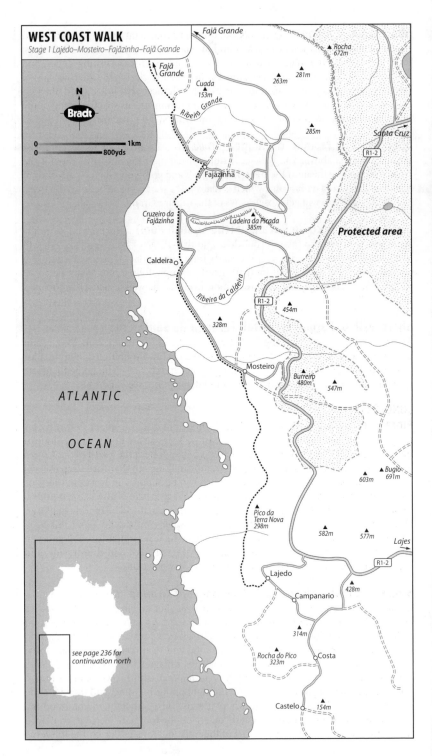

WEST COAST WALK
Stage 1 Lajedo–Mosteiro–Fajãzinha–Fajã Grande

Fajã Grande

Fajã Grande

N

Bradt

0 _____ 1km
0 _____ 800yds

▲ Rocha 672m

▲ 263m   ▲ 281m

Cuada 153m

Ribeira Grande

▲ 285m

Santa Cruz

R1-2

Fajãzinha

Protected area

Cruzeiro da Fajãzinha

Ladeira da Picada 385m ▲

Caldeira ○

Ribeira da Caldeira

R1-2

▲ 454m

▲ 328m

Mosteiro ○

Burreiro 480m ▲   ▲ 547m

ATLANTIC

OCEAN

▲ Bugio 691m
603m ▲

Pico da Terra Nova 298m

▲ 582m   ▲ 577m

Lajes

R1-2

Lajedo ○

▲ 428m

○ Campanario

see page 236 for continuation north

▲ 314m

Rocha do Pico 323m   ○ Costa

Castelo ○   ▲ 154m

234

of the Atlantic winds without interruption all the way from the Statue of Liberty, and when I last saw it, was about to go into orbit.

Follow the cobbled trail keeping left at the junction you come to in a couple of minutes. From here route finding is straightforward, always following the main trail which varies from cobbles to grass. In approximately 30 minutes a second stream crossing is reached, the first one being only very small. The water can be heard but the dense vegetation makes it almost impossible to see. You are actually crossing an old stone bridge said to have been built by the Castillians some 500 years ago. Try to peer back through the trees and undergrowth, where the path has been left, to see the two stone arches.

In about another 30 minutes the next stream crossing comes as a surprise; it is flowing down your trail with no obvious onward path. Walk upstream on the boulders, keeping to the left side, and after a couple of metres the vegetation opens to reveal your onward path sharply off left. Climb up and out of the valley. Continue climbing, soon with a closer view of the basalt rock, and onward to Mosteiro. On reaching the asphalt road turn left, walk downhill, soon reaching the church and a tiny square with seats, a good spot for a break after 1½ hours.

Continue on downhill on the asphalt road; when it bends right you go straight ahead on a wide paved path which quickly bends right and crosses a river bridge. Continue on the grassy path which soon climbs uphill and rejoins the asphalt road. Turn left and continue along this quiet coast road. Soon it drops downhill and goes around the uninhabited hamlet of Caldeira, before climbing again towards another hilltop, with a mast. Approximately three-quarters of the way uphill watch carefully for the grassy path off left signed to Fajãzinha. Sometimes the sign has fallen down or is simply not there! Look for the path! Follow this path all the way. At its highest point there are spectacular views ahead of the next deep valley, the Ribeira Grande and the latter part of your walk; also the mountainous inland cliffs and waterfalls. The path down is mostly in trees and vegetation; it is steep but not difficult. Once in Fajãzinha you will soon reach a tiny square with a tree, and in summer a table and chairs. As you enter the square there is a shop on the right that doubles as a coffee bar. You are now about 2½ hours into the walk.

Continue on out of the square and take the narrow road down towards the sea; a second shop/coffee bar is on the corner. A new black asphalt road has been constructed down to the sea where before there was a simple unsurfaced track. To avoid this new road look out for a cobbled grassy path on your left, marked with a wooden post and red band; it joins the asphalt road at the bottom of the hill. Continue along the road until the sharp left-hand bend. You now have to cross the Ribeira Grande; there is now a very smart bridge, but before it was interesting when the river was in spate and tossing the boulders around. The path cuts inland of the small round hill ahead and reaches an asphalt road. Turn left and walk downhill through the village of Fajã Grande. At the end of the road, past the junction on the right signed to Ponta da Fajã, there is a bar and restaurant on the right, also a picnic area and pebble beach, while ahead there is a concrete quay used by swimmers. From here in summer you can telephone for a taxi.

Stage 2: Fajã Grande–Ponta da Fajã–Ponta Delgada (*Time: about 4hrs; distance: 12km*) This walk begins with a cliff ascent of 350m. It is never very steep or difficult, nor has it any vertiginous drops. It continues across high moorland often surrounded by a sea of blue hydrangeas in June–July and finally descends through pastures to Ponta Delgada. Throughout the walk there are many stream crossings, occasionally running along the path, creating short wet/muddy sections. There are

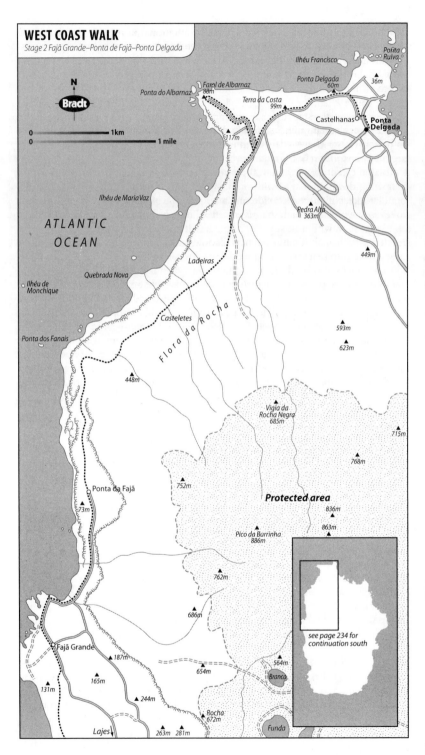

WEST COAST WALK
Stage 2 Fajã Grande–Ponta de Fajã–Ponta Delgada

N

Bradt

0 ——————— 1km
0 ——————— 1 mile

ATLANTIC
OCEAN

Ilhéu de Monchique

Ilhéu de Maria Vaz

Ponta do Albarnaz
Farol de Albarnaz
88m

Ponta Delgada
60m

Ilhéu Francisco

Ponta Ruiva

36m

Terra da Costa
99m

Castelhanas

Ponta Delgada

117m

Pedra Alta
363m

449m

Quebrada Nova

Ladeiras

Casteletes

Flora da Rocha

593m

623m

Ponta dos Fanais

448m

Vigia da Rocha Negra
685m

715m

768m

752m

Protected area

836m

863m

Ponta da Fajã

73m

Pico da Burrinha
886m

762m

686m

Fajã Grande

187m

165m

244m

654m

564m

Branco

see page 234 for continuation south

Rocha
672m

Funda

Lajes

263m 281m

directional signs, but the walk should not be attempted in mist or cloud as good visibility is essential to find your way across the middle section of high moorlands.

Either take a taxi to the *balneario* (bathing area) in Fajã Grande, and begin your walk with a coffee at the restaurant (in summer) and then walk round the beach to pick up the road into Ponta da Fajã, or take a taxi to the church at the far end of Ponta village.

From the church start the walk where the vehicle road ends and take the rocky track between stone walls. In a few minutes you are climbing up a wide grassy cliff path. Apart from a few wet areas as mentioned in the introduction, the path is fairly easy to follow. Observe the cloud level and if visibility is poor, when you reach the top of the cliff think seriously about postponing the walk and returning to Fajã Grande.

After approximately 35 minutes a junction is reached, the walk bends right and uphill into woodland; look out for goldcrests here in June. A wooden marker post confirms the way.

After a further 35 minutes, a gate is reached which is the end of the cliff path. The views from here are excellent across the northwest corner, to Maria Vaz Island, the lighthouse at Ponta do Albernaz and Corvo Island beyond.

From the gate, follow the grassy path which has turned inland. After approximately five minutes, you meet the first of many stream-bed crossings. Scramble upstream for a few metres to find the ongoing path which veers left from the stream bed.

Ten minutes later, you reach a wet stream bed which can be easily crossed on small boulders. The ongoing path remains clear throughout the walk except after a grassy section where the ground drops down ahead – this is another stream crossing, approximately one hour 50 minutes from the start – the path goes down right, crosses the stream and bends back left and continues. Much of the time you can see Corvo directly ahead; the path runs parallel with the coast but slightly inland. There are many stone walls, hydrangea hedges and heather bushes, plus a number of rustic gates to pass through. Occasionally you will see a blob of red paint on a rock that confirms the way.

Further on, the grass path continues between two walls, the path becomes more stony and there is a very short steep descent. The path soon drops down through pastures. Some 2½ hours from the start, there is a short wet muddy section with a stream running along your trail (this cannot be bypassed and is not quite as bad as it first appears) and soon after a clear stream is crossed.

Approximately three hours from the start, the path emerges onto a new cement road. From here you have about 4km to walk to a café and the end of the walk. Turn left and follow this cement road. After 1.4km you might see a sign on your left marking a path to Ponta do Albernaz and Quebrada Nova dos Furnais. DO NOT take this! It can be a very difficult walk, and all it does is take you to the sea at the bottom of some forbidding cliffs. Continue straight and very quickly you come to an asphalt road, better described as an asphalt track. If you turn left, it is a 0.5km walk to the Albernaz lighthouse, where you get a good close view of the large Ilhéu de Maria Vaz just offshore, and, beyond, Ilhéu de Monchique. You will have to return to the junction. Alternatively, simply turn right and follow the asphalt track contouring past pastures and hedgerows with Corvo getting ever closer, and after about 1km begin descending. Ignore an asphalt track coming in from the right and continue straight down between stone walls. Turn left downhill to the village of Ponta Delgada and reach a crossroads. If you turn left in 100m you have a view of the tiny harbour and the village. Return to the crossroads and go straight across uphill. Continue on until you come to the *império* building and then a water

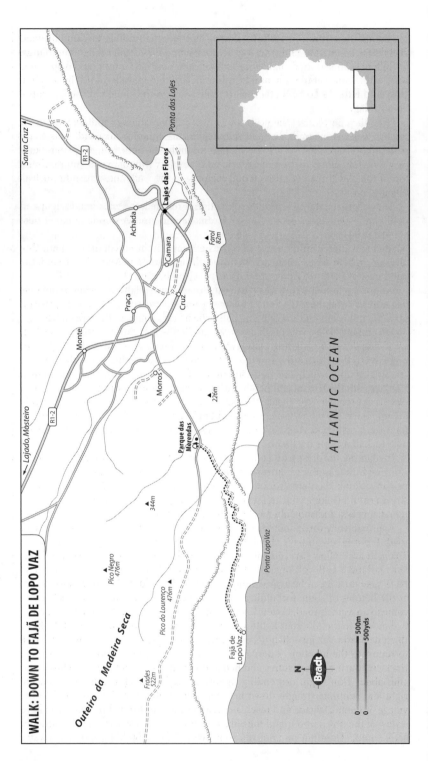

fountain, followed by a small general shop and the new Casa do Povo, all on your right. Turn left at the junction and in 100m come to a blue-and-white café, Café do Sr José Adao, from where you can telephone for a taxi.

Down to Fajã de Lopo Vaz (*Time: 45 mins each way from the clifftop, total 4km; 2½hrs to Lajes, 8km*) This walk descends from a small attractive picnic park to the largest beach on Flores (pebbles and sand) some 300m below. It claims to be the hottest area with a 'microclimate tropical' and bananas are grown.

The most pleasant way is to take a taxi the short distance from Lajes up to the picnic site above the *fajã*, the Parque das Merendas. This is a pleasing spot, with lovely views over the countryside and out to sea, with picnic tables, barbecue and toilets beneath myricaria trees.

The walk down the cliff to the beach takes approximately 45 minutes each way as the descent needs care. The path down has more than 300 uneven stone steps; there are also well-formed sections of path on grass or earth. At times the drop off to the left is sheer but it is mostly well protected by vegetation, though not recommended after rain. There is no onward path from the beach and no road access and also no facilities. There is an occasional house and parts of the beach may be suitable for swimming when very calm – there is a strong undertow. It was one of the sites adopted by the early settlers, and gives a good feel of how hard life must have been in such an isolated place. The path is one of the oldest manmade constructions on Flores; some 500 years old.

For the return to Lajes, simply puff back up to the main road, and choose any route down – you will see the town laid out before you.

Parque Florestal, Fazenda de Santa Cruz (*Time: 1½hrs*) This is a charming park set in a valley surrounded by evergreen forest and dates from the time when the then extensive common lands were cleared and converted to more productive pastures and timber in the early 1960s. In addition to a small formal garden with azaleas, there are picnic tables and a barbecue area, a children's play area and toilets. Maybe less to your liking are the caged birds (pheasants) and a deer enclosure. A short walk leads up to a viewpoint overlooking a small dam. By taxi it takes eight to ten minutes. You could also go slightly further on and ask to be put down at the dam. This is a peaceful spot with picturesque views, good for a picnic, and you can easily walk back to the park. If you cross the dam you will see a cobbled path leading steeply uphill beneath the trees. Should you follow this it goes between stone walls and hydrangeas and comes out after about 30 minutes into pastures where you get a fine view of the Ribeira da Badanela. Return the way you came.

Parque Florestal da Fazenda to Santa Cruz das Flores walk (*Time: about 2hrs; distance: about 6km*) This is a glorious, easy, rural walk in magnificent pastoral country surrounded by high valley sides and largely sheltered from wind. Magnificent on a sunny day if you want to be idle and take a long time over an easy walk, splendid on a windy or cloudy day, and absolutely perfect in winter.

Although the distance can be covered in a couple of hours, try to allow longer because it is so tranquil and you could extend the walk by combining it first by visiting the Parque Florestal (see above) and then walking back to the road fork to the start of the walk.

Take a taxi to the Parque Florestal, but at the fork leading down to the park by the wooden carved signpost pay off your driver. Take the left fork, which is a cinder road, going uphill between evergreen trees. You slowly climb up the valley of the

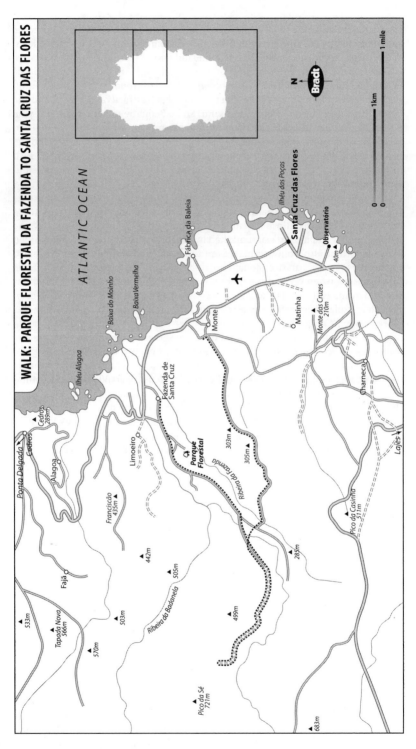

WALK: PARQUE FLORESTAL DA FAZENDA TO SANTA CRUZ DAS FLORES

ATLANTIC OCEAN

Ponta Delgada
Cedros
Cedros 889m
Alagoa
Ilhéu Alagoa
Baixa do Moinho
Baixa Vermelha
Fábrica da Baleia
Ilhéu das Poças
Santa Cruz das Flores
Observatório 40m

533m
Tapada Nova 566m
Fajã
570m
503m
Franciscão 435m
442m
Limoeiro
Fazenda de Santa Cruz
Monte
Matinha
Monte das Cruzes 210m

Ribeira da Badanela
505m
Parque Florestal
Ribeira da Fazenda
303m
305m
499m
285m
Charneca
Pico da Casinha 511m
Lajes

Pico da Sé 721m
683m

N
Bradt

0   1km
0   1 mile

240

Ribeira da Fazenda, the trees of pittosporum, acacia, eucalyptus and cryptomeria sometimes totally enclosing you, at other times opening to present intimate views of the valley. Look back from time to time and you will see the ocean. Towards the head of the valley the road ends and levels off, and you have glorious views all around you, except eastwards where lies the sea. Maybe it will remind you of the French Pyrenees. At a double green gate you see a *levada*, or water conduit, contouring off up a small side valley. Look up and slightly to your right and you will see the Pico da Sé, the highest point, in view. You have also reached the highest point of the road, and soon you descend for a short distance to find the road ending by some trees. Follow the tiny path down and you come to the stream and a most enchanting place where the sparkling water gurgles over smooth boulders and then cuts its way deeply down through the rocks. There is a pool deep enough for a refreshing splash and to leave a bottle of wine to cool in time for your picnic. Endemic plant species you can find around here include juniperus, rhamnus, faya, tree heath, vaccinium and viburnum.

To return to Santa Cruz should take you no more than 1½ hours. When you are ready to continue, walk back down the road to where the trees begin, and start looking out very carefully for the first break in the trees on your right. You will see the start of a broken cobblestone path. Once this had been cemented, but at the time of writing it is now broken and has washed down the trail. Descend steeply below low stone walls under the pittosporum trees and soon you will arrive at the valley bottom. Cross the stream, the Ribeiro da Fazenda, and then ascend along a path between two walls which more or less goes diagonally up the valley side. On your left the view of the Fazendas Valley gets better at every step. This path eventually becomes cemented and you simply follow it to the top and continue when it changes to a cinder road at a place known as Beija Mão. In just over another kilometre you will be in the centre of Monte, where you drop down to the road junction and turn left. Santa Cruz town looks like a children's model laid out below you. Shortly, take the right turn steeply down at a small green-and-white-painted water tower and come to a T-junction. Turn right to join the main road again and soon you will see a mirror on the bend. At the side of the mirror take the steps down to São Pedro, to come out near the whale factory.

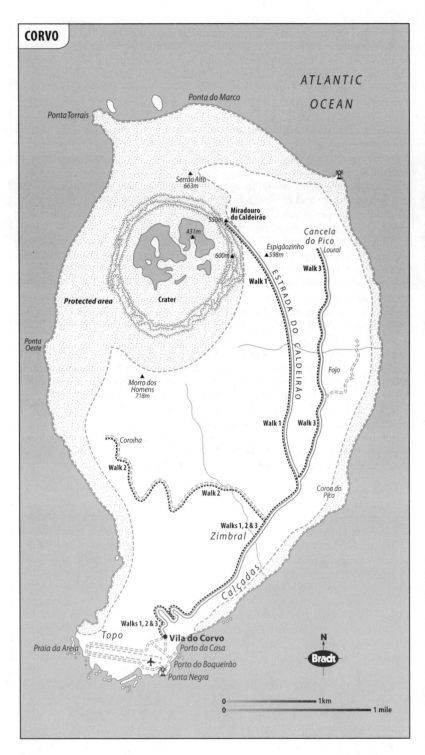

CORVO

ATLANTIC OCEAN

Ponta do Marco

PontaTorrais

Serrão Alto
663m

Miradouro
do Caldeirão

550m

Cancela
do Pico

431m

Espigãozinho
▲598m

Loural

600m

Walk 3

Walk 1

Protected area

Crater

Ponta
Oeste

ESTRADA DO CALDEIRÃO

Morro dos
Homens
718m

Fojo

Walk 1

Walk 3

Coroiha

Walk 2

Coroa do
Pico

Walk 2

Walks 1, 2 & 3

Zimbral

Calçadas

Walks 1, 2 & 3

Topo

Vila do Corvo

Praia da Areia

Porto da Casa

Porto do Boqueirão

Ponta Negra

N

Bradt

0 _____ 1km
0 _____ 1 mile

11

Corvo

Corvo is by far the remotest island of the archipelago and must surely rate as one of the most isolated places in all Europe. This ancient volcanic remnant is surrounded by an often cruel and savage ocean, and inaccessible for months at a time from its nearest neighbour until the very recent advent of the aeroplane. It is the tiny elusive gem at the apex of the Azores crown. Day visitors from Flores making the boat crossing in settled summer weather are increasing, but for the true traveller intent upon getting a feel for this island there are eight rooms in a small *residencial* or a simple camping site available.

Whether you arrive by plane or boat, you land in the island's only settlement, Vila do Corvo. It is the only suitable place at sea level, a lava delta where the last eruption occurred. Little has changed in the eastern segment of the town, the narrow cobbled streets between dark basalt walls of the houses all huddle tightly together in mutual protection against winter storms and to save valuable arable land much as they have always done. The only road snakes steeply up the hill to the cow pastures, and continues ever upwards to the caldera, a distance of 6km.

On a day visit there should be time enough to walk to the road's end to enjoy the view down into the crater which, at 300m deep and 2km across, is among the largest in the Azores. However, be warned: it is often shrouded in cloud. For those with more time, there are three walks to do, plus sea activities, and it is the Azorean highpoint for autumn birdwatching, but the greatest delight must surely come from simply being on Corvo and freeing your senses to absorb its atmosphere.

To make my first visit I had to charter a boat, and I gave a lift to an emigrant who had returned from California to Flores for the first time in 26 years. He was desperate to get to Corvo to see his 84-year-old aunt. Arriving at the little jetty, a small drama ensued with much embracing and tears between him and about a dozen islanders, and it was equally emotional when we departed four hours later. The boat's captain was given bunches of onions, and as we drew away from the harbour we were all sadly watching the tiny town grow smaller and smaller and the mists come down ever lower.

As well as being the remotest island in the Azores, Corvo is also by far the smallest, at just 17.13km². It is also the smallest parish in Portugal: 430 people, 1,500 cows. The island consists of a volcano summit in the northern half of the island with a caldera, in the bottom of which are small lakes. Given its size and isolation it is perhaps just as well that today there is no noticeable seismic activity and it is considered to be inactive. Since the western islands are the first obstacle that the Atlantic Ocean meets for over 1,000 miles, Corvo has been substantially eroded, so that the island now confronts the ocean with precipitous cliffs 700m tall, especially in the north and northwest, which are the tallest in the Azores.

In 2009, UNESCO declared the island a Biosphere Reserve, encompassing all the land area above sea level and a surrounding marine zone totalling 25,853ha. The landscapes and biological value are considered to be of regional, national and international importance, and take in the previously protected sites.

BACKGROUND

GEOLOGY Like Flores, Corvo can be divided into two complexes, the oldest comprising submarine eruptions one to 1.5 million years old, and a superior complex of above-sea-level volcanism dating from around 700,000 years ago. The island appears to have a much simpler structure than Flores, and is the emerged summit of a basaltic stratovolcano (one that is a steeply sided cone of alternate layers of lava and other basaltic fragments). It would have been about 1,000m high before the caldera collapsed, and the highest point is now 718m.

The caldera's now smooth and gently sloping sides suggest it could be one of the oldest in the Azores. The cinder cones within it, some up to 30m tall, are the result of later eruptions.

The last eruption occurred 100,000 years ago in the area of Pão de Açúcar and its lava flows created the lava delta where Corvo village and the airstrip are now located.

HISTORY Corvo means 'crow' or 'raven', but probably the name derives from a pre-Portuguese designation of Corvimarini or similar. Along with Flores it was the last of the islands to be discovered by the navigators, sometime around 1450. Initial attempts at colonisation failed and it was not until 1548, when its donatory, Captain Gonçalo de Sousa, imported slaves, probably from Cape Verde, that permanent settlement was achieved. Because of its size, no safe harbour and isolation, it has remained an agricultural-based society, and today livestock farming and fisheries, both subsidised, together with subsistence agriculture, are the mainstays.

GETTING THERE AND AWAY

This is not a straightforward process. Weather conditions are all-important, and the visitor should always allow for delays when planning a holiday itinerary. However, just because it is too windy for a plane to fly or the sea is too rough for a ship to come into port does not imply bad conditions on land.

I had some magnificent weather, changeable and exhilarating, for ten days one December. Exactly according to schedule SATA Air Açores flew me from Ponta Delgada via Terceira to Flores and a week later from Flores to Corvo. This time it was just me and a policeman as passengers. An hour later a storm blew in, and the next day I watched fascinated as 12m waves crashed over the end of the runway and I began to see myself on Corvo for Christmas. Twenty-four hours later and so typical of the Azores, the wind dropped long enough for the plane to land, fly to Flores and back, and take me to Faial exactly as printed in the timetable and displayed on the airline's website. At the same time high seas had prevented the usual supply-ship crossing from Flores for over three weeks, and the island was very short of fresh fruit and vegetables, though I was assured there was still three months' supply of beer in stock. It was a fun experience, but a visit in summer should be easier!

SATA Air Açores flies regular but not daily flights connecting Corvo with Flores, Horta and Terceira. See page 228 for ferry information.

Early communication with Flores was by fire, the number lit coded for a doctor, priest or other urgent need. Money entering the island's economy had to come from outside and in the time of the pirates and corsairs it seems an unofficial relationship was established with them to everyone's mutual advantage. In exchange for water, food supplies and ship repairs, the islanders gained protection and luxury items.

The advent of the American whalers in the 18th and 19th centuries attracted able men to help crew the ships, and later land-based open-boat whaling generated some cash income. In 1830 there were some 3,000 sheep grazing the island. The first boys' school opened in 1845, followed by one for girls in 1874, thanks to a bylaw passed in Lisbon. Around the turn of the century imports included sugar, flour, coffee, wine, vinegar, *aguardente*, port wine, cheese from São Jorge, figs, candles, soap and leather. Important exports were cows and hides, but it was also a time of yet more emigration, to Brazil, the other islands, but mostly to North America. In 1864, the population was 1,095; now it is over 400 after a recent modest increase, and occupies just one page in the Azores telephone directory. Beef cattle are winched from the quay into a boat during the summer months for transfer to Flores, where a larger ship takes them onwards. With an excellent new school, easily identified by its windows and doors most attractively framed in traditional blue and yellow, the new generation maintains contact with the outside world via the very latest technology, and has far better internet access than I have in rural England. At age 14, the pupils go to Terceira or São Miguel, boarding with families for which the parents have to pay.

GETTING AROUND

Walk! If this really does not appeal, it is said there are now two taxis on the island.

WHERE TO STAY

Guesthouse Comodoro (8 rooms, 1 apt) Caminho do Areiro, 9980 Vila do Corvo; 292 596 128; e corvoazores@yahoo.com. About 5 mins' walk from the airport, everyone can tell you the way, but the guesthouse offers a free transfer. Rooms come with private bathroom, free internet service & cable TV. A 2-star-equivalent hotel. €

CAMPING There is a good, flat, grass field at the end of and just above the airstrip, and by Corvo's tiny boulder-and-sand beach. There are simple facilities including a barbecue, all free of charge.

WHERE TO EAT

Restaurante A Traineira Rua da Matriz, by the harbour; 292 596 207. With fish soup a speciality & always fresh grilled fish. In Dec, to my considerable dismay, the proprietor left for Flores on the plane I arrived on, so the restaurant was closed & I have no first-hand experience. One of the hazards of winter travel!

Restaurante O Caldeirao Carminho dos Moinhois
Snack Bar Irmãos Metralha Rua Joaquim Pedro Coelho. Basic village bar.
Bar dos Bombeiros Av Nova

WHAT TO SEE AND DO

ENVIRONMENTAL INTERPRETATION CENTRE (*Canada da Graciosa;* 292 596 051; e *parque.natural.corvo@azores.gov.pt;* http://parquesnaturais.azores.gov.pt/corvo;

Corvo is so small and with so few people that celebrations here seem like a big house party. The most important festival is that of Our Lady of Miracles in August. The dates of festivals may vary each year, so please check with the tourist information office.

Festa de Santo Antão last weekend of May
Festa de São Pedro last weekend of Jun
Festa do Dovino Espírito Santo 2nd weekend of Jul
Festa da Sagrada Família last weekend of Jul
Festival dos Moinhos and **Festa de Nossa Senhora dos Milagres** 14 & 15 Aug
Festa da Senhora do Bom Caminho 2nd weekend of Sep

⏲ *09.00–12.30 & 14.00–17.30 Mon–Fri*) The exhibits and custodians provide the visitor with an understanding of life on the island, an experience that will enhance any visit. The recently restored building shows the traditional architecture, and is appropriately located in the town's historic core. In addition to the exhibition area, there is a media library and a workshop to support field activities.

WALKING The best way to explore the island is to walk. Three walks are described on pages 247–8.

BIRDS AND FLOWERS It seems you should never relax but keep alert for birds all the time; what little tree cover there is is on the eastern side – look here for passerines, and the caldera lakes for ducks and waders. Peter Alfrey has written a most vivid and exciting (even for a botanist!) description of his visit in October 2005 that puts birdwatching on a totally different plane (see page 268). In that year 16 species of mostly Nearctic passerines new for Macaronesia were recorded, and more since.

THE SEA For anything to do with boat trips, fishing or diving, contact **Nauticorvo** (*Rua da Matriz, 9980 Corvo;* ✆ *292 596 287;* e *corvomarinho@nauticorvo.pt*).

VILA DO CORVO There is only one town, **Vila do Corvo**, and no villages or other settlements. If you have come just for the day, as do most visitors, then Vila do Corvo certainly justifies an hour or two. Wander around the old part of town enjoying the details: from the harbour, the narrow streets called *canadas*, the play of sun and shadow on the cobbles, and the Church of Nossa Senhora dos Milagres – Our Lady of Miracles – with origins dating back to the 16th century. The present church was built between 1789 and 1795, and paid for by the Corvo population together with remittances from emigrants; the first priest was appointed in 1796, who came from Urzelina on São Jorge. Corvo was the first island to publish and have approved in 1984 a strategic development plan and all the old part of Vila do Corvo is a conservation area. The new half is not without interest, and reflects the enterprise of the islanders. If you explore the south coast below the airport you soon come to an old slipway by the windmills; this was where whales were brought up before the factory was built on Flores, and the blubber was reduced on the shore in the open. If the clouds are high, then the other thing to do is to ascend the only road to the high ground to see the caldera, the crater with its lake and small islands; see *Walk 1*, opposite, for details.

WALKS

Corvo offers three very easy and very satisfying walks. Most visitors will want to go to the highest accessible point and see the caldera. Certainly if you are a day visitor crossing by boat from Flores this is the easiest to do for it follows an asphalt road all the way so that if the clouds come down you can easily find your way. The summit frequently is in clouds, but do not be put off as these often clear for short moments, enough to give you a window to see down into the caldera, and on the way up or down there are views across pastures, the sea, and even as far as Flores. The second walk is again very easy, and is both picturesque with all the pastures and at the same time dramatic because of the steep slopes above and below the path, the views of the sea and across to Flores, and the fact that you can be in such a glorious place and yet in the middle of the Atlantic Ocean. The third walk contours along on the east coast below the road to the caldera, and is a peaceful, easy walk, again surrounded by more pastures but this time you will also discover Corvo's few trees and patches of forest.

WALK 1: VILA DO CORVO TO THE CALDERA (CALDEIRÃO) (*Time: 4hrs; distance: 12km*) Leave the harbour and turn right past the Restaurante Traineira and follow the narrow black-cobbled Rua da Matriz all the way up until you join the main road, also cobbled. Turn right for the caldera, and ascend. You rapidly get a fine view of Vila do Corvo, especially of the old, original part of town easily distinguished by the houses of natural stone, weathered pantiles, and the tiny *canadas* or lanes between them. Note the rear walls of the houses are virtually windowless, to protect them from the harsh winter winds. Soon the road changes from a cobbled surface to black asphalt, which continues all the way to the edge of the caldera. Walking along a road is a bore but it is little used and the scenery more than compensates, for you are in a land of pastures, stone walls, hedgerows and views to the sea.

After almost 2km you will see a temporary bar, the Formidável, open in summer only, among the pastures up on your left – the post and rope fence leads the way to the dance floor. Sadly neither currently function. Opposite is a wooden signpost to Fonte Doce. If the clouds have come down and visibility is poor, continue along the asphalt road. To avoid walking all the way along the main road you can take the cement road going up left between two houses and a prominent cement-rendered wall on the corner, just beyond the bar building. Soon you pass the old butter factory and at the end of the cement road turn right (for *Walk 2*, turn left).

This cinder road goes between walled fields and comes out again onto the asphalt road; turn left to continue to the caldera. You will come to a wide cinder road leading straight on where the asphalt road bends left (this is *Walk 3*). Continue on the asphalt road and look out for another small road off on your left. You should be able to see where this goes, for it is another short cut, relieving you of the asphalt road. Rejoin the main road and continue up to the caldera. If mist and cloud are absent, the caldera is rather beautiful with its two lakes and their irregular margins and islets, and the inner slopes covered with pastures clearly divided by immaculate stone walls and hydrangea hedges. The lakes drain to a waterfall into the sea on the west coast.

To return to Vila do Corvo, retrace your steps.

WALK 2: VILA DO CORVO TO THE PASTURES BELOW MORRO DOS HOMENS (*Time: 3½hrs; distance: 4km from the asphalt road leading to the caldera (Caldeirão), 6km from Vila do Corvo, 12km there and back*) This is magnificent. As for *Walk 1* as far as the closed Bar Formidável. Just beyond the bar take the cement road going up left

Corvo WALKS 11

between two houses and a prominent cement-rendered wall on the corner. Soon you pass the old butter factory and at the end of the cement road turn left. Continue until you come to two stone posts and a cattle grid. Do not turn right, since this leads to the new reservoir providing drinking water to Vila do Corvo and is a closed area. Turn left, and follow the cinder road. Soon you get wonderful views to Flores. As the road bends round you can discern Corvo's second volcano crater, or part of it since the west side has been eroded away. Almost at the end of the road you will see a small watercourse running down below on the left – it is partly lined with hydrangeas and gingers. There will also be, passing beneath the road at this point, a large grey plastic drainage pipe. From this point, if you look carefully about 60m down towards the watercourse, you should see a natural spring. Here you can either drink the water or better still, cool your wine to accompany a picnic. To return to Vila do Corvo either retrace your steps or follow the signposts of the official Caro do Índio walk, graded as medium difficult.

WALK 3: AN EASY WALK PASSING PASTURES AND WOODLAND (*Time: 3½hrs; distance: 4km from the asphalt road, 6km from Vila do Corvo, 12km there and back*) From Vila do Corvo continue as for *Walk 1* until a wide cinder road leads off on your right from the main asphalt caldera road. Follow this farm road until it comes to an end in pastures and woodland. It simply provides access for the farmers, but it is a lovely quiet walk more or less on the level.

Appendix 1

LANGUAGE

Portuguese is notoriously difficult to pronounce, takes much practice, and ought to be mastered before trying to use any vocabulary. Fortunately, you will meet plenty of friendly Azoreans happy to coach you to say a phrase to the point where they can recognise it!

Many words can be guessed from English or Spanish and some Spanish speakers get along quite well with a mixture of *português* and *espanhol*. Examples include many words ending with -ion or -on in English and Spanish respectively which are similar in Portuguese but end in -ão (plural usually -ões) – *televisão, associação*.

Take care, though, for some similar Spanish and Portuguese words have completely different meanings: *niño* (Spanish = child) versus *ninho* (Portuguese = nest); and it is best not to describe an ordinary man as *ordinário* as this implies he is common or vulgar.

PRONUNCIATION

ã + a followed by m	nasal (similar to 'ang').
c	ss before i or e; k elsewhere
ç	ss
cc	ks
ch	sh
g	soft j before i or e; hard g elsewhere
j	soft j (as in French)
lh	ly (as in Spanish ll)
nh	ny (as Spanish ñ)
o or ô	oo when unstressed
o or ó	o when stressed (as in hot)
ou	o sound (as in both or window)
õ + o followed by m	nasal (similar to 'ong').
qu	k before i or e; kw elsewhere
s	z or sh (at end of word)
x	sh or s
z	soft j

ESSENTIALS

Hello	*Olá*	Yes	*Sim*
Good morning	*Bom dia*	Yes please	*Sim, por favor*
Good afternoon	*Boa tarde*	No	*Não*
Good evening	*Boa tarde*	No thank you	*Não obrigado*
Goodnight	*Boa noite*	(masculine)	
Goodbye	*Adeus*	I am sorry	*Desculpe*

That is all right	Está bem	excellent	óptimo
good	bom		

Excuse me (to pass someone)	Com licença
What is your name?	Como se chama?
My name is…	Chamo-me
You're welcome	De nada
	(ie: 'it's nothing' – reply to thank you)

Please	Por favor
Thank you (masculine)	Obrigado
Thank you (feminine)	Obrigada
Thank you very much (masculine)	Muito obrigado
Thank you very much (feminine)	Muito obrigada
It is very kind of you	É muito amável

QUESTIONS

How?	Como?	How much (cost)?	Quanto custa/é isso?
How much?	Quanto?	What?	O quê?

NUMBERS

0	zero	16	dezasseis
1	um	17	dezassete
2	dois	18	dezoito
3	três	19	dezanove
4	quatro	20	vinte
5	cinco	21	vinte e um
6	seis	30	trinta
7	sete	40	quarenta
8	oito	50	cinquenta
9	nove	60	sessenta
10	dez	70	setenta
11	onze	80	oitenta
12	doze	90	noventa
13	treze	100	cem
14	quatorze	1,000	mil
15	quinze		

DAYS, MONTHS AND TIME

Sunday	Domingo	Thursday	Quinta-feira
Monday	Segunda-feira	Friday	Sexta-feira
Tuesday	Terça-feira	Saturday	Sábado
Wednesday	Quarta-feira		

January	Janeiro	July	Julho
February	Fevereiro	August	Agosto
March	Março	September	Setembro
April	Abril	October	Outubro
May	Maio	November	Novembro
June	Junho	December	Dezembro

after	depois (de)	now	agora
before	antes (de)	today	hoje

day	dia	tomorrow	amanhã
never	nunca	yesterday	ontem

GETTING AROUND

aeroplane	avião	right	à direita
bus	autocarro	road	estrada
car	carro	Stop here, please	Pare aqui, por favor
closed	fechado	straight on	em frente
here	aqui	street, road, highway	rua
left	à esquerda	there	ali
lorry, truck	camião	Where is it please?	Onde é que é, por favor?
open	aberto		
		Which way?	Para onde?

ACCOMMODATION

bathroom, toilet	casa de banho	cold/hot water	água fria/quente
bed	cama	hotel	hotel
guesthouse	residencial	toilet paper	papel higiénico

EATING AND DRINKING This includes sufficient restaurant Portuguese to help you through the usual menu.

In a bar/café

I would like …	Queria …
a beer, please	uma cerveja, por favor (for types of beer, see Drinks below)
a sandwich, please	uma sanduíche, por favor (these almost always come as rolls filled with ham, cheese or mixed: fiambre, queijo or mixta)
mineral water, please	uma água mineral, por favor (com gás = carbonated; sem gás = still)
two coffees, please	dois cafés, por favor
some more coffee, please	mais café, por favor
the bill, please	a conta, por favor

In a restaurant

For two, please	Para dois, por favor	dinner	jantar
The menu, please	O menu, por favor	dish of the day	prato do dia
Enough, thank you	Chega, obrigado	the wine list	lista de vinhos
lunch	almoço		

Drinks Coffee comes in many forms: café com leite = white coffee; café bica = small strong black coffee; café galão = white coffee served in a long glass; for more details, see page 59.

tea	chá (chá da Índia = India tea; chá de camomile = chamomile tea)
fruit drink	um sumo de frutas
iced	fresco
house wine	vinho da casa (tinto, red; branco, white)
bottled beer	cerveja de garrafa
draught beer	cerveja de pressão or fino or imperial

Fish (*Peixe*) See also *Appendix 3*, page 264.

clams	*ameijoas*	salmon	*salmão*
common sea bream	*pargo*	salted cod	*bacalhau*
forkbeard	*abrotea*	sardine	*sardinha*
horse mackerel	*chicharro*	shellfish	*mariscos*
lobster	*lagosta*	shrimps	*camarão*
mussels	*mexilhões*	squid	*lula*
octopus	*polvo*	swordfish	*espadarte*
prawns	*gambas*	tunny fish	*atum*
red fish	*boca negra*	wreck fish	*cherne*
red mullet	*salmonete*		

Meat (*Carne*)

beef	*carne de vaca*	rabbit	*coelho*
chicken	*frango*	sausage	*salsicha*
chop	*costeleta*	smoked pork	
kid	*carne de cabrito*	sausage	*linguiça*
liver	*fígado*	spiced sausage	*chouriço*
loin	*lombo*	tongue	*lingua*
pork	*carne de porco*	veal	*carne de vitela*

Cooking methods

baked/roasted	*no forno*	smoked	*fumado*
boiled or *pot-au-feu*	*cozido*	steamed	*suada*
fried	*frito*	stewed	*estufado*
grilled	*grelhado*	tinned	*conserva*
roast/roasted	*assado*	with a sauce	*com molho*

Azorean/Portuguese foods

apple	*maça*	lemon	*limão*
beans	*feijão*	lettuce salad	*salada de alface*
beans with mixed		lupin seeds (usually	*tremoços*
meats	*feijoada*	in a saucer on the	
beef	*bife*	bar counter)	
biscuits	*biscoitos*	mixed salad	*salada mista*
bread	*pão*	olive oil	*azeite*
bread soup	*açorda*	olives	*azeitonas*
butter	*manteiga*	omelette	*omelete*
cabbage soup	*caldo verde*	orange	*laranja*
cake	*bolo*	peanuts	*amendoins*
caramel custard	*flan*	potatoes	*batatas*
chicken	*galinha*	rice	*arroz*
egg	*ovo*	sauce	*molho*
fruit	*frutas*	soup	*sopa*
fruit salad	*salada de frutas*	sugar	*açúcar*
garlic	*alho*	tomato salad	*salada de tomate*
honey	*mel*	yoghurt	*iogurte*
ice cream	*gelado*		

HEALTH

casualty department	*banco de socorros* (*SAU – Serviço de Atendimento Urgente*)	diarrhoea	*diarréia*
		to hurt (or ache)	*doer*
		doctor	*médico*
hospital	*hospital*	ill	*doente*
		fever	*febre*

OTHER USEFUL WORDS

battery	*pilha*	mountain	*montanha*
book	*livro*	night	*noite*
change	*câmbio*	nothing	*nada*
child	*criança*	on the beach	*na praia*
church	*igreja*	rain	*chuva*
currency	*devisas*	sea	*mar*
enough	*bastante*	shop	*loja*
hill	*colina*	small	*pequenho/a*
house	*casa*	to swim	*nadar*
lake	*lago*	too much	*demais/demasiado/a*
large	*grande*	town	*cidade*
a little (not much)	*pouco/a*	travellers' cheques	*cheques de viagem*
a lot (very, much)	*muito/a*	village	*aldeia*
market	*mercado*	you	*você* (polite, formal),
money	*dinheiro*		*tu* (familiar)

LANGUAGE COURSES The University of the Azores (*Rua da Mãe de Deus, 9500 Ponta Delgada;* ☎ *+351 296 650 000;* **e** *cursoverao@alf.uac.pt; www.uac.pt*) offers summer Portuguese-language courses at beginner, intermediate and advanced levels on São Miguel. There are also courses in Azorean culture, society and art on São Miguel, Terceira, Faial and Pico. Courses run for two to five weeks between June and July. Accommodation is provided in university hostels and fees include costs of field trips and social events.

Appendix 1 LANGUAGE

A1

Appendix 2

FLORA

Given that there are some 850 flowering plants and ferns in the Azores, the following 60 have been selected as those most likely to strike the eye of the visitor. Books that describe European flowers will identify most of the Azorean flora apart from the endemics, and the well-illustrated *Mediterranean Wild Flowers* by Marjorie Blamey and Christopher Grey Wilson, published by Collins, London, is helpful. The most difficult plants to identify confidently are the evergreen trees and shrubs. As always, the one plant you really would like to name will not be included!

The Latin name is given in italics, followed in brackets by the Portuguese vernacular where known, and by the common English name if there is one, and then the family.

EVERGREEN TREES AND SHRUBS

Myrica faya (faia) **Myricaceae** Evergreen shrub or small tree up to 8m. Leaves lanceolate, leathery, dark green, margins often toothed towards the apex and frequently rolled backwards. Flowers are unisexual and borne on axillary catkin-like spikes, male and female on the same plant; overall colour olive-green, withering to brown. Fruit small, rounded and very hard. All Azores islands, Madeira, Canaries and Portugal. Often a coastal shrub, but found up to 700m. At higher altitudes a member of the laurisilva association. Can form pure stands, but is often out-competed by alien *Pittosporum undulatum* and you can frequently see the two species fighting for dominance. Makes a good shelter hedge and was once used around orange orchards. Isolated trees make good garden specimens.

Ilex perado **ssp.** *azorica (azevinho;* **Azorean holly) Aquifoliaceae**
Tree up to 5m, with a smooth grey bark. Leaves dark and glossy, stiff, elliptic-oblong, sometimes with a few spines. Madeira and the Canaries also have their own subspecies. Usually found above 500m, and an important member of the laurisilva forest; can be seen as isolated specimens or in hedgerows. Formerly encouraged by farmers for winter cattle feed. On all the islands apart from Graciosa.

Laurus azorica (louro; **Canary laurel) Lauraceae** Dark, glossy green, evergreen tree up to 10m, sometimes taller, with a dense crown. Young shoots clothed in dense brown downy hairs. Leaves alternate, varying between five and 15, 3–7cm, broadly lanceolate-elliptic, hairless above, softly hairy beneath at least when young, strongly aromatic when crushed; in the axils of the midrib and main veins are tiny, gland-like projections. Flowers creamy yellow, fruit ovoid, 1–2cm, broadly ellipsoid, green turning to black when ripe. Usually grows above 500m and a key member of the laurisilva forest.

***Picconia azorica (pau-branco)* Oleaceae** Evergreen tree or shrub, leaves opposite, leathery, without hairs, two to three times as long as broad, with small white flowers on inflorescences from the leaf axils. Found mostly between 300m and 600m, once widespread and used for house building, its presence now rather scattered. Endemic to the Azores, but not found on Graciosa.

***Frangula azorica (sanguinho)* Rhamnaceae** Large deciduous shrub or small tree with a wide spreading crown; branches little divided and leafy only towards the end. Leaves broadly elliptic, up to 15cm long with distinct parallel lateral veins. Flowers small, yellowish, in clusters from the leaf axils. Generally around 500m and up to about 1,000m altitude it is a member of the laurisilva forest, and also remnant hedgerows. On all islands except Graciosa and Corvo, now extinct on Madeira.

***Prunus lusitanica* ssp. *azorica* (*ginja*; Azores cherry laurel) Rosaceae** Evergreen small tree to 4m, leaves somewhat leathery, to 10cm, oval and tapering at each end, dark green and shiny above, paler beneath, possibly finely toothed, leaf stalks red when young, the whole plant without hairs. Flowers rounded, white, in racemes of up to 20–30 from the leaf axils. Fruit cherry-like, oval to almost round, turning red at first, finally ripening purplish black. Above 500m in deep ravines or in dense laurisilva forest. Endemic and rare.

***Myrsine africana* (*tamujo*; African boxwood) Myrsinaceae** Dense, low evergreen shrub to 1.5m, leaves 0.6–2cm, roughly egg-shaped with small teeth on margins. Flowers small, pale brown in clusters of three to six, followed by bluish-lilac 6mm-diameter fruits. Generally above 400m, it favours the shelter afforded by dense laurisilva forest where it can be abundant, but it also occurs in more open vegetation. Occurs from east and South Africa, and the Himalayas to China.

***Persea indica* (*vinhático*) Lauraceae** Evergreen tree up to 15–20m tall, with a broad, rounded crown. Shoots finely hairy when young. Leaves without glands, 10–20 x 3–8cm, elliptic, leaf stalks up to 3cm, reddish; whole leaf becomes reddish when old. Inflorescence on stalks shorter than the leaves, flowers small, whitish. Fruit about 2cm. Ellipsoid, bluish-black when ripe. Found above 200m, introduced long ago (from the Canaries?), now naturalised. *Persea americana* is the avocado.

***Clethra arborea* (lily of the valley tree) Ericaceae** Evergreen shrub or small tree to 8m with a bushy crown, twigs have obvious leaf-scars, and young twigs, leaf stalks and flower stems all densely covered in rusty hairs. Leaves about 12 x 5cm, somewhat crowded towards the shoot tips, leaf margins with forward pointed small teeth, with fine hairs on veins on underside, leafstalk often reddish. Flowers in simple or branched racemes up to 15cm long, erect, the flowers to

8mm, nodding, white, cup-shaped, scented. Endemic to Macaronesia (Madeira), probably introduced into São Miguel where it has rapidly naturalised on the hills above Furnas.

Pittosporum undulatum (*incenso*; **Victorian box, orange berry**) **Pittosporaceae**

Vigorous tree to 14m, leaves 10 x 3cm, narrowing to a point, shiny dark green above, pale beneath, young leaves yellow-green, margins wavy. Flowers bell-shaped, about 1cm diameter, creamy-white in clusters, sweetly scented, February. Fruit orange when ripe, the pale brown seeds very sticky. Native of southeast Australia, it was introduced as an ornamental and used as a hedging plant to shelter the orange orchards but is now widely naturalised throughout the archipelago and is a major and aggressive component of the tree cover, especially on Santa Maria and Pico.

Hedera helix ssp. *canariensis* (**Canary ivy**) **Araliaceae**

The familiar plant with climbing or creeping woody stems and evergreen leaves with three to five short, triangular lobes. Yellow-green flowers in many flowered umbels, fruit rounded ripening black. Widespread between 100m and 1,100m, most common at mid altitude, and most luxurious in laurisilva forest. Also found in Madeira, Canaries, Portugal and northwest Africa.

Viburnum tinus ssp. *subcordatum* (*folhado*; Azorean laurustinus) **Caprifoliaceae**

Evergreen shrub with oval leaves and small white to pink flowers in large terminal convex clusters, spring. Fruits are at first a vivid deep metallic blue, turning black as they mature. Associates with laurisilva forest, but can be seen in remnant hedgerows on Pico; generally above 400m and up to 900m. *V. tinus* is native of southern Europe, with a closely related species in the Canaries, but absent from Madeira. The Azorean subspecies differs from the mainland species by its more vigorous habit, more glossy leaves and larger inflorescences.

Vaccinium cylindraceaum (*uva da serra*) **Ericaceae**

Deciduous shrub generally less than 2m tall, with 20–50mm-long finely toothed, narrowly oblong leaves; when young these are attractively red-tinged. Flowers borne in clusters, yellow-green tinged red; just how red the flowers are varies, partly due to age, and the combination of young red leaves and good red flowers in June puts this among the most attractive of the Azorean endemic plants. Grows generally above 400m and is conspicuous among the laurisilva forest, and often may be seen in old hedgerows. Occurs on all the islands. Fruits locally harvested for preserves.

Euphorbia stygiana **Euphorbiaceae**

Many-stemmed soft wooded shrub up to 2m tall with conspicuous narrow leaves 10–15cm long, apple-green and waxy with prominent pale midrib. Flowers terminal, yellow-green. Most easily seen in association with laurisilva, where it is moist and the surrounding vegetation provides shelter. A very noticeable plant of attractive form. Endemic.

Daboecia azorica **Ericaceae**

Dwarf, heath-like evergreen shrub less than 15cm tall with alternate leaves to 8mm long. Flowers in terminal loose racemes, nodding, bell-

shaped, ruby-red. Mostly above 500m, can be found in grassland but is most spectacular on the upper slopes of Pico, where it forms magnificent carpets with *Thymus caespititius* in midsummer. Endemic.

Erica scoparia ssp. *azorica* (*urze*; besom heath) Ericaceae
Stout, evergreen shrub or small tree with narrow 4–7mm-long leaves in whorls. Insignificant reddish-brown flowers in interrupted terminal groups. Grows from sea level up to about 2,000m on Pico, at its best above 500m when part of the humid laurel forest. Long used for fuelwood, fencing poles, and woven shelter screens and brooms. Endemic, on all the islands, but large old specimens now rare.

Juniperus brevifolia (*cedro-do-mato*) Cupressaceae
This endemic conifer was once a major tree in the laurisilva forests, producing a superb timber from trunks 40–60cm in diameter; these may still be seen as roof beams in old buildings. Today they are small trees or mostly shrubs with crooked stems affected by exposure and are to be found in remnant cut-over forest associated with other laurisilva species or sometimes surviving in hedgerows or as forlornly isolated specimens. The branches are short and numerous, densely foliate with needle-like leaves in whorls of three with two white stomatal (breathing pore) bands on the upper surface. Found usually above 500m, but also lower and on Pico they reach up to 1,500m. On all the islands except Santa Maria and Graciosa.

Arceuthobium azoricum (*espigos-de-cedro*; dwarf mistletoe) Viscaceae
A genus of partly parasitic mistletoe found on conifers. The whole plant is yellowish-green with scale-like leaves and grows upon *Juniperus brevifolia*. At first difficult to find, the rather sickly colour of the small bunches of tangled stems becomes apparent from among the dense green leaves of its host. Above 600m altitude, it is found scattered in large laurisilva stands and is most easily discovered on Pico. An intriguing curiosity, it can be cultivated by taking cuttings of infected juniper when, after three years or so, the parasite will develop from the host tissue.

Lantana camara (*cambará*; shrub verbena) Verbenaceae
Evergreen shrub to 2m, leaves oval, shortly pointed at apex, up to 6cm long, margins toothed, surface wrinkled, rough to the feel with a strong, pungent, lemony smell. Flower in hemispherical heads to 3cm across, yellow to orange or red often with a brighter 'eye'. Native to tropical America, this attractive flowering shrub has escaped from gardens and is naturalising and becoming a pest as it has in so many other places worldwide; poisonous to cattle.

Solanum mauritianum Solanaceae
Large shrub or small tree up to 4m tall with foetid, softly hairy leaves ovate-elliptical, pointed at apex, up to 30cm long. Flowers up to 2cm across, violet-blue with yellow anthers, in many-flowered heads. Fruits round, 1.5cm across, deep yellow. Native of Central America, it is frequently found near habitation and on waste ground.

HERBACEOUS PLANTS
Rocky coastal areas, formed by variously aged lava flows or volcanic ash
Crithmum maritimum (perreexil-do-mar; rock samphire)
Umbelliferae A short, bushy plant with fleshy, hairless, once- to twice-divided greyish leaves. Flowers yellowish-green in umbels 3–6cm across. Usually seen growing alone or with few other species in lava close to the sea and tolerant of sea spray. Britain and western Europe.

Gnaphalium luteo-album (perpétua-silvestre; Jersey cudweed) **Compositae** Shortish, white-woolly annual. Clustered yellow-reddish flowers. In sandy soils and lava cliffs. Rare in Britain, occasional in Europe, and in warm temperate regions worldwide.

Solidago sempervirens (cubres) **Compositae** Fleshy with leaves ending in small broad points at the tip. Flowers yellow in a closely branched panicle. Found as a coastal plant and occasionally elsewhere, particularly noted on the sea cliffs of Flores. Native of northeast America, and spread to the Azores in prehistory times.

Tolpis succulenta (visgo) **Compositae** Perennial herb with a woody base and becoming shrubby with age. Up to 30cm but can be as much as 100cm. Leaves narrow to broadly elliptic, often toothed, somewhat succulent. Flowers yellow, late summer/autumn. Grows near the coast on sea cliffs and gravelly places, as scattered individuals. To be found on all the islands, but in few localities, and on Madeira.

Azorina vidalii (vidalia; azorina) **Campanulaceae** Soft-wooded shrubby perennial with a main stem and branches to 50cm. Young plants form ground-hugging rosettes. Leaves dark green, often shiny, narrow, edged with forward-pointing rounded teeth, the whole plant somewhat sticky. Flowers nodding, bell-shaped, waxy, greenish-white to white to pink in an elongated raceme. Coastal plant in rock crevices and sandy places – even grit on the edge of asphalt roads. Most abundant among the rocks and sand below the airstrip on Corvo where it gets frequent sea spray. On all islands except Graciosa and Faial, but is often difficult to find. One of the loveliest endemic Azorean species, it is becoming increasingly popular in Britain as a tender garden plant.

Silene uniflora (bermin; seacampion) **Caryophyllaceae**
Hairless, prostrate, much-branched perennial herb up to 30cm. Leaves without a stalk and often covered with a waxy bloom. Flowers with a bladder-like calyx, petals white, from March to late summer. Widespread coastal plant, also on Madeira, and in west and northwest Europe. Also found around the summit of Pico, but this may be a subspecies.

Plantago coronopus (dia-belha; buck's-horn plantain) **Plantaginaceae**
Small herbaceous annual, biennial or perennial plant with rosettes pressed closely to the ground. Leaves somewhat fleshy, usually 2–6cm, linear-oblong, not lobed or with a few teeth or often twice-lobed. Flowers yellowish-brown, 3mm, borne in long, dense spikes on

curved stems that are longer than the leaves. Very common in coastal habitats and an early coloniser. Can also be found inland on dry, waste ground.

***Juncus acutus* (sharp rush) Juncaceae** Tall, up to 150cm, robust grassy perennial making dense prickly tussocks with stiffly pointed stems and reddish-brown flowers in a compact inflorescence. Although a widespread species – Madeira, Mediterranean, Britain, North America – it is included here because it is a typical plant of the coast.

***Festuca petraea* (*bracel-da-rocha*) Graminae** Grass with narrow, stiff leaves 30–50cm tall, flowers in whitish-green panicles. Coastal plant on cliffs, on lava and in sandy places often exposed to sea spray. Forms pure colonies but these are now rare because of human interference along the coast and this species is found commonly mixed with other species. Endemic to the Azores and found on all the islands.

In laurisilva forest and at habitats generally above 400m
***Leontodon filii* (*petalugo-menor*) Compositae** Perennial herb with up to five 20cm conspicuous, more-or-less elliptical leaves, toothed and hairy, bearing one to five yellow flowers on a branched stalk. Associated with the laurel forest, it likes wet, open places, often in grassland, usually above 600m, lower on Flores. Endemic, but not found on Santa Maria or Graciosa.

***Senecio malvifoliius* (*cabaceira, figueira-brava*) Compositae** Perennial herb up to 120cm with rounded, lobed leaves 10–15cm, often found growing among shrubs which provide support. Flower colour varies from pale purple, bluish to white all on the same inflorescence, summer. An attractive plant usually growing in wet shady places, but I have seen it in a sunny hedgerow on São Miguel. Endemic, but not on Graciosa or Flores and Corvo.

***Tolpis azorica* Compositae** Perennial herb up to 70cm, leaves crisp-looking, hairless, oblong, up to 15cm, margins deeply toothed. Flowers yellow on a branched inflorescence. To be seen in laurel forest and on constantly moist grassy slopes where it is conspicuous, generally above 600m. Endemic, but not on Graciosa.

***Erigeron karvinskianus* Compositae** Perennial, stems slender, flat on the ground with erect tips. Leaves to 3cm, flowers varying from white through pink to red-purple. A pretty little daisy from Mexico that has escaped from gardens in numerous temperate places worldwide; in the Azores it is adaptable to different habitats.

***Cardamine caldeirarum* Cruciferae** Included here because it is endemic and widespread in the Azores above 400m (but not on Graciosa). In northern Europe it has bittercress relatives that are the weeds and curse of garden centres. Herb up to 50cm tall, basal leaves with five to six pairs of leaflets, flowers white. Likes wet places.

***Centaurium scilloides* (perennial centaury) Gentianaceae** Low, spreading perennial with non-flowering decumbent (flat, tips turning up) shoots, found usually above 400m. Upper leaves lanceolate, about 1cm long. Flowers white, solitary or just a few together in summer. Likes moist habitat, often with grasses. Could once easily be seen at several viewpoints, but seems to be disappearing, maybe due to visitor trampling. *C. scilloides* occurs in western Europe, generally with pink flowers, but some authorities classify the Azores plants as subspecies *massonii*, in which case they would be endemic. Francis Masson, Kew Gardens' first professional plant hunter, collected in the Azores in 1776 and this became one of the first plants from the Azores cultivated in England.

Hypericum foliosum **Guttiferae** Deciduous shrub to 0.5m with crowded narrowly ovate leaves and conspicuous yellow flowers 2–5cm diameter in terminal inflorescences. Normally above 400m, a member of the laurisilva forest but survives where this has been destroyed, and can also be found on steep grassy slopes. Endemic, on all the islands.

Thymus caespititius **(*erva-úrsula*) Labiatae** Dwarf, mat-forming plant with woody growth and upright flowering shoots to 5cm. Leaves to 6mm, narrow, spoon-shaped. Flowers in lax, small heads varying in colour from white through rose to almost lilac. Grows from low altitude to high on Pico, often in crevices on lava flows and on sandy banks. On the upper slopes of Pico it makes a spectacular summer display with *Daboecia azorica*.

Anagallis tenella **(bog pimpernel) Primulaceae** If you are looking at this in detail you will either be bored or very keen. Mat-forming, slender perennial with mostly opposite rounded to elliptical leaves. Flowers pink to whitish pink, somewhat bell-like on slender stalks, opening fully only in sunshine. Around 500m in wet or moist places, often near lakes. Western Europe.

Lysimachia nemorum **ssp. *azorica* (*palinha*; yellow pimpernel) Primulaceae** Evergreen herb with procumbent stems, quickly creeping and rooting at the leaf joints. Leaves opposite, more or less egg-shaped. Flowers solitary on slender stalks. A pretty, modest plant most often found in moist grassland and happiest above and around 500m. *L. nemorum* is found from Britain through to the Caucasus, the endemic subspecies *azorica* is found throughout the archipelago.

Ranunculus cortusifolius **(*bafo-de-boi*) Ranunculaceae** A handsome buttercup being an erect, up to 1m-tall herbaceous perennial, with slightly leathery basal leaves, lobed, rounded and heart-shaped up to 21 x 30cm. Flowers shining yellow up to 50mm diameter in a branched inflorescence. Usually above 500m but lower on Flores in permanently moist areas especially in the shelter of laurisilva forest in ravines, and occasionally in roadside gullies. Also found on Madeira and the Canaries.

Polygonum capitatum **Polygonaceae** Prostrate perennial with rooting stems, often forming large ground-covering carpets. Leaves 2–5cm oval, green with purple V-shaped band, often covered with glandular hairs. Flowers pink in dense, stalked, more or less globular heads. Native to the Himalayas, it was introduced and has escaped on many of the islands, happily colonising young lava flows, stone walls and waste places.

Rubia peregrina (*rapa-língua;* wild madder) Rubiaceae

Distinctive, trailing or scrambling, hairless, rampant evergreen perennial. Stems square and rough with downturned prickles, leaves in whorls of four to six. Flowers yellowish-green, 4–5mm, forming a leafy inflorescence. Fruit rounded, ripening black and fleshy. Widespread, also in west and south Europe, north Africa.

Luzula purpureo-splendens Juncaceae

This charming woodrush is a perennial, leaves grass-like, wide and up to 60cm long with fine hairs along the margins; flowers brown-purplish in clusters. Found usually between 500m and 1,100m altitude, preferring a moist grassland habitat, often on slopes, and among moss carpets around remnants of laurisilva forest, but also can withstand drought. Endemic, on all islands except Santa Maria and Graciosa.

Platanthera micrantha (Azores butterfly orchid) Orchidaceae

Basal leaves two, about 10 x 4cm, erect to spreading. Stem leaves two to six, much smaller. Flowers in a rather dense narrowly cylindrical inflorescence, 8–13cm high and about 1cm across. Individual flowers numerous, small, yellow-green. Found between 200m and 1,000m but mostly above 600m in moist places in full sun to semi-shade; I have most often seen it in grass on roadside verges. The plant's characteristics are variable and some authorities recognise a second, similar species *Platanthera azorica* that is more stocky with larger leaves and a more lax inflorescence of whitish-green flowers. Of the orchids recorded for the Azores' *P. micrantha* is the species most likely to be encountered; the other is a Tongue orchid.

Trachelium caeruleum (throatwort) Campanulceae

Perennial herbs up to about 50cm tall with numerous small slender blue or lilac flowers in much-branched, leafless, broad flat inflorescences. In walls, roadside verges, etc, São Miguel, Terceira and Faial, west and central Mediterranean.

Arundo donax (*cana;* giant reed) Graminae

A tall (to 5m) perennial rhizomatous grass, leaves 60 x 6cm, grey-green. Flowers in large terminal, feathery inflorescences, autumn. Introduced long ago, it thrives in volcanic sands around the coast and is used widely for shelter hedging. Strongly invasive, it quickly spreads if not strictly controlled. When grown in ideal conditions in the south of France the canes are supplied to make the reeds for musical wind instruments.

FERNS

Asplenium marinum (*feto maritime;* sea spleenwort) Aspleniaceae

A coastal, tufted, plant with a short, thick rhizome with dense blackish-brown scales, the whole growing tightly in among the rocks. Leaves 20–30cm long, pinnate, mid green and glossy above, dull and paler below, thickened and rather stiff; tolerant of salt spray. Madeira, Britain to western Mediterranean.

Blechnum spicant (hard fern) Blechnaceae

Evergreen fern forming attractive crowns of long, sterile, pinnate leaves with a herring-bone appearance lying close to the ground; the young leaves are flushed red. The fertile fronds have a longer stalk, are much narrower, and are erect.

Widespread in northern temperate lands, it is one of the commonest and most distinctive ferns in the Azores, usually above 300m.

Woodwardia radicans (chain fern) Blechnaceae
Found from the Azores to Java, this fern is one of the most attractive of the archipelago's fern flora. The fronds are 1–2m long and up to 0.5m wide and often hang down over gullies and banks. The fronds produce bulbils towards the apex and these form new plants, hence the common English name. Usually found above 400m in moist places.

Culcita macrocarpa (feto-do-cabelinho) Dicksoniaceae
Conspicuous large fern with strong erect stems up to 100cm tall. The frond is triangular in outline, often shiny and frequently of a yellow-green colour. Found mostly above 500m but also down to 150m. It is associated with laurel forest and can be readily seen between the tree stems on the lava flows of Pico, but it also survives the loss of forest cover and can be found beyond the laurisilva. It has a prostrate rhizome covered with hairs, which were once collected and used for stuffing cushions, etc. Found on all the islands except Santa Maria and Graciosa, it is native to Macaronesia and the Iberian Peninsula.

Lycopodium cernuum (clubmoss) Lycopodiaceae
A distinctive curiosity of a plant and a fern ally, its long creeping, looping stems rooting at intervals often spread over several square metres. Overall colour is yellowish-green and the tiny leaves are spirally arranged along the stems. The fertile leaves (sporphylls) are arranged in terminal cones (strobili). Generally found above 400m, frequently associated with laurel forest, but often also on steeply sloping banks where it can be a pioneer species on recently exposed surfaces. Also occurs by hot water springs. On all islands, except Santa Maria and Graciosa. In central Europe the strobili of clubmosses used to be collected, dried, and the fine yellow spores kept for use as a medicated talcum powder; sensitive to pollution, they are now rare and strictly protected there.

Osmunda regalis (feto-real; royal fern) Osmundaceae
Large tufted fern with upright fronds up to 1m tall and 30cm broad, pinnate. Sporangia produced on some of the terminal pinnae of the fertile fronds. It has a distinctive, short, massive, erect rhizome and a tangle of wiry roots, once popular in mainland Europe until mid last century as compost for growing orchids. Growing in wet places, often in water, and found on all islands except Graciosa.

CULTIVATED PLANTS
Agapanthus praecox Liliaceae
Perennial herb forming dense clumps from strong fleshy rootstocks with long strap-like leaves and large heads of blue flowers on leafless unbranched stems up to 60cm tall. Seeds black when ripe, borne in pendulous capsules. Native to South Africa, widely planted in towns and along roads, often naturalising.

Amaryllis belladonna (beladona; bellandonna lily) Amaryllidaceae
South African bulbous perennial with strap-shaped leaves in two ranks. Large funnel-shaped pink flowers produced in late summer before the leaves appear, six or more together on stout 60m stems. Frequently planted in public gardens and along roadsides, also naturalised.

***Abelia x grandiflora* Caprifoliaceae** Attractive semi-evergreen shrub to 2m with long arching branches, the young leaves at first markedly bronze-pink; flowers tubular, five-lobed, in clusters, pink to white, flowering over an extended period from summer. Frequently planted on road verges.

***Aloe arborescens* Liliaceae** Perennial succulent from South and east Africa with 60mm long grey-green leaves having sharp forward-pointing teeth. Inflorescence unbranched to 80cm, flowers tubular, 4cm, scarlet tipped greenish-white. A good ornamental thriving in hot dry places in private gardens and public places.

***Acacia melanoxylon* (blackwood) Mimosoideae** Fast-growing Australian tree with leaves modified to reduced simple, flattened leaf stalks up to 14 x 2.5cm. Flowers in nearly spherical heads in branched racemes, very pale yellow, late winter. A much-desired timber tree for high-value products. Seedlings are abundant on disturbed land, mature trees in gardens and woodland.

***Metrosideros excelsa* Myrtaceae** Dense evergreen tree that in maturity develops massively heavy branches and trunk with many aerial roots swinging from its branches. The dark leathery leaves are silvery on their undersides, and in summer terminal flowers burst into a spectacular show of scarlet-stamened pin cushions, seldom all over the tree but in large patches. Called *pohutukawa* by the Maoris, in its native New Zealand it often begins life as an epiphyte and is commonly found on sea cliffs. Very tolerant of salt spray, this tree is often to be seen in public gardens and squares on most of the islands.

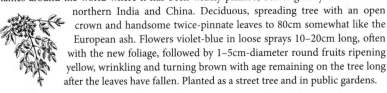

***Melia azedarach* (Persian lilac) Meliaceae** This tree has many local common names around the world where it has been widely planted, but originally it came from northern India and China. Deciduous, spreading tree with an open crown and handsome twice-pinnate leaves to 80cm somewhat like the European ash. Flowers violet-blue in loose sprays 10–20cm long, often with the new foliage, followed by 1–5cm-diameter round fruits ripening yellow, wrinkling and turning brown with age remaining on the tree long after the leaves have fallen. Planted as a street tree and in public gardens.

***Araucaria heterophylla* (Norfolk Island pine) Araucariaceae** A stately conifer endemic to Norfolk Island attaining 20m or more, with spreading branches in whorls. Leaves scale-like to 1cm, somewhat triangular, overlapping like roof tiles. Planted widely throughout the islands, they are all protected and special permission is necessary before they can be felled. Captain Cook on his second round-the-world voyage in the 1770s discovered them and enthused about their potential use for ships' masts but sadly the wood proved too spongy and heavy. In their natural state they grow to 60m with a trunk circumference of over 8m on dry but fertile shallow volcanic soils. This drought tolerance the Victorians soon realised made it an ideal house plant when young, and it is again coming back into fashion. Dating back to the Jurassic period 225 million years ago, they were browsed by dinosaurs, but in the Azores they are vulnerable to lightning strikes.

Appendix 3

FISH ON THE MENU

There are some 50 species of fish found in the waters around the Azores that can be eaten. Those more likely to be found in the islands' restaurants are detailed below in alphabetical order according to their Azorean common name. Resilience is an indication of how much exploitation a species can tolerate and how long a minimum population takes to double in time. Very low = more than 14 years; Low = 4.5–14 years; Medium = 1.4–4.4 years.

ABROTE Greater forkbeard *Phycis blennoides*. Commonly up to 45cm, max size 110cm long, max weight 3.5kg. Found over sand and mud bottoms, a deep-water fish 10–800m, usually seen in caves, very shy, gentle fish; young more coastal. Feeds on crustaceans and fish. Eastern Atlantic, Iceland down to west Africa, and the Mediterranean. Resilience medium. Served as transverse steaks or filleted.

ATUM Tuna or tunny. Three different ones are commonly eaten in the Azores: *Thunnus obesus* is mostly squeezed into tins while albacora, yellowfin tuna, *Thunnus albacares*, and Bonito, skipjack tuna, *Katsuwonus pelamis*, are served under Atum in restaurants. The yellowfin tuna reaches a max size of around 230cm and weight of about 180kg, and the skipjack 90cm and 23kg.

BADEJO Island grouper *Mycteroperca fusca*. Max size 80cm, max weight 3kg. Subtropical, found above rocky areas, depth down to 200m. Azores, Madeira, Canaries and Cape Verde Islands. Resilience low. Served stewed, maybe grilled or baked in the oven.

BICUDA Yellowmouth barracuda *Sphyraena viridensis*. Max size 128cm, max weight 8.2kg. Depth 0–100m. Tropical, eastern central Atlantic. Feeds on fish, cephalopods and crustaceans. Resilence low. Eaten best as a transverse steak, also whole baked in the oven.

BOCA NEGRA Blackbelly rosefish *Helicolenus dactylopterus*. Max size 47cm, max weight 1.5kg, reportedly living for around 40 years. Depth 50–1,100m. Deep-water fish found in soft-bottomed areas of continental shelf and upper slope, feeds on crustaceans, fish, cephalopods. Venomous. Eastern Atlantic Iceland to South Africa, western Atlantic. Resilience very low. Served whole, good grilled or fried.

BODIÃO VERMELHO Ballan wrasse *Labrus bergylta*. Max size 65cm, max weight just over 4kg. Found around rocks and offshore reefs to a depth of 50m. Feeds on crustaceans and molluscs. Eastern Atlantic. Born first as female, then changes sex after four-plus years old. Resilience low. Served grilled.

CHERNE Wreckfish *Polyprion americanus*. Max size 210cm, max weight 100kg. Deep water (40–600m), solitary, likes caves and shipwrecks. Feeds on large crustaceans, cephalopods and fish. Wide distribution, eastern and western Atlantic, southwest Pacific. Resilience low. Best served as transverse steaks, when thick and simply grilled a gastronomic highlight.

CHICHARRO Blue jack mackerel *Trachurus picturatus*. Max size 60cm. Depth to 270m, a schooling species favouring shallow coastal waters of islands, banks and sea mounts, feeds on crustaceans. Eastern Atlantic, Bay of Biscay down to Tristan da Cunha. Resilience medium. Eaten small, about 10cm, fried really crispy they are quite yummy.

ESPADA Silver scabbardfish *Lepidopus caudatus*. Max size 2m, max weight 8kg. Depth 100–600m. A deep-water school-forming fish found usually over muddy or sandy bottoms and migrates into midwater at night, when it is most often caught. Eastern Atlantic France to South Africa, southern Indian Ocean, southwest and southeast Pacific. Feeds on crustaceans, squid and fish. Resilience medium. Eaten as fillets.

ESPADARTE Swordfish *Xiphias gladius*. Max size 4.5m, max weight 650kg. Depth 0–800m. Oceanic, occasionally in coastal waters. Migrates to temperate or cold waters in summer, returns to warmer waters in autumn. Feeds on fish, also crustaceans and squid, using their sword to kill prey. Atlantic, Indian and Pacific oceans. Resilience low. Usually served as a transverse steak, too often cut measly thin; like a good beefsteak, it should be thick.

GAROUPA Blacktail comber *Serranus atricauda*. Max size 43cm. Depth 1–90m, found over hard bottom; carnivorous, distributed eastern Atlantic. Resilience low. Served whole, usually grilled.

GORAZ Garapau or Peixão blackspot seabream *Pagellus bogaraveo*. Max size 70cm, max weight 4kg. Inshore waters to a depth of 700m, feeds on crustaceans, molluscs, worms and fish. Eastern Atlantic. Resilience low. Served grilled or baked in the oven. Locally regarded by some as 'horrible'.

MERO Dusky grouper *Epinephelus marginatus*. Max size 150cm, max weight 60kg. Depth 8–300m, subtropical, likes reefs and rocky bottoms, solitary and territorial, feeds on crabs, octopus and fish. Eastern Atlantic and western Indian Ocean, and western Atlantic. Resilience low, endangered. Served as fillets rather than steaks but also good poached or cooked in the oven.

PARGO Common seabream *Pagrus pagrus*. Max size 91cm, max weight 7.7kg. Depth down to 250m. Subtropical, found over rock or sandy bottoms, feeds on crustaceans, fish and molluscs. Eastern Atlantic north to the British Isles, western Atlantic, down to Argentina. Resilience medium, endangered. Served whole or as transverse steaks. Excellent covered with sea salt and oven baked.

ROCAZ Large-scaled scorpion fish *Scorpaena scrofa*. Max size 50cm, max weight 2.9kg. Depth 20–500m. Subtropical, solitary, sedentary over rocky, sandy or muddy bottoms, feeds on fish, crustaceans and molluscs. Venomous. Eastern Atlantic. Resilience low. Very expensive but very nice! Served whole, grilled or poached.

SALMONETE Striped red mullet *Mullus surmuletus*. Max size 40cm, max weight 1kg. Depth less than 100m. Found over rocky places and also sand and soft bottoms, feeds on shrimps, molluscs and fish. Eastern Atlantic. Resilience medium. Eaten whole.

SERRA Atlantic bonito *Sarda sarda*. Max size 90cm, max weight 11kg. Depth range 80–200m, subtropical schooling species, cannibalistic, feeds on squid, shrimps and fish. Widespread Atlantic. Resilience medium. Served as fillets or transverse steaks.

Appendix 4

FURTHER INFORMATION

MAPS *Azores* published by Turinta in their regional series. Folded map, scale 1:75,000. A topographical map of the islands with tourist information, lots of detail and easily readable; £8.95

BOOKS There are numerous publications on technical topics about the Azores, but they are almost all in Portuguese. In English there is virtually nothing readily available that is specific to the Azores, but there are several coffee-table books for sale in the local shops, together with outline guides with lots of pretty pictures. One exception is the guide to Flores:

Bragaglia, Pierluigi *Flores–Azores–Walking Through History* Author's publication, 2009; www.argonauta-flores.com
Nemésio, Vitorino *Mau tempo no Canal* (1944), translated as *Stormy Isles: An Azorean Tale* (1998). Nemésio's novel provides an intriguing window into early 20th-century Azorean life and society, with coastal whaling at times a prominent feature. It is a story of unrequited love and two warring families in locations on Pico, Faial and São Jorge, and the intervening channels, and may still be available in Ponta Delgada bookshops.

Nature
Bento, Rita and Sá, Nuno *Diving Guide Azores* Ver Açor, Ponta Delgada. Available from the Centre for the Arts and Marine Sciences, Pico. A 192-page guide with photography by Nuno (265 photos). A total of 53 diving sites are described.
Cas, R and Wright, J *Volcanic Successions* Springer, 1987
Clarke, Tony *Birds of the Atlantic Islands* Christopher Helm, 2006. The first comprehensive field guide to the birds of the Macaronesian islands – Canaries, Madeira, Azores and Cape Verde. Illustrated by Chris Orgill and Tony Disley.
Rodrigues, P and Michielsen, G *Birdwatching in the Azores*. Detailing habitats and distribution with many excellent colour photos and illustrations. Pbk, published by Azores Tourism but currently out of print.
Scarth, Alwyn and Tanguy, J-C *Volcanoes of Europe* Terra, 2001
Schäfer, Hanno *Flora of the Azores* Margraf Verlag, Weikersheim, 2002. In English, with 380 colour photographs and brief descriptions of 650 native and introduced species.
Soares de Albergaria, Isabel *Gardens and Woodlands of the Azores Islands*. Pbk, published by Azores Tourism but currently not for sale. In the format of a travel guide the 692 descriptions are liberally illustrated by excellent small photographs, old postcards and engravings, together with location maps and opening times. Most interesting and informative is the introduction in which the historical and social background sets the scene for the intriguing snippets appearing in the individual garden descriptions.

General reading

Abdo, Joseph C *On the Edge of History* Tenth Island Editions, 2006. The story of the Dabney family, American consuls to the Azores during the 19th century.

Ashe, Thomas *History of the Azores or Western Islands: Containing an Account of the Government, Laws and Religion, the Manners, Ceremonies and Characters of the Islands* Kessinger, 2009

Birmingham, David *A Concise History of Portugal* Cambridge University Press, 2003

Boid, Edward *A Description of the Azores: Or Western Islands from Personal Observation* London, 1835. Kessinger Legacy Reprint.

Gordon, J S *A Thread Across the Ocean* Simon & Schuster, 2002. A fascinating account of entrepreneurial determination to lay the first Atlantic cable.

Robertson, Ian *A Traveller's History of Portugal* Cassell, 2002

ARTICLE

Alfrey, P 'American vagrants on the island of Corvo, Azores', 2005, Birding World 18(11): 465–74

WEBSITES
Tourism

www.visitazores.com Site in English and Portuguese giving details of travel agents, accommodation, etc, run by the Azores Tourism Authority.

www.azores.com User-friendly site run by Portugal Online Corp, a company promoting Portugal on the internet.

www.azores.gov.pt Official website of the Government of the Azores, which gives up-to-date information about the Azores and government activities and, under 'About the Azores', tourist information.

www.casasacorianas.com Owners of rural accommodation website, giving property details and booking online.

www.hostels.com/pt.az.html Azores youth hostels.

www.destinazores.com Simple 'guidebook' in English, German and Portuguese giving very limited background information plus some accommodation and eating places.

www.azores.com Information on travel, hotels, tours, etc.

www.azoresinfo.com Details of restaurants, local agents offering activities, and other useful information.

www.atlanticoline.pt Inter-island ferry services.

www.meteo.pt All you need to know about the weather in the Azores, including a 10-day forecast.

www.transmacor.pt Inter-island ferry services.

www.sata.pt For direct flights from the UK and inter-island flight schedules.

www.flytap.com For flights throughout the year via Lisbon to the Azores.

www.noonsite.com/Countries/Azores/ Yachting information.

http://news.bbc.co.uk/weather Under 'search', type in 'Azores' for a five-day forecast.

www.meteo.pt/en A fascinating site from the Instituto de Meteorologia Portugal giving all the information and more about the weather in the Azores, seismology, marine meteorology and atmosphere.

www.allyoucanread.com/azores-newspaper-portugal/ Online newspaper.

Activities

www.teatromicaelense.pt For programme details of the theatre in Ponta Delgada.

www.cineclube.org For information on films being shown in the Horta theatre; see page 189 for details.

www.angrajazz.com For details of the jazz festival on Terceira.

www.trails-azores.com Government site giving details and updates on all the official walking trails.

www.montanheiros.com Website of the Sociedade de Exploração Espeleológica whose headquarters are on Terceira.

www.azoresweb.com/diving_azores.html Details of diving companies.

www.marinasazores.com Official website of Sea Week.

Natural history and conservation

http://parquesnaturais.azores.gov.pt/en/index Gives details of all the nature parks.

www.spea.pt SPEA: the society for the study and conservation of birds in Portugal.

www.birdingazores.com Excellent website, initialised in 2004 by two Swedish birders to collect information and describe the bird fauna of the Azores, and to create a source of information for visiting birders. Gives birding sites, bird photos, trip reports, checklist and more.

http://azoresbs.weebly.com Records bird sightings and disseminates interesting bird news from the Azores.

www.wdcs.org Whale and Dolphin Conservation Society, the world's most active charity dedicated to the conservation and welfare of all whales, dolphins and porpoises.

http://whale.wheelock.edu/whalenet-stuff/Azores Shows satellite-tagging observation maps for sperm whales in the Azores, part of a programme to monitor migration of selected species.

www.ospar.org For the past 40 years OSPAR has been identifying threats to the marine environment and has organised programmes and measures to combat them. Their Biological and Ecosystems strategy aims to restore, where practicable, marine areas adversely affected, and to create marine protected areas.

www.azoresbioportal.angra.uac.pt An important and wonderful working tool providing a database for about 5,000 species, often accompanied by images. Groups include lichens and fungi, bryophytes, flowering plants, marine invertebrates, arthropods, and vertebrates.

www.horta.uac.pt University of the Azores, Department of Oceanography and Fisheries.

NOTES

NOTES

Index